THE QUEEN CHARLOTTE ISLANDS
1774-1966

Copyright © Kathleen E. Dalzell, 1968
All rights reserved

First printing 1968
First paperback edition 1981
Second paperback edition 1988
Third paperback edition 1993

Harbour Publishing
Box 219
Madeira Park, B.C. V0N 2H0

Printed and bound in Canada by Hignell Printing Ltd., Winnipeg

Canadian Cataloguing in Publication Data

Dalzell, Kathleen E., 1919-
  The Queen Charlotte Islands

  ISBN 0-88894-312-1 (v.1). — ISBN 0-88894-313-X. — ISBN 1-55017-008-2 (v.3). — ISBN 1-55017-011-2 (v.2: 1989 print.). — ISBN 1-55017-312-1 (v.1: 1993 print.)

  Contents: V.1. 1774-1966 — v.2. Places and names — v.3. The beloved island.

  1. Queen Charlotte Islands (B.C.) — History. 2. Queen Charlotte Islands (B.C.) — Biography. 3. Queen Charlotte Islands (B.C.) — Description and travel. I. Title.
FC3845.Q3D34 1989   971.11'2   C89-091334-X   F1089.Q3D34

The
QUEEN CHARLOTTE
ISLANDS
Volume 1
1774-1966

Kathleen E. Dalzell

"THE QUEEN CHARLOTTE ISLANDS – 1774 to 1966"

To my own pioneers,
Meta and Trevor Williams,
for whom these beloved
Islands were Shangri-la

ACKNOWLEDGMENTS

Without the generous help of the many interested people who, over the past five and a half years, have provided information, pictures and hospitality, this book could not have been written.

To all of you whose names have been recorded in these pages with the stories you have told — and in many cases retold again and again so that I might more fully understand — thank you for entrusting these priceless first-hand recollections to me.

I am also deeply indebted to Mr. Willard Ireland and his staff in the Provincial Archives in Victoria who have gone out of their way to make information available to me; to the B.C. Historical Association who sponsored me for the Leon and Thea Koerner Foundation grant which enabled me to travel to many places to interview Islanders and ex-Islanders; to Mr. Howard Phillips of Masset who picked up the tab for the hundreds of historical pictures which were copied and filed; to the Queen Charlotte Islands Chamber of Commerce for their interest and endorsation of this book; to all the government departments, private companies and newspapers who assisted in making their files available; to Professor Wilson Duff who gave valuable advice in connection with early Haida history and to Chief William Matthews of Masset who supplemented this information; to Mrs. J. W. Gibbs of Sidney who has been so helpful in the final editing of the manuscript; and, for their co-operation and understanding during these past five and a half years, when this project meant such a theft of time from our normal family activities, I am deeply indebted to my husband, Albert, and our children, Glenn, David and Joan.

Special thanks to my dad, T. L. "Timber Limits" Williams, for laboriously transcribing the old diaries he had written in court shorthand over fifty years ago. Without the accurately documented information they contained and without his countless letters to me patiently answering in detail my numerous and persistent questions, it would not have been possible to have undertaken this history of the Queen Charlotte Islands.

Lastly, but most importantly, my most sincere appreciation to Charles Merson Adam, one of the earliest pioneers of the Queen Charlotte Islands, whose invaluable assistance has caused this book to be printed.

Five such volumes could not contain the wealth of information which resulted from this all out effort to retain at least some of the history which was being lost all too quickly — in fact it was almost too late when this book was undertaken.

Kathleen E. "Betty" Dalzell

THE ISLANDS

Land of azure northern skies
Of geese and their haunting cry,
Land of ancient monarch spruce
Of the ocean's moaning sigh.
Land of the wapitis' bugle call
Of spawning salmon streams
Land of the warrior Haida tribes
Of settler's broken dreams
Land of the trumpeter swan's retreat
Of clean, salt-laden air
Land of thunderous rolling surf,
Of otter, seal and bear
Land of the wheeling sea-gulls scream
Of shooting Northern Lights
Land of the flaming sunsets
Of soft, short summer nights
Land of the loon's mournful call
Of treasure-laden sands
Land where man can plainly see
The prints of his Maker's hands
Land that sends forth stalwart sons
Yet never sets them free
But calls them back again and again
To these Isles of the Northern Sea.

—by Dorothy Richardson
Tlell, January 1966.

Frontispiece caption: As Tow Hill watches out to sea in the distance (see page 159),
a newer visitor to the beach looks for treasures in a favourite rock hound site on the
North Beach of Graham Island.

TABLE OF CONTENTS

TABLE OF CONTENTS

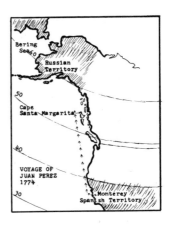

CHAPTER ONE

BRIEF ENCOUNTER

From time immemorial islands have held a strange and compelling fascination for man. And few islands are more intriguing than the unique and beautiful group known as the Queen Charlottes.

Remote and beckoning, they lie like an inverted triangle about fifty miles off the nearest mainland point in northwestern British Columbia. The warm Japanese Current swirling in from the Pacific Ocean on the west keeps the climate invigoratingly temperate all year round.

Geographically they offer all the variety a heart could desire. Numerous wonderful inlets and sounds divide the Charlotte group into an archipelago of over one hundred and fifty islands and inlets of every shape and description. One small island has a near-boiling mineral spring on it — as yet completely unspoiled. Miles of crescentic sandy beaches fringe the northern and eastern shoreline of the largest island, Graham, stretching in an almost unbroken line from the ancient Haida village of Old Masset (1) on the north to historic and picturesque Skidegate Mission in the south.

On the west coast, rugged mountains rise straight from the ocean floor hundreds of feet below. Born during a period of violent volcanic upheaval eons ago, the main backbone of the Islands, about 155 miles long, is part of the same submerged mountain range which runs from the Olympic Mountains in Washington, U.S.A., and continues along Vancouver Island.

With the ever present sea surrounding the Charlottes, boats have always played a vital part in their history and, appropriately, there is a lighthouse at each extremity. Separating the Islands from the mainland on the east, there is the shallow and capricious Hecate Strait which causes tricky and dangerous overfalls and tide rips as it meets the Pacific off Cape St. James, and again where it meets Dixon Entrance on the northeast, off long-nosed Rose Spit — the *Ne'koon* of Haida legends.

Through Dixon Entrance, which runs right across the north end of the Islands,

(1) Known as HAIDA today.

13

lies the International Boundary line at "fifty-four forty" and divides the Charlottes from Alaska, some forty miles away.

Lonely, wind-swept Cape St. James Lightstation guards the southern extremity of the Islands and warns mariners of the hazards. While up on the far northwestern tip of the Charlottes — like a pennant flag — shines the important light of Langara Lighthouse, beaming out to sea for many miles.

Strangely enough it was from this extreme northwestern tip — not from the east nor from the south — that the Islands were first discovered. It was in 1774 that Juan Perez sailed up the western coast of the continent, under orders from the Spanish Viceroy, to look for new land to claim for Spain. Rumors of Russian advances down the Alaska Panhandle were causing great anxiety to the Spanish governments in Madrid and Mexico and in anticipation of more aggressive advances the Spanish had already set up ports in California — the most northerly being Monterey. It was known that the Russians had come down as far as Cape St. Elias, near the 60th parallel, so Juan Perez was instructed to take his expedition up to that point and establish ownership of the intervening area for Spain.

Just what lay between California and Cape St. Elias was completely unknown at that time. Only a blank was shown on the charts on June 6th, 1774 — the day Perez left Monterey in the corvette *Santiago*. In addition to his pilot, Estevan Martinez, and the crew of eighty-six men he had on board two Franciscan priests, the Reverend Fathers Juan Crespi and Tomas de la Pena, who were to keep an official record of the journey.

It was a miserable trip.

Encountering very heavy swells and fog most of the way, Perez was forced to keep far off the coast. Only briefly did they see land dimly in the distance, when their log recorded the sighting of what must have been the high peaks of the Coast Range on the mainland. But soon the heavy mist closed in again. Day after weary day there was just the grey emptiness of the ocean.

Constant bouts of sea-sickness plagued the Reverend Fathers throughout the trip and before long tell-tale signs of the dreaded scurvy appeared in the crew. Added to this, the water supply — which they had hoped to replenish — was running dangerously low.

Aloft in the crow's-nest, a lookout peered endlessly over the horizon to the north — to the east — and to the west. Then, as they reached the vicinity of the 54th parallel, he unexpectedly gave the loud cry which electrified the whole ship. . . "Land ahead!"

All hands rushed on deck. Even Father Crespi rallied from his awful seasickness, and scrambled up to see the wonderful sight of solid earth once more.

Sure enough, there to the north and east, they could see the unmistakable outline of land far in the distance. Elatedly Juan Perez sailed his ship in as close as he dared before darkness set in. It was July 17th, 1774 — almost two hundred years ago.

The next day they could clearly make out a prominent headland and ordering his ship hove-to, Perez gave this part of the world its first recorded name — Cape Santa Margarita. (1) ". . .because it was the day of that glorious Saint when we

(1) *Langara Lighthouse was built on part of this historic site. Information from Mr. R.B. Young, Dept. of Mines and Technical Surveys, Victoria, B.C.*

14

first set our eyes on this new land," recorded Father Crespi.

This remote headland, on the still unnamed Queen Charlottes, was the first place in British Columbia to be discovered and named by a European. It was, in fact, the first place along all the coast — from Monterey, California, right up to Cape St. Elias in Alaska — to be discovered, named and *recorded.*

Spirits were high on the *Santiago* for Perez had decided to make a landing here as soon as the weather permitted and to plant the marker — a huge wooden cross prepared by the ship's carpenter with the inscription "INRI" (Jesus Nazarenus Rex Judaeorum) and Carolus III Hispaniarum, rex año de 1774" claiming the new land for Spain, although it was far short of his directed 60th parallel destination. But they were running out of food and water too quickly to be able to continue much longer without landing.

The weather was extremely squally, rendering closer approach inadvisable, and for three days the vessel remained hove-to in the area hoping for improvement.

During this time they were the objects of great curiosity for several boatloads of Haida Indians — both men and women. They had come out in sleek canoes from a village on the shore to have a look at this strange craft which had entered their waters. Watching them in return, the Spaniards were impressed, not only with the grace and design of the Indian canoes ". . .which are made but from a single tree trunk," but also admired the marvelous dexterity with which they were handled. These Indians were supreme boatmen, obviously.

As the first canoe approached the *Santiago* the occupants began to sing, and one of the Indian men stood up to scatter feathers ceremoniously on the water before the canoe. The friendly gesture was unmistakable, wrote Father Crespi. The Haidas circled the *Santiago* viewing her from every angle for a considerable time, then attracted by the Spanish sailors proffering handkerchiefs, beads and other trinkets, the canoes were paddled to the lee of the ship. Here, by mutual agreement and the use of sign language, some trading began. The Indians offered woven bark mats, plaited hats and dried fish in exchange for the Spaniard's articles of trade. (1)

Scarcely had the bartering begun when a stiff breeze blew up, freshening to a gale. Hurriedly the Indians concluded the dealings and paddled swiftly for the shore — while Perez's vessel was forced southward by the fury of the wind, despite all he could do.

This time he was able to see clearly much of the west coast and noting a high mountain range southwards along the Charlottes, he gave to it the name of Sierra de San Christoval after the ". . .Saint who was so tall." The storm worsened, driving his ship ever farther down the coast and soon out of sight of land. The wooden marker prepared with such care was never erected.

In fact it was destined never to be erected at all on this voyage. As he sailed homeward after leaving the Charlottes, Perez decided to attempt a landing on Vancouver Island — once again in the hopes of replenishing his dwindling water and food supplies. But this, too, was unsuccessful owing to adverse weather and hostile natives. On Vancouver Island he applied the third name of the voyage to Estevan Point.

The Viceroy in Monterey greeted Perez's return home with dampened

(1) There are varying descriptions of this meeting.

enthusiasm. However, intrigued by the possibilities that the voyage had opened up, he decided to order a second trip for the following spring — 1775. Once again the *Santiago* was pressed into service, but with Bruno Hecata as captain now. Perez went along as second in command. To accompany the *Santiago* Viceroy Bucarelli chose the *Sonora*, a bare thirty-six feet long. Bodega y Quadra was to be in charge of her. Quadra was very anxious to make the trip in spite of the obvious unsuitability of his vessel for such a voyage. He reasoned that the stiffer the odds, the greater the glory — and he was looking for rapid advancement.

Owing to a succession of adversities which plagued both ships, it was not long before Hecata decided to discontinue the voyage and turned his ship *Santiago* homeward after a comparatively short distance. It was the last voyage our discoverer Juan Perez would ever make, for he died when on his way back to San Blas from Monterey, after the trip.

The intrepid Quadra in his tiny *Sonora* kept doggedly on. They must have had a fearful journey according to all accounts, but they did manage to get well above Perez's 54th latitude mark — going as far as the vicinity of Sitka before turning homeward.

As he sailed southward, Quadra crossed Dixon Entrance, naming the waters as he did so Entrada de Perez. This entrance was to be renamed many times, other names being Douglas Entrance, Granitza Sound, Kygahne Strait and its present Dixon Entrance. Quadra could see Perez's *Cape Santa Margarita* quite clearly but believed, as Perez had done, that it was all part of the mainland.

However, the earlier voyage of Perez in 1774, as it was the first voyage to be properly recorded, gave to the Charlottes several distinctive firsts. In addition to being the first area on the coast between Alaska and California to be visited by a European, the Charlottes were also the first to receive not one, but two of the names given to any point in British Columbia by an outsider. (1) They were also the scene of the first trading and meeting of native Indians with outsiders in British Columbia waters.

Although the Perez trip is the first *authenticated* visit of Europeans to the Queen Charlottes, knowledge of them may possibly have been recorded more than two hundred years earlier than Perez. However, this is still disputed. But on an interesting map by Zolteiri, bearing the date 1566, without latitude or longitude, three islands appear — and according to some historians (2) they are not unlike Baranof, (the island Sitka is on); the Queen Charlottes; and Vancouver Island. If so, then this map is the earliest known record of the Charlottes.

Furthermore, over one hundred years before Perez's visit, Bartholomew de Fonte is thought to have entered Masset Inlet. . . although de Fonte wrote so many fanciful and greatly exaggerated stories that anything he said is open to question. However, Dr. G. M. Dawson in his geological report of 1878 pointed out that in de Fonte's description of the ". . .unique inland lake, connected to the sea by a long narrow inlet. . ." parts of the narrative are close enough to actual fact to be interesting.

For instance, when that early mariner describes his ship as being, "Opposite Myhasset on September 5th, 1640", he could, according to Dr. Dawson, very well mean the island of Maast at the entrance to Masset Sound. The latitude

(1) Confirmed by Mr. W. E. Ireland, Provincial Archivist, Victoria, B.C.
(2) "The Great Company", Beckles Wilson

16

given by de Fonte is reasonably close. In his account of the trip de Fonte tells of how one of his officers, Bernado, ". . .examined a river nearby with three Indian boats, each made of a tree 50 to 60 feet long, accompanied by two Jesuits, twenty of his own people and thirty-six natives." The description could well have fitted the Haida canoes of that day.

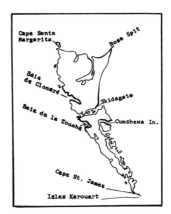

CHAPTER TWO

A PATTERN FOR NAMES

If there be any question as to which European first learned of the existence of the Charlottes there is, on the other hand, absolutely no doubt at all as to who named them. It was Captain George Dixon who, on August 3rd, 1787, in seafaring tradition gave them the name of his ship the *Queen Charlotte,* a sailing vessel of some 200 tons. This was thirteen years after Perez's historic trip.

Actually a great deal of the history of the Charlottes has been retained in their nomenclature. The rich, sometimes tongue-twisting, often melodic names of the inlets, capes, bays, mountains and villages would make a history in themselves. Haida, Tsimpshean, Spanish, French, British, American and Canadians are among the nations represented in this heritage. Although early visitors named so many of the places, they did not publicise the fact and consequently there was much renaming.

By the time George Dixon had arrived on the scene Nootka, on Vancouver Island, was developing into an important trading centre. The beautiful pelts of the sea-otter were one of the most sought after commodities, as prices being paid for them in the Orient were fabulous. In the keen competition for this extremely lucrative trade men were coming from all quarters of the world — with each ship's company searching for new areas to buy the precious furs.

Although many expeditions sailed by the western shores of the Charlottes, going up and down the coast looking for likely fur areas, the Islands themselves lay strangely alone and untouched by this "invasion" for a full twelve years after the initial encounter with Perez.

It was not until 1786 that three ships got close. The first to arrive was Captain James Hanna's tiny brig of some 60 tons, the *Sea Otter,* out of the port of Macao in Portuguese China. Hanna came as far as the 53rd parallel and did some trading in the area at the south end of Moresby Island. (1)

That same year Captains Laurie and Guise said that they had sailed their ships, the *Captain Cook* and the *Experiment,* down an ". . .inland waterway"

(1) Dawson Report, 1878.

(Hecate Strait). There was strong evidence that they had traded around the south end also, but they were close-mouthed about this, for there was no point in advertising a good trading area.

Then romantic "Around-the-World" La Perouse, the French explorer who had been looking vainly for the elusive Northwest Passage, came sailing southward along the west coast and was interested in what he saw.

Crossing the broad entrance of a large bay on Graham Island, he named it the "Baie de Clonard." Sailing a little farther down the coast, another large bay warranted a name he decided — and to this one he gave the intriguing title of "Baie de la Touche," (1)

Gradually passing down the rugged coast, he was surprised to see that it came suddenly to an abrupt end near a lonely cape. Naming this "Cape Hector", he cautiously sailed around the string of rocky islets leading out from it. Swarms of huge copper-colored sea-lions could be seen and heard — splitting the air with raucous barking on this favorite spot of theirs. To these islets Perouse gave the name "Isles Kerouart" and through the years of constant naming and renaming of Island points, only this last name has come down to us in its original context.(2)

Both Baie de Clonard and Cape Hector were to be renamed the very next year by Dixon — the first being changed to Rennell Sound, and the latter to Cape St. James. Lovely Baie de la Touche at the entrance to what is now known as Gold Harbor, was called Englefield Bay by Captain Vancouver a few years later.

After passing the islets of the Kerouarts, La Perouse did not continue southward as might have been expected — instead, his curiosity aroused, he turned his ship eastward. He was amazed to see such a vast expanse of water between the land he had just passed and the distant shore, which was 75 miles or more to the east. For the first time he raised the suggestion that this part of the land might ". . .indeed be separated from the mainland shore completely!"

Upon leaving the area which had interested him so much, Perouse continued his journey around the world — which he was fated never to complete. After touching at Monterey in California, the Hawaiian Islands and then Botany Bay in Australia, he was never heard from again and was presumed to have been lost in a storm with his ship and all hands. This was just a few months later.

It was in search of new and undiscovered territory for furs that Captain George Dixon decided to have a closer look at the Charlotte area. He had been on the west coast, off Hippa Island, the year before — just after Perouse. That was in September, 1786 and he was accompanied then by his partner Captain Nathaniel Portlock of the *King George,* but the whole region had seemed so deserted the two ships left almost immediately — going on to spend the winter in the Hawaiian Islands.

Returning to Prince William Sound (Alaska) in the summer of 1787 they decided to separate and trade. Accordingly, Dixon set his course for the south. He crossed Quadra's Entrada de Perez, which next year was named Dixon Entrance by Sir Joseph Banks, and then rounded Perez's Cape Santa Margarita.

As he was attempting to manoeuvre his ship into the large bay to the south of the cape, a canoe-load of Haida Indians, on their way home from a fishing trip, came to look at the British ship.

(1) Dawson Report, 1878.

(2) Named Isles Kerouart by La Perouse in 1786. Adopted as Kerouard Islands and name applied in 1897 by Dr. G.M. Dawson, Director of Geological Survey of Canada.

Seeing the beautiful fur cloaks that the Haidas wore, Dixon's pulse quickened. This looked like trading territory — completely untouched. He tried to interest the Indians in trading, showing them a great variety of goods, but they wanted no part of it. It was the ship that took their eye, instinctive boatmen that they were. Round and round they paddled, looking the *Queen Charlotte* over from every quarter, gesticulating and discussing her among themselves. The British seamen, for their part, were just as impressed with the graceful canoe and the infinitely skilful manner in which it was handled, as Juan Perez had been some thirteen years before.

And as it had been with the Spaniards, so it was with Dixon — not until the Indians had completely satisfied their curiosity about the ship could they be tempted to trade. Once interested, however, they gave their complete attention, later on bringing out more people in loaded canoes from a small village in the bay.

As he had suspected, Dixon found that this was virgin fur territory — for obviously no trading in furs had been done here before. It was a buyer's market all the way.

"In less than half an hour," recorded William Beresford, purser on the *Queen Charlotte,* who kept a journal of the trip, "we had purchased three hundred of the finest pelts we had ever seen. The furs being neatly sewn into cloaks which the Haidas wear."

Aware of his bonanza, Dixon was careful to see that each customer was completely satisfied. "Toes", a type of adze seemed to be the articles most in demand by the Haidas at this time.

When he left the area on July 4, George Dixon was so impressed with the whole proceedings, that he named the waters there, Cloak Bay, to commemorate the memorable event. Then he named the island the bay was on, North Island. The *Queen Charlotte* was to leave a legacy of still more names for this vicinity, for the names of many of the officers on this voyage can still be found on current maps of the region. In addition to purser *Beresford,* they were — John *Carew,* 1st mate; James *Turner,* 2nd mate; George *White,* 3rd mate; William *Lauder,* surgeon; Henry *Forrester,* steward; John *Gatenby,* boatswain; and John *Sadler,* carpenter. (1)

Leaving Cloak Bay, Captain Dixon sailed southward. He tried to enter what is now Parry Passage, but was prevented from so doing by the strong tide flowing out. Instead, he came out around the point of Cape Knox and down the west coast. Noting signs of habitation near Frederick Island in the village of Susk, he stood in a short way to see if some of the inhabitants would come out. He was not disappointed.

After spending two days trading there, July 5th and 6th, he hoisted sail once more and went on as far as Nesto Island. He was intrigued with the structure of a house which reminded him of the fortlike hippas of the New Zealand natives, and accordingly he christened this island Hippa Island on July 7th.

Crossing the outer part of La Perouse's Baie de Clonard he named that Rennell Sound — the first in the series of renamings, so persistent in Queen Charlotte Islands history.

Standing well off the entrance to Skidegate Channel, they could see signs of

(1) British Columbia Coast Names", Walbran.

more villages so cautiously came in closer. Haidas from Chaatl and Kaisun came out to see them and more trading was instituted. It was here that Dixon was able to secure a labret from one old lady — for both men and women came out on the trading parties. Labrets had been a keen source of fascination for everyone on the ship and were an ornament worn by the Haida women in their lower lip, which was especially pierced for the purpose. The one that Dixon obtained was 3—7/8 inches long by 2—5/8. Oval in shape, it was cleverly inlaid with pearly shell and decorated with a rim of copper.

Father Crespi had made note of the lip ornaments in his journal at North Island when on the historic trip with Juan Perez, for they had also been a source of interest to the Spaniards who had never seen anything like them before.

One of the Indians who came out to barter in the Kaisun area was a tall, homely man, who had taken a great liking to a light-horseman's cap. Dixon made a present of it to him, which seemed to make a big hit.

By July 23rd, the *Queen Charlotte* was riding off Anthony Island and the ship's company was delighted when a party of eleven canoes containing one hundred and eighty people paddled out to see them. Although they had left no record, it was soon apparent that this was where Laurie and Guise and Hanna had traded earlier, for these villagers knew instantly how to go about trading and at once came out with canoe-loads of furs. They had no fear or curiosity about the strangers. This contrasted with the villagers further north. Although Dixon didn't know it, these were the most warlike of all the Haidas. It was their exploits, in the main, which gave the whole of the Haida nation its reputation for fierceness.

After trading there for two days, George Dixon began to think of continuing his journey and set about rounding the hazardous rocks and islets of the Kerouarts. It was July 25th, 1787, St. James's Day, and purser Beresford wrote in the log, ". . .the Captain has decided to distinguish the land off which these rocks lie, by the name of "Cape St. James". So now the Charlottes were guarded north and south by two saints.

Turning his vessel northward, Dixon soon came to a wide channel which he named Ibbertson's Sound. (1) Records show that he journeyed at least as far as Cumshewa Inlet and perhaps even to Skidegate Inlet. As he progressed he became increasingly aware that he was circling a group of islands.

Not only from the nature of the territory, for he was recognizing mountain peaks here that he had seen from the west coast, but also because in Cumshewa Inlet he met the same tall, homely Haida he had seen on the west coast, who had taken such a liking to the light-horseman's cap.

Apparently the man was a chief of some importance on this side. But at this meeting with Dixon he was disconsolate. Evidently he had been overpowered in a fierce fight, and showed Dixon the wounds he had sustained trying to keep possession of his beloved hat. George Dixon, seeing the special attachment the chief had developed for the cap, dug deeply into his seaman's chest and produced another . . .to the joy and sincere appreciation of the old Haida.

The date was now August 3rd, 1787, and satisfied that he was definitely sailing along the shores of a group of islands, Dixon gave them their name — THE

(1) Now Houston Stewart Channel

QUEEN CHARLOTTE'S ISLANDS — for his ship and for his queen.

Sailing east towards the mainland he encountered Captains Colnett and Duncan in two ships of his own company — the King George Sound Company. Enthusiastically he told them of his profitable trip to the Islands, for he had secured 1821 skins with a market value of over $90,000.

Hearing this news, Captain Duncan lost no time in setting his own sails for this new "land of good fortune". And this was only the beginning, for the area was soon to gain the reputation of being the best source for furs on the coast. It was the forerunner of a business which was to prove too lucrative for its own good.

CHAPTER THREE

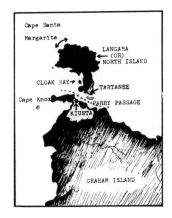

KING GEORGE'S MEN
AND THE BOSTONIANS

By 1825 more than 230 vessels had visited the coast for purposes of trade — many returning year after year. It would not be possible to follow the various traders who came to the Islands at this time, but there were several whose visits did tangibly contribute to the pattern of history.

For the first few years trading was dominated by the English, who were called King George Men by the Indians, but there was an increasing number of Americans — the Boston men, and some French and Spanish.

The majority of the early traders treated the Indian with esteem, finding him to be a shrewd and intelligent bargainer and in every way a force to be respected. For the Indians, it ushered in a period of prosperity that resulted in what might be termed their golden age of culture. Their distinctive art form was already well established, but the new wealth led to more frequent feasts and ceremonies. This stimulated their artists and craftsmen to supply more and even better carved spoons, dishes, poles and other items. With the acquisition of better tools for their work (through trade for furs), their skill had full scope. Most of the magnificently carved poles which rose in the larger villages were erected in the years following the white man's arrival.

By 1788, the year after Dixon's trip to the Charlottes, news of the trading possibilities in the Islands area was beginning to leak out. In August of 1788 ex-British Navy man, John Meares, who was established at Nootka, decided to send one of his ships up to the GREAT ISLAND as he called the Charlottes. He delegated Captain William Douglas to go with the *Iphigenia* and scout the territory.

It was on this trip that Douglas first met Chief Blakow-Connehaw, the powerful chief of Kiusta — near North Island. (A successor of Connehaw's, Chief Albert Edward Edenshaw, was to become well-known in later years of Island history.)

Douglas coasted eastward along the north shore of the Islands rounding, as he did so, the remarkable promontory on the northeast corner of Graham. This spit stretching nearly five miles out into the water is caused by the meeting of the currents of Dixon Entrance and Hecate Strait — and has been the Nemesis of countless boats of every size. Known as Ne'koon or Needle-nose by the Haidas, it was christened that year Point Rose by William Douglas in honor of George Rose, a well-known political figure and writer of that day.

At the other end of the Islands, George Rose was also to be remembered in another spot that year when James Johnstone, a member of Colnett's ship, the *Prince of Wales,* named Rose Harbor for the popular politician. When a whaling station was built there in the early 1900s, the name Rose, applied to the harbor, contrasted so markedly to the usual breath-stopping odor that lay heavily in the air, it became the object of endless puns.

Although the Charlottes had been discovered several years previously, it was not until 1789 that we have any record of a European actually setting foot on land there. In April of that year an American trader, Captain Robert Gray, of the *Lady Washington,* a sloop of 90 tons, sailed up to the Islands. Unaware that Dixon had already named them, or of Meares "Great Island" caption, Gray decided to christen them WASHINGTON'S ISLAND, believing them to be one big island in the main. This name was used on American charts for some time.

In the Cloak Bay region, Captain Gray made one of the most notable barters for furs that was ever made with the usually shrewd Haidas. He obtained two hundred prime pelts for the price of just one chisel each. It was a fantastic profit.

Later, sailing down the west coast of the Islands, the *Lady Washington* stood in to have a look at the large inlet opening up at the south end (Houston Stewart Channel), which Gray named for his ship's owner, Barrell's Sound.

Manoeuvering in here, they encountered Haidas from Anthony Island who were coming out quickly to take advantage of some possible trading with the Americans, for by now these Indians had become experienced bargainers. Anchoring near the island, a brisk trade was shortly in full swing. In contrast to the usual demand for ironware elsewhere, these Haidas wanted clothing in trade for their furs. The date was June 11th, 1789.

Leading the bartering for his people was the important chief of the Raven Crest, Chief Koyah, the Raven. This distinguished man, chief of the dominating tribe of the area at that time, soon became so well-known to traders that the whole region was referred to as Koyah's Place.

During the visit, young Robert Haswell, mate on the *Washington,* was anxious to stretch his legs ashore and to do some exploring in the picturesque village on Anthony Island. Writing in the ship's log, ". . .this place has been visited by quite a few vessels before us and relations with the Haidas here are very congenial. . ." young Haswell went ashore to have a look at a Native fort, (1) and so became the first white man known to have set foot on the Queen Charlottes.

However, about this time William Douglas was making a return trip to the north end of the Islands in his *Iphigenia* and he also went ashore on this visit. Arriving off Masset on June 19th, 1789, he named the large outer bay McIntyre's Bay, noting as he did so, the wonderful sandy beach stretching all along the shore from Rose Point to Masset.

Hove-to off the Masset Bar, Douglas traded with the Masset Haidas for a short time before proceeding to North Island. The channel between North Island and

(1) "Anthony Island, A Home of the Haidas", Wilson Duff

26

Graham (still unnamed) had greatly interested him on his visit the previous year and he wanted to make a closer examination.

Dropping anchor off Blakow-Connehaw's village at Kiusta on the 20th of June, it was not long before the *Iphigenia* was recognized and the chief came out to visit. He remembered Douglas from the year before and now welcomed him with great and dignified ceremony.

In a strong resonant voice Connehaw began to sing the solo of a Haida greeting song — beckoning to about two hundred of his tribe on the shore to join in each chorus. The vibrant, moving rhythm made a deep and lasting impression on Douglas. After the greeting ceremony was over, the two exchanged names — and the name of Douglas has been handed down in that Haida family ever since.

Early next morning Douglas began exploration of the channel which had captured his interest, and named it Cox's Channel for the partner of Meares, John Henry Cox, who lived in Macao, China at the time. It has since been renamed Parry Passage in honor of the famous Arctic explorer.

After the friendly and obviously sincere welcome given to him by Connehaw upon his arrival, Douglas was dismayed to learn that during the same night two canoes had come out furtively to the *Iphigenia* apparently hoping that all the sailors would be asleep. Realizing that watch was being kept and they were discovered, they hurriedly made for shore. Although the action was highly suspicious, no order was given to fire, and they were allowed to make their getaway without interruption.

But when a similar attempt was made on the second night, (having been forewarned by some of the women who were visiting the ship that it might take place as soon as the lights on the ship were extinguished), Douglas ordered the gunner to fire a few rounds over the heads of the Haidas as soon as the canoes began to steal out from shore. This worked like magic, and there were no more attempts of this sort.

When the sailors went ashore in the morning for wood, they were met by Chief Blakow-Connehaw, who wanted them to know none of his people were involved — for he wanted no part of this type of thing.

Douglas apologized for having fired, but the chief cut in to say that he approved entirely of that action and added that if it happened again the British should shoot to kill. Connehaw told Douglas that the midnight visitors were not of his village, but of the one on the opposite shore — and he had suspected some such behavior from them. It was on his instructions that the women had been told to warn the British sailors of the impending repeat visit from the scallywags — who had murder and plunder in mind.

A few days later the *Iphigenia* crossed to a sheltered cove on the north side of the channel and named the place Beal's Cove. Lying at anchor, Douglas noted that from the cove they could clearly see "...the great wooden images of Tartanee, (1) bearing east and one quarter north."

When they went ashore in Tartanee to view more closely the superbly carved poles, Douglas found that they were about forty feet high and were part of the structure of the huge lodges, for through an opening, ingeniously forming part of the mouth of one of the lower figures, was the entrance to the house. The

(1) The early name for Dadens, on Langara Island (North Island).

27

Britishers were impressed with the size of the huge timbers and excellent construction of the Haida house. Going inside they could see that in the centre there was a deep depression, in the form of a square pit. The various levels leading up to the ground were lined with hewn timbers. At one end of the village there were also a few smaller mortuary poles, wonderfully carved.

Another surprise for the British was a patch of well-cultivated land in the village. Douglas later concluded that Captain Gray had preceeded him in this area and taught the Indians to garden. Most later historians do not agree, and think that it was a patch of Indian tobacco. In any case, Douglas himself planted some bean seeds and, "hoped the villagers would enjoy the benefit of them." He spent about a week in the Parry Passage area, and except for the one incident, enjoyed excellent relations with the Haida people there.

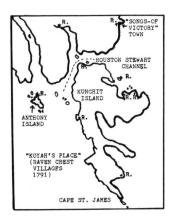

CHAPTER FOUR

THE END OF A CHIEF

At the other end of the Islands, in Houston Stewart Channel, Captain John Kendrick (a senior partner of the Captain Gray who had preceeded Douglas) began a chain of events that would undo many of the good intentions of these earlier traders and the good relations set up by the leading chiefs who had welcomed the strangers.

For scarcely had Gray, his junior skipper, left Anthony Island area in the *Lady Washington* when Captain Kendrick entered the Houston Stewart Channel in the larger (about 220 tons) vessel *Columbia.* It was common practice for most of the trading ships to "sweeten the pot" by giving a few gifts to the chiefs. However, Kendrick, an arrogant moody type of man — entirely lacking Gray's more winning personality — had no such policy. He was out to make all he could and "free gifting" made no sense to him.

But the Anthony Islanders were also tough bargainers. Kendrick's high-handed manners and unprincipled tactics got him nowhere with these Haidas. During the unfruitful negotiations there had been a bit of petty pilfering on the part of the Indians (perhaps to compensate for Kendrick's not having given anything to the chiefs). With their new interest in European type clothing, some laundry hanging out on the deck to dry, proved irresistible to one light-fingered Haida. Unfortunately it happened to be the captain's personal washing that he swiped.

By now Kendrick was becoming increasingly annoyed and short-tempered about the frustrating trading and when he noticed his laundry had been stolen from under his nose, he lost his temper completely. Livid with rage, he roared hoarsely, "Damn you! You black thieving savages!"

"Seize the chiefs," he bellowed to members of his crew nearby, "we'll teach the scoundrels a lesson in manners!"

Chief Koyah was as usual leading the trading talk, assisted by lesser Chief Skulkinance, when suddenly they were both roughly overpowered and thrown unceremoniously to the deck. The other Haidas backed off in alarm at this unexpected indignity to their most important chief.

Angrily Kendrick told his sailors to bind and tie the two Indians tightly and

29

place a leg of each into the carriage of a cannon. Then threatening to blow them to bits if they didn't comply, the chiefs were ordered to tell their tribesmen to return all of the pilfered articles plus any furs not yet traded. For these Kendrick named his own niggardly price.

But what may have seemed to be only the "teaching of a lesson" to John Kendrick, was a shattering insult to the two Haida chiefs. Most especially so in the case of proud Koyah, the Raven. He had been reduced to the status of an "ahliko" or one of the lower class in the eyes of his people by the violation of his person in Kendrick's action.

Once ashore, Koyah broodingly deliberated his untenable position. It would take an elaborate and costly potlatch or a complete revenge to remove the stigma from his name. The capture of a trading ship might be the answer. Skulkinance's help was enlisted, for although his fall was not quite as great as Koyah's, since he hadn't as much prestige to begin with, still he had lost the status he had. A bond was struck, plans tentatively laid and then the long wait for the opportune moment began. It was not to come for another two years.

During that time scores of trading vessels visited the area. Then on June 16th, 1791 — almost two years to the month — the little *Lady Washington* once again came nosing into Houston Stewart Channel. But she was not under the genial command of Captain Gray this time. As the Indians went out to trade, Koyah's pulse quickened when he recognized the acid-dispositioned Kendrick as the master on the smaller ship. The knot in his stomach tightened. A feeling of exhilaration was hard to keep down when he realized that Kendrick was not nearly as sharp now as he had been on the earlier trip in the big *Columbia.* For John Kendrick had begun to have bouts of excessive drinking — and was well along in one today. (1) Perhaps because of this, his guard was down. At any rate he permitted an unusually large amount of Haidas to come on deck — well over 50 were on the ship, with more than 100 in the canoes close by. The dreaded cannon was dismantled, for the gunner had been cleaning it. Added to this, many of the crew were below decks.

It was Koyah's chance.

More Haidas were beckoned to come aboard from waiting canoes and then the steady chant of a war song began, growing into a frightful din. It was a chilling sound and sobered Kendrick up quickly. But the moment was Koyah's. And how he savored it!

Daggers appeared from Haida sheaths, and not being able to resist it, Koyah began to taunt Kendrick. Standing on the dismounted cannon he jeered, "Now try to put me in your gun. . ." In the delicious moment of revenge, Koyah too became careless.

The sailors below deck had pistols and realizing what had happened, were able to creep up. Under the now sobered Kendrick's direction they opened up a merciless fire. The Haida daggers were no match for the firearms — and blood flowed freely.

Frantically the Indians left the ship — in canoes or by jumping into the water and swimming furiously to get out of the range of the guns. It was a massacre.

When a few survivors managed to get beyond range of the gunfire, Kendrick

(1) *"Anthony Island, A Home of the Haidas", Wilson Duff*

ordered his sailors to jump into the longboats and pursue them relentlessly. Not many Haidas escaped. Over sixty Indians were killed that day, and most of the others maimed and crippled forever. Somehow both Koyah and Skulkinance escaped alive from the carnage, but the defeat was crushing for Koyah. In addition to the heavy casualties for his tribe, he lost two brothers, his wife and two children. And both he and Skulkinance were badly wounded. (Ironically, Kendrick lost his own life the next year from a cannonball when in the Hawaiian Islands.)

For Koyah, the Raven, it was the beginning of a savage struggle to regain some of his former prestige — a desire that was now greater than life itself to the once proud chief. Two months later accompanied by the faithful Skulkinance, he began by leading a war party on his old traditional enemy Chief Skidegate. Then during the next four years he attacked three more trading ships. Twice he was successful.

He was responsible for the overpowering and killing of the crew of the American brig *Eleanora* and repeated the atrocity when a large British ship put into the Houston Stewart Channel with a broken mast. Some of his blazing fanaticism for revenge must have been evident — for he was referred to as Old Scorch Eye.

In June 1795 his bloody trail finally and mercifully came to an end when he attacked the *Union* a trading vessel of about eighty tons. Koyah had badly underestimated his adversary in Captain John Boit, and besides the forty or more Haidas who were killed in this unsuccessful attack — Koyah was himself killed.

Of the ten known attacks on ships in which there was loss of life, Koyah's rank significantly. No other chief succeeded in capturing more than one ship and his victories may have encouraged others to follow his example. His failures only added to the bad blood on both sides.

And so the episode of the stolen laundry had triggered a monstrous chain reaction. The oldest sea chantey known to have been written about the Pacific Northwest was about the battle in Houston Stewart Channel in 1791 and was written soon after the massacre. It has fifteen verses. The last two are:

"And now unto old China we're fastly rollin' on
Where we shall drink good punch for which we've suffered long;
And when the sixteenth day of June around does yearly come
We'll drink in commemoration what on that day was done.

And now for to conclude, and make an end unto my song,
Success to the commander of the *Lady Washington.*
Success unto his voyage wherever he may go,
And may death and destruction always attend his foe."

Another skipper who acted impetuously and unwisely was Samuel Crowell of the brig *Hancock.* This was around the same time as the 1791 fiasco when Koyah attempted his first revenge with Kendrick.

Captain Crowell was trading in Cumshewa Inlet, when for some trifling offence he fired on the trading party, killing three of the Haidas. The seed sown by these two men, Kendrick and Crowell, was to be reaped by unsuspecting Captain Gray, who had always got along well with the Haidas.

He entered Cumshewa Inlet shortly after Crowell had left for Masset, and in need of wood for his ship, Gray sent three men ashore. Evidently the Haidas in this area assumed that all white traders were cut from the same cloth and fell on the shore party — killing them all.

The body of only one, a Mr. Caswell, was recovered and it was buried there with Captain Gray performing divine service — the first European style funeral held on the Charlottes. Gray, mystified by this unexpected hostility from the Haidas did not learn the reason until he caught up with Crowell at Masset a short time later. (1)

(1) "Queen Charlotte Islands", B.C. Heritage Series, Volume 1

CHAPTER FIVE

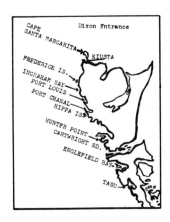

SLOWLY GROWS A MAP

By 1791 boats were flocking to the Charlottes for the superb quality of the sea otter pelts taken in Island waters was becoming well known. With the ships came the inevitable problem of unchartered waters and unnamed points.

In the years from 1791 to 1793, four men corrected this situation to a marked degree. They were Ingraham, Marchand, Caamano and the master chart-maker, George Vancouver.

First to arrive was Joseph Ingraham in the American trading brig *Hope*. Ingraham was fascinated by the Islands and made many excursions ashore exploring, collecting and writing about it all carefully in his log. He was content, apparently, to leave all the trading to his supercargo (purser).

Arriving in June, Ingraham spent most of the summer of 1791 cruising Island waters, and left quite a few names for the charts. First of all was Craft's Sound (now Virago Sound), then Hancock's River, which seems to have been applied at that time to what is now Masset Sound.

On southwest Moresby he named Magee Sound after the owner of his ship. A large bay on the northwest side of Graham was dubbed for himself, and the well-known Frederick Island was named for his son Frederick. This was not the Frederick Island that we know today. Owing to misreading his chart he evidently applied the name to the already named Hippa Island. When Vancouver charted the coast he used the name Frederick for the island just north of Hippa. (1)

A few months after Ingraham's visit, a second "around-the-world" French explorer came along. This was Captain Etienne Marchand who in his ship the *Solide* — a vessel built expressly for the cruise by the wealthy house of Baux in Marseilles — sailed into Cloak Bay in August of 1791. The *Solide*, a ship of 300 tons, was fitted in the most complete manner for a scientific voyage as well as a commercial one.

The first accurate charts of any Q.C.Islands harbors were prepared by this excellent navigator. His officers explored Parry Passage in detail and then he sent

(1) *Although Hope Point on Frederick Island is for Ingraham's ship, it was not so named until 1908 when Captain Learmonth was surveying the region in the EGERIA.*

a boat down the west coast as far as Rennell Sound with 2nd Captain Prosper Chanal in charge. Chanal added three more names — still in use today. He named Otard Creek for one of his friends, then the snug harbor of Port Louis was christened in honor of Marchand's brother, Lieut. Louis Marchand. Finally the channel to the south of Port Louis was named Port Chanal for himself. Incidentally, Captain Chanal is credited with being the first white man to sail through Hippa Passage.

The next year, 1792, there were three interesting events. The idea of a permanent trading post for the Masset area was first suggested by our old friend, Captain Gray, in his report dated May 18th, 1792. But it was many years before this idea was implemented.

Joseph Ingraham returned for his second visit and added two unique innovations. Realizing that the Islands had no predatory animals such as wolves or cougars and also that there was not much variety in quadrupeds, he decided to experiment. In Magee Sound he put ashore three pigs, a boar and two sows, hoping they, "would thrive and increase in the temperate climate". As an added protection he sealed a bottle and nailed it to a tree asking future visitors not to molest the animals. Nothing was ever heard of the pigs again.

He journeyed to Cloak Bay and feeling quite at home in Island waters now, Ingraham conducted the first and possibly the most unusual July 4th celebration ever held on the Charlottes. At ease with the people there, the crew of the *Hope* decided to "whoop it up a bit" in honor of the occasion. Hearing that Samuel Crowell was in the area, word was sent asking him to attend. Then making a special trip to Kiusta, Ingraham ceremoniously invited Chief Blakow-Connehaw to be guest at the proceedings. Connehaw, the master diplomat, said that he would be delighted to help the Americans celebrate their holiday.

Ingraham chose a nice spot on the beach near a shady tree and ordered a huge fire to be lit. A whole 60-pound pig was put on a spit to be barbecued for the festivities. Promptly at 12 noon, guns fired a salute from the ships and on shore the American flag was raised with a flourish. Everyone present gave three rousing cheers with great gusto to commemorate the occasion suitably.

A countryman of Juan Perez's came to the Charlottes that summer. He was Spanish Lieut. Jacinto Caamano who made a brief trip along the north end of the Islands in his corvette the *Aransasu,* and left several names. He applied Point Ymsible to Rose Spit, and Estrado to a lagoon near Masset. A group off Virago Sound was called the Mazerredo's, and lastly he named Dixon's North Island after Admiral Langara of the Spanish Navy — Isla de Langara. Only the last two names have survived.

Because Langara Island is so important navigationally, the Geographic Board has officially adopted the Spanish name, feeling that it is a more distinctive way to designate it on the maps. But it is Dixon's name of North Island that is used locally.

In September of the following year, 1793, Captain Vancouver who was in the course of his extensive survey and explorations of the whole coast of B.C., sailed down the West Coast of the Islands to chart that part of the coastline. True to accepted procedure, he began changing names.

He renamed Perez's historic headland Cape Santa Margarita, North Point, and surely a less distinctive name could not have been found for this important headland. This section of rugged coastline named both by Perez and Vancouver takes in a considerable portion of the northwestern part of Langara Island, for it includes Langara Point (where the lighthouse is) and St. Margaret's Point about a mile away to the east — which is the point farthest north. (1)

In the course of this survey, Vancouver reapplied the name Frederick Island, as mentioned earlier, and added Hunter Point for his friend, Dr. John Hunter. La Perouse's beautiful Baie de la Touche was changed to Englefield Bay for Vancouver's other good friend, Sir Henry Englefield, the scientific writer and Cape Henry was also named for him. Buck Point and Cartwright Sound were others named by Vancouver, all of which are in use today.

(1) St. Margaret's Point was named by Captain Learmonth in 1907.

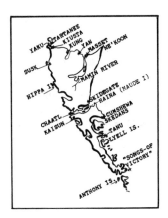

CHAPTER SIX

HAIDA VIKINGS

By the year 1800 an estimated 7,000 Haidas were living on the Charlottes with about 1,700 more, known as Kaigani in southern Alaska. The Kaigani were the group of Haidas who had migrated from the Charlottes about the time of the first white contact. Some of the Kaigani who went to the most northerly Haida village in Alaska, the town of Kasaan, were members of the same branch of Haidas who, at that time, also occupied the most southerly part of the Charlottes, on Kunghit Island. These were the Sand-Town-People.

Considered to be among the world's most distinctive peoples, the Haida had elaborate and well-functioning patterns of social organization long before the first Europeans arrived. Representing the elite of coastal Indians, they were a bold, vigorous and resourceful race, with the complete self-assurance which is born of proven ability.

Extremely creative, theirs was one of the most richly ornamented societies on the continent. Everything they used was carved or decorated in the vibrant style of their unique art form. They were described as being, "somewhat fairer skinned than other tribes and the women exceedingly comely."

On the sea the Haidas were supreme. As "Vikings of the Northwest Pacific" they raided or traded at will up and down the coast in their big canoes — and there were few attempts from the mainland tribes in retaliation. The remoteness of their Island home added to the effect their trips created and heightened the aura of glamor forever associated with their name.

Living on Islands that produced the finest stand of cedar in the world, the inventive Haida took every advantage of his heritage. Its straight grain and softness made it ideal to carve and to hew out the poles and timbers for their great lodges, and to fashion the huge canoes which became legendary. In addition, the pliable bark of the cedar provided material for serviceable garments, sails, baskets, woven mats and many other items of daily and ceremonial use.

One of the most useful and cleverly fashioned articles was a box which was made from a single piece of cedar. Ingeniously grooved, then soaked, steamed and shaped, it was finally sewn together so skilfully with cedar or spruce roots

37

that it was completely watertight. The matching close-fitting lid was similarly made and fitted with exactness into the specially cut-away parts on the sides of the box.

Iron (1) was already known to them long before any fur traders appeared, as the earliest explorers found iron tools in habitual use along the coast. This fact has intrigued anthropologists and most of them feel that iron must have come by way of aboriginal trade routes from Asia in prehistoric times — as did the iron which was in use a thousand years ago by the western Eskimo.

And so the seafaring Haida was completely attuned to his island environment, and whenever he felt inclined, the world was his to travel almost at will wherever there was a waterway for his renowned canoe.

(1) "Contributions of Marius Barbeau to West Coast Ethnology", Wilson Duff

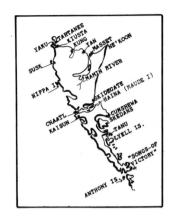

CHAPTER SEVEN

CANOES BY CRAFTSMEN

Many of the graceful, beautifully balanced Haida canoes, about which we have heard so much, were longer than the sailing ships of those who came to trade. They were works of precision, unmatched anywhere, for Island Indians were the master shipbuilders of the coast.

Ranging in length from a huge seventy-five footer with a seven foot beam, which could carry 40 people and about two tons of baggage, down to the everyday ones of twenty-five feet or so, they were also much sought after by the mainland tribes, who considered a Haida canoe to be an article of great value. Although the Haida did not use sails before the coming of the white man, it did not take him long to adopt the idea once he saw them on the early ships. If canvas was not available, he used woven cedar bark mats.

Wiggs O'Neill, (1) whose stepfather, J.M.L.Alexander, was a Hudson's Bay Factor at Masset in 1890, could remember when his family lived there that soon after Christmas they would see all the canoe-building families of Masset sail away up to Inlet to the Mamin and Yakoun River areas — the land of the giant red cedars. Each family carefully selected their tree, then pitched camp and set to work felling the huge cedar. To this day, timber cruisers in that region occasionally come across cedars that were anciently marked for canoes, but for some reason left to stand. And once in a while, in the two areas mentioned, one can find the remains of partially hollowed-out canoes, now rotted and with new trees growing on them.

When the big tree had been felled, then came the work of fashioning the canoe in the rough, shaping it and hollowing out the centre. By careful teamwork, it must now be manoeuvred from its forest home to the water's edge — quite an engineering feat in the case of the larger trees. Once in the water the new canoe was towed to Masset in its rough state, there to be pulled up on the beach in front of the village, well above high-tide mark. The long finishing process then began.

(1) Wiggs O'Neill correspondence.

This finishing was done mainly by using a home-made adze with a blade about 1½ inches wide and attached to a curved handle about 18 inches long. The handle was made from a natural tree crook, especially sought for this purpose, and was usually of yellow cedar.

From early morning to dusk each day the continuous tap tap of the little adze could be heard fashioning the canoe. When this work was finished and the canoe ready for the final stages, it was an odd looking apparition. It was cocked up at each end for bow and stern and humped up in the centre – and the whole canoe was much narrower at the top than anywhere else. When they were ready for the final stage, canoe builders along the beach worked together.

They built big fires on each side of the canoe and heated dozens of rocks. Several buckets of water were poured into the canoe and as soon as the rocks were red-hot, quick hands shovelled them into the canoe where they fell with a great hissing and spitting into the cold water. Swiftly cedar bark mats were spread over the top of the canoe. In a short time the hot rocks made the water in the bottom of the canoe boil and the big mats prevented the steam from escaping.

At the right moment, when the body of the canoe was steamed through and had become flexible, the man in charge gave the signal. "Now!" Then eight men skilfully grabbed the gunwales and pulled gradually and carefully on either side.

"Before your very eyes," remembers one old timer, "the sides would come out to the proper beam they desired and the big hump in the centre would disappear, leaving the canoe in beautiful symmetrical lines."

While the wood was still hot, cross braces were deftly positioned to ensure that the desired shape was retained as the wood cooled and the canoe permanently set. The thwarts were fashioned and fitted, and lastly the carved ornamental bow and stern were fastened into place.

Only very special canoes were decorated with paint, since it was rarely available – instead the Haidas would scorch the whole surface, making it a mottled black. This method of applying fire to the cedar wood made it much more durable. Strange to say, in the early days they did not think of bending ribs into the canoes, which would have added strength and would have helped to keep the wood from splitting. Quite a few drownings were directly attributed to this.

When the canoes were finished and before the people departed to the mainland to market them – along with products of dried halibut – there would be many feasts in Masset before all the final farewells were said. Some of the older people can remember watching the unforgettable sight of the graceful flotilla of canoes departing from the village, paddles dipping in unison. They kept close together to cross the unpredictable waters of Dixon Entrance and the more treacherous Hecate Strait. Every canoe had two masts and each mast had a square sail. There were many paddlers, some of the women even better than the men.

Few canoes were built once the settlers began to arrive, for they brought with them sailboats, schooners and other types of craft. The laborious job of building the famous canoes was not worth the months of effort – it was much more practical to buy boats. But they were still the superlatively skilled seamen and as such, it was the Haidas who operated most of the boats plying to and from the Islands and the mainland in the days of haphazard steamer service.

However, in 1908 the Seattle Exposition commissioned Alfred Davidson, the

40

red-headed Haida craftsman, to build a genuine Haida war canoe for their fair. It was a beauty. Sixty-six feet long, with a six foot four beam and wonderfully decorated with paint — it took Mr. Davidson and his young brother Robert eight long months of painstaking work to complete.

People who remember this canoe being built, still talk of the large chunk of rot Davidson found in one end of the cedar trunk. He replaced it with a large plug so skilfully that it was impossible to tell where he had done so.

When at last the canoe was finished, Henry Edenshaw's schooner *Josephine* was engaged to tow it to Prince Rupert for shipment to the United States. The weather was uncertain as they started out from Masset, but when they rounded the long nose of Rose Spit a furious gale blew up. In the cross tides and overfalls the tow line suddenly snapped.

In minutes schooner and canoe were out of sight of each other. Captain Edenshaw had all he could to to guide his ship safely into port in Prince Rupert, after a gruelling trip across the Straits.

He could hardly believe his eyes, therefore, when he came in to tie up and saw the big canoe already safely moored in Prince Rupert. She had beaten the Josephine by several hours and had a fine trip. Evidently, when the tow line broke, the Haida and his wife who were in the canoe, just hoisted a sail. The big sixty-six foot canoe glided along on top of the waves with great speed before the wind — whereas the shorter *Josephine* ploughed into every wave, making heavy weather all the way.

In the final bargaining the Davidsons felt that the price of $200 offered by the Seattle people was far too low for all their months of work, and would not sell. The canoe was brought home to Masset. Word of the situation was sent to Ottawa and the Canadian Government offered Mr. Davidson $500, which he accepted. For its final trip to the mainland, the big canoe was carefully slung on board the *Henriette*. It was shipped across Canada on flat cars to be put on display in Ottawa. (1)

A few years later, "Father" Hogan, that beloved Anglican missionary, who was soon to lie, "with my Haida braves. ." in the little Masset cemetery, wrote a column for his church paper in which he mused,

"How strange it is that the old Haida of over 300 years ago, arrived at the lines of a truly fast boat from just battling around the waters of these Islands, whereas the white man with all his advanced knowledge has only just arrived at these lines in the past thirty years. For both the *Mauritania* and the *Lusitania* are built to the same proportions as the Haida canoe was, 10 to 1." (2)

(1) *Information from Mr. Robert Davidson of Masset,*
    who had helped in the building of the canoe.
(2) *1911 Report for the Diocese of Caledonia, Rev. William Hogan.*

CHAPTER EIGHT

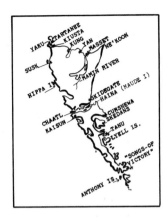

LEGENDS IN WOOD

In addition to the graceful war canoes, which were built long before any white contact, there are many other proofs of the highly developed Haida culture and creativity which was present when the European first arrived.

One is in the description of the superbly carved poles at Tartanee (Dadens) which intrigued Captain William Douglas so much when he visited there in 1789. There are several other records of early visitors who wrote of the carved poles at Kiusta, Skidegate, Skedans, Masset and Anthony Island (1) – and all these writings were before 1800.

A unique totem pole "raising" took place in 1794, when the American trading brig, *Jefferson,* out of New England and under the command of Captain Josiah Roberts, actually helped to erect a Haida Memorial Pole in Chief Blakow-Connehaw's village at Kiusta. (2) At the request of the chief they planed smooth a tall pillar and erected it, using ship's tackel. Three weeks later they helped to place a large carved figure of a bear, generously inlaid with abalone shell, on top of the pillar.

A sketch made of the pole five years later, by a member of the ship *Eliza,* showed it to be about thirty feet tall and massive in proportion. A pole of this type, but not as tall, stood for many years on the Masset Reserve outside Henry Edenshaw's home.

In general there are six recognized types of totem poles. The House Pole, which formed part of the house structure; the Mortuary Pole, which contained the remains of a deceased chief or other high ranking person; the Memorial Pole, which was equivalent to our tombstone and usually raised to a chief by his successor; the Heraldic Pole, recording the mythological history of the family; the Potlatch Pole, which was the largest and was the one over which much rivalry developed. It was sometimes distinguished by having from one to three high-hatted figures on top. The sixth type of pole was known as the Shame Pole,

(1) Hoskins, 1791; Bishop, 1795; Ingraham, 1791; Marchand, 1791.
John Bartlett sketched one of the Tartanee poles in 1791.
(2) "Contributions of Marius Barbeau to West Coast Ethnology", Wilson Duff.

and it was erected to ridicule or shame some person of high standing for not having lived up to his obligations. Often the subject of derision was carved upside down.

The famous black slate, or argillite, carvings were not made until about 1820. Developed exclusively for the curio trade, and not a part of tribal custom or ceremony in the way of the large wooden poles, these exquisite miniatures have from the beginning been eagerly sought after by collectors from all over the world. These carvings came into existence after a special type of slate was accidentally discovered near Skidegate by two white prospectors in the early 1800s. (1)

By this time Haida lads were being signed on as crew on some of the ships coming to trade, and later joined the crews of sealers and whalers. During the long months at sea the white sailors whiled away the monotonous hours by doing scrimshawing, or carving on bone and wood. The creative young Queen Charlotte Islanders were not long in following suit. Then when the Haida learned that the white man's penchant for trinkets was as insatiable as his own, he resourcefully capitalized on this by converting the unique Skidegate slate into excellent carvings to sell.

In the beginning these argillite carvings were influenced by the scrimshaw work of the white seafarers, but it was not long before Haida motif took its rightful place. Today the most popular argillite piece is a miniature totem pole.

---

(1) "Haida Myths", Marius Barbeau

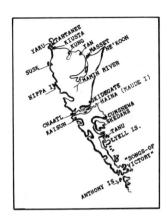

CHAPTER NINE

TO EACH LODGE A TITLE

Never a "wigwam Indian", the noble Haida liked plenty of space and comfort, so built his home accordingly. The giant crossbeams and supporting posts of these big houses have always been a source of wonder to Europeans. The very size of the beams and planks used necessitated the co-operation of many hands. The erection of a house, therefore, in all its stages from the cutting and hewing out of the beams in the forest to the launching and towing of them to the village, and then their final erection and fitting, were occasions for celebration. Natives from other villages were usually invited to join in the Potlatch ceremony of a house-building, which was the giving away of property by the person for whom the labor was done.

There was usually a set price for each worker. So many blankets for the men who dug the holes, so many for those who cut the beams and so on. It was hard work, but there was plenty of entertainment too, celebrations varying, of course, in extent and lavishness according to the wealth of the house owner.

Most of the lodges were about forty-five feet square, but several were larger. Where soil permitted there was a large excavation in the floor, sometimes two or three tiers below ground level. Each tier was planked and wide enough for a person to sleep with his feet towards the central fire. According to Chief Matthews of Masset, the main reason for the excavation was the draftiness of the ground level owing to innumerable cracks between the wall timbers.

The smoke-hole in the roof was directly over the central fireplace. In the summer villages, much smaller houses were built with no central excavation. Many a prospector who had permission to use these summer cabins found them extremely comfortable. The fireplace worked well; as long as the door was shut the smoke went straight up and out of the hole in the roof.

It was customary to give the large houses names. If a family moved from one village to another, and built a home in the second location, they often took the name of the house they had occupied in the old village for the new house. At Yan (opposite Masset) one of the houses was known as Gambling House and this name had been brought from the old village at Rose Spit by a family whose old

45

home was known by that name because the owners gambled so much.

The welcome mat idea was used by a chief in Haina (Maude Island) when he called his lodge, The-House-Always-Looking-For-Visitors. And on the east side of Lyell Island in the old Eagle village of Chicken Hawk Town, the house of the chief was so large there was a different name for each side. One half was named, Halibut-Drying-House and the other side was called Rock-Slide-House. It was said that they had cut so many planks for this house from the trees on the hillside that it looked as though there had been a rock-slide. The house pole for this unique house was covered with abalone shell. (1)

One of the chiefs at Grizzly Bear Town, Skedans — who, it was reported, had potlatched ten times — had a house with five successive steps under it. Its name was, The-Clouds-Sound-Against-It-As-They-Pass-Over. Tanu had a house called, Port-Simpson-House, because it was stockaded like the Hudson's Bay House at Port Simpson. When a newer house replaced it, the two posts nearest the door bore the figures of white men at the top. (2)

For many years the remains of a large Indian lodge could be seen on the Richardson Ranch at Tlell. Even in 1878, it was considered almost legendary because of its size, according to Dr. Dawson. (3) It had been erected by a Skidegate chief, stories of whose size and powers were told and retold in many Indian tales. The region came into the possession of that Chief Skidegate as the property of his wife, but was afterwards given by him to the Chief Skedans of that day as a peace-offering for the wounding or killing of one of the Skedans women. Its name was translated to mean, The-House-Chiefs-Peeped-At-From-A -Distance-Because-It-Was-Too-Great-To-Let-Them-Come-Near. In contrast, another house belonging to the Skidegates at Tlell was called simply the Steel-House. (4)

In Masset, young Henry Weah, who was born around 1852, became Town Chief of that village in 1882 because of his immense popularity. He was fortunate to have survived to achieve this, as he had three very narrow escapes from drowning as a young man and shortly after becoming chief, he met a bear with murder in its heart. Young Henry Weah killed the bear with his naked hands. Brought up a pagan, he was converted by Collison and became a good church worker. When he died in 1932 at the age of eighty-two, he was succeeded by his nephew William Matthews — who in turn has become a much respected and revered chief. Henry Weah's predecessor had lived in a good sized house in Masset, but when young Henry became Town Chief he built a huge home — so big that it was known as the Monster House. Henry's successor, Chief Matthews has a new home in Old Masset on the exact site of this Monster House, and the giant beams from the first house can still be seen in his basement.

Decorations, often of a practical nature, were introduced into all sections of the big houses. For instance, on one house at Kiusta the front end of the stringers were carved in the shape of sea-lion heads. Each stringer was grooved along the top to carry off the rainwater which ran through the sea-lion's mouths. Thus they formed gargoyles. (5)

(1) (2) (4) (5) "The Haida", J.R.Swanton
(3) Report of 1878 by Dr. G.M.Dawson

CHAPTER TEN

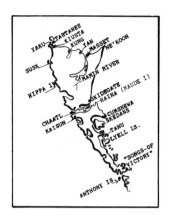

RAVEN MUST THE EAGLE WED

In the well-defined Haida plan, the whole of this nation was divided into two basic clans — Ravens and Eagles. Each of these clans was again subdivided into numerous families and subtribes — which sometimes took their names from towns or camping sites.

When it came to weddings exogamy was strictly adhered to. This meant that people belonging to the Raven group *could only* marry someone of the Eagle clan. Marriage within one's own clan was regarded as incestuous. Following a matriarchal system, the children always belonged to the mother's clan, and even in death a wife and children would lie with the wife's people.

This explains why a chief's son was never his successor — for the boy would be of the opposite clan. Chieftainship was passed down, first to the chief's brother (if he had one) then to the eldest son of the chief's eldest sister. In view of this a man tended to regard his sister's children as closer than his own, as they would inherit. Where nature did not provide a suitable descendent, an adoption would be carefully arranged.

The special calling of Shaman would also be passed on this way. Although an uncle might instruct his nephew how to become a Shaman, or medicine man, it was still necessary for the aspiring Shaman to have visions and hallucinations before being one and he had to undergo severe rituals for at least a year. They believed implicitly that disease was caused by evil spirits, and treatment consisted mostly of mystic practices devised to overcome these spirits and drive them out of the body of the patient. Visions, fasting, singing and special dancing aprons and rattles were part of the occult art.

The fee for doctoring depended on the wealth of the family or upon the anxiety of relatives for the medicine man to do his best and could be ten blankets or just one. If the patient died, the blankets must be returned. Being a medicine man was no easy task. One story is told of a medicine man being brought to the side of a sick woman that two other Shamans had failed to cure. His visions showed him that her problem was a canoe in her chest. Now this presents a special technique for removal, as anyone would admit. But by massage

47

of her abdomen and the utmost in incantations he was able to draw the canoe up and out to the surface of the chest. Walking in a circular fashion, all the while massaging and incanting, he was suddenly able to deftly grab the canoe, pull it out and transfer it to his own bosom thereby breaking the spell. In two days the woman was well. Because he had succeeded where two others had failed, his reputation was established, and from then on he was in great demand.

Each family had certain crests, names and so on which could be handed down by heredity, or purchased from another family. Crests were the visible symbols that set the various kin groups apart and were exhibited on all manner of belongings: costumes, feast dishes, house fronts and, most prominent of all, on totem poles. They were a heraldic device to mark the family and social position of the wearer. Clans of outside tribes such as Tlingit, Tsimpshean and other groups with matriarchal kinship would compare crests to see if they could marry a person in another tribe, for crests were more important than names.

Generally speaking wives and children were treated with much affection and tenderness, and the women took an active part in any matter affecting economics. Much attention was paid to the advice of the aged, even elderly slaves being respected for their wisdom.

The social organization was based upon kinship and rank. Rank meant three distinct classes — nobles, commoners and slaves — and as in any society, the bulk of the people were from the middle group.

The group known as slaves were the captives taken in war and no difference was made between those speaking Haida and any others. They were the absolute possession of their owner. In general they were not treated unkindly, although there were instances of grossly inhuman treatment. This usually occured when a man wanted to make a big impression on others and thought some form of cruelty would be dramatic. A case in point is the odd time when a slave might be killed in connection with a house building potlatch to be buried — sometimes alive — under the House Pole. And there were owners who forced them to do extremely heavy work and undergo severe privations.

Occasionally a slave might escape by running away, but upon returning to his own village he was treated as the lowest of the low. To have been a slave gave one a very bad name, and only an excessively brave deed or some distinction such as artistic ability would ease the burden. In the case of a person of the upper class he would need to acquire enough wealth to give successively large potlatches. The road back was never easy.

In the Monster Lodge of Chief Henry Weah there were three slaves that his nephew, now Chief Matthews, remembers well. Mr. Matthews lost his father at an early age and was brought up by his uncle. Two women and a man, the man was a captive from Bella Bella and was put in charge of young Matthews. Great was the bond of affection between the two, so much so that for many years the young boy actually believed the older man was his grandfather and loved him dearly. When he prepared to embrace Christianity, Chief Weah offered his slaves their freedom, but the old man from Bella Bella wouldn't take his, for he had become too much a part of the family. (1)

(1) Told to the author by Chief Matthews of Masset, 1965.

Slaves could be bought and sold. If they had children by marrying other slaves the children were also slaves and belonged to the owner of the mother. The greatest number of slaves were owned by Chief Albert Edward Edenshaw who not only inherited a great number but whose wife brought many with her to add to the household. Being a very wealthy man, he was able to purchase as many more as he wished.

The chiefs always came from the upper class and were of three kinds; Town Chiefs, Family Chiefs and House Chiefs. The Town Chief was only found in the larger villages, and he would be a Family Chief as well, but could rule only in his own village.

The Family Chief, on the other hand, could be a chief of families in more than one town, but not a Town Chief, although in smaller villages he would be put in the role of Town Chief. In the larger villages he was merely one of a group in which the Town Chief ranked first. A House Chief was a Family Chief in miniature.

There was no overall or absolute chieftainship, such as emperor or king, among the Haidas and the chieftainship was never the absolute and despotic authority sometimes attributed to an Indian chief. He was the head or president of the various family combinations, but unless his decisions carried the assent of the other leaders, they did not have much weight.

If there was more than one choice for Chieftainship the richest man was generally the one with the best chance. Town Chiefs would often marry out-of-towners in looking for a wealthy match — for sometimes wealth as much as ancestry determined class and the noblest Haida was he who could provide the most lavish potlatch. Those families who maintained prestige by successive generations giving potlatches had the highest status — more so than those whose rise was comparatively recent.

Feasts and potlatching were the two principal means of increasing one's social position among the Haidas. Feasts were expected from all the upper class families and Town chiefs. The Potlatch was the giving away of property — in reality the public witnessing for payment of debts. When a man died, his wife's clan conducted the funeral. Then when his successor made a Potlatch to put up the Grave Post, he would invite all of them to it. But the biggest affair was usually the one in connection with a house-raising, and here the chief beneficiaries were members of his own clan.

Property divisions were clearly defined and respected. Certain rivers, berry patches and beaches belong to certain families and no one else used them without permission and payment. Chief Matthews drew the map divisions (shown on page 332 in map section of this book) illustrating how this division was done for the north part of Graham Island, and it will be realized from this that very little of the land was not in full use.

The southern part of the Islands was similarly divided. In general however, the Haidas used the shoreline and not the interior of the Islands. According to stories, land as well as ownership of a town might be exacted in payment for injuries — as was done in the case of the lodge at Tlell. Land could be legitimately parted with by the family in possession.

The story of Masset is the story of a gift of a town. In very early days it was a Raven village and its chief was Seegay. This man decided that he wanted his son

49

to be the next town chief. The boy was in line to inherit the Eagle chieftainship of Weah, and could not become heir to Seegay's Raven title. So Seegay transferred the whole town to his son Weah, and the town chieftainship passed to the Eagle lineage of Weah. This boy was the uncle of Chief Henry Weah, to whom the title was later passed. (1)

In the ancient days, each town was inhabited by one clan only. The women of the town all belonged to outside towns — to which they and their children would later return. But as time went on, some children remained in their father's town — and also many of the social activities during the winter required the presence of each clan — and so the larger villages became occupied by members of both the Raven and the Eagle clans. The village, however, would be known as belonging to the traditional owner.

Summer camping places were occupied by only one clan. The carved poles were not found in these temporary sites but only in the more permanent winter locations. (2) The one exception, perhaps, is the sea-otter hunting camp, just north of Susk. This was Tledo and there was at least one totem pole here.

(1) Information from Chief Matthews and Prof. Wilson Duff.
(2) Map with village sites and main camping locations may be found in map section of this book. Owing to lack of accurate records the map is far from complete.

CHAPTER ELEVEN

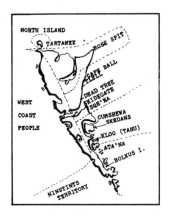

IN THE BEGINNING ...

In the absence of any written history, Haida origin is still a subject of speculation. A popular theory is that they were part of a migration from Asia, via Alaska. But there are also arguments supporting the idea that they may have come accidentally from Asia by way of the Japanese Current, when trading prehistorically in boats on that far shore.

Regardless of where or how the original inhabitants did arrive, undoubtedly the Queen Charlotte Islands have been the established home of the Haida Indians for centuries.

Although they did not have a written language, Haida children were well-educated by their elders. Legends and tales of history were repeated endlessly, until the youngsters had committed them to memory, word for word. In this way the history and customs of the race were handed down intact from one generation to the next — almost by rote.

About 1900, a keenly interested anthropologist, Dr. J. R. Swanton of the Smithsonian Institute made one of the most extensive researches ever made into Haida history. After an exhaustive study of the legends, tales and myths gathered at great length from elderly people living then, it was his opinion that the Raven clan might represent the true Haida, with the Eagle branches coming into the picture a little later. According to legends, the original seats of the Haida race seem to have been on the east coast of Moresby Island and at Rose Spit.

Taking the Raven legends first, there were three main points of Raven origin, Bolkus Island, House Island and Rose Spit. Four main ideas were the basis of all their legends which were as follows:—

No. 1.   After the Flood (which was raised by the supernatural being at Cape Ball) began to subside, a reef in Skincuttle Inlet rose to the surface. This was on or near Bolkus Island. And on this reef sat the Foam Woman who became the ancestress of all the Middle-Town-People. (Some of these were the Striped-Town -People who took their name from a rock there.)

No. 2.   About this time another island, Ata'na (House Island), near Hotspring Island, also came to the surface. Upon this island there was a cockle shell, and from this shell came a woman who is the grandmother of all the Sand-Town -People, and also a branch known as Those-Born-At-Dead-Tree. Some of the Dead Trees used to say that they had been washed ashore in a cockle shell (and free from impurities), but they all felt that the woman from Ata'na was their ancestress.

No. 3. One Rose Spit tale says that when the Flood began to subside only Rose Spit and Bolkus Island were showing. There is another which says that the Flood never covered Rose Spit, and that there were two humans there and from them came all the Rose Spit families:— Point-Towns, Rear-Towns, and Standing-Water-People.

No. 4. A fourth legend tells that the story town of Sqe'na, just south of Sandspit, was the origin of all the Raven tribes plus a few of the Eagles, and that they took their names according to the row of houses they lived in, such as Rear-Town, Middle-Town, Point-Town and so on.

In the case of the Eagle legends, however, Dr. Swanton found that their stories did not have the same strong pattern that was found in those of the Ravens, and so tracing the Eagle tribe movements can be only a broad generalization as is the separating of their ancestry into three approximate points of origin. There was a noticeable mainland influence in many of the Eagle names and legends.

Separating the people of the Eagle crest roughly into three divisions, going from south to north, would result in:—

No. 1. The group of Eagles of Ninstints Territory.

No. 2. Those descended from Property Woman.

No. 3. The large group of Those Descended From Labret Woman.

As the tribes became intermingled, (1) geographically they fell into six groups, the southern or Ninstints group; the people of Skedans, Kloo and Cumshewa; the people of Skidegate Inlet; the West Coast people; the people of Rose Spit and North Coast; and the people of North Island, who became the Kaigani.

There was very little difference in the dialect of the Massets and Alaskas — but a marked difference in the Massets and Skidegates. Then a lesser difference between that spoken by the Skidegates and the people in southern parts of the Islands.

Before leaving the tribal divisions, it might be appropriate to say a word about the group known as the Kaigani. Kaigani stock was composed of Ravens from Ata'na, Bolkus, Rose Spit and the West Coast. The Eagles joining them came from Kayang (2), and from a village near the stream north of Yan (3), and there was also an Eagle group from Scotsgay Beach, near Skidegate, among the migrators.

The migration is generally presumed to have taken place just after the time of the first white contact — since Captain Douglas spoke of the North Island village by its old name of Tartanee and said it was a thriving, well-inhabited town. Whereas after the migration it was known as Dadens, and was only irregularly

(1) See Appendix One for Haida migrations
(2) Kayang was the small village to the south of Uttewas,
  and later these two villages became the one village of Old Masset.
  Today it is commonly called Haida.
(3) On the opposite side of the Inlet to Old Masset, and slightly to the northwest.

inhabited and seems to have had a fire which destroyed the large houses and poles which were mentioned by Douglas as well as other early visitors.

There are several versions of the quarrel that precipitated the flight to Alaska but, according to Dr. Swanton, the Haida branches who migrated had been moving northward for generations, and this corner of the Islands was becoming over-populated. The mountains of Alaska can be seen very clearly from here on a fine day, and it needed only a small inducement to make the people move northwards again.

CHAPTER TWELVE

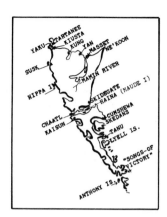

THE "COMPANY"
OFFERS A CHALLENGE

As 1799 turned the corner into a new century, the fur trade was booming along the North Pacific coast. Ships of many flags were crowding the seaboard – and dreams of a rosy-hued future appeared to be becoming a reality in the mounting prosperity for buyer and seller alike. The magic formula to wealth lay in the glossy pelt of the sea-otter – and right in the heart of all the trading were the Queen Charlotte Islands.

Europe was being swept by the Napoleonic wars with the result that few vessels from the Old World were seen on the Pacific coast and, except for the few posts established by the Russians in the north, the whole of the maritime trade was dominated by the "Gentlemen from Boston."

But this monopoly was soon to be vigorously challenged.

In 1821 George Simpson, the energetic governor of the newly amalgamated Hudson's Bay Company (with the Northwest Company) cast a practised eye at the coastal trade and liked what he saw. Skilled from years of inland trading, the officers of the Company shrewdly assessed the best means of wresting the profitable trade from the Yankees. To be worth while, it would have to be a long range plan.

A series of strategically located trading posts plus a regular canvass of the more remote areas by their own ships would put them on the spot to corral all the business, they thought.

So in 1825 the first post went in at the mouth of the Columbia River, and the little *William and Anne* was sent north to harvest furs. She went to Skidegate and Cumshewa on the Islands, the two most important trading areas there. Other vessels followed her lead.

Six years later Captain Aemilius Simpson was sent to establish a second post at the mouth of the Naas River. The post was no sooner completed when the dapper little captain became violently ill on a trading trip to Skidegate and died. He was buried at the Naas post which was then named Fort Simpson in his honor.

The site was so difficult for sailing ships to approach that in 1834 the post was relocated on the Tsimpshean penninsula. The body of Captain Simpson was reverently exhumed and transferred — together with the name — to this new site which rapidly became an important trading center for the north.

The turn of the century marked the zenith of the lucrative sea-otter trade. This animal has a low reproductive rate and the indiscriminate slaughter could have but one inevitable result. Some idea of the wholesale destruction which took place was graphically illustrated in the 1802 account of one Boston trader who collected over 15,000 skins in a short summer's trading. And William Sturgis, master of another vessel, claimed to have purchased 6,000 in a single voyage to one region.

Competition among the traders became increasingly keen and tough. In an effort to win favor among the Indians, traders offered them drinks of rum. At first the Indians abhorred the taste but, once the initial revulsion had passed, desire for it became intense.

The Fort Simpson post did not offer liquor or arms for trade. This policy was enforced not necessarily because of any moral scruples on the part of the H.B.C., but because they had long range trading plans and knew that liquor and trade simply did not go together. Guns were not offered for the obvious reason that there was still too much unpredictable hostility in the air. (Later, in 1852, they had to revise their policies, for when the miners began to arrive the whole aspect changed.)

Before long the H.B.C. realized that their post on the Columbia River was not as convenient as they had thought and in 1843 James Douglas was sent to establish Fort Victoria on the south end of Vancouver Island. Called Camosun until 1846, this post grew rapidly into a lusty seaport — and it was the lure of the "bright lights" of this city that was to have such a devasting effect on the Haidas, and ultimately lead to a change in their destiny.

The first Haidas to go down that way were the sophisticates of the trading world, the Indians from the southern part of the Charlottes. Not being able to get the coveted liquor at Port Simpson they rarely went to that northern post as they found it was always available in Victoria — for a price.

The logs of captains of trading vessels had begun by now to unfold the story of changing trade, showing that instead of only sea-otter peltries, they were buying a variety of items from the Haidas such as fur seals, marten, bearskins, fish and potatoes. Potatoes were being purchased in increasing quantities as even in 1825 the Indians on the Island had a number of patches under cultivation. (1)

By 1834 the sea-otter trade had dwindled to almost nothing and in search of other possibilities the H.B.C.'s vessel *Vancouver*, under Captain Alex Duncan, sailed to the north end of the Charlottes. Caught in a storm off Rose Point, his unwieldy ship struck the long bar of Rose Spit and began to break up. The crew managed to get off safely, but were unable to save their ship. This was home ground for the Haidas living nearby, so they went on board and took everything of value off before she was completely lost.

The Hudson's Bay Company were irate over this unauthorized salvage and confiscation of their possessions but there was not much they could do about it. Realizing that sailing ships operate under a handicap, the Company was prompted to order a steamer for trade along the coast. In 1836 the first

(1) According to Marius Barbeau, the Haidas called the potato "Skuseet"
and obtained the seed from the Hawaiian Islands.

steamship to be used on the Pacific coast, the *Beaver,* arrived at their Columbia River post, and early in the spring of 1837 she made her first trip to the Charlottes, going as far as Skidegate.

CHAPTER THIRTEEN

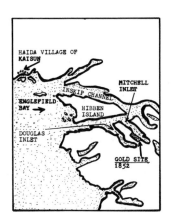

BRITISH COLUMBIA'S
FIRST GOLD RUSH

Some of the first gold to be 'mined' in British Columbia was promptly thrown into the sea by a small Haida boy who grew weary of waiting for his parents.

The H.B.C. had suspected for some time that the Haidas had knowledge of a source of gold. An occasional sample had been shown in Victoria, and quite a few pieces turned up in Fort Simpson. How to ferret out the source of it without arousing undue interest posed a problem.

The Chief Factor at the Fort Simpson post was puzzling about this when he saw Albert Edenshaw (1) enter the store one afternoon. Aha! thought the factor — here is my answer. Not only does Edenshaw know the Charlottes almost as well as the back of his hand, but also he is a "potlatching" chief on the way up. Feeling sure that Edenshaw would be interested in adding to his fortune, and would keep his silence — if it was worth his while — he approached the chief with an ore sample and asked him if he knew of any more like it. Edenshaw turned the rock over in his hand and, ever the bargainer, parried, "You want more?"

"Yes" replied the factor, "and I'll pay well for it."

"How much?" grunted Edenshaw, thinking it pretty doubtful that anyone would pay much for just a piece of rock.

The factor made the shape of a large box with his hands and said, "you bring me this much and I'll give you enough blankets for a potlatch."

Edenshaw turned quickly to look elsewhere and hide his gasp of astonishment from the Hudson's Bay man. *That* much payment for a box of rocks! It looked as though he surely must have hooked the proverbial "live one".

When he regained his composure, he said offhandedly that he would think about it and see what he could do. He could hardly wait to get home and make discreet inquiries. It was not until he attended a celebration in Skidegate a few weeks later that he had any luck.

Sitting around the fire there, he casually brought out the sample of ore the

(1) English name adopted by Edenshaw following baptism, many years later

Hudson's Bay man had given him and asked if anyone had ever seen anything like it. No one had. Then one old lady left the fire and went to look among her treasures and sure enough she did have a piece — of even better quality than Edenshaw's sample. Edenshaw told her that he liked this kind of rock very much and would like to get some more of it, if she would show him where it came from.

Flattered by the attention of this wealthy chief from the north end of the Islands, the old lady agreed to guide him. Accordingly they set off early next morning for what is now known as Mitchell Inlet in Gold Harbor, just Edenshaw, his wife, their small son Cowhoe (1) and the old lady. By catching the tide at the right stage through Skidegate Channel, they were at their destination in a few hours.

Leaving the four-year-old Cowhoe in the canoe, the others clambered up on to the ledge. Edenshaw started chipping the golden ore from the quartz rocks, and his wife carefully gathered it up in a basket. It was very hard, tiresome work, but at long last the basket was full. Envisioning the exorbitant payment that had been offered him and the fact that there were still a few hours left before they needed to return, Edenshaw tried to fill a second basket.

His wife was sent to empty the first into the bottom of the canoe and wearily they set about filling the basket once more. It was back-breaking, but eventually they had enough. Stumbling back to the canoe they gasped in utter dismay, for there were only two or three pieces of the first basketful left. Their small son had been amusing himself during the long wait by throwing piece after piece of the pretty rocks into the "salt chuck.".

In his rage Edenshaw would have thrown the boy into the water too, had not his wife been able to calm him. It was too late in the evening to gather more, so they went back to Skidegate with what they had. Later Edenshaw took it to Fort Simpson and, true to his promise, the factor gave him a huge cargo of blankets in return. (2)

Word of Edenshaw's bonanza was not long becoming known among the other Haidas who also took samples of the "rocks" to Fort Simpson. The prices they asked were so steep the H.B.C. asked Factor John Wark to see if it would be profitable for the Company to mine it for themselves.

Guided by Edenshaw, Wark set off by canoe in the spring of 1851. Upon his report of that visit the Company ordered the *Una,* under Captain "Wullie" Mitchell, to go with Wark and look the region over more closely. Going as traders so as not to alarm the Indians, the expedition went to Gold Harbor (as it became generally known) in July 1851. There were Indians encamped there, and they had dug out quite a bit of the ore.

The H.B.C. representatives began bartering for it, and took advantage of the opportunity to see just what there was in the way of a vein. It looked very good indeed. The bartering proved too expensive, for as soon as the Haidas realized how interested the white men were in the rocks they raised the prices out of all reason. Only about $1000 worth of gold was obtained on this trip.

H.B.C. headquarters in Victoria wanted more — but at cheaper rates. In October of the same year they sent Wullie Mitchell to the site in the *Una* once

(1) Anglicized version of the Haida name.
(2) Version given to author by Mrs. Fred Nash, Edenshaw's granddaughter.

more, and with him some miners who had a crude drill and blasting powder. Under John McGregor, an expert collier who did his best with the rude equipment, work was begun. There was great excitement when the blasts were set off and the huge chunks of rock flew into the air. For a few days everything went well.

Then as the Haidas realized how much the miners were taking, they were afraid they would be left on the losing end. And after all this was *their* land. As soon as the blasts went off they rushed out — almost before the dust settled — and scrambled for the dislodged rocks before the miners could get to them. Inevitably feeling turned hostile and there were several rough skirmishes.

Fearing bloodshed, the H.B.C. withdrew — taking with them about $75,000 of the gold ore. It was not the business policy of the H.B.C. to antagonize unnecessarily any natives in their trading areas.

The *Una* with her precious cargo set sail and Wullie Mitchell promised to have the men in Victoria for Christmas Day. The day before the feast day, as she entered Neah Bay, the *Una* grounded with a grinding crash on an uncharted reef. Her plight did not go unnoticed by some Indians and they came out to gather the spoils. After a fierce fight, the men on the *Una* were rescued in the nick of time by an American vessel, the *Susan Sturgis* under Captain Matthew Rooney. Strangely enough, Rooney was on his way to investigate the rumors of a "gold field" on the Queen Charlottes — a rumor which had been spread by a discharged H.B.C. employee.

This first gold to be mined in B.C. by white miners was destined never to be used by them, and it ended, as had Edenshaw's, in the sea. As the crew of the wrecked *Una* were taken aboard the *Susan Sturgis* (1) an Indian set fire to the *Una*. Slowly she burned to the water-line, then suddenly slipped from the reef and slid to the bottom of the bay, taking her golden cargo with her.

Gold had an irresistible lure to which the staid H.B.C. was not immune. Undaunted by the loss of their ship, they sent out another expedition the next year, 1852, in their schooner the *Recovery*. This time they sent a strong party with the ship to repel any hostile attacks by the Haidas. It was not needed, for the men were able to establish friendly relations with the Indians. The work of mining commenced in earnest — to be met with disappointment, for the apparently rich vein proved to be only a small pocket. Added to this, their blasting operations the second time were inefficient and more of the dislodged rocks fell into the harbor than on land.

Not only was the gold prospect disappointing but to the H.B.C. an even more sinister prospect was looming. Their old rivals the Yankees were swarming to the area. As the *Recovery* began operations six schooners arrived from San Francisco and anchored in the harbor. Two more arrived at the end of the week, adding to their concern. Most of the ships were carrying men fresh from the gold fields of California and it began to have the earmarks of a gold rush. When the Americans saw the H.B.C. at work they fanned out in all directions looking for new sites.

One of the American ships was the two masted brig *Eagle* belonging to Cyrenus Mulkley and his partners Abraham Way and Andy Burge. It was on this trip that Cy Mulkley, while tramping the beaches, found an outcropping of rock ledge, which when assayed showed "$16,000 to the ton". He was never able to

(1) "Pageant of B.C." — B.C.McKelvie

find the place again, although he tried several times. For years stories were told and discussed at length as to the whereabouts of Mulkley's "Lost Mine", which was said to have been a "day's sail from Skidegate."

When Governor James Douglas of the H.B.C. post in Victoria heard about the number of American ships going to the Charlottes he became alarmed — mindful of the squeeze that had gone on in Oregon earlier. He asked the Colonial Office to issue a proclamation excluding all foreigners from the Islands, effective immediately. He pointed out that not only were they attempting to mine but, also

> "I have just received information to the effect that the master of the American brig *Susan Sturgis* lately cut and carried off a cargo of spars from Queen Charlotte's Islands, a liberty that no British vessel would be permitted to take on American coasts."

The Colonial Office did not think that excluding all foreigners from the Islands was justified, but they did accede to Douglas's request for the *H.M.S. Thetis* under Captain Kuper to go to the region. The vessel would be engaged in making sketches and surveys during her visit, formally establishing the fact that this area was under the British flag.

Douglas, convinced that the American interest in mining on the Charlottes could be a cloak for the deeper purpose of annexing the Islands to the United States and mindful of his duty to the Company to protect their trading interests, finally had his efforts rewarded in a measure.

Early in 1853 he was appointed Lieutenant Governor of the Queen Charlotte Islands. His only real power in the office was the issuing of licences to search for gold. In March and April of that year he issued a proclamation of the Crown's ownership of all the precious metals on the Queen Charlottes, and required all miners to pay a specified fee, monthly. Buying of a licence acknowledged British Sovereignity over the Queen Charlottes. (This set a precedent for the Cariboo Gold Rush later on.)

The duties of Douglas's new office were easily filled; he did not have a single application for a licence. The Americans were not able to find any more gold than the H.B.C. had, once the small pocket had been exploited. And so the "Gold Rush" on the Queen Charlottes was over.

CHAPTER FOURTEEN

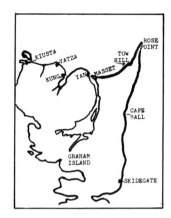

CHIEF EDENSHAW
AND THE SUSAN STURGIS

No history of the Islands would be complete without a short item about one of the most flamboyant of all Haida chiefs — the man who in later years became known as Chief Albert Edward Edenshaw.

He was born about 1822 (1) in the village of Althins Kwun, on the promontory of Cape Ball and, until he became chief, he bore the name of Gwai-gu-unlthin which meant He-who-rests-his-head-upon-an-island. His youth was spent in the stirring times of the Haida heyday and with two older brothers, who were considered to be exceptionally fearless men, young Gwai-gu-unlthin strained to his utmost to be considered just as brave.

The two older brothers were enjoying early manhood when they were killed in an ambush and Gwai-gu-unlthin, who was eighteen at the time, grieved bitterly over the loss of their stimulating companionship. But he was soon to have even more to think about. His mother was the sister of the powerful chief at Kiusta who bore the hereditary name of Edenshaw, (2) and when the two older brothers died the aging Edenshaw immediately directed that young Gwai-gu-unlthin should be brought to Kiusta to prepare for succession to the chieftainship of the Edenshaw tribe.

(1) The date used on his monument after careful reckoning but this is an approximate date as Haidas did not keep records of such events.

(2) The head chief at Kiusta, known to all early explorers, was Chief Blakow-Connehaw who exchanged names with Capt. William Douglas in 1789. (Chapter Three). As the migration to Alaska gained momentum Connehaw, with his family, became one of the Kaigani. To succeed him as head chief of the important village of Kiusta, a chief of the Sta'stas family was chosen whose hereditary name was Edenshaw, an Anglicized version of the Stikine name meaning, "The place where a glacier meets the sea — at the spot it begins to melt." As chief, Edenshaw moved to Kiusta, although he still maintained his house in Tow Hill, and celebrated his new station by erecting such a big housepole that his lodge was known as, "House-With-The-Pole-Reaching-To-The-Sky". (Information from Prof. Wilson Duff and from "The Haida" by Dr. J.R.Swanton.)

63

According to the Haida custom of chieftainship descending to the chief's sister's eldest living son (see Chapter Ten), he would be well cared for by his uncle and trained in every aspect deemed necessary for the position he was to assume. It was also the established practice for such a young heir-apparent to marry the chief's daughter (who by our standard would be his first cousin, although not so by the Haida's reckoning). This was to keep the property, title and wealth in one family to make it stronger. As old Edenshaw had no daughters for him to marry, it was arranged that young Gwai-gu-unlthin should marry the daughter of an excellent and powerful chief in Alaska. (1)

Before 1850 dawned, old Edenshaw was called to his "last voyage", and as his spirit joined the ancestors of long ago, young Gwai-gu-unlthin succeeded him, inherited all his property and officially took the name of Edenshaw.

The big Potlatch held at his succession was one of the grandest and largest distributions of goods and articles of value (including slaves) that had ever been known. Young Chief Edenshaw's inherited property included twelve slaves, male and female, and when he became united to his wife, his wife's father gave his daughter ten more, so the Edenshaw domestic establishment was liberally supplied with attendants. It was an auspicious beginning.

Being now his own master, he had full scope for the terrific energy and capacity he possessed. Taking every advantage of his good fortune, he soon added considerably to the prestige he had inherited. Knowing that the chief who could make the most potlatches was unanimously accorded supremacy, he set out to gather wealth. And as he had strained in his youth to equal the feats of his older brothers, now he would put that fiercely competitive nature to work in an attempt to equal, and perhaps even surpass, the greatness of the legendary old Blakow-Connehaw of Kiusta.

Wealth in those days consisted chiefly of slaves, blankets, furs and coppers (2) — a copper being worth ten slaves. It was said that he never captured slaves himself, but he constantly bought and sold them, obtaining them from Skidegate mostly and then going as far as Sitka to sell them. It was on one of these trading parties that he nearly lost his life.

He had been chief only a short while when he went with a large party to the Naas to sell a slave and a large copper. The Naas people recognized the slave as one of their own and claimed him — without payment. This led to an angry dispute and Edenshaw and a Tsimpshean chief engaged in a hand to hand struggle. One of the bystanders raised his gun to shoot Edenshaw, who adroitly swung his opponent around so that he received the bullet. The Tsimpshean chief fell dead. Although Edenshaw immediately raced for his canoe, he received two bullets in his flesh as he did so — and carried them there to the end of his days.

In the prime of his life he was said to have been a most impressive looking man, not tall, but very well built and handsome. On state occasions he travelled in a large canoe, elaborately painted at both ends and manned by a great number of slaves and attendants. He had an instinctive flair for the impressive entrance to any ceremony — plus the money to back up his claim to power. For by means of constant shrewd trading, he accumulated a large amount of property and gave a total of ten lavish potlatches in the course of his life — on a par with the

(1) "Haidas and their Legends" XXI, Charles Harrison
(2) See Appendix Two for description of copper.

great Ninstints of Anthony Island fame.

In 1853 (1) he established his head village at the mouth of Naden Harbor, and the village of Kiusta was vacated. The new village was known as Kung and according to Dr. Dawson, who visited it, Kung was a well-constructed and sizeable village. Building a lodge there to adequately house his entourage resulted in Edenshaw's Kung house being called House-That-Can-Hold-Many-People. (2) When times became slim, around 1875, he decided to move to a new site near Shag Rock, and called this village Yatza or "knife village". Edenshaw hoped the new site at Yatza would be an easier place to attract trade from Alaska.

Dr. Dawson reported that, when he was there in 1878, about ten houses had been built in this new location, and with a customary flourish, Edenshaw was planning a big potlatch to officially launch the new village. Invitations had been ceremoniously delivered to Alaska Haidas to come and take part in the celebrations there.

Never an indolent rich man, Edenshaw was an extraordinarily capable seaman, who liked plenty of activity, and many were the early ships that he guided in Island waters. Perhaps the one that was to become best known was the *Susan Sturgis*. Matthew Rooney, skipper of the *Susan Sturgis* had been trading in Skidegate Inlet when he decided to go around to the North Island region, and here in his own words is an account of what happened:— (3)

"On Thursday, September 23, 1852, sailed from Skidegate's harbor, east side of Queen Charlotte's Islands, bound to Edenshaw's harbor at North Island. We had on board the chief, Edenshaw and his wife and child, with two of the Skidegate Indians, one of whom had been to California with us, his name is Winnett. Nothing extraordinary happened until we rounded Point Rose on Saturday, September 25, when a canoe came alongside the vessel. They told Edenshaw they were from Fort Simpson and were bound to Massett Harbor. He asked me to allow them to come aboard, but I refused. They then traded some fish for some tobacco and went away. On the following morning some canoes came off from Massett Harbor, we being about four miles off to the northwest. I commenced trading with them for fish, believing that to be their object, as nearly all the canoes had more or less fish in them. I now counted twenty-five canoes around the ship — but never suspected an attack, having had a similar number around her before. I therefore, continued trading on the starboard side of the quarter-deck.

The chief, Edenshaw was passing the tobacco into the canoes, one of the seamen lowering the fish into the hold and another on the main deck at the port gang-way. While in this scattered position, a large canoe came along the port side, and one of the Indians jumped over the nettings on the deck. I ran from the quarter-deck to stop him and make him leave the ship, but at this signal the vessel was boarded simultaneously on all sides by at least one hundred and fifty men. I was in a moment, completely surrounded and overpowered. I rushed at the first Indian who boarded and was about to fire at him, but was seized by two others from behind, thrown on my back and dragged towards the stern of the vessel.

(1) Information from Professor Wilson Duff.
(2) "The Haida", Dr. J.R. Swanton
(3) "Ballou's Pictorial", Boston, May 2, 1857

Here I managed to break away from them, but was immediately covered by five or six muskets pointed at my breast, and was only saved by Edenshaw's wife forcing herself between the Indians and myself. Chief Edenshaw then came up to me and by dint of force dragged me away from them towards the cabin. A sudden rush was made, by which the cabin was immediately broken open and a fight ensued between the Chief and one of the other men, in which the former had his nose nearly cut off."

The chief of the Massets making the attack was old Chief Weah (not Henry Weah, but his predecessor) and now Weah told Edenshaw to stand aside, for the ship was in his territory and therefore his rightful prize. Edenshaw protested vigorously saying that as he had undertaken to guide the ship, he could not allow its capture when in his care. The situation was ugly.

For powerful as Edenshaw was, he was so completely outnumbered that his own life could be in jeopardy if he persisted. There was only one way to outwit Weah, and cannily he appeared to resort to the old, "if you can't lick 'em, join them", policy. Now to continue with Rooney's story:

"During this time I managed to make my escape to the after cabin, where I found four of my men secreted, all being stripped naked and one slightly wounded in the side by a musket ball. However anxious the chief Edenshaw and his party may have been to preserve our lives, they now appeared equally anxious to share in the plunder with the Massett tribe, for on our departure from the cabin, they began to ransack the whole vessel, cut down all the sails and let go the anchors. They removed all the spare sails from the hold as well as the fish and stores. They also took the safe out of the lazarette (which was placed there for safety) containing $1,500 in gold and silver, besides several amounts of private cash. During this time they were shouting most vigorously for my life.

I was therefore obliged to keep myself secreted as it was the intentions of those Massetts to shoot both me and my men, if we made our appearance. Edenshaw tried to make a treaty with them to spare our lives for a quantity of cotton and tobacco. But they grew angrier and overpowered Edenshaw and his men and forced us to quit the cabin. I was taken prisoner by a chief named Scowell, who told me in pretty good English that his wife's father was a Boston man and that he would protect me."

Edenshaw apparently agreed that Rooney should go with this Masset Chief, because Chief Weah was taking the attitude that it would save trouble and future repercussions if they merely killed the whole crew and burned the ship, thereby destroying all evidence.

By now the tide had carried the vessel onto the beach outside Yan. Edenshaw, the master bargainer, now held a long conference with Weah, offering him compensation to spare the men's lives and pointing out that undoubtedly the H.B.C. would pay a handsome price in ransom for the men. Edenshaw's offer to negotiate with the H.B.C. on Weah's behalf, asking $250 for the captain and $30 for each crew man (1) was the final inducement to get Weah's co-operation. Weah agreed — but none too willingly. Later Edenshaw sent word, officially, that he would dispatch a powerful war party to Masset immediately if the agreement

(1) Ransom would be paid in blankets, not cash.

was broken and the Americans harmed in any way.

That Matthew Rooney credited Edenshaw with saving his life is shown in the document, still in possession of Edenshaw's grandchildren.

"Fort Simpson, October 10, 1852.

The bearer of this, Edenshaw, is chief of the tribe of Indians residing on North Island. I have reason to know that he is a good man, for he had been the means of saving the lives of me and my crew, who were attacked by Massett Indians off the Harbor of that name. He and his wife and child were on board that vessel coming from Skidegate Harbor round to North Island, when on September 26, 1852, we were surprised by some canoes alongside. We were so overpowered by numbers and so sudden the attack, that all resistance on our part was quite impossible, but after gaining the cabin, this man and his wife and two or three of his men who happened to come off in a small canoe, protected us for seven hours until he made some terms with them for our safety. He saved my chronometer and several other things, which he brought to Fort Simpson and gave to me without ever asking for any remuneration. I hope that if this should be shown to any master of a ship, that he will treat him well, for he deserves well at the hands of every white man.   "Matthew Rooney"
                           Former master of the schooner *Susan Sturgis"*

In 1853 two government boats visited Edenshaw's territory and their commanders interviewed him. One of these was the captain of the *H.M.S. Tricomalee,* Captain William Houston Stewart, who reported that he found Edenshaw "to be a man of great influence in the neighborhood and I advise that he be treated with great consideration".

The steam sloop *Virago* under Commander J. C. Prevost also visited the area and concurred in this, added that Edenshaw was also far and away the best pilot he had ever met on the coast. Prevost took a great liking to little Cowhoe, (1) Edenshaw's son, and when he returned in 1859, on the *Satellite,* he gave the lad a book of Testament, inscribing on the fly leaf that he hoped he was "casting bread upon the waters" in doing so.

It was almost prophetic, for not only did Cowhoe treasure this book, which he could not read, but in later years he was the first Haida in Masset to become a professed Christian and was baptised George.

Both of Edenshaw's sons were outstanding men. George died in 1890, but the younger son, Henry, lived to be part of the difficult transition from old Haida customs to the adoption of the white man's religion and way of life. Chief Edenshaw was finally converted by his sons, and when he was baptised he took, appropriately, a name from the royal family of Britain, Albert Edward. Like all new converts, once the decision had been made he gave it his heart and soul, thereby influencing his people to follow his example in a large measure.

He still had a great deal of influence over his people, long after confidence in Haida chiefs waned in other areas, and it was because of his influence and that of young Henry Weah of Masset, that the North Coast Haidas were the last to be affected by the ravages of civilization.

In 1882 Reserve Commissioner O'Reilly laid out a reserve for Edenshaw at

(1) As with all written Haida names, it is an Anglicized version.

his Yatza village, (1) but by the next year he had joined with the other tribes on the north end of the Charlottes to form one big settlement at Masset, where Henry Weah, one of Masset's most popular Town Chiefs, had recently spread out the welcome mat. Edenshaw henceforth made Masset his home and died there on November 16, 1894.

For many years a large monument stood in the main street of Old Masset beside the much-photographed Bear Totem outside the house of Henry Edenshaw. It had been presented by the British Government (2) in recognition of the remarkable Chief Edenshaw. The inscription now partly effaced, reads:—

"In Memory of Albert Edenshaw, head chief of
Born 1822, Died 189
A member of St. John's Church
A staunch friend to the White man
He heroically saved the life of Capt. Rooney
and his crew of the Sch. Susan Sturges
attacked by Indians, Sept 26, 1852,
for which he is held in grateful remembrance."

The monument was intended for the Chief's grave when he died, but it was so heavy that the family erected another marker there and the historic memorial was moved to the garden of his granddaughter, where it stands today.

When Edenshaw died the chieftainship passed, according to tradition, to his nephew. This was Charlie Edenshaw, one of the most noted Haida carvers of all times.

(1) Information from Professor Wilson Duff, U.B.C.
(2) Information from Mr. Norman Brodhurst, Brentwood Bay.

CHAPTER FIFTEEN

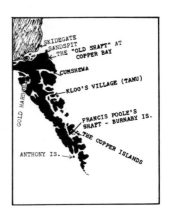

DOWNIE, TORRENS,
WADDINGTON AND POOLE

Although the flurry over gold possibilities on the Charlottes had died down by 1859, the head office of the H.B.C. in Victoria could not resist one last experiment. In July James Douglas commissioned William Downie to go to the old gold site on Mitchell Inlet.

Downie, an experienced miner from the 1848 California goldfields, took 27 men and provisions for three months. A diligent search of the old gold pocket, as well as the shorelines of Douglas and Skidegate Inlets, proved fruitless. All he could find of value, he reported, was some coal in the Skidegate Inlet region. This first mention of the mineral, which was to create such a stir later, went unnoticed.

About the same time as Downie left Victoria, Captain R.W. Torrens was encouraged by James Douglas to take a smaller party — eleven men — and search for gold on the Charlottes. Late in July Torrens and his men left Fort Simpson by canoe for Rose Spit. Working their way south along the east coast of Graham Island they found evidence of "color" in the black sands at several locations.

Calling in at Skidegate to pay their respects to the head chief, Nestacanna, they were invited to spend the night in the village, and anxious not to offend, Torrens accepted. The tent was set up, dinner prepared and Nestacanna and several of the other chiefs were asked to be guests for the evening meal. They had scarcely finished eating when a disturbance took place outside and the tent was surrounded by a crowd of Indians wrangling among themselves about the Torrens group. One man, Naskilkengan, was especially hostile and soon had numerous supporters.

"Several suspense-filled hours passed before Chief Nestacanna was able to calm the hostile ones sufficiently for us to make a move for our canoes," wrote Torrens in his report. "Hasty as our departure was, we did not get away before several shots were fired at us. Had it not been for Nestacanna's help, we would all undoubtedly have been murdered, for our interpreter said that the hostile Naskilkengan was telling the crowd, "These white men are come to take our

69

lands and our property from us. Come! assist me to put them to death. Not one of them will be living in five minutes." There were a large number of Skidegates fishing at Gold Harbor, and not knowing what their feelings would be towards us we deemed it advisable to return to Fort Simpson."

Upon hearing how Torrens had been treated at Skidegate, the Gold Harbor people sent a deputation to Fort Simpson urging him to return – assuring him of their good will. Sending two of his men with Chief Edenshaw to go to the Copper Islands, by way of Chatsina, Tongay and the northern Q.C.I., and leaving three of his group at Fort Simpson to prospect, Torrens took the remaining six men with him and went to the Charlottes for the second time. The party soon became discontented however.

"The place was condemned before a single blow had been struck," he wrote. The party on board the *Island Queen* which we had passed on our way to Gold Harbor, had become completely disorganized from disappointment. They had expected to get ingots for the mere trouble of picking them up and were disgusted to find that the quarts reefs in Gold Harbor would require hard labor. Their feeling of depression soon extended to my own men and after seven days I was forced to leave. The men refused to stay in the place any longer."

However the men who had gone with Edenshaw to the Copper Islands had been more successful. They had found copper, samples of which assayed 96 pounds to the ton – valued at $7,000. "No labor of drilling or blasting had been used to procure them," he reported to James Douglas, upon his return to Victoria.

The Torrens report was still very much the topic of conversation when a twenty-five year old Englishman, Edmund Cosworth Waddington, arrived in Victoria in 1862. Waddington, (who was related to the well-known B.C. pioneer Alfred Waddington, first Inspector of schools) had done some mining in Australia and was in Victoria lured by the Cariboo gold rush which was under way. The excitement about copper on the Charlottes intrigued him. Impulsively he went up there instead.

South of Sandspit he found his spot – a small copper outcropping. For the rest of that year, he and his men worked at putting down a shaft on the north side of what became known as Copper Bay. Returning to Victoria for the winter, they came back early in the spring to work once more on the *Old Shaft* as it became known locally through the years.

All this news of possible copper on the Islands interested the Wharf Street merchants in Victoria. They engaged Charles Smith, brother of the politician Amor de Cosmos, to go to the Charlottes to see what he could find. Smith prospected the whole of the southern part of the Islands and, being in the Skidegate Inlet area in August, he went to see how young Waddington was getting on.

The scene was one of bustling activity with the shaft down sixty feet, and the men working night and day to drive down farther. Noting the small outcropping on the surface, Smith could not refrain from asking Waddington why he was going to so much trouble and expense for such a small sign of ore.

"Oh, I expect to strike a large body of copper when I get down deeper," replied Waddington confidently.

But what he did find deeper is not known, for abruptly at the end of 1863 he covered up the shaft and returned to Victoria. In a short time he was on his way back to Australia — never to be heard of again.

The Old Shaft lay untouched until 1907, when two men named Sheldon and Shabot bonded it to D.R. "Windy" Young and his associates. In the Provincial Mining Report for that year, it was noted that Young was "employing a white man and two Indians to unwater it." They had unwatered to about 90 feet, it was reported, where they found that two cross cuts had been made, one to the east and one to the west, extending about 25 feet from the shaft. The foreman said that he had sounded a further depth of at least 45 feet.

In 1908 the foreman, Mr. McPhail, said they had reached the bottom — 190 feet — and found good showings of copper. Later that year the launch *Eola* took a Mr. Blackstock and party from Jedway, who were interested in the proposition of the Shaft. By 1909 it was once again abandoned, and as far as is known it was never again used. The site can be clearly seen near the road going to Copper Bay, even to this day, although the Shaft itself was filled in with earth several years ago as a safety precaution.

About the same time as Edmund Waddington was preparing to sink his shaft in 1862 at Copper Bay, the Queen Charlotte Mining Company of Victoria sent a young engineer named Francis Poole to the Charlottes to see if all the stories about copper were true.

Poole fell in love with the Islands and later dictated a book about his stay there. On every page he sings the praises of his beautiful Island setting. As the boat which took him there, the *Rebecca,* dropped her anchor in Skincuttle Inlet on August 11, 1862, Poole remarked, "As far as the eye can see either way, this land is a picture of loveliness."

Many names in the Skincuttle area can be attributed to Poole's visit — among them Burnaby Island, Rock Island and Skincuttle Island, which are still to be found on current maps.

One of his first friends among the Islanders was Kitguen who had just succeeded to the head chieftainship of Laskeek after his older brother was killed in a fight. Kitguen was now the hereditary chief Kloo (1) (of Tanu) and henceforth would be known by that name. Kloo assisted Poole many times during his stay, and was a big help in smoothing the way for introductions to other chiefs.

The first shaft was sunk on Skincuttle Island, then a larger one was begun on southeast Burnaby Island. After a year, the first shaft seemed to be hardly worth the effort, and Poole was weighing the idea of abandoning it when the decision was made for him.

The dreaded smallpox broke out among some of the Haidas who were camped on Skincuttle — and when several of them died there, the rest panicked and fled, leaving the dead where they lay. Poole buried the dead Haidas (possibly the first time a Haida was ever interred), then set fire to the camp buildings and shacks the Indians had used to prevent further spread of the dread disease.

Shortly after this he went to Victoria to make a report on his efforts to the Mining Company which had engaged him. Returning to the Charlottes in the

---

(1) From the Haida Xeŭ, meaning the 'southeast'; "The Haida", Swanton.
Word corrupted to Kloo and has a variety of English spellings.

spring of 1863 he passed by Bella Bella, and Poole was shocked to learn that this tribe had been almost completely decimated by smallpox.

"Many mournful hours of reflection did it give me," he said in his book, "when I came face to face with the enormous sacrifice of life I had unwittingly brought about through my unfortunate exploring party earlier in the Cascades, for we had introduced the disease in their neighborhood then. Remembering the shocking havoc of the Smallpox amongst the Q.C. Indians, plus my misfortune in carrying the plague to the tribes along the north and south Bentick arms — a similar fate seemed to be pursuing me. For now we picked up a sick European to go to Victoria via the Q.C. Islands. And what should he have but smallpox!"

The skipper insisted on putting the sick man ashore at Burnaby Island, despite all Poole could do, and in no time the newly arrived band of Ninstints Indians caught it. It wreaked havoc amongst them, raging in full force until it was spent.

As health was gradually restored to the area, a few of the Haidas had begun once more to congregate around the "diggings", when one day the supply ship *Nanaimo* was sighted. The Indians jumped into their canoes and went out to meet her; among them was Chief Kloo, who was delighted to recognize four of his own tribe grinning down at him from the schooner's taffrail. Poole's description of the incident reads:

"Great was the pleasure and pride of Kloo, for these fellows had been down at Victoria all winter. Kloo knew by instinct that his tribe would have a "dram all round" of the infernal "fire-water", whilst the Cape St. James Indians would be condemned to look on with envious eyes and watering mouths. Even Skid-a-gate and his lot getting only a sop; and so it eventuated. This quadruple piece of rascality had come back, sporting no superfluous luggage, but carrying between them, just as one might treasure ingots of gold, a large barrel of whisky, which pint by pint, I may say, they had earned and stored up at Victoria with a view to a single day's gratification at Home. What was the result? No advice, no entreaty, nothing availed from me. Swallow the "fire-water" they would and should. And hence within an hour's time after the first appearance of the schooner, Kloo and all his tribe had drunk themselves mad."

In April of 1864, eighteen months after he had first landed, Poole became increasingly discouraged by continuing trouble with his miners, who were perilously close to mutiny. Ironically, if he had not been able to enlist help from the Haidas, especially Kloo and some of the Skidegate encamped there, he would have been shot by his own men. So he arranged with Chief Kloo to take him back to Victoria by canoe, leaving the miners to go back on the supply vessel when it would arrive later.

He described Kloo's canoe as being large enough to carry Kloo, Poole and thirty-five braves, plus about two tons of freight. It carried three jury masts with a fair amount of sail, and although it could be a hazardous journey at that time of year, April, he was impressed with the cheerfulness of the Haidas, who sang most of the way. He was moved to say, he wrote, that he had never enjoyed anyone's company more — and it was a sight better than his miserable miners had been.

Exactly one hundred years later, in 1962, Mac Merrican International Mines

Limited began surveying and drilling on almost the same spot as Poole's original Burnaby Island work, but to date this newer operation does not seem to have been much more rewarding than the first try there, so many years ago.

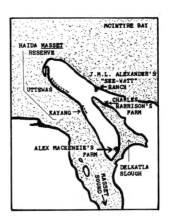

CHAPTER SIXTEEN

TRADING POST DAYS

The initial discovery of gold and copper had created a good deal of interest in mineral possibilities on the Charlottes, but it was still the Islands' fur trade which was the major concern. The H.B.C. post at Port Simpson had developed into a large enough centre by the 1860s to attract any of the Haidas who did not go either to Victoria or to Sitka, and the Company was aggressively pursuing all aspects of the fur trade. As a result, independent traders who made rounds on the Charlottes frequently found slim pickings.

An enterprising American decided on a bold course of action to forestall the H.B.C. Loading his sloop with trade goods he left for Masset to establish his own trading post − right on the Islands. He would get the furs from the Haidas before they left for mainland points.

It so happened that when he arrived in Masset most of the villagers were away and only a minor chief was left in charge. A persuasive spiel about the advantages of a trading post in their own village, so that the people would not have to cross the stormy waters to the mainland − plus a few lavish gifts − secured the chief's permission and assistance to set up a store. Having heard about the Haidas reputation for unpredictable hostility, the American had his store constructed in the form of a strongly timbered block-house − in case his welcome was short-lived. He arranged his stock for trade and, as an added precaution, placed a small loaded brass cannon in a position commanding the door. Then he opened for business and since his stock contained a goodly supply of "hootchum", he did a roaring trade.

News was flashed to Port Simpson, "Charley the Langleyman has built a house at Masset and is trading liquor for bears and seals!" (1) − causing consternation in the H.B.C. headquarters. When the rest of the Massets arrived home with the leading chiefs and found what the introduction of so much "fire water" had done to their village they were not happy with the situation either.

As darkness descended that night they decided to run their unwelcome visitor

(1)*From an H.B.C. Journal*

out of town and surrounded the block-house, demanding his surrender. Getting no answer they began to fire into it. But after the first shot Charlie fled via a secret entrance and under cover of night made his way to the beach. It was a hundred miles to Skidegate along the coastline, but panic lent speed to his journey and he covered the ground with amazing rapidity. In Skidegate he engaged a canoe to take him to Port Simpson, where he offered what remained of his house and stock to the H.B.C. (1)

The Hudson's Bay Company jumped at this opportunity to establish a post in Masset. Charlie's invasion of their territory had come as an unpleasant shock, and they had heard that Boscowitz was planning to put a station over there also. Trader McKay from Victoria, another thorn in the Company's side, was reported to have a small station near Cumshewa. On April 26, 1869, Chief Factor William F. Tolmie wrote from Victoria to ask Captain Herbert G. Lewis of the Company steamer *Otter*,

". . .engage if you can Mr. Rudland of Metlakatla as Indian Trader at a salary of about $40 a month and if he agrees, to place him with some trade goods at Masset Harbor. Make the best arrangement you can in the meantime for his accommodation so as to avoid the expense of building until the prospects for Trade there can be better ascertained." (2)

Apparently Mr. Rudland declined. The H.B.C. discovered that finding someone to run the newly acquired post after the row caused by its first owner would be extremely difficult. It was not until the next year that they were able to engage a man who not only would agree to do it but, more important, one who would be acceptable to the Masset people. This was Martin H. Offutt, (3) and his biggest asset was his Tsimpshean wife who was well-known and liked among the Haida. *Only* if she accompanied him would they permit the reopening of the post.

Mr. Offutt was ideally suited for the job. A hard-living man, who had made and lost more than one fortune, he had travelled all across the American continent in his day. At one time he had owned the land where Sacramento now stands and kept a prosperous saloon there during the California gold rush days. (4) Once again losing his wealth almost as soon as he had gained it, he became disillusioned with his life and drifted up the coast, thinking to prospect for gold in Alaska.

On the way up he stopped for awhile in Port Simpson where he met his wife. The ways of her people offered Offutt the contentment that his battered spirit craved and he adopted their life whole-heartedly. Settling down among them he soon came to be accepted almost as part of the tribe — and so fitted into the subsequent Masset arrangement very well. The Masset chiefs agreed to a permanent operation of the post as a result. From 1871 to the summer of 1874 Mr. A. Cooper was in charge of the Masset post (5) with Mr. Offutt replacing him in autumn of that year. In addition to fur seals and sea otters, the Company was buying a considerable amount of fish oil, which the Indians rendered themselves from the dogfish livers. When Factor Robert Williams made an

(1) "In the Wake of the War Canoe", W.H.Collison
(2) H.B.C. Archives B.226/b44/
(3) H.B.C. Archives and Mrs. E.C.Stevens, Skidegate, B.C.
(4) "In the Wake of the War Canoe", W.H.Collison.
(5) H.B.C. Archives B.226/b/45. fo.206

inspection trip to Masset, Offutt told him that he was having a hard time to attract trade to the post as the Company did not keep him supplied with trade goods and he was indebted at that time to the Indians for about $1,500. Williams said he would make a strong report about the matter, and noting that Mr. Offutt, his wife and two children were having to use the block-house for their dwelling place as well as a store, he told Offutt to build himself a house − at company expense. But he also told the Masset trader that the Company was going to pay only seven dollars instead of ten for prime large skins in future. Offutt shook his head at that news.

When the fur seal season opened the next spring Boscowitz sent up his schooner to catch, as well as trade for, seals − and Boscowitz's agent offered 50% more than the H.B.C. would let Offutt do. That year when furs were put on sale in London prices were down greatly and the Company's secretary notified all its branches that they were to reduce further prices given to the Indians for furs. Knowing the difficulties Offutt was having in obtaining furs after the first reduction, Factor Williams was afraid that the newest prices would finish things, causing the Indians to cross over to the Mainland in search of more profitable markets. It was June 1876 when he visited Offutt to break the news − and learned that there were three schooners engaged in fur-sealing off Masset, one of them was McKay's from Cumshewa.

In 1876 another white man came with his family to live at Masset − this was Rev. W. H. Collison. Collison was somewhat shocked at Offutt's unorthodox way of living for a white man, but soon became very fond of him and affectionately called him the "Squire". Offutt was due to retire so Collison suggested that the H.B.C. send as his replacement an officer commissioned Justice of the Peace as there were numerous disputes arising from time to time that needed to be properly settled.

In December 1878 Alexander McKenzie had replaced the retiring Martin Offutt as the H.B.C. agent at Masset − and became the Queen Charlotte Islands' first magistrate. The tall Scotsman had been formerly connected with the Company and was well-known to the Masset Indians from his time on the Skeena River and in the vicinity of Port Simpson. McKenzie did an excellent job during his time in office, helping to smooth out the rough spots during the difficult period when the old Haida ways were stymied in the attempt to cope with the relentless inroads of civilization. To help keep the peace, he organized a local police force of four stalwart young Haida men − each over six feet tall. These were Edenshaw's eldest son, Cowhoe; Steilta, successor to the great Chief Steilta; Kinaskilas, another name which was famed in many Haida tales of action; and the fourth man (unnamed by Collison) whose tattooed face evidently gave him a very fierce appearance. The little hut used for storing salted furs was the jail.

By 1883 the posts of Bella Bella and Bella Coola had been closed and Masset had been scheduled to close also − but amazingly this post showed a good profit that year − so it was "deemed advisable to continue the operation of the post at Masset for the present at least". (1) The low prices offered by the Company for fur seals, the staple trade of Masset, not only deterred the Indians from hunting them to any extent but also encouraged them to trade some of their smaller

(1) H.B.C. Archives D.13/14 fos 643-649

catch to competitors offering higher prices. Thus the trade managed by McKenzie continued under difficulties. Cunningham's schooner *Skeena* was taking quite a lot of the Masset trade, and in 1887 R. H. Hall, in charge of Port Simpson, suggested that the Q.C.I. post should have a like schooner to cruise the area, especially in March and April, to wrest the trade from Cunningham.

Mr. Hall's suggestion was approved by the Governor in London, but fears that the vessel might be seized in the fisheries dispute between the British and American governments changed the situation.

On August 1, 1887, Roderick Finlayson Dodd took over the post from McKenzie, who had been so captivated by the charm of the Islands he couldn't think of leaving. He purchased, and was Crown Granted, 1,015 acres surrounding Delkatla Slough, (1) built a house for himself near the entrance, and put in a big garden which did exceedingly well. The Islands had their first white settler.

He was so enthusiastic about the possibilities for successful ranching on the Islands that he was able to interest two other H.B.C. men, R. H. Hall of Port Simpson and C. W. D. Clifford of Hazelton, to form a partnership and set up a cattle ranch on the North Beach end of McKenzie's land. McKenzie and Clifford supplied the land and Hall undertook to do the actual ranching as soon as he could make suitable arrangements.

Charles Harrison, the Anglican minister stationed at Masset then, shared McKenzie's feeling about this land. Purchasing the grasslands area at the head of the Slough from McKenzie, Harrison built his home there when he left the ministry, and became the Islands second white settler.

Harrison had an edge on his neighbor in the farming venture. McKenzie resigned as J.P. and Harrison was appointed. Whenever a strong able-bodied offender came before Magistrate Harrison, he would be sentenced to work on the Harrison farm. In a short time Harrison had his land cleared and buildings set up at no cost to himself for labor. As the prisoners liked it much better than languishing in the tiny jail everyone was satisfied.

Roderick Dodd had been promised by the company leave for each year after he took charge of the Masset post — but in 1890 the company still hadn't got around to sending him a replacement to enable him to have his holiday. The isolation was beginning to tell on the thirty-five year old man.

In May of 1890 the steamer *Sardonyx* brought the large Alexander family to Masset. R.H. Hall, having had second thoughts as to the wisdom of cattle-ranching had persuaded his brother-in-law, J. M. Lindsay Alexander to buy into the venture, resign his position with the H.B.C. and go over to run the ranch. Alexander was the Senior Factor with the Company at the time, with Hall only a Junior Factor — and came after Alexander in any company promotion. But so persuasive was Mr. Hall, that despite anything Mrs. Alexander could say, her husband gave up his seniority in leaving the company at the time, to move to Masset. Hall was to resign the next year and both families would join actively in the ranching. But he never did. Instead he stepped into the senior position which was opened by Alexander's resignation. "My mother always told the old man he was an easy mark," recalled Wiggs later, "he couldn't see the

(1) *Lot No. 7 – which was registered to him in 1886.*

skulduggery when it was as plain as day." (1)

When Roderick Dodd learned that Alexander was an ex-H.B.C. man, he lost no time in capitalizing on this streak of good luck.

"Please — just take over for me for two months, I simply have to get away for a break," he begged and pleaded his cause so well that soft-hearted Alexander agreed. There was no way of letting the Company know, so it would have to be French leave, but Dodd would go by way of Port Simpson and explain. He left by canoe with a group of Haidas the next morning on his long overdue holiday.

The cattle had been already shipped to the Masset area prior to Alexander's arrival and although Alexander was anxious to get at his ranching, he moved his large family into the big H.B.C. house in Masset to tend the store for the two months Dodd was to be away. Two months and more went by, but there was no sign of, or word from, Mr. Dodd. Mr. Alexander was now obliged to hire someone to go out and look after the cattle and ranch while he kept an eye on the store.

What could be keeping Dodd?

Not until the following spring did he learn the answer. When the steamer *Danube* arrived with supplies for the store it had on board Crawley Stevens, a widower with two children, who told Mr. Alexander that he had been appointed to manage the Masset store. Dodd would never return. He had gone to San Francisco for his holiday and on his way back to Masset had his leg broken in a railway accident. Infection set in and he died of blood poisoning. Communications were so poor in those days no word had reached Mr. Alexander.

The Alexanders were at last free to move out to the ranch, "which we named See-Watt," recalled Wiggs O'Neill. "We all loved the life and everything was going nicely. There were no predators on the Islands, plenty of good grazing land and a mild climate so we didn't need much in the way of barns. The cattle grew sleek and fat and multiplied and there seemed to be no obstacles. But a vital factor had been overlooked in all the big plans — markets for beef were non-existent in those days.

Reluctantly, after a few years — for he had fourteen mouths to feed in his family — Mr. Alexander realized he had no option but to abandon the enterprise. He arranged with George Williscroft, of the Georgetown sawmill, to bring the *Nell* and take twenty-one steers to the mainland, planning to bring the rest of the cattle over in gradual stages.

"When the *Nell* arrived, bad storms broke and she was stormbound at Masset for ten days," remembers Wiggs, "but finally got away with a load of steers and the whole of our family aboard. On the mainland side the *Nell* pulled into Elizabeth Island and dumped the steers overboard in a bay and let them swim ashore. At $70 a day, step-dad was finding the expenses too much for him to handle. He moved us all to Port Simpson to live, then went back by rowboat to butcher the steers to try and get back some of his money peddling the meat. He did get a few on the first try but learned shortly after that a large portion of them had been drowned trying to swim over to nearby Porcher."

The remaining cattle on the Charlottes were abandoned. These amounted to

(1) J.M.L.Alexander had been a widower with nine children and shortly before going to Masset had married Mrs. O'Neill, a widow with three children — one of which was the well-known writer, the late Wiggs O'Neill. R.H.Hall was the brother of Alexander's first wife.

about four hundred, and were the progenitors of the famous "wild cattle" which roamed the northeast beaches of Graham Island.

Shortly before the Alexanders left Masset, Mr. Harrison brought the sad news to them that his old neighbor, McKenzie, had been drowned the night before. Evidently he had been visiting Harrison and returning late appeared to have slipped and stunned himself on a log whilst crossing a creek and drowned in the water below. Mr. Alexander and Harrison dug a grave in Mr. McKenzie's much beloved garden near the edge of Delkatla Slough, (1) then with Willie Alexander and Wiggs O'Neill as the only other mourners, the Islands' first settler was laid to rest. Rev. Keen, incumbent at Old Masset, walked the four miles from the village to take the service. (2)

Crawley Stevens was having as much difficulty as his predecessors in keeping the Masset post in the black, as a report to Commissioner C. C. Chipman from R. H. Hall in December 1892 indicated,

"...our efforts have been directed to putting our affairs on such a footing that we may be able to close the post at Masset without serious loss.

The trade is small and prices are regulated by those obtained on the mainland of Alaska, where American products are sold at rates with which we cannot compete. There is no Customs Officer on Q.C.I., and the natives are able to buy their supplies in Alaska without contributing in any way to the Canadian Revenue. The attention of the authorities has been frequently drawn to this matter, but the Coast line which would require protection against smuggling is so vast that, till there is a larger population on these Islands, there is not much hope of remedy." (3)

In autumn 1894 an agreement was made between the Company and Mr. Stevens for him to purchase the post's stock and to rent the premises. R. H. Hall wrote to Chipman recommending the transaction,

"...if anyone can succeed at Masset, Mr. Stevens will. When the Indians go away he will close the post and go fishing for dogfish, making probably three or four hundred dollars on the oil. He will also provide for his own wants of salmon, halibut and &c, and he is satisfied to live almost exclusively on the produce of the Island." (4)

Before coming to Masset in 1891, Mr. Stevens had been an H.B.C. employee at Hazelton, where he had met and married his wife. In 1882 their daughter Irene was born, and two years later Eddie arrived. The children were only seven and five years of age when their mother died. Stevens was a silent morose man who seemed to take little interest in his children, and Bishop Ridley persuaded him to send the youngsters to be cared for and educated in the new Ridley home in Metlakatla. Irene — or Rene as she was called — was the first child to be registered in the Ridley Home. (She married Walter Rudge, and their daughter, Elsie, became matron of that same home in 1930.)

(1) The late Mr. C.Smith of Masset remembered having the site
    pointed out to him by Charles Harrison, it was in the vicinity
    southwest of the present Anglican rectory.
(2) Information in a letter to author by late Wiggs O'Neill.
(3) H.B.C. Archives, B.226/b/81; Report from District Officers.
(4) H.B.C. Archives, B.226/b/94 (R.H.Hall to C.C.Chipman).

Both Rene and Eddie came to live with their father when they finished their schooling. When the H.B.C. closed the Masset post for good on June 1, 1898 (1) Mr. Stevens stayed on for a very brief period to sell the remains of his small stock, but his health was failing too much for him to continue operating even a small store. The site of the old H.B.C. post and residence is now occupied by the Primary School in Old Masset.

Captain Hugh McKay, who operated a rival post on the Charlottes, was no stranger to the coastal trade. He had first come to Victoria in 1852 where he went into the cooperage business with William Spring at Sooke for a few years. With the purchase of several vessels later on, they had branched out into the general coasting trade, operating mainly on the west coast of Vancouver Island.

In 1868 Captain McKay bought a fine new "fore and aft" schooner, the *Favorite,* of 125 tons, and entered the sealing industry. Plying his trade up and down the coast the idea of a small trading post permanently based midway on the Charlottes took shape. In 1869 he took up supplies to build a house near the entrance to Cumshewa Inlet. Laying in a good supply of trade goods, he engaged a Mr. Hargreaves to run it for him.

The little base was reportedly quite popular and soon the bay became generally known as McKay's Harbor. The post is known to have been operating in 1874, but four years later when Dr. G. M. Dawson visited there, it had closed down. However, the store building was still intact and in good repair. Dawson referred to the place as McKay's Cove after Trader McKay, but in 1921 when the *Lillooet* made a survey of that region — true to form — they changed many names. Captain McKay's name was taken from the chart to be substituted by McCoy's Cove, in honor of a Liverpool fireman aboard the *Lillooet.* (2)

There were two other stores operating on the Islands before 1900, one at New Kloo on Louise Island and another at the Oil Works in Sterling Bay, Skidegate Inlet. But they were not trading posts in the sense that the H.B.C. store at Masset and McKay's were, in that they were instituted primarily to collect furs. The stores at New Kloo and Sterling Bay were operated for the convenience of the residents, although for their size and isolation they carried a surprisingly good stock.

(1) C.C.Chipman's Report for outfit 1898-99.
(2) Information supplied by Mr. W.E.Ireland, Provincial Archivist, Victoria, B.C.

CHAPTER SEVENTEEN

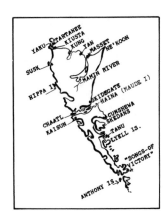

THE CRUSADERS

It is commonly said that the British Navy brought religion to the Northwest Coast. This is due to the influence of Commander James Prevost. When Prevost had come up to Masset on the *Virago* in 1853 to look into the *Susan Sturgis* incident, he had been distressed over the lack of church influence in the area.

Being a very religious man he felt it was imperative that, if the Indian was to be exposed to the seamier side of the white man, he should also be shown a way of coping with the moral degradation that could result from this contact. If not checked it might utterly destroy what was now an intelligent, creative and physically superb people.

The successive waves of smallpox which had accompanied the coming of the white man had carried off thousands of Indians already — particularly on the mainland side — leaving in its wake a land of desolation. The sickness brought with it poverty in marked contrast to the era of wealth which had preceded it. Now the lure of the cities was stronger than ever — with the readily available "fire-water" to blot out realities. As confidence in the old ways began to wane, so did the influence of the chiefs and older people, who tried in vain to stop the drain of young people from the villages.

The Charlottes at this time had not been as badly affected as some mainland areas, being somewhat protected by their isolation. But signs of the new trend could be seen, especially on the southern part — and would undoubtedly spread with devastating rapidity. The comeliness of the Haida women who had "gone to the south" made them particularly sought after for the age-old profession in the lusty seaports along the Sound and in Victoria — and the temptation of easy money was proving irresistible. Those Haidas who might be able to survive smallpox might not be so fortunate in overcoming the other diseases of civilization, thought Prevost.

He began a crusade to interest the Church Missionary Society in the situation and was successful. In 1857 when he returned from England on the *H.M.S. Satellite* he brought with him the first missionary for the Northwest Coast — young William Duncan. *(Church of England.)*

83

On advice, Duncan went to Port Simpson to set up his first Mission, as it was felt that this would be the most central place from which to work. He found the environment there anything but conducive to spreading the gospel, however, and after five years moved south to the Indian summer village of Metlakatla in 1862. He had intended to try to keep up a token contact with Port Simpson, but his heart was really in the new mission — which soon became a thriving center.

Some sixteen years later, Duncan began tentatively to talk about opening a new Mission in Rupert's Land. So in 1873 Rev. W.H. Collison and his bride — the first white woman to live in Metlakatla — arrived to take over Duncan's duties. With the rugged experience of having nursed in the Franco-Prussian war, Mrs. Collison's skilled hands were invaluable in the little community.

However, before he could be of any use, Collison had to learn the Tsimpshean language of his new charges and, as he did so, he soon heard many stories about the Haidas — mainly of their fierceness and fearlessness.

It was not until June 1874 that Collison had a glimpse of these fabulous Islanders. This was the first time he witnessed a Haida fleet coming into Port Simpson from the ocean and he never forgot it. Forty graceful canoes, each with two white sails, expertly handled, came gliding over the rolling waves before a stiff westerly breeze. As soon as the canoes neared the shore the sails were furled, and upon reaching the beach out jumped the occupants to drag the canoes above high water mark.

What a superb-looking people they were! Most of the men were over six feet and although many had tattooed faces, their complexions were markedly fairer than those of the mainland tribes. The women nearly all wore nose rings and anklets and many had several beautifully engraved bracelets on each arm.

Collison was delighted to find that he could talk to one of the women, who turned out to be the Tsimpshean wife of the young Raven chief, Chief Seegay, from Masset. Through her he was able to open conversation with the chief himself. Winning their interest, he invited them to visit him in the old Anglican Mission House at Simpson. The couple eventually visited Collison several times during their stay and the minister took advantage of every opportunity to plant a little missionary seed. He doubted that it would take root for Seegay was very reserved and non-committal.

That year, 1874, the Methodist Church opened a Mission in Port Simpson as the Anglican effort there was too weak to be considered even token. Duncan now changed his mind about leaving his beloved Metlakatla, which meant that Mr. Collison was free to strike out in new fields. He was drawn to the idea of establishing a mission among the Haidas, who had so captured his interest and admiration, but the Church Missionary Society was opposed to the idea, feeling that the long months he had spent in learning to speak Tsimpshean would be wasted.

When the same Haida fleet returned the following year, Collison was pleased to be able to renew his acquaintanceship with Seegay and his wife. He found now a troubled and anxious Seegay who asked many searching and difficult questions of the young minister about the new concepts of living that the missionaries were teaching on the mainland. Collison's seed had apparently fallen on more fertile soil than he had realized.

Brought up in the traditional Haida way, Chief Seegay was immensely proud of his heritage and people, and he was a very popular and much respected chief in his village at Masset. Well-versed in the stories of the "Power-Of-The-Shining -Heavens" of his forefathers and of the special calling of the Shamans, Seegay, nevertheless, even before he had met Collison, had begun to have grave doubts about some of the things he had been brought up to believe. For none of the entreaties or incantations of even the most powerful of Shamans had been able to halt the dreaded smallpox which had wiped out whole Haida villages. Nor could they overcome the strange and awful power of the white man's whisky which was doing so much damage among his people.

Although the old customs had been well defined and workable for centuries they could not cope with the new pattern of things. Seegay had been stunned to learn that the great and fierce tribe of Ninstints on Anthony Island who had feared no one, nor anything on earth, had been almost wiped out. Only a handful of people remained in that village, and it had been predicted that by 1886 even these few would be gone.

Skidegate, once so populous that there was barely room to launch a canoe from its beach, was now a mere skeleton of its former days — more than half the houses abandoned and falling down. The chiefs there were deploring the way their young people were going to debauch in Victoria. At Masset and along the North Coast of the Islands, Edenshaw and Weah and other chiefs were still influential enough to stop their people from going to Victoria (which was then represented as a den of iniquity) — but how long would this last? Seegay had seen what had been accomplished among the Tsimpshean by these missionaries and was impressed.

"Here among the Tsimpshean you now have two white churches. (1) But my people too, are in great need. Why do you not send someone to teach among the Haida as you have done for the Tsimpshean?" His point-blank request was all that Collison needed to spur a renewal of his plea to be allowed by the Church to go to the Haida.

In June, 1876, when the fleet came over from the Islands, Seegay was not in the group. But he sent a message to say he was very ill and anxious to talk with Collison once more. His wife also sent an entreaty, begging Mr. Collison to come to her husband, for she feared he was dying and desperate to talk once again with the missionary. Collison lost no time in rounding up a Tsimpshean crew to take him to Masset by canoe.

After many long and weary hours they arrived and were taken to the Town Chief's lodge. This was Chief Weah (2) of the Eagle Crest. Everyone crowded in to have a look and hear why the traveller had come. Weah understood some Tsimpshean, so Collison was able to explain why he had made the trip and with Weah's consent was taken to see Seegay. Seegay's wife had not underestimated the seriousness of her husband's illness, for it was obvious that he was in the final stages of T.B. — another illness that was to wreak havoc among the native people.

---

(1) *The Methodist church at Port Simpson and the Anglican one at Metlakatla.*
(2) *The descriptive Tsimpshean word for "great wind".*
   Name said to have been acquired from the Tsimpsheans by the Haidas. "The Haida", Swanton

Seegay, believing his days were over and confused about the old beliefs of his people, wanted to know more about the Great Chief who meant so much to Collison. After spending many hours satisfying the dying man, Collison returned to Chief Weah's lodge.

There he was grudgingly permitted to make the speech telling them he would like very much to come to Masset, and of the new way of life he would tell them about when he came, of how Seegay had sent word to him "across the waves" and that now he had come, his words of the new way had made Seegay very happy. Evidently the sincerity of his words created a favorable impression for some of the hostility faded and many of the older men nodded saying, "Yes, yes – it is so. But why did you not come when you came to the Tsimpsheans?" Then Chief Weah signalled his intention to talk and all were quiet as he began.

"Smallpox has killed many of our people. It came first from the north (from Russia via Alaska), and then when I was a young man, it came from the south. Many fine and brave men have died. You have come too late for them. Now another enemy has arisen. The spirit of "fire-water". It is really bad medicine. It came from your people. If the white man had this good news that you say – why did you not send it to us first, and not these evil things? You have come too late. Yes, it is too late now to help." And he sat down, sadly.

Collison showed him his dark hair (in contrast to Weah's grey head) and said, "See, I am still young. I could not come before. But Chief Seegay's call brought me instantly and I was not too late for him. I am not too late for you either – or for your children." But with a shaking of heads he was told, "No, it is too late, we cannot give up our old ways now." Then surprisingly they added, "But perhaps you can help our children." It was a touching moment.

Sensing the threat to their influence the medicine men were openly hostile and tried to talk down any idea of Collison's coming, but it seemed that the missionary was going to be permitted by the chiefs to have his chance, at least on a trial basis. Now it would be up to him.

The day after the meeting the great Chief Edenshaw from Virago Sound arrived on a peace-making visit with the Massets. Hearing about Collison and how much his visit had pleased the dying Seegay, Edenshaw sought out the missionary. Speaking Tsimpshean, Edenshaw told Collison that his nephew was also dying of T.B. Would Mr. Collison go and see what happiness he could give him? Collison consented, then asked Edenshaw to interpret for him later when he made another speech to the Haidas.

During the interpretation Edenshaw began to falter, and Collison was sure his message was not getting across, so he asked for an explanation – which he got in no uncertain terms. Edenshaw did not think much of this Christianity idea. He had been told that when the mainland people had embraced it they had been required to free all their slaves. He had worked all his life building up his collection – the largest in the north – and he had no intention of any such foolishness as those mainland chiefs had been talked into, he declared emphatically.

Concluding his visit to Masset, Collison returned to the mainland to decide where to set up his church. Permission had finally been granted by the Missionary Society for him to try among the Haidas. He must choose his base carefully for, with only one pair of hands, it would have to be the best possible location from which to evangelize in such an isolated area.

"Skidegate would seem to be the most central village," he wrote explaining the situation, "but the tribes of the southern Charlottes have suffered so much from their constant resorting to Victoria that I fear I would be fighting a losing battle. The northern Haidas are healthier and more vigorous, with a much greater proportion of women and children. And I feel that in them lie the hope of the Haida nation. Then too, the tribes of southeastern Alaska are close and it seems to me that under the circumstances, Masset is the best location."

On November 1st, 1876, when the steamer *Otter* arrived at Masset to pick up the last furs for the season from the H.B.C. post there, the Collison family were on board. For by now the Collisons had a small son, Will — the first white child to be born in Metlakatla. The Captain of the *Otter* was absolutely aghast at the idea of the family being left for the winter among the fierce Haidas. "You'll be murdered in your beds before the week is out!" he predicted. "At least," he begged Collison, "Let me take your wife and child back to the mainland. . .these people are still savages." But Mrs. Collison would not consider such an idea. If her husband was willing to try this new venture then she and Will would be at his side.

The furs were taken aboard at Masset and the Collisons went ashore. To their surprise they learned that the H.B.C. trader there was a white man. This was Mr. Offutt, who had been permitted to live in Masset under the protection of his Tsimpshean wife.The Collisons had only a tent to sleep in so the Offutt family invited them to stay with them, and then said that if they liked to clean up the tiny 10 feet x 12 feet hut used for storing the salted furs (now shipped out on the *Otter*) it might serve as a temporary home.

Next day Mr. and Mrs. Collison set about making the hut habitable. A crowd gathered to watch them. There was no hostility apparent, except from the medicine men, but there was an inordinate amount of curiosity, especially about Mrs. Collison who was the first white woman many of them had ever seen. They peered in the half window at the back, crowded into the hut, looked over all the items that were being unpacked, passed things around for interested inspection and tried on any garments that took their eye. There was barely room to breathe in the tiny hut, let alone move. As soon as he was able Collison put a new door in place — building a Dutch door, so that the bottom could be kept locked. Visitors could still satisfy their curiosity about what the newcomers were doing, and yet there was room for the three Collisons to move about. They were very conscious of a responsibility to create a good impression at all times — not only for themselves, but also laying the foundation for those of the Church who would follow later.

Attempting to learn the difficult Haida language, Mr. Collison visited every evening from house to house and talked to the people. It soon became apparent to him that what he really needed was a central meeting place. He was able to buy an old dance house that had fallen into disrepair, and with gifts of tobacco soon found many willing hands to help restore it.

That first winter young Will became very ill with typhoid fever causing grave anxiety to his parents. Hardly was he out of danger when Mr. Collison was stricken with the same illness. He was desperately ill and near death. The medicine men were delighted. Their powers were greater than the white man's. Boldly they went about foretelling his death. His unexpected recovery did nothing to endear him to them after this embarrassment. It began to look as though Collison's "Great Chief" had stronger powers than anything they could conjure up — for the minister should have died, all their signs pointed to that.

This escape from death by typhoid brought home to Collison the need to persuade the Haidas to change their burial habits. When the great Chief Steilta lay dying, he talked at length with Collison about Christianity. One of the Eagle Crest chiefs, Steilta, a tall, well-built man blamed his premature death on "too much hootchum". Collison was able to suggest interment and to his surprise obtained the chief's consent. Death was not long in coming — but his tribe were violently opposed to interment for their chief. How could his spirit roam free if he were under the ground? But Steilta's father said that his son had wished upon his death-bed to do this thing. . .and so be it.

The first burial combined some of the ancient Haida rites with the Anglican church customs. Swans-down was scattered on the coffin, a death dance was performed together with the traditional wailing. As the coffin was lowered into the ground and the simple service recited by Collison — a cannon was fired.

Since Christmas the canoe builders had been hard at work along the beach and by March all the canoes were ready for the mainland market. Mrs. Collison, who was pregnant, was suffering from a painful ailment which required surgery so Collison decided to take advantage of the large flotilla going to Port Simpson and take his family over to the mainland.

It was March 31st when the fleet left Masset, and a beautiful day. The Collisons were in Chief Weah's canoe — for Weah was friendly to him now, and had even encouraged the missionary to visit his aged mother. She was a dear old lady with a head of white woolly hair, which greatly intrigued Collison as it was in contrast to the usual straight Haida hair.

The lead canoe was in command of Chief Edenshaw. As they neared Rose Spit, Collison was surprised to see Edenshaw suddenly make for the shore, because the weather seemed to be fine, only one small cloud showed in the sky. It was a significant proof of the esteem in which Edenshaw's seamanship was held among his people, that not a single Haida argued the point, but quickly followed his canoe to shore. Edenshaw's instinctive alarm about the weather was soon justified, for scarcely had the canoes landed when a sudden frenzied squall was upon them. In the violently churning waters off Rose Spit, they wouldn't have had a chance. This master seaman from Virago Sound knew his Island waters.

When they returned from the mainland visit, Mr. Collison began to build a proper Mission House for his family as their second baby was due in August. He enlisted help from the villagers and had just put up the framework when they had a visit from Mr. Robert Williams on June 7th. He was on an inspection trip of the H.B.C. posts, and as Collison had some business to see to on the mainland he arranged to go back with Williams when he returned. The night before they were to leave a strong wind came up, blowing down the carefully placed rafters of the new Mission House. Collison could not bear to leave the place in such a mess, so changed his mind about accompanying Williams. We can only imagine his feelings when he learned that Mr. Williams had been drowned on the return trip when his canoe overturned in a sudden gale off Rose Spit.

In August of 1877 a baby girl, Emily, was born to the Collisons — the first white child to be born on the Queen Charlotte Islands.

That summer Collison went down to Skidegate with Chief Edenshaw and his son Cowhoe and held an evangelical meeting at Skidegate, the first service to be held there. Sometime later a few of the Skidegates sent a request to Duncan for a missionary to come to them. Edward Mathers, a Tsimpshean, was sent. He brought his wife and two children and built a house in Skidegate — ready to begin teaching. But the Skidegates were resentful as they had wanted a white teacher. Their village had formerly been just as important as Masset, they said, and they felt they were entitled to the same treatment. They had wanted a "Medicine Man from the Iron People" as it was customary to refer to white missionaries. It is possible that they were not all in favor of having Christianity at that time because Edward Mathers did not stay for very long.

In the spring of 1879 Bishop Bompas visited Masset and brought over a young native teacher from Metlakatla to take Collison's place temporarily. William Duncan was ill and Collison was needed to assist in Metlakatla. In the early summer George Sneath came out from England to take over the Masset Mission, and Collison went over with Sneath to help him get the lie of things. It was barely three years since Collison had first taken his family to Masset and the Captain of the *Otter* had predicted that they would be murdered in their beds before he could return, in six months.

Among all the other things that he had been able to accomplish, one thing that pleased Collison very much was being able to unite the Offutts in Holy Matrimony. Seeing how much it meant to Collison, Offutt had obligingly humored the young missionary, although by now he had two grown daughters and cared little about propriety.

Mr. Sneath was in Masset for nearly two years, and his replacement was Reverend Charles Harrison. Harrison was the son of a well-to-do minister in England. Educated and clever, he was planning to follow in his father's footsteps but had become a heavy drinker. To straighten him up, his people had persuaded him to try Canada in the hope that a change of environment and the challenge of a mission church might accomplish what love and prayers had failed to do.

At twenty-one he married his sweetheart, a shy quiet girl of nineteen, and on October 21st, 1882, the newlyweds left London for a new life. It was December before they reached Metlakatla and the weather was so stormy it was not until the end of March that they could leave for Masset. Harrison put in the months learning Chinook.

There was no steamer to take them to Masset so they went by canoe with nine Indian paddlers. Crossing the wild, wind-tossed waters of Hecate Strait in an open craft in March was a nightmare trip for Mrs. Harrison, who had led a most sheltered life in England. Several times they were almost swamped, but her large wooden trunk lashed in the center of the canoe provided the extra buoyancy needed to steady the craft. She lost count of how many miserable, bone-chilling hours it took to cross those endless waves. When they finally arrived at Masset everything they had in the canoe was soaked. It was March 31st, 1883.

Six months later on the 28th of September, she was delivered of their first baby, a girl. Her only attendant was her young husband. They named the tiny infant Maude Alice. She lived for a week.

Harrison industriously set about evangelizing and, according to the accepted way in those days, as each Indian became baptised he was given an anglicized name, for not only did the white men have no idea how to spell the Haida names — they couldn't even pronounce most of them. The white man's custom of handing names down from father to son was introduced, and to a people who had always followed the matriarchal system the result was confusion for everyone concerned.

Mr. Harrison had learned to speak Chinook fairly well, but was looking forward to delivering his first sermon in Haida. He enlisted the help of good-natured Mary Ridley, who was to help so many white people learn her language. The words for numbers were giving Harrison some difficulty. One of the Haidas known as Cultus Johnny had been fishing halibut and brought a whole string for Mary to prepare for drying. Harrison pointed to the fish one by one and said carefully, "one, two, three . . . etc." and asked Mary to give him the Haida names for them.

That Sunday he proudly delivered his sermon in Haida using the new words in the appropriate places. But the instant reaction of giggling amongst the congregation was an indication that something was not quite right. After the sermon, Mary approached him and said in a puzzled way, "Harrison, how come you alla time preach about halibut in church today?" Evidently he had been saying, "When three or more halibut are gathered together . . . and so on." With the wonderful sense of humor that the Haidas have — this story has been told and retold with infinite relish for many years.

In 1886, three years after they had arrived in Masset, the Mission House burned to the ground and the Harrisons lost everything. The kindly Haida people rallied to the rescue, quickly erecting a temporary shelter and furnishing it as well as they could for the young couple. It was felt that now was the time for Masset to have a proper church. During the year blankets and cash sums were collected in the village to the amount of $2,620 — and building was begun.

On May 3rd, 1887, a second baby was born to the Harrisons, and was named Constance May. She was a bonnie baby. A few days later, on May 7th, the new church was formally opened. It was named St. John the Evangelist's Church and in honor of the occasion Bishop Ridley came to officiate at the consecration.

There was a fine choir of thirty-two members for the opening service and when the offertory plate was passed around, a total of $150 was put in. Whilst in Masset the Bishop baptised eighty-two people, confirmed sixty-three and eighteen young couples were united in wedlock. It looked as though the Church was a success in the Masset Mission.

But if the church movement was meeting with success, this could not be said of its incumbent minister. He was fighting a losing battle with his old enemy the bottle. As it was hardly an example for a minister to set, his superiors were concerned. After each reprimand, Harrison would try to straighten up, but in March of 1889 the Harrisons received a crushing blow when two months before her second birthday, their adored little daughter became ill with pnuemonia and died. This was the final straw for Harrison who was hardly to draw a sober breath at times. Bishop Ridley and Harrison did not get along too well at the best of times, as Harrison staunchly defended William Duncan's actions at Metlakatla when Ridley and Duncan had fought so bitterly over whether church ritual should be imposed that, in 1887, Duncan took his followers and moved to Alaska. Harrison's heavy drinking now was too much for Ridley to excuse in addition to his insubordinate hostility. He recommended that Harrison be defrocked.

The Church Missionary Society did not do this. They requested Mr. Harrison's resignation, to be effective on December 12th, 1890.

For Mrs. Harrison the months had become an agony. The tragic loss of both her baby girls, and the strain of watching her clever young husband becoming an uncontrolled drinker had brought her almost to breaking point. The realization that she was to have a third baby made the longing for her own people too acute to be denied. She left for England.

Harrison stayed on in the Mission House at Masset to await a successor. Believing that the Islands had a future without par he decided to invest in some real estate and purchased a large tract of grassland at the head of Delkatla Slough from Mr. McKenzie, the ex-H.B.C. man, who had retired to live on the islands as mentioned earlier. (Chapter Sixteen) (1) There were rumors of a man coming in to run a cattle ranch on the North Beach, close to Harrison's newly purchased land.

The big Mission House was a lonely place so when the J.M.L. Alexander family arrived to run the North Beach cattle ranch Harrison invited them to stay with him until they could get a house built at their ranch. But when Alexander took over the H.B.C. post to let Mr. Dodd have a holiday, the large family moved into the Company residence and Harrison was on his own once more. As soon as Rev. and Mrs. Keen arrived to take over the Masset Church in late 1890, Mr. Harrison lost no time in leaving. He went to France for a year as a chaplain, but before he left the incumbency at the Masset Church he completed one more task. Mary Kinaskilas, who helped so diligently in the school the church had set up in Masset, and her husband (one of the special constables) had lost two of their babies at about the same time the two Harrison babies died. Instead of the customary tombstones, Mr. Harrison had persuaded the Kinaskilas's to combine with him in putting in two small stained glass windows in remembrance of their children. When the old church was replaced in Masset, these two windows were carefully removed to the new church and are there today, high up in the back — the only known record of the two Harrison babes who died so long ago. They were buried just outside the old church, but with the passage of years the graves have been bulldozed over for a playground and the small headstones ground into the soil.

The Islands had not heard the last of Charles Harrison by any means, and what "Windy" Young was to Queen Charlotte City, Harrison was to Masset. Banishment from the church did not seem to bother him one whit. He was soon back in Masset on his Delkatla farm. Should an emergency arise he was still permitted to give sermons — and he never lost a chance for he dearly loved to get up and preach. It is said that he delivered a cracking good sermon, though he was a square peg in a round hole ecclesiastically.

(1) When Mr. McKenzie died, Harrison bought the land he had owned
as well as the North Beach section which had been jointly owned by
Clifford and McKenzie — thus becoming owner of the whole of
Lot 7, containing 1,015 acres.

On his return to Masset the "country squire cum entrepreneur" role suited him admirably. He thought he was now able to control his drinking and sent for his wife to have another try in these circumstances. She came at once bringing Percy, the small son who had arrived in the meantime. Percy was not the joy to Mr. Harrison that he was to his mother. Brought up with Haida lads, he loved the free and easy life and wanted no part of the niceties of civilization such as formal school. Harrison practically disowned the boy after awhile concentrating all his affections on the fourth and last child to arrive, Cyril, who was born in 1892. As for the wonderful Mrs. Harrison, her kind understanding helped more than one pioneer bride over the rough spots in adjusting to the sometimes bewildering conditions of frontier life.

In September 1890, Rev. and Mrs. J. H. Keen arrived to take over the Masset Mission and remained for eight years. During this time Rev. Keen translated the Gospels of St. Luke, St. John, and the Acts of the Apostles into an anglicized version of Haida. For this undertaking he had the able assistance of Henry Edenshaw, younger son of Chief Edenshaw. When George Edenshaw died of T.B. in 1890, Henry was able to step into his brother's shoes and take over the teaching in the school and the many other duties that each Anglican minister entrusted to the capable young men.

The Keens left Masset in 1898 and for eight months, Rev. William Hogan of Metlakatla filled in. He was the huge six-foot-four, three hundred pound parson who was to become so beloved. In the interim, Will Collison, the man who had spent the early years of his life here as a small boy, had become an ordained minister. He returned in August, 1900, with his sister Emily (who had been born at Masset) to take charge of the Mission his father had begun in 1876.

Along with his evangelizing, Will became enthused with the idea of becoming a land-holder on the Charlottes. To this end he bought, and was Crown Granted, Lot 750, which adjoins the old Indian Village of Kung at the mouth of Naden Harbor. Will proposed to make his land into a townsite. He must have reconsidered, for in a few years the land had reverted. In 1909 he was transferred to Stewart, and the Bishop appointed the big parson from Port Simpson to succeed at Masset. The stories about "Father" Hogan are legion and merit a whole book to do them justice. When he died in his eighty-third year at Masset in February, 1914, he left footprints that would be hard to fill.

One of the first things said of Hogan was, "Beware of his handshake!" Evildoers dreaded his closed fist and his friends evaded his open palm with its warm, paralyzing grasp. Said one writer of that day,

"His limbs are like full-grown firs, and his great shoulders — like the foreshoulders of a buffalo, strain through the tightfitting homespun clothes. His fists are like weights. But above everything else is the way he shows his head, well above the crowd, set back and poised like a Senator's. He faces every man the same way — with a dauntless and steady gaze, and within his eye lurks a fine humor and impatient understanding."

Born September 4, 1831, in Clifden County, Galway, Ireland, (1) he was the son of a member of the Royal Irish Constabulary. In the region where he grew

(1) Documents loaned by Mr. Hogan's niece,
    Mrs. J. Ticehurst, Toronto, Ontario.

up, it was often customary not to baptise people until they "were old enough to know their own minds," so it was not until his twentieth birthday in 1851, that William Hogan was accepted for baptism. This fact resulted in a wonderful gain for the New World.

On July 17, 1877, when in his late forties he married pretty Margaret Louisa Hutchinson, who always called him Willie, despite his great size. She was twenty-one years his junior. In 1881 they became the proud parents of a baby girl, May Eva, (who married Dr. Horace Wrinch of Hazelton in 1927). Actively interested in St. Matthias Church, Dublin, the Hogans were teachers in the church school there and were the Master and Mistress for eight years, from 1885 to 1893.

During this time Hogan heard of the need for missionaries in Canada. He was greatly attracted to the adventure and desperately wanted to become part of it. With Hogan, if a thing needed doing and it was a right thing to do, he did it. The fact that the age limit for missionaries was forty-five and he was over sixty then, was the sort of red tape that never did mean much to him. He knew that a baptismal certificate was accepted as proof of age so he presented his, lopping twenty years off the actual date of his birth. Those who knew him would fully agree with what he did, for he was a physically superb man and easily equal to men twenty years his junior.

In June of 1893, St. Matthias Church presented the Hogans with many testimonials of the high esteem in which they were held and then regretfully bade them godspeed. The Church Missionary Society sent them first to Metlakatla to help Bishop Ridley. Ridley made him a Deacon in August of that year and a priest the following summer. He was at Metlakatla for five years, then eight months at Masset and in 1899 was posted to Port Simpson to succeed Rev. Stephenson. Rev. and Mrs. Hogan spent ten happy years in Port Simpson and this was where he acquired the affectionate nickname of "Father", although he was most definitely a Low Church Anglican parson.

He was fond of giving what he called a "powerful sermon" and as he stood in the pulpit preaching, "Dearly Beloved, the Scripture moveth us. . ." he would thunder upon his flock all the meaning of the Law and the Prophets as it affected them in their daily lives. He would intimate that with his own hands and with all his heart he would see to it that the Law and the Prophet were accorded all that mortal man can accord them, ". . .that all might be made men, real men, capable of self-control, worthy of self-respect and of offering worship to God."

If an oratory did not accomplish the desired end he took the simple and direct way of correction. The story is told of Mr. Hogan hearing that two men were engaged in a vicious fight. He came hurrying down the road "making six feet to a stride", and oblivious of the knives and clubs the combatants had, he picked up the men by their collars and knocked their foolish heads together with a resounding thwack.

When he was posted to Masset in 1909, the flaming red beard and shaggy head were now white, for Hogan was seventy-eight years of age, but the great strength was ever there to be used in aid of righteousness, or when ordinary people were just too slow. As was the case recalled by Mrs. Jesse Bridden, one of Delkatla's pioneers. Hogan had arranged to pick up her husband in his boat. Mr. Bridden, a larger than average man himself, had forgotten his gum-boots and as Hogan's boat was too deep draughted to get close in on the flat beach, he began looking about for a plank to use to get out to the boat. Hogan, impatient with the delay, strode ashore and unceremoniously picked Mr. Bridden up, tucked him under one arm and strode out again to the boat. The sight of her husband's long legs dangling from Hogan's side was something Mrs. Bridden would never forget. Hogan was eighty at the time.

On Sundays everyone in the village (1) went to church, making a congregation of some 350 to 400, oldsters down to babies. "I don't care if the babies cry in my church, I can always talk a little louder," he would say to a hesitant mother. He loved to sing stirring hymns, and especially hymns of the sea. The congregation could be sure that every Sunday would include either "Eternal Father Strong to Save" or "Jesus Saviour Pilot Me". A fledgling town had appeared some three miles up the Inlet, soon to be called New Masset, and Hogan was required to take services there each Sunday as well as in his own church. This meant a row of six miles, or an equal distance walking along the beach in every kind of weather. In all the years he was there he never missed a Sunday, come rain, storm, sleet or snow.

Charles Harrison, who could give the service if needed, would stand hopefully by . . . perhaps this time he would be late. Although Hogan thought very highly of Mrs. Harrison he disapproved of her husband, especially his tippling habits. Possibly it was the thought that Harrison *might* hold forth in his place that spurred Mr. Hogan each Sunday.

One December day when he was visiting the Old Masset cemetery — a little island known as "God's Acre" — Mr. Hogan suddenly turned and said to the friends who were with him, "Bhoys! I don't ever want to leave these wonderful Islands. Promise me that when I die, you will bury me in that southeast corner over there, so that I may lie forever with my Haida braves." The earnest request demanded a promise — to be fulfilled too soon. After Christmas he caught a chill which developed into pneumonia and within weeks beloved "Father" Hogan was dead. The whole area was stunned.

The Haidas, claiming him most especially for their own, asked to be allowed to make the casket. Lay Reader Nigel Sherwood of Delkatla, told of going down the night before the funeral to see how they were getting on with the casket.

"I looked into the Town Hall to see a scene which would have brought infinite pleasure to our Father Hogan. Men, women and children of all ages were in on the building of the casket. Men preparing, planing and whittling of the narrow boards to build it, and the women getting the meals or sitting in groups and the youngsters running and playing, making it a live community.

Board by board, yellow cedar and red — although of conventional shape, it was built up as you would a boat. Then varnish applied, polished vigorously, gilded badges, diamond shapes, gilt handles fastened on. The whole work stood when finished, a flame of amber and gold — a happy sign of their love and respect for their beloved. I have never seen such a coffin before — it was a triumph of Haida workmanship and art. At the service the remains were put in that radiant casket and it was set in the Nave to be covered with wreaths made from mosses and ferns gathered from the woods." (2)

---

(1) Village here refers to the Haida village of Old Masset.
(2) Account written by Mr. Sherwood, in the office of the Anglican Synod in Prince Rupert.

Preceded by the Masset Indian Band in full uniform, the body was born to the cemetery followed by almost the entire population of Old and New Masset and a very large representation from Woden, Nadu, Queenstown (now Port Clements) and Sewall. Bishop du Vernet read the final services, with responses by Canon Rix and Rev. Will Collison, and Rev. Heber Greene and Rev. Bygraves to help. Father Hogan was buried February 5, 1914, in the spot he had chosen just scant weeks before.

Rev. Creary was appointed to take over the Masset Mission, and he was succeeded in 1916 by Rev. A. E. Price. The Prices left a member of their family in that same cemetery when their young son died the next year at Old Masset.

After the war, tightening budgets permitted the Anglicans to have only one minister on the Islands and he had to look after both the Massets, plus the settlements along the Inlet and Port Clements. The rectory in the Haida Masset was sold and proceeds used to buy a house in New Masset as it would be more central to work from. From that time until lately there has been no minister living in the Indian village. However, with the threat of other churches moving in on Anglican territory, it was decided that the village, which has 1000 band members now, warranted a full-time minister and so a new Rectory has been built on the Masset Reserve and Vicar H. R. Kreager installed.

CHAPTER EIGHTEEN

AMOS RUSS SHOWS THE WAY

The first Haida to be converted to Christianity came not from Masset, but from Skidegate, and he was drawn into the Church several years before Collison appeared on the scene. This was Gedanst, favorite grandson of the leading Eagle Crest chief, who had the lad under his special care preparing him for succession to the Chieftainship at Skidegate.

Gedanst, who was born in 1849, had heard so much about the city of Victoria that one summer, as a lad of seventeen, he accompanied a group of his villagers on a trip there. Wandering about the streets of the city, he encountered a Miss Pollard of the Methodist Church. She had recently opened a class in Victoria to try to spread the Gospel, for the Methodists, too, were concerned about the effects of civilization on the Native people. Miss Pollard coaxed young Gedanst to come in so, with nothing else to do at the moment, he agreed. He became converted to principles which were to turn his life upside down.

Returning home with these new concepts, the once favored grandson was now subjected to every persecution and ignominy that his people could think of in an effort to change his mind. He was able to stand resolutely against them, although tearful pleading by his beloved grandfather nearly caused him to falter in his determination to follow a different life.

The old chief, deeply concerned about the drastic changes taking place among his people — the terrible onslaught of smallpox and the even more insidious debauchery of so many of the young — felt that the future of his race lay in the leadership of strong young men like Gedanst. To this end he had been training the lad rigorously, that he might emulate former great Haida chiefs and lead the people to greatness once more. He was extremely angry and sick at heart at what had come over the boy.

Like Seegay of Masset, Gedanst knew by heart the traditions and history of his people and was aware of their fine heritage. He had also heard the older people deploring sadly what was happening these days. How Haidas, who once were counted in the thousands, now were reduced to hundreds, and how the end of the race was a certainty unless something was done. Because he was so sure

97

that only in the gospel way of life lay the salvation of his people, not in the old ways, he was able to resist all entreaties and could stand firmly for what he had decided to do.

Gradually the persecutions ceased and a truce was declared. Gedanst was even able to break a little soil with his new ideas — which is undoubtedly why Rev. Collison did not encounter as much resistance as might have been expected when he took his first trip down there in 1877. Although the old chief did not live to see it, his hopes for his grandson to lead the people out of their decline came into reality.

As he reached manhood Gedanst, (who was baptised, and renamed for the pioneer Methodist missionary, Rev. Amos Russ) went to live for a few years in Port Simpson, where he became a valuable assistant to Rev. Thomas Crosby who had set up his mission in 1873. It was here also that young Amos Russ met his wife.

She had been born in Masset as Agnes Hubbs, and when her mother and father (who was an American) went to live in Alaska the Masset grandparents were so attached to the little girl that they persuaded the parents to leave her behind with them. When Agnes came of marriageable age her grandparents arranged for her to marry the handsome and important Eagle, Chief Steilta, but they were married only briefly when Steilta died (mentioned in an earlier chapter as being the first Haida to be interred at Masset). After his death his young widow went to live in Port Simpson with one of the Offutt daughters, Mary, and subsequently went to work helping Mrs. Crosby in the Crosby Girls' Home. (1)

The Crosbys were delighted at the idea of a wedding between Amos and Agnes, two fine young people, and arranged a big celebration for the event. They were married on November 10, 1879 by Rev. Crosby with Josephine Russ and David Swanson as witnesses. Although they were dedicated and able church. workers, the Russ's did not completely abandon all of the fine old Haida traditions, and when their eldest son Willie was in line for the hereditary succession to Chief Seegay (through his Raven Crest mother) he was encouraged to accept the honor.

Mr. and Mrs. Russ eventually had eleven children, and all turned out to be fine, respected people. Amos Russ died at the age of eighty-five in 1934 and his wife lived until 1964, when she slipped away in her sleep at the grand old age of one hundred and five. During their life they were instrumental in laying most of the ground work for the missionaries and had a hand in the building of three churches — Skidegate, New Kloo and Haina (Maude Island). (2)

After their wedding in 1879, Amos and Agnes Russ helped Rev. Crosby for some years, then returned to Skidegate to live and by 1883 were able to persuade the grandfather of the need for missionary guidance in his village. The chief finally gave his permission for a missionary to come and teach in Skidegate. (A few years earlier there had been an abortive attempt at this, as mentioned previously, when Edward Mathers had been sent by the Anglicans. This was not successful due to lack of co-operation by the chiefs.)

(1) *Information for the history of Mr. and Mrs. Russ was provided by their eldest daughter, Grace (Mrs. E. C. Stevens), also from books written by Rev. Thomas Crosby and Captain Oliver.*
(2) *Sometimes called New Gold Harbor.*

In November of 1883 when Amos Russ brought the news of his grandfather's new turn of mind, Mr. Crosby was disconsolate at having to turn him down. There was absolutely no money to finance another missionary undertaking. Realizing what a breakthrough Amos Russ had achieved, however, it seemed unthinkable not to back him up and George Robinson, who was teaching at the Port Simpson school, offered to go over with Mr. Russ on a purely voluntary basis. The two men left by canoe next morning for Skidegate, where Robinson remained for two years rendering yeoman service in the new mission.

The first thing they did was to build a church, and at the same time Mr. Robinson instructed Mr. Russ so well in English and the Bible that Russ could teach on his own. He went to Haina on Maude Island, but the people there wanted no part of it, saying

"Let the Skidegates give up the way of the Indian if they want to, but we *never* will. What has the white man got anyway that we need? All he has is a bible. We have our dances, potlatches, medicine men and a wise chief as well as our Shaman's powers. We don't need the white man's ways."

Wisely, the Methodists did not force the issue but the improvement in Skidegate was so noticable within the first year that the people of Haina realized they would soon be left behind. So they sent word that they would like to have a teacher come to live with them. The Methodists urged them to move to Skidegate for there were not enough children to have a school at each place. They refused, adamantly. Their village was just as good as Skidegate, they said, and they wanted to have the same things.

In the summer of 1885 the *Glad Tidings* dropped anchor one day off Haina and put ashore the young Tsimpshean Indian teacher, George Edgar, with his wife and two children. The Hainas had asked for, and expected to have, a white teacher as in Skidegate. A meeting was held to decide if Mr. Edgar could stay or not. After some haranguing it was decided to give him a chance and Amos Russ stayed nearby to lend a hand and smooth out the path. (In later years Mr. Edgar became an ordained Methodist minister.)

In October of 1885 another big meeting was held at Haina in Chief James Watson's house. George Edgar was instructed to write to the Church saying that the people on Maude Island planned to build a church. It would be forty-four feet long and twenty-eight feet wide, with three windows down each side and one on either side of the front door. It would face the water. A collection was taken to pay for the building and Chief Watson led by contributing 20 blankets, while his wife gave a treasured headdress. The final yield was 236 blankets, 5 headdresses, 1 dance blanket, 2 other blankets and 1 large flag. By next year the little church was a reality, and there was now a minister at Skidegate to take the services.

This was Mr. G. F. Hopkins, who had been appointed to Missionary status by the Methodists in June of 1884. Although Mr. Hopkins was stationed mainly at Skidegate, he was called to help out for the winters in Bella Coola. In August of 1866 he married Miss Mary Green, sister of Rev. A. E. Green of the Naas River and they took up residence at Skidegate. In 1887 Mr. Hopkins was ordained, making him the first ordained Methodist minister to evangelize on the Queen Charlottes. However in 1888, Rev. Hopkins was compelled, by the decline of his wife's health, to leave his isolated appointment and was succeeded by Rev.

A. N. Miller who stayed four years and left in 1892. A lay teacher, Mr. S. Lazier, filled in for part of the next year. Rev. B. C. Freeman arrived in Skidegate in 1893 and stayed fifteen years. He was subsequently succeeded by the venerable Dr. John Clark Spencer who left an indelible mark behind him on the Islands when he was transferred to the Port Simpson post in 1914.

It might be appropriate to mention a bit about the *Glad Tidings* at this point. When it was realized that Rev. Crosby had to have a boat to get around effectively, and as usual the church was short of funds, a young Scottish carpenter in New Westminster volunteered to build the boat at cost. This was William Oliver who made no secret of the fact he had been a swashbuckling drunk in his days as a roving seaman. However, he had come under the influence of Rev. Ebenezer Robson, another early Methodist minister, and to Mr. Oliver's great credit he had completely reformed. Now working for the church was the thing that gave his life meaning, and certainly no local history of the Methodist church could be written without his story.

William Oliver put his very best work into this first boat. He built her in New Westminster in 1884 and then took her to Victoria to have the engines installed. Drawing 8 feet of water, she was 71 feet long with a beam of 15 feet. Her steam engines were of 300 nominal horsepower. The engine-room was amidships and forward there was a freight hold. The foc'sle had accommodation for two crewmen until 1892 when the cabins were placed on deck, an improvement for both passengers and crew. Rev. Crosby was skipper and Capt. Oliver engineer until Mr. Crosby was transferred to the Lower Mainland, and then Oliver became skipper.

As he piloted the boat along the shores of the southern Charlottes (for it was tacitly agreed that Anglican territory lay along the northern part of Graham and Methodists would handle the southern Charlottes) Rev. Crosby was distressed at the conditions he found in Cumshewa and at Ninstints. When he called in at Tanu (Kloo) he found things just as bad there. Several of the Kloo people approached him and asked for his advice and help. They realized how greatly Skidegate had improved since a white teacher had gone there. Could Mr. Crosby help them too?

There was a big meeting that night and the village tried to decide what to do. A spokesman got up and said earnestly –

"If only we had a teacher in our village now, our people would stop this going to Victoria. Victoria has been a place of death and destruction for our village, most especially our young women. There are almost none left now to be wives to our young men. And we shall soon have no children. We are a dying and doomed people. Already our graveyard is overflowing."

Mr. Crosby tried to persuade them to move to Skidegate where Rev. Hopkins would be able to teach and guide them. But like the people of Haina, they felt they could not do this. They wanted their own village. As it seemed imperative to get them away from their present environment for the sake of morale – a site on Cumshewa Inlet was suggested. This was on the north side of Louise Island and it met with favor.

In 1887 the whole village moved to the new location which was named New Kloo. Among those moving were the Calder family who were sending their daughter Agnes out to Port Simpson to school. The *Glad Tidings* helped in the move and later in bringing lumber and supplies to build the new town. Once again Amos Russ was the able adviser and helper in setting up this new community. With liberal donations of blankets, coppers and other treasures, enough money was raised to build a church — the foundation of the new village. These villagers had decided to adopt the new way of life with all their hearts and to the best of their ability now the decision had been made.

Early in 1893, Captain Oliver took time off from the *Glad Tidings* to go and live in the little village which, though doing fairly well, was nevertheless in need of another source of income. Oliver, a practical man, had noticed the success of the Oilery at Image Point (near the Skidegate village) which was being capably run by Mr. and Mrs. Bob Tennant. The waters of the Cumshewa region teemed with dog fish, so it seemed to be a good idea to install a plant for the extraction of liver oil at New Kloo, similar to the one operated by the Tennants.

He had to go to Victoria for his financing and on December 11, 1895, the little Oilery at New Kloo received official status when the Memorandum of Association of the Queen Charlotte Oil Company was signed. It was stated that the object of the company was, "to carry on the work of an oilery and the business of storekeeping and trading at Clue, Q.C.Is." Capital stock was $14,000, with head office at Victoria and trustees were Thomas Shotbolt, Druggist; W. H. Dempster, Canner; and Samuel Williams, Master Mariner, all of Victoria.

Although labor unions were unknown at that time Captain Oliver soon had his troubles in the new venture. His crew of seven men refused to work any longer unless he secured a new cook. And so it was that the Captain in his difficulty thought of young Agnes Calder, who had spent years training at Port Simpson under Mrs. Crosby in the Girls' Home. She agreed to take over the cooking for the crew, and so well did she manage that not only were there no further labor troubles, but the Captain became more than interested in the young lady herself. After a period of cooking for the men, Agnes worked in the Kloo General Store which Oliver had established there. During this time they became better acquainted but, mindful of the twenty-three years difference in their ages, William Oliver waited two years before asking her to become his wife. They were married in April, 1896.

By now the people of New Kloo had become reconciled to joining the others in Skidegate and in 1897 the final move was made, uniting all the southern Haidas in one village. The Olivers went to live in Port Simpson and the Oilery lay abandoned. In August, 1911, a report was filed in Victoria addressed to the three original trustees, Shotbolt, Dempster and Williams, notifying them that the Queen Charlotte Oil Company Ltd. was to be struck from the register. (1)

Skedans, around the corner from New Kloo on the east side of Louise Island had been visited by missionaries and the people asked to be included in the new scheme, but they too refused to live in Skidegate. However, they were agreeable to a suggestion that they go to Haina, and sometime between 1888 and 1890 they moved there.

After Rev. Freeman arrived, everyone in Haina concluded that they might as well go to Skidegate to live, as it would be more convenient for all. In 1893 the Maude Island village was abandoned and, as mentioned, in 1897 the New Kloos

(1) B.C. Archives.

joined them in Skidegate. Lumber from the churches at New Kloo and Haina was used to enlarge the church at Skidegate and to build a school.

So now at the turn of the century there were only two villages occupied on the Islands, Masset and Skidegate. From a population of 7,000 or more at the beginning of 1800, a hundred years later there were only 600 left. (1) These were divided, 400 in Masset and the remaining 200 in Skidegate — but the tide had been turned. The relentless decline of the Haida had been stopped. Ended, also, was a way of life.

From the vantage point of hindsight, the descendents of those who made the early policies and decisions can see many errors, but it was a time of great emergency and there were no rule books. Anyone who reads the diaries and writings of those who were concerned cannot help but realize that the actions were taken with complete sincerity and purity of motive. This applies to both the helpers and those being helped.

As confidence in the chiefs' ability to act wisely on their people's behalf began to wane in the changing times, more and more Indian affairs were left to Government supervision. There *is* doubt as to sincerity and purity of motive here, for political expediency played no small part in many of the subsequent decisions.

In 1854 the Colonial Government denied any necessity to extinguish Indian titles before making land grants, and in 1867 Governor Douglas issued a proclamation saying that title to all the land in British Columbia resided in the Crown. To protect Indian interests to some degree Commissioner Peter O'Reilly allotted reserves to the Haida bands (among others) in 1882. These were surveyed in 1887 by a Mr. Jemmett. More reserves were allotted by the 1913 - 1916 commission. In general they were the old villages and camps that had formerly been used by the Haida. The Indian Land question is, however, still unfinished business. (2)

With the turn of the century, as the new era began on the Islands, a period of adjustment, with many growing pains, was necessary as the various tribes united in the two main villages. Under the new scheme, although hereditary chieftain-ship still brought respect, it was the elected chiefs and councillors who made the decisions for the people. The passing of the potlatch ceremonies and other traditions meant that masks and ritualistic paraphernalia were no longer needed. Crests were out of fashion, so there was no reason to carve the giant totems. Ceremonial items, formerly seen only by participants, were now not only freely shown to strangers but were also for sale.

It was not long before collectors and anthropologists from all over the world came to gather the rich harvest of historic treasures. The best of the towering totems were shipped away and today there are few important museums that do not display items which were created by one of the most artistically advanced and superbly creative peoples on the Pacific coast. There are not many historic items left on the Charlottes today.

Knowledgeable Islanders of both Haida and non-Haida heritage are dismayed

(1) In addition to the estimated 600 Haidas on the Q.C.I., there were
   300 Kaigani Haidas in Alaska at this time.
(2) Information in this paragraph from Professor Wilson Duff, U.B.C.

by the misguidance given to the Haidas by government officials entrusted with their welfare. There was far more interest in making the right appointment politically than any concern about qualifications and knowledge of those put in charge.

For instance, although Anglican and Methodist missionaries have been blamed for influencing the removal of the big totem poles, research does not bear this out. In fact they deplore the loss in several reports. (1) Most of the poles were sold during Indian Agent Thomas Deasy's term of office (2) as even the most casual study of his records will show. Deasy was a devout Roman Catholic and a business man. Perhaps it was the basic fact that there was a good market for items no longer in use and the sellers were having a hard time financially that motivated the actions of political appointee Deasy.

He seems to have had the willing co-operation of his uninformed charges in many instances and to have been persuasive in others. In 1933 the B.C. Government stepped in to forbid the sale or shipping of any of the large totem poles outside the province, but they had no objection to their being taken wholesale from the Charlottes to Prince Rupert, Vancouver or Victoria – and offered no advice against it.

In fact they footed the bill for several expeditions to remove poles expressly from the Islands, feeling that the carvings could be better preserved and enjoyed by people in the capital city than they could be among the descendents of the carvers. This is strange, since Haida creativity and skill has never waned, and in a multitude of ways still shows up today as clearly as it ever did.

(1) *It is commonly said that the missionaries did not like the totem poles because they believed the Indians worshipped the images carved on them. It is strange how this misconception could have arisen with regard to Q.C.I. poles. Books and reports written by all early Island missionaries make it clear that they were fully aware of the heraldic and lineage significance of the poles. One explanation for the erroneous impression might be that in the zeal of conversion some of the Haidas rid themselves of all old-fashioned (to them at that moment) paraphernalia and their uninitiated neighbors said, "See, this is what the missionary makes them do . . ." Since it was felt that epidemics of typhoid, which were taking a heavy toll, might be prevented by better sanitation there is no question the missionaries did encourage and coax the Indians to bury their dead. This would lead to the abandonment of the use of grave houses and mortuary poles, contributing to the idea the missionaries did not like the use of such things, which was true, but not for the reason that was represented.*

(2) *Thomas Deasy took up his duties as Masset Agent in 1910, succeeding Charles Perry who was in Masset from Dec. 31/09 to May 1910.*

PART TWO

CHAPTER NINETEEN

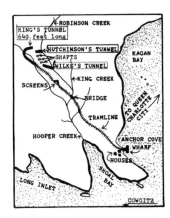

COWGITZ AND
THE "OIL WORKS"

The Crown Colony of Vancouver Island had not yet merged with the mainland Colony of British Columbia when the Charlottes were usurped by officialdom.

The government began making real estate deals on the Islands six years before British Columbia officially became a province, as Joseph Trutch was acting on behalf of the Colony of B.C. when he signed the lease on November 7, 1865, granting the Queen Charlotte Coal Company of Victoria 5,000 acres in the Skidegate Inlet region — and thereby set in motion the first government land transaction to take place on the Islands.

It might have been assumed, logically, that since this land was still very much in Haida occupancy and, as they had been the sole traditional owners for centuries, it would have been the Haidas who would have been the vendors But, as mentioned earlier, the "government" had taken over. From this time all decisions, permissions and policies affecting the Charlottes were made in Ottawa or in the capital city of B.C. Needs and hopes of resident Islanders were to be of little consequence — except perhaps in the golden glow of pre-election solicitudes.

It may have been the frustrating knowledge that "off-Islands" political expediencies did so often play a controlling part in their destinies that provided the common bond between Haida and non-Haida — this plus a shared appreciation of the way of life which is possible on the remote and lovely Islands that they both call home. But it is interesting to note that although during the fur trading days the Haidas had acquired such a wide reputation for unpredictable hostility it was considered foolhardy to venture near any of their villages without a loaded cannon, yet when the white man actually took up residence on the Islands beside them there were no incidents of violence at all.

High expectations were held in 1865 for this first coal mining venture on the Charlottes by the Victoria company, and George Robinson of the Vancouver Coal Company was engaged to supervise the operation. These were the coal measures which had aroused so little interest when William Downie had first reported them in 1859. (1)

(1) See Chapter Fifteen

Narrowing the vast acreage to the section which seemed to be most promising, the coal company staked 1150 acres in the Kagan Bay area (west of Queen Charlotte City) and had it surveyed by F. W. Green, a Victoria surveyor who completed the work on October 9, 1867. It was designated as Lot No. 1, and became the first registered lot on the Islands when it was Crown Granted to the Coal Company on November 14, 1868. The land as surveyed then, is intact to this day and is represented by the oldest document on record in the Prince Rupert Land Registry Office.

Named the Cowgitz Coal Mine, the venture was under way as soon as financing could be arranged. There was so much evidence of good quality anthracite coal at Cowgitz that it was felt quite in order to invest a sizable amount of capital to get the mine into initial production. Backers would soon have their money returned in full — plus a good bonus.

Several tunnels were driven and tramways constructed to tidewater in Anchor Cove, a short distance away. A good wharf and buildings to accommodate the men were erected, together with screens and all the appliances for a large output.

But the undertaking seemed to be so perpetually beset by delays and problems that in September 1870, the Victoria office sent engineer William Russell up as trouble shooter. Five years had passed since the company had been organized and, although a great deal of money had gone into the project, there had not been a single shipment of coal to show for it, and financing was becoming shaky. Company directors said they must have a good-sized shipment of coal by the end of that year at the latest.

Mr. Russell found evidence of inefficiencies at Cowgitz everywhere. They had been caused in the main by short-sighted, skimpy building practices, in an effort to get into production as soon as possible.

The most glaring one was the huge sag in one of the two tramlines. There had been numerous accidents here as the cars flipped off the tracks with almost monotonous regularity, and twice loaded cars had careened down the whole length of the line and gone over the end of the dock. This meant laborious building of new cars.

The gleeful delight of a few Haida lads who sneaked over after dark to joy-ride the cars down the rickety roller-coaster did not help matters. Finally the sag became so bad and accidents so frequent the whole roadbed had to be rebuilt.

It was a vexation for Russell who knew that he had only four months to get a shipload of coal ready. However, with the rebuilding of the entire roadbed for the tramline, repairing breakages on the cars, time lost by injury plus the time-consuming operation of cleaning coal which had been carelessly thrown into the chutes without being cleaned, resulted in only 435 tons ready for the steamer *Lulu* when Captain Knowles brought her into Anchor Bay on Christmas Day, 1870. (1)

Mr. Russell was well aware of the long faces that would meet the party loaded ship when Knowles brought her back into port in Victoria — but it was the best

(1) Information from diaries of Thomas Russell, published in the
Victoria Times in 1911. And from Dr. G. M. Dawson's "Geology report"
of 1878. Additional information was supplied by Provincial Archives
of British Columbia.

that could be done. And their problems were not over, for the ship had not left Cowgitz many weeks when Russell was told that, owing to a serious miscalculation, food supplies at the mine were running dangerously low. So much so, that in February he decided to row down to McKay's Trading store in Cumshewa.

It was a grim trip, taking two full miserable days each way, a fruitless mission as the supply ship for the store had not yet arrived. Trader Hargreaves (in charge there) had barely a week's supply for himself. The hungry situation of the miners was remedied only by a chance visit from some Gold Harbor Haidas who sold them a quantity of halibut and crabs.

Mining continued, but the promising coal seams were found to be faulted and in places metamorphised to such a degree that extracting good quality coal proved difficult and tedious. One of the last reports of the engineer explains how, through the loss of a sailing ship loaded with coal sold to a firm in San Francisco, the company finally became involved in insurmountable financial difficulties which resulted in the closing down of the property. The load of coal was expected to supply the company with enough money to pay for a shipload of machinery coming from England via Cape Horn and overdue wages. Operations at Cowgitz stopped in 1872.

From time to time over the years speculators have looked at the old mine site with a view to reopening it. Although it changed hands several times there was little subsequent activity.

The closing down of the Cowgitz was not the last of the big plans for Queen Charlotte Islands coal — these continued and will come into the story again. In the meantime another industry came into existence in the Skidegate Inlet area — and in contrast to Cowgitz — this one met with success for a number of years. In fact the history of what is known today as Skidegate Landing may be said to date from the humble venture, which was begun at the site in 1876, when William Sterling and J. McB. Smith set up the pilot plant for the extraction of oil from livers of the dogfish which teemed in the waters of that region.

The results of this experimental oilery were so rewarding that in 1879 a company was organized to go into the oil manufacturing business on a larger scale. To be known as Skidegate Oil Company's Steam Oil Works, its first registered shareholders were William Sterling, C. Morton, J. McB. Smith and H. Trenholm, and the operating capital was given as $24,000. That year Sterling had applied to have Lot No. 2 (Torrens Island), Lot No. 3 (Skidegate Landing) and Lot No. 4 (Alliford Bay) surveyed. Choosing Lot No. 3 for his base of action, he arranged for the steamer *Skidegate* to take a load of machinery and supplies in April of 1879 to build a larger plant.

Andy McGregor was hired as foreman and he had three experienced fishermen, Clyde Edmund, G. C. Dyke and Sam Poole, to help him organize the whole operation. The rest of the labor was obtained from local Haida residents. Evidently they did their job well because the B.C. Directory of 1882 reported that the oil manufactured by this plant was so pure and clear that, "it has been very highly recommended by all who have used it," and there were numerous testimonials as to its value by engineers and machinists. The output of 40,000 gallons a year sold at excellent prices.

In 1882 the plant consisted of four wooden buildings, the main one with an area of 2,000 square feet on the ground floor. This contained the steam boiler, three retorts, drying pans, settling pans and so on. The site was variously known as the Oil Works, Sterling Bay, or by the Haida name of Gontha.

In 1885 the newly-wed Mr. and Mrs. Robert Tennant bought out the Sterling Company and ran it for sixteen years. They put in a clam cannery as well after a few years, and this was under the joint managership of Mr. Tennant and a Mr. Dempster. All the cans had to be hand-soldered, and the wood for making charcoal to heat the soldering irons was obtained from a small island off what is now Queen Charlotte City.

Bob Tennant built a comfortable home for his bride (which is now the residence of Mrs. E.C. Stevens), enlarged the store and the couple are remembered as exceedingly kind people. They had no children, but Mrs. Tennant's unique pet, a tame otter, was a source of great interest.

A post office was badly needed in the area and numerous applications had been made from the Haida village of Skidegate to have one installed. Bob Tennant decided to capitalize on this when he made his application and gave the name of his proposed post office as Skidegate. His application was granted, and from that day on the Sterling Bay settlement was known as Skidegate. (1) The original Haida Skidegate, just a few miles to the north of Sterling Bay, became known as Skidegate Mission. In recent years a water taxi to serve the airport at Sandspit has run between Skidegate and Alliford Bay and the old Oil Works site is called Skidegate Landing now, locally.

Around the turn of the century William Oliver, who had operated the small oilery at New Kloo mentioned earlier, came back to the Islands with the idea of setting up a similar plant in Skidegate Mission. Rev. Freeman, who was in charge of the church there, was in favor of this but he persuaded Oliver to make it a co-operative arrangement. On January 4, 1901, the Skidegate Oil and Trading Company of Skidegate Mission was officially registered with William Oliver as president and Rev. B.C. Freeman the secretary. (2)

In the working out of a scheme of operation, bickering developed in the embryo company and Oliver, who was never a patient man, impulsively resigned, sold his interest and pulled out of the organization. He had heard that the Tennants wanted to sell and retire, so he made arrangements to buy their business. His partner was a good-looking young batchelor, Johnnie Mathers, who had come up to look at the old Cowgitz mine.

Young John was not to have his single status for long after joining forces with Captain Oliver. Oliver's sister, Mrs. Charles Bruce, who was living in Victoria, had arranged for her niece Jean Hall to come out from Scotland and live with her. Jean's parents sent a younger sister, fourteen-year-old Elizabeth along to keep Jean company. The Olivers, who by now had settled into the comfortable Tennant home at Skidegate, took such a liking to young Elizabeth she was invited to come up and live with them in Skidegate. When she was eighteen years old Elizabeth married Johnnie Mathers, going to Port Simpson for the ceremony, performed by Rev. B. C. Freeman visiting there at the time. Elizabeth's elder sister Jean married John Haan in Victoria. (3)

(1) *Information from Mrs. E. C. Stevens, Skidegate, B.C.*
(2) *From data supplied by the Provincial Archives, Victoria, B.C.*
(3) *Information from Agnes, eldest daughter of John Mathers.*

Skidegate now became the hub of the Islands, and in a short time a fair-sized settlement developed there — complete with jail. Captain Oliver, still keenly interested in church work, was determined to discourage drinking. As Charlie Adam now of Terrace, B.C. recalls "Every time the *Amur* landed, Captain Locke, her skipper, held "open house" in the ship's bar, and in short order everyone in town with any loose cash usually got good and lit . . . 75¢ bought a good bottle of whisky in those days."

John Mathers took over the running of the Oilery's store, post office and the newly established Sub-Mining Recorder's office. His family responsibilities increased also when a baby girl arrived in 1903. This was Agnes, the first white child to be born in Skidegate Landing and she was greatly admired and fussed over by everyone in the community. Captain Oliver had invested in timber property at Sandspit and when cruisers came up to inspect it, he moved over to be nearer the activities. The Mathers moved into the big Tennant house. Such glowing accounts to life in Skidegate had gone home to relatives in Scotland that several members of the Hall family came out to visit, both with the Olivers at Sandspit and with the Mathers at Skidegate. First to arrive were Grandma and Grandpa Hall, who made their home with the Mathers.

In 1907 Simon Leiser formed a company and made such a good offer to Mr. Mathers and Capt. Oliver for their business that they agreed to sell out to the Victoria company. Mr. and Mrs. Mathers moved to Sandspit to join the Olivers as homesteaders on the picturesque northeast tip of Moresby Island.

One of the partners in Leiser's company was Captain John Haan, (Mr. Mather's brother-in-law) who sold his home in Victoria and moved his young family to Skidegate. Captain Haan owned the 85 foot tug *Ranger.* His engineer, Billy Rhineheart, was also from Victoria and their work was to tow the dogfish sail or rowboats to the fishing grounds in Hecate Straits, going as far north as Cape Ball and south to Cumshewa. (1)

Skidegate was a popular place in those days and dances as well as meetings to discuss the topics of the day were often held in the big net loft of the cannery. In 1908 Mr. W. J. Leary was appointed manager of the Oil Works in Skidegate and when he arrived with his wife and their large family of five daughters and two sons, they were a welcome and lively addition to the community.

"It was March 1908 when our family arrived at Skidegate on the *Amur* with Captain Locke as the skipper," recalls Lottie Leary, now Mrs. Roy Field of Courtenay, B.C. "It was 4 a.m. and someone on the shore shouted, 'Look out for the hole in the wharf.' Like Swiss family Robinsons we came well supplied with livestock and took up quarters in the Company House, as it was called. Mr. and Mrs. Tennant had lived in it and lovingly made a wonderful old-fashioned English garden, where flowers bloomed in a riot of color. At the back and sides of the house were fruit trees and small fruit bushes. We all of us loved that garden," adds Mrs. Field, "but it was an especial delight to my mother."

The Oilery at Skidegate was a successful concern, and the co-operative venture in Skidegate Mission was also doing fairly well. They, too, were canning clams in addition to manufacturing oil and had put in a small store for the convenience of

(1) Information from Capt. Haan's eldest daughter, Jean, who is now
Mrs. W. Singer, Parksville, Vancouver Is.

the villagers. Rev. Thomas Crosby writing about this in his book, said:

"A substantial and well-finished wharf runs out on piles some 300 feet to deep water. They have a main building of 40 feet x 60 feet which contains 2 huge retorts, refining and storage tanks, steam hoist and a car used in the process of refining the oil. Then in another part are crates, racks, hand-soldering machines and other apparatus used in the canning of clams. At the rear is a boiler, woodshed, blacksmith shop with its outfit, and a water tank with a ½ mile of flume. In addition to this they have three small cabins to accommodate employees. In their first years of operation they were able to put out 19,000 gallons of first class dogfish oil, plus a quantity of clams. Nearly all the men and a number of women are shareholders in the company, and feel a commendable pride in the enterprise."

CHAPTER TWENTY

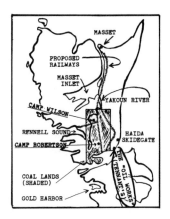

FROM "STAKERS"

TO . . . . . RAILWAYS?

The spirit of adventure ran strong in the veins of Scottish born William Robertson. Coming to Canada as a youngster with his parents, he had grown up to experience a varied career in this new land. Among other things he had gone across the border to fight as an officer in the Union Army during the American Civil War and had been taken prisoner by a force under the command of Stonewall Jackson. After the war he lived in California for several years, then drifted up to the seaport town of Victoria.

Here he met and married his adored wife who presented him in quick succession with seven healthy children. For the first time in his life Robertson had to settle down, and to support his growing family he opened a blacksmith shop in the capital city.

He was nearly fifty-three years old when he learned about a Provincial Government offer of $300 for someone to examine and report on the unknown Masset Inlet area of the Charlottes. The humdrum life of a blacksmith shop with its meagre income paled beside the irresistible lure of adventure and fortune. The stories about the H.B.C. find at Mitchell Harbor in 1852 had intrigued him for some time, and the yearning to try his luck there also had only been held in check by his extremely restricted financial resources. The $300 would provide cash, and the trip to Masset Inlet the opportunity. It was too good to pass by.

When his application was accepted he immediately got in touch with his friend Jimmy Shields, an ex-sealer, who was finding life ashore mighty dull. On July 7, 1885, the two adventurers left Victoria for Masset Inlet with a full measure of buoyant optimism in their hearts.

In the course of prospecting the Masset Inlet area for the government, they found outcroppings of lignite coal and reasoned that it was likely there would be more between this region and the Cowgitz mine site. They decided to go overland down the centre of Graham Island, following the banks of the Yakoun River which, they had been told, flowed almost to Cowgitz.

The river was reported to be so full of log jams and debris that it was impassable by boat after the first mile or so, but Mr. Robertson felt that it would

111

be well worth their while to purchase a small canoe and try by this method. They set off up the Yakoun, which has been described as one of the most beautiful rivers to be found anywhere in the pre-logging days. (Present-day logging operations in the lush timber of the Yakoun Valley have left the usual desecration of unkempt logging slashings.)

They were only a few miles upstream when they rounded a bend and saw a dazzling yellow shaft on the west bank of the river. This was the unique Golden Spruce. It stood majestically in the brilliant morning sun, a blaze of unexpected beauty which was enhanced by the dark green of its neighboring trees. (1)

Robertson and Shields found that the reported log jams in the river had not been exaggerated and would have discouraged the travellers except for the rewarding discovery of float coal in many places. On the fifth day they came to a huge hump of coal in the river bed. This looked like pay dirt.

They lost no time in making camp and investigating. There was evidence of coal all over this region and it burned so well on their campfire it appeared to be of excellent quality. Camping for several days, they staked out the whole locality and put up their coal claim notices. (In later years this site became known as Camp Wilson.)

Cheered by this find the two men continued up the river and three days later arrived at the serene and beautiful Yakoun Lake and had the honor of being the first white men to have made this overland trek. In the lake area they found many more signs of coal which might warrant future investigation.

Now they stowed their canoe and climbed to the peak of a mountain to have a better look at this new country. The view was panoramic. To the south side lay the island-studded Skidegate Inlet and to the north stretched the long Yakoun Valley. They estimated their coal discovery to be about sixteen miles from Skidegate Inlet. It posed a transportation problem. But over the mountains to the west the huge bight of Rennell Sound ran well inland. This might present the solution for it was much closer to the coal site and there appeared to be natural draw through the coastal mountains that might be utilized.

As Mr. Robertson was still anxious to have a look at the old gold site in Mitchell Harbor, it was arranged that they would go to Skidegate and hire a canoe and two guides. While Robertson prospected the Mitchell Inlet region, Jimmy Shields would take the canoe and guides and go on to Rennell Sound. If the harbor looked as good from ground level as it did from this mountain crest, Shields was to stake out a townsite there to tie in with their coal claims.

It was getting dark so they camped for the night on the side of the mountain and proceeded towards Skidegate on the following day. On the way they met four Haidas who were going into the slate quarry to get argillite for carving. The Indians were astounded to learn that white men had come *overland* from Masset Inlet.

At the Oil Works in Sterling Bay, Bob Tennant was preparing to take over but found time to help them hire a canoe and two guides from Skidegate. It was a very rough trip to Mitchell Inlet, making Mr. Robertson extremely happy to be

(1) In 1966, it is still the only known tree of its kind in the world.
A successful graft has proved that it is a distinct species of Sitka
spruce and not a chloritic accident as has been sometimes suggested.

112

put ashore on dry land to begin his search for gold possibilities. The rough waters did not bother the old ex-sealer Shields or his experienced Haida guides, so they went north along the coast to Rennell Sound.

When they returned three days later, Shields reported that the harbor was a good one so he had staked out a townsite there as planned. Shields Island was named at this time as well.

For his part, Robertson had to report that the gold mining prospects were not promising. It would take a good deal of money and supplies to do much with the Gold Harbor proposition. Although he had found signs everywhere of former prospecting activities, that was all he had found.

After looking around Cumshewa Inlet and spending some time at the old Cowgitz workings, Shields and Robertson returned to Victoria and, on the strength of their Yakoun coal discovery, formed a company and each applied for 480 acres of coal lands in that region. The company included Thomas Russell, James Robinson, James Shields, Thomas Earle and W. Robertson.

The need to support his large family sent Mr. Robertson back to blacksmithing but if the partners were to capitalize on their coal find they would have to prove up on it. Jimmy Shields agreed to build a cabin and cut a trail from Skidegate Inlet to the site; then two miners, Tom Lewis and Petter Irving, were engaged to open up one of the seams. The three men were there until January of 1887 completing this assignment.

With one coal field waiting for a buyer, Robertson itched to have a better look at the Yakoun Lake region, but as usual he was short of money. He was so positive that he would find another good coal field there he was able to persuade Dr. Powell of Victoria to grubstake him $200. It was agreed that if another field was discovered Powell would get a Los Angeles financier, Mr. Freeman, to put up capital to develop and work the subsequent mine with Robertson and Powell to share half the resulting profits for their part in initiating the venture.

With $200 in his pocket, Mr. Robertson lost no time in closing down the smithy and getting back to the Yakoun. It was spring, 1887. He had little difficulty in locating the coal fields known as Camp Anthracite and Camp Robertson, both just a few miles east of Yakoun Lake, and staked out nine sections, three each for Powell and Freeman and the remaining three for himself. He had grave misgivings as to the scruples of his new partners, however. Having been swindled in a similar position once before he decided to play it safe and staked the choicest looking sections for himself.

When he returned to Victoria, Powell and Freeman indicated they were still behind the scheme and would provide the financial aid promised. They agreed to Robertson's suggestion of engaging James Parkinson, an English coal expert, to evaluate this latest find although Robertson would have to pay for this out of his own pocket for the present. Taking his son, Bill, and Petter Irving with him, Robertson went back to cut a trail, build a cabin and develop their newest coal find.

Freeman's son came up to check on things during the summer and made arrangements with Bob Tennant to give credit (in lieu of wages) to any local help Robertson had to engage. At the end of the summer things had reached a stage where a more definite business arrangement was required to pay for surveying and other expenses. Now he found that his premonitions about his

113

partners' honesty were justified, for they refused to let him have any money at all unless he signed all rights to his own sections over to them. After much feinting and sparring the whole deal fell through and Robertson was left on his own with a huge pile of unpaid bills.

In the fall of 1887, with no money to work his coal fields, he was persuaded to take a fling at politics and ran for the Dominion House of Common. His defeat was mitigated by meeting the wealthy William Wilson.

Wilson, interested in the coal mining prospects that Robertson had opened in the Charlottes, offered to back him to the hilt. This was wonderful news. Mrs. Robertson had become desperately ill with cancer and he was sorely in need of money to obtain medical care. With Wilson's backing Messrs. T. S. Gore and Mahood were engaged to survey the coal properties and Robertson was able to buy and receive a Crown Grant for nearly 3000 acres of coal lands.

In January 1892, Mrs. Robertson died. Her disconsolate husband now buried himself in the development work on the coal properties. Mr. Wilson took an active interest in the whole affair and engaged Mr. H. Parrish, a mining engineer, to supervise. They proved up so well on their claims that they almost sold the lot next year for a clear profit of $10 per acre. Then to Robertson's dismay, Wilson drove such a hard bargain that the would-be purchasers called the deal off.

During the next few years several good options were taken on the properties and in support of one in 1901 Michael King and John Irving of Victoria, well-known business men, had a Private Bill passed in the Legislature to incorporate the Graham Island Railway Company. According to Dr. T. B. Marshall's report for 1902 it was to go:

". . .from the north end of the coal fields and follow the level bed of the Yakoun River to a pass, called Yakoun Pass, and thence out to Rennell Sound where the terminal would be sheltered by Shields Island."

By 1909, interest in the Queen Charlotte Island coal fields had reached the point where not just one, but a total of three separate charters were applied for — to run railroads down the centre of Graham Island more or less from the mouth of the Yakoun River to the neighborhood of Queen Charlotte City with branch lines, one to Rennell Sound and the other to extend up past Port Clements (which was then known as Queenstown) as far as Masset.

In February of 1910 all three charters were granted to:

1. The ISLAND VALLEY RAILWAY COMPANY who planned to build 37 miles of railway — this company was represented by one of the directors, Mr. Castleman of Vancouver.
2. The QUEEN CHARLOTTE RAILWAY COMPANY, who would build 35 miles of track — this petition was put forth by W. T. Kergin, M.L.A. The original name of this company was the Graham Island Railway Company, but they agreed to a change of name to avoid confusion with the third charter being granted to —
3. The GRAHAM ISLAND RAILWAY COMPANY, which was having its original 1901 charter revived and confirmed. This company was also granted an extension of time, until December 31st, 1911, for spending $10,000 on its preliminary work.

It looked as though transportation problems for Graham Island were a thing of the past.

114

Ample money was being set up in capital funds for a number of companies who were investing in the coal lands. In 1909 Mr. Robertson's properties were finally sold for enough to enable him to retire at seventy-seven years of age, free from the money worries which had plagued him most of his life. (1)

(1) *All references to Mr. Robertson in this chapter were taken from his memoirs on file in the Provincial Archives, Victoria, B.C.*

CHAPTER TWENTY-ONE

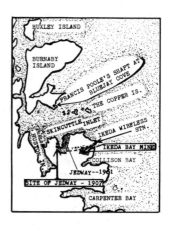

JEDWAY AND IKEDA

The big word in speculation at the south end of Moresby Island in the early years of the 1900s was copper. It was the magic chance to, "Make a real Pile."

This all began many years before with our old friend Francis Poole. When Poole returned to Victoria from the Bella Coola district in 1862 he had said confidently,

". . .from observations and calculations I've made on the mainland just across from the southern part of the Queen Charlottes, I am positive that there is copper over on those islands in paying quantities."

The statement caught the imagination of a group of Victoria mining men to such a degree they formed the Queen Charlotte Mining Co. and liking the sincerity and apparent ability of the young English mining engineer, they awarded him the contract to sink several shafts on the Charlottes to see if his "calculations" would bear fruit. It was July 31st, 1862.

As we know, Poole sunk his first shaft on the eastern end of Skincuttle Island and put up a log cabin there with a view to making this his headquarters. He soon found that the main course of the veins lay on nearby Burnaby Island – in the Bluejay Cove region – so he moved his operations over there. He reported to his company that besides Skincuttle and Burnaby Island, he had also found good copper signs on the west end of George Island and on Copper Island, as well as some on the west side of Harriet Harbor.

However, the Q.C. Mining Company did not pursue their interests in the Charlottes and by 1864 had abandoned their activities. Very little prospecting was done again in this area until 1889 when the pioneer prospector, Abe Heino, located his Skincuttle and Golden Gate claims. When the shafts he sank gave evidence of promising returns and word got around that he had located good copper properties, prospectors Hendrickson, Grant, Harper and Raper came up in 1901 and they too found satisfactory locations. One of Mr. Raper's claims was the site of Poole's original test shaft on Skincuttle Island.

This marked the beginning of the "copper rush." L. T. "Lucky" Watson who had been doing prospecting work for Victor Vigelous in the black sands region of Cape Fife (near Rose Spit) heard the news and as he had lived up to his nickname of "Lucky" so well earlier — he was able to interest Vigelous in grubstaking him to try his luck prospecting for copper.

When he arrived in the Skincuttle Inlet area, Mr. Watson teamed up with another old hand in the prospecting game. This was a former Yukoner of the days of '98, "Ike" Thompson. In 1905 they made the first important copper find of the district — the Copper Queen group at the head of Harriet Harbor. (1) They quickly found a buyer, J. S. McMillan of Seattle, who took it off their hands for the excellent price of $125,000.

By 1906 many prospectors were beginning to drift into the region and quite a cluster of cabins was built on the west side of Harriet Harbor which was known by the Haidas as Gigawai, meaning a snare or trap. The name was applied more loosely in this instance to mean the dangerous nature of the bay in the southeasters when sudden sharp squalls would sweep along the waters causing havoc to the unwary. Gigawai was adapted into the word Jedway by the white man and became the name of the new settlement.

It was during a storm in the Jedway area that Arichika Ikeda, of the fishing firm of Awaya, Ikeda and Company of Vancouver, came ashore to talk to some of the prospectors, and this visit to socialize became one of his most profitable.

Although feelings about Orientals in general was prejudicial, Archie Ikeda was popular with all prospectors in that region. He was an affable and willing fellow and had performed many favors for them bringing mail, supplies, donating fresh fish and other similar services. One of the prospectors who had found ore in the area showed a specimen to Ikeda and suggested he do a little prospecting on his own. Perhaps he could try the adjoining bay? He explained to Ikeda how to examine the ground for signs of ore, and said that if he did find any he could sell his discovery for a good price in Vancouver.

Ikeda thought this sounded like a good idea, much better than chasing elusive fish. It was too rough for fishing so he called together the other Japanese who were working for his firm and explained the proposition. Not one of them knew anything about prospecting, but they reasoned that given enough men to the square mile not too much would be overlooked.

This logic bore fruit in a surprisingly short time when, at the head of a creek in what is now Ikeda Bay, Mr. Ikeda discovered a surface outcrop of the prettiest copper ore anyone could have fancied. Carefully following what were thought to be the main veins, the group staked out 47 claims and went to Vancouver to form a company. It was 1906.

Their initial mining methods were appallingly crude and backbreaking, but within a year the Ikeda Bay Mines were shipping first class copper ore in good quantity. Improvements were made steadily until by 1908 there were 118 Japanese and two white men working. Well over $60,000 had been spent putting in a good wharf, bunkers, tramway, office buildings and dwellings and in converting the old sternwheeler Dawson into a comfortable bunkhouse. A Japanese doctor, in residence, was a great asset to that isolated location. Archie Ikeda remained popular and well-liked as he had always been. All the papers of that day had many favorable comments about his conduct both as

(1) Information from the Provincial Archives, Victoria, B.C.

mine manager and good neighbor.

The mine continued unter Japanese management and ownership until 1910, when Ikeda Bay was sold to a Vancouver firm for a reported $250,000. The company's president was Mr. R. P. McLennan, of McLennan, McFeeley and Co.; vice-president was Mr. W. C. Nichol, publisher; and Mr. J. J. Plommer of Nicola Valley Coal and Coke, the secretary-treasurer. The four directors were W. R. Phillips, of Hopper-Phillips, bankers; C. J. Peter, Manager of Galt Bros.; Senator The Hon. J. H. Ross of Ottawa; and A. Ikeda of Awaya, Ikeda and Co.

In October 1909 the Dominion Government steamer *Quadra* took a party of thirteen men to build a much needed wireless station at Ikeda Point. When completed, at a cost of $12,205, the station had dwellings, operating house and a huge 228 foot mast — the highest on the coast. Two miles of trail connected the wireless station with Ikeda Bay Mines.

It was here that the first telephones on the Charlottes were installed, with the line running from the Ikeda Wireless Station into the office of the Ikeda Bay Mines, and then over the hill to the Jedway Hotel — a total distance of about four and a half miles.

Eleven years later, in September 1920, the wireless station closed down. So was the mine which had begun as one of the most promising ventures in this field on the Islands. In its day many thousands of tons of high grade copper ore were shipped from Ikeda's busy docks.

The Cinderella success of Archie Ikeda and his fishermen friends was an added spur to the efforts of the score of prospectors going into the region. It was backbreaking work, not without its hazards. At least two young men lost their lives in 1908. In Huston Inlet, Jack Allison was killed helping his partners put in a tunnel, and up in Sewell Inlet Pete Peterson was killed by a falling tree when clearing a section to work on his claim. The possibility that a fortune could lie just a finger's breadth away brought it into the realm of high adventure. Everyone tried — from genuine prospectors to passing fishermen and even sea captains. Canadian Pacific's Captain Louis P. Locke was among those who used the opportunity of a lay-over for bad weather to go ashore and stake out a claim.

One of the men who tried his luck in the fall of 1906 was Walter Dass. The weather was too poor for prospecting the rest of that year, recalled Mr. Dass, and in the spring of 1907 he took on the job of foreman, constructing a hotel in Jedway. This was to be built for Marsh M. English, cannery manager of Port Essington, who thought he saw good prospects in this feverish activity. It was agreed that upon completion of the hotel, Mr. Dass was to have the job of managing it for two years. (1)

The *North Coast,* which was published in Port Simpson, ran an item in its Nov. 23, 1907 issue saying,

". . .and the new hotel at Jedway is finished and Walter Dass, the foreman has the best wishes of all the boys for his good work and judgment in handling his men. There are eight bedrooms, sitting room, dining room, office, kitchen and the swellest little buffet north of Seattle, where guests can get anything from ice water to champagne."

Profits were ensured when absentee owner English was granted a liquor licence

(1) *Information from Mr. W. Dass in a letter, July 1964, from Toronto.*

for his hotel. It looked as though he had invested his money wisely — perhaps much better than poking around in the hills looking for a copper mine — as a further report in the *North Coast* in December says,

"The hotel at Jedway is doing a rushing business. The past week they have been unable to care for all the travellers and some have had to double up and several were put in outside cabins. Manager Dass is complimented on his table, and it is said that he really knows how to handle a crowd."

From the small cluster of cabins in 1906, Jedway grew rapidly into quite a little metropolis. By the end of 1907 there was the hotel, a good general store run by Mr. A. Sivart, and his son-in-law, C. A. Bourne, was operating a sawmill at full capacity to keep up with the local demand for lumber. Houses were going up at a great speed, a clam cannery was built, as well as a fine wharf, a post office, a deputy mining recorder's office and a pokey. Tom Daykin, a good-natured prospector from Collison Bay, was appointed acting lawman until Constable Charles L. Cullen could arrive from Atlin to take over his duties. Cullen was transferred soon afterward to be replaced by Constable Walter Prescott — a physical culture devotee who drew much interest in his daily excercises — part of which consisted of rowing a boat across the bay three times a day, rain or shine.

Prospecting activities had reached such a peak in April of 1908 that an Order-in-Council was passed to be effective the next month, which detached the Q.C. Islands from the Skeena Mining Division and formed the Islands into a separate Division with official headquarters at Jedway. E. M. Sandilands was put in charge, and he was also made a stipendary magistrate for that area.

Lucky Watson had bought the first of his boats, the *Jedway,* and engaging Charlie Crawford as engineer, kept it busy transporting men and supplies in the new rush. J. S. McMillan had ordered work pushed ahead as fast as possible in developing the Copper Queen properties which he had bought from Watson and Thompson. His superintendent, Frank Watson, was putting in the tramline from the water's edge to the mine entrance where Mr. Dodd had two shifts at work driving in a tunnel.

Copper strikes were being reported from every side now — from Klum-Kwoi (Lockeport) to Huxley Island, Huston Inlet, Carpenter Bay and even down on Kunghit Island. Many were wishful thinking, but a few had good enough showings for sizeable amounts of cash to change hands.

In April of 1908 Stanley Boys of Vancouver, owner of the plant which printed the *North Coast* in Port Simpson, announced that he was thinking of moving the press to Jedway to begin publication of a newspaper.

Over the hill from Jedway the little community of Collison Bay had its group of hopefuls and it was here that the Daykins sold one of their claims for $10,000 and Joe Tritheway sold one for $15,000. When J. H. Gordon and Captain Locke sold their Black Prince to a Seattle syndicate for $60,000 things honed to a sharp edge. Joe Tritheway thought it might be smart to open up more on some of his other holdings, so he engaged the Daykins to build a large float for unloading supplies and then went south to bring ten men to build a tramline into his Treasure Box and Cash Box claims and to erect a two-story house for accommodations. When he hired two women to run his "eating house" it created a real surge of interest in that all-male community. As one man said, "There's nothing like the presence of two ladies to make the boys spruce up and clean out their ears."

Jedway, too, had its feminine residents, as Mrs. Thompson had come up to join Ike, and both Mr. Bourne and Mr. Sivart had their wives there. Then Fred Dolmage of Port Essington, who had a contract to get out logs for the Jedway sawmill, brought not only his wife over in June of 1908, but also his four children — Jennie, Olive, Bill and baby Charles.

Jennie (now Mrs. McGregor of West Vancouver) was only eight at the time but has vivid memories of those days. Jedway seemed to be a bright, sunny place — but windy. How the wind would sweep up under the cabin floor and blow the linoleum right up off the floor! Mrs. Dolmage would rush around trying to nail it down and as fast as she did, tacks would give way in another place, to the glee of the four small people looking on.

She remembers how concerned Mr. L. T. Watson was at the lack of fresh milk for the children — so much so that he sent to a farm and had two cows shipped up to Jedway. They arrived safely on the boat, but as there was no fodder to be found on the wooded shores of Harriet Harbor, they gave no milk. In fact it was obvious that they would perish if left there, and so after a short time, with great reluctance, the kindly colored man had to have them sent back to the farm. Jennie McGregor recalls how heartbroken the Dolmage children were to see the soft-eyed animals go, and wept copiously as they were hoisted aboard the *Amur*.

Mr. Sivart had little in his store for children, but as soon as he began to stock a few dolls, teddy bears and so on they all turned up at the Dolmage home, despite anything Mrs. Dolmage could do. She was distressed at the prospectors spending their money in such a way, knowing that some of the most generous were also the ones who could least afford to part with cash, for they were still living on dreams of making a strike.

Gradually, in that year of 1908, other children came to live at Jedway. Mr. H. L. Robertson of Hartley Bay, a builder, found so much work in Jedway that he brought up his wife and daughters. Tom Wilson, the new foreman for McMillan, brought along his family. Then in July the first baby arrived when a twelve pound son was born to the C. A. Bournes. Dr. Nogero and his family moved into their new Jedway home in September. Travelling minister Rev. Keyworth came often to hold services in the Jedway Supply store. He kept his services simple, non-denominational and lively and the whole town turned out to sing familiar hymns and give him rousing support.

L. T. Watson had a flotilla of boats by 1908, the largest of which was the *Elola* which had sleeping quarters for eight, and all the bunks had the new spring-filled mattresses. Captain Anderson was engaged to skipper her, with Jack Scotland as the engineer. Mr. Watson hired Mr. Harvey to take over the job of keeping his boats in good repair, and the Harvey family moved in to swell the Jedway population. In the fall of 1908 Marsh English had such a good offer for his hotel that he could not resist it. He sold out to Ben Metcalfe, who arrived in November with his wife, daughter and son-in-law, (Mr. and Mrs. Armitage) to take over and run the hotel. So Walter Dass was out of a job, despite English's firm assurances when he had needed someone to take over building the hotel. It was not for long because Walter soon became skipper of the 23-man fishing boat *Flamingo,* the first of many Island boats Mr. Dass captained during his long years of residence on the Charlottes.

Although there were several children in Jedway, there was still no school as most of the youngsters were either too young or were sent "out" to get their education. This was a matter of grave concern for the diminutive Mrs. Emily Dolmage, as she had two children ready for school and she felt that their education should not be delayed. She decided that she would have to undertake the job herself and in lieu of orthodox teacher training she would use her own good common sense in preparing lessons.

All instruction was conducted on the kitchen table, and Jennie McGregor still remembers the white oilcloth on the table, with the blackboard hung on the wall, and rows and rows of arithmetic sums to do. They had no text-books (for money was scarce in the Dolmage home), so they made do with English books sent from grandmother and some American books that a friend had loaned.

Mrs. Dolmage was a wonderful person. Born near Plymouth in England, she was only seventeen years old when she was sent to accompany her elder sister to live on their brother's farm in Alberta. Here she met Fred Dolmage and a year later they were married. Mr. Dolmage, who was tall and good-looking, had come from Ontario and did not care for life on the prairies so after a few years he packed up his family and moved to the lively little Skeena River town of Port Essington. With frequent engagements to go out on timber cruising or prospecting trips, he was seldom at home, so the formidable job of raising her young family under pioneering conditions fell almost wholly on the shoulders of the tiny, five foot Emily.

Fortunately she had been taught to sew expertly as a young girl in England and she had one of the very few sewing machines in Jedway. How those nimble fingers flew as she made nearly every stitch of clothing her family wore! Most of the garments were fashioned pain-stakingly from discarded adult clothing.

With the more than full-time job of teaching, baking, sewing and caring for her family, the days were so full that there was never time to be lonely. Mrs. Dolmage was completely happy so that when they went to live in Vancouver a few years later, Jennie says the children would often find their mother crying, and through the tears she would say, "Oh, I just miss those Islands too much . . . sometimes I don't think I can bear it any longer down here in the city."

In 1909 the Pacific Coast Fisheries began building a plant in a bay off Selwyn Inlet. Using the first two letters of each name in the company's title, the $300,000 plant was christened Pacofi. Fred Dolmage was up in that region timber cruising, and when he learned that there was a house available at Pacofi, just along the beach from the plant, he moved his family up from Jedway. They were the only white family in Pacofi and so once again the children were made much of by all the men working there.

In the fall of 1910 there were mysterious talks between mother and father, and one November day, after a series of gales had swept the coast, Jennie heard her father say, "I don't think we'd better take a chance on the *Amur,* she's liable to be stormbound — I'll go down to Jedway and get Maggie Wilson to come up." It was calm when he left, but by evening a gale broke over the region. How it lashed the trees, whipping the branches wildly and up-rooting many of the smaller trees in its fury! However, the Dolmage cabin was snug and warm and the children settled into the carefree sleep of youth.

It was still howling fiercely and the sky an inky black when Jennie felt her mother at her bedside shaking her gently but firmly. "Jennie, I want you to get up, I am not well, dear – you will have to go up to the bunkhouse and get Scotty Fraser for me." Then as a strong gust shook the frame house she clutched the child tightly and said, "Oh, how I hate to let you go dear – but this is very important. You must take the "bug" (a candle set into a jam tin, or one of similar size) and go along the water's edge – don't use the trail tonight."

The young girl sensed an imperative emergency, different from anything she had ever known, and despite her terrible apprehension at venturing into that wild dark night alone, knew she must – somehow. Never will she forget that night. The candle blew out in seconds, but luckily there was still a dim light showing from the bunkhouse to give her direction as she fumbled and fell over the log-strewn beach. She could hear boughs crashing to the ground from the trees along the beach and knew why her mother had said not to go by the forest trail.

Just as she got to the bunkhouse door, the light went out. She knocked hard upon the door and the grumbling astonishment as the lamp was relit faded into concern when the men saw the little girl there. She gave the message to Scotty – and he seemed to know what was wanted. Telling Jennie to remain with the men, he lit a storm lantern and went out around the bay to the Indian settlement. Jennie can still recall seeing that light bobbing all along the beach, sometimes lost to view as Scotty went behind the huge logs on the beach. Then she could see a light come on in one of the Indian houses. Shortly after, Mr. Fraser's lantern once again bobbed all the way back along the beach. When he reappeared in the bunkhouse door, he had an Indian woman beside him.

"Keep Jennie here for the night, and some of you boys come with me and we'll bring over the other three." Strong arms carefully wrapped up the other young Dolmages and tenderly carried them over to stay the night in the bunkhouse under the attentive care of the fish-plant men.

Later that night Pacofi had a new citizen. In the morning Charlotte Dolmage lay in her mother's arms, the first babe to be born in Pacofi.

By the next day the storm had subsided and Fred Dolmage returned with the doctor from Ikeda Bay and the stout Maggie Wilson to care for his family. Maggie had very rigid ideas about "raisin' kids" which she immediately put into practice. First it was a hot bath to "clean 'em outside", then a huge dose of castor oil to do the job inside. All four children were lined up for the oil, but the usually tractable Jennie absolutely balked – earning Maggie's ire and despair as a result. The feud went on for the full time she was there, and neither gave an inch.

It was logging also, rather than prospecting, that brought another well-known early pioneer to the Islands. This was Fred B. Jones – much better known as "Jiggeroo" Jones. He came up with his two older boys and young thirteen-year-old Weaver to log on Burnaby Island for the Jedway sawmill in 1907. Jiggeroo was a big strapping man with a head of flaming red hair and beard to match, and with an immense sense of fun which made him a welcome visitor everywhere he went.

Jones' life, like that of so many of his contemporaries, had been full of adventure. Born in New Brunswick in 1860, he had come west by almost every means of transportation – covered wagon, horse and shank's mare. He had set his sights for Washington State, and when he came to Lake Chelan, he and a friend persuaded an Indian to paddle them across the lake and they blazed a trail through the woods to the Skagit and Mount Vernon region.

Here he met Ida Tingley, the attractive sister of another equally well-known Masset Inlet pioneer, Freeman Tingley, Senior, and a distant relative of Bert and Eli Tingley of Port Clements' pioneering days. Mr. Jones married his Ida and they took up homesteading and raised a family. Five sons were born to them, Samuel, Oliver, Morton, Weaver and McKinley.

After ten years of homesteading on the Skagit, Fred Jones's feet itched to move again — and this time B.C. lured him to Vancouver Island. He logged there until 1907, when he and his sons went to Burnaby Island, on the Charlottes. They couldn't be in that area for long without catching the prospecting fever. The place they chose is one of the loveliest spots on the Islands, Hotspring Island. The Hotsprings had become a resort in the early days for everyone in the region, and Archie Ikeda had built a comfortable cabin for the use of visitors which by all accounts was well patronized.

The Jones staked and applied to pre-empt Hotspring Island in 1907, going up from Burnaby Island every so often to work on their claim. When the mill at Jedway burned down in 1909 there was no longer a market for their logs so, sending the two other boys back to live at home, Jiggeroo and his son Morton went to work in earnest looking for their lode on Hotspring. When they finally abandoned it in 1910 they had not found anything there, despite the sinking of a good sized shaft.

To keep his family in the meantime, Jiggeroo took on other jobs, mainly timber cruising and guiding speculators into prospecting sites. Old timers say he was one of the most able timber cruisers in the country and could go through the most jungle-like growth as though it were of no consequence — inevitably emerging with his whiskers full of spruce needles and leaves. There were few places on the Charlottes that he had not been when he finally left the Islands in 1910. His wife passed away that year and Jiggeroo went to Plumber Bay, Vancouver Island, where he remained until his death in 1937.

It was said that he acquired his nickname because of his habit of referring to people whose names had slipped his memory as, ". . .that jiggeroo". His son says that he had also been known in the Vancouver Island logging camps earlier, as "Dirty Face Jones" — a title which he apparently enjoyed. (1)

The poem "Tale of the Moveable Mine" by George Winkler was based on Jiggeroo's episode when he staked out part of the black sands near Cape Fife only to have an exceptionally high tide wash away all traces of the placer gold he had found there.

In February of 1908 while he was on Hotspring Island, Jiggeroo left with Tom Pollard, a Haida, to go to Jedway, telling young Morton that he would be back the next day, or if the weather became stormy Morton was to allow five days. Ten long days passed and there was no sign of his father. Morton rowed all the way down to Jedway in a state of apprehension and, as he had feared, there had been no sign of Jiggeroo.

There was no one to authorize the chartering of a boat to search for the missing men, and it was kind-hearted L. T. Watson who came to the rescue with his launch *Elola*. They finally found Mr. Jones in Skidegate — miles away from his

(1) All information about Jiggeroo from his son Weaver Jones, Bellingham, Washington.

original destination. When they left Hotspring, he and Pollard had been caught in a series of storms and despite anything they could do, were forced northward. He well knew how anxious the boy would be and heaped profound thanks on the embarassed Lucky Watson for his help. This was not the only instance of neighborly help extended when Government hands were seemingly tied by the red tape of "Lack of Authorization" in human emergencies.

As mentioned earlier the "staking" rush resulted in a busy headquarters in the office of the Mining Recorder. It looked as though some thought should be given to laying out a properly organized town to take care of the expected "boom town." In November 1908 John Elliott, B.C.L.S., laid out a townsite on the opposite side of the harbor.

The first building to go up on this new townsite was a fine new Mining Recorder's Office for the Gold Commissioner, together with a wharf and float. It was the only building to go up there, as it turned out.

In June of 1909 the mill at Jedway burned to the ground. A fire started near the boiler and was extinguished — so it was thought. But several hours after, it broke out again and had made such headway that in a short time it was beyond control. The entire mill and equipment were destroyed and were only partially covered by insurance. This marked the beginning of the end for Jedway.

Copper, which seemed to lie everywhere, was mainly in small pockets and veins, many of which were so faulted that it was uneconomical to mine. One by one the claims were abandoned as people drifted away. In 1908 a growing voters list had fifty-four names, but in 1910 only ten names remained. In April of 1910 the Jedway office of the Gold Commissioner was closed. It reopened the following year in the newly booming townsite of Queen Charlotte City.

Even Mr. Sivart, Jedway's pioneer storekeeper, decided to close up shop and move to New Westminster where he planned to go into the hardware business. But the veteran prospector Abe Heino was still there in 1912 and had ten men working for him on his Copper Island claim, and was making small shipments. Ike and Mrs. Thompson still stayed in their beloved little town. In fact they stayed on for many more years, as Ike was still listed as the sub-mining recorder there in 1922. Assessment work on a few of the more promising properties was kept up and recorded until 1926.

Since then, several Japanese salteries located in the area ran for a number of years and there was also an abalone cannery in a nearby inlet for a short time. But gradually the weeds and forest growth began to take over Jedway and it eventually became one of the many ghost towns of B.C.

That is until 1961 when the whole region was revitalized with the opening of a good market for another mineral which was present in abundant quantities in that area. This was iron ore.

The Jedway Iron Ore Limited company was formed in April of 1961 with its head office in Vancouver. They had a contract with Sumitome Shoji Kaisha Limited of Japan to supply 2,000,000 long tons of iron ore over a five year period. Once again this part of the Islands sprang into the news with successful open-pit mining and a growing townsite. The Jedway of 1961 was built on the eastern side of Harriet Harbor, using the old site surveyed in 1908. Once again, also, prospectors were everywhere in the hills. Several companies were formed and on the strength of a drill going in, glowingly descriptive brochures were mailed to the public, urging them to buy shares and "cash in on the boom." But only the Jedway mine has come into actual production.

CHAPTER TWENTY-TWO

TASU AND LOCKEPORT

In 1966 another iron mine is on the verge of going into action — and this, it is rumored, will surpass Jedway in output. Located in Tasu Harbor, it is anticipated that by 1967 on Gowing Island a town of one thousand people will be an actuality.

Tasu also began as a copper site discovery. The first prospecting was done there in 1907 and the next year trails were cut in from Lockeport, Crescent Inlet and Sewell Inlet, so that prospectors might have an easier access from the east side of Moresby and not have to make the trip — often stormy — up the west coast.

One of the first companies to buy into this area was the Elliott Mining Co. In 1909 they bought out all the holdings of Henry Moody and his partners and soon had their foreman, James D. McKenzie, with a crew of thirty men putting in a tunnel. In June of that year Arthur Gowing went to Prince Rupert to hire eleven men to add to the fifteen he had at work on his property. Mr. Gowing reported that Skidegate's Albert Jones had good showings on his claim at Tasu — with copper and gold to the value of $43.50 per ton.

In 1910 the Granby Consolidated were developing properties they had purchased in the harbor, according to their superintendent, A. B. W. Hodges. The newly formed Tassoo Mining and Smelting Company had driven a 225 foot tunnel into their mine. R. R. Hedley was the manager, and he had hired E. T. Crawford of the Vancouver Machinery Depot to install an aerial tramway from tidewater to the mine entrance part way up the mountainside.

Working conditions were so difficult it was becoming impossible to hold men, but eventually the mine opened and worked until 1914. They were able to ship one boatload of ore, only to find that the copper contents were too low to cover expenses and they closed down — leaving all the crew waiting for their pay. Charlie Hartie, one of the Island's early arrivals, told how he barely escaped being one of that waiting crew.

In December of 1913 he had decided to go home to Vancouver Island for Christmas and boarded the *Prince Albert* in Queen Charlotte City for the trip. When the boat called at Lockeport there were several passengers waiting to go south. These were men from the Tasu mine who had quit the job and hiked over the trail to catch the boat. The mine boss was on the *"Albert"*, which was to go around the south end of Moresby and thence up the west coast to deliver a load of supplies to Tasu.

At Lockeport the boss tried in vain to induce the men to go back on the job, but it was no use. "He then asked me," says Mr. Hartie, "and several other passengers if we would like a job — offering much higher wages than was usual." Charlie liked the sound of those extravagant wages, but was not happy with what he heard the ex-workers say about the place, so he said he'd let the mine boss know his decision when they docked in Tasu.

It was a rough trip all the way up the west coast and the *"Albert"* heaved and plunged in the heavy seas. When they at last docked in Tasu, Charlie met a number of his Queen Charlotte City friends there — Archie Duval, Joe Renner, Ed Anderson and Charlie Golden. They were not happy with conditions. The cook for the outfit was Teddy Clark, "a pint sized Cockney with a pug nose that someone's fist had bashed up some more," said Charlie, "so he always looked as though he was smelling something he didn't like."

Trying to make up his mind, balancing those high wages against his own feelings that things weren't as good as they should be there, Mr. Hartie asked Teddy how he liked Tasu life. Teddy was kneading a batch of bread dough and as Charlie talked to him, he could see a drip forming on Teddy's pug nose. The drip grew larger and larger and finally dropped into the dough. Teddy paid no heed — and another drip followed the first, and then another.

This was enough for Mr. Hartie. He sought out the boss in a hurry and said, "no thanks." When he heard later that all the men who had stayed after this lost their pay, he says he always felt he was saved, "by a drip," from a similar fate.

When they left Tasu that noon, they ran into one of the worst storms of the *"Albert's"* crossing — it took five days to get to Vancouver. Ben Metcalfe of Jedway was a passenger and became so ill on the trip that when they eventually docked in Vancouver he had to be taken ashore on a stretcher.

In 1911 there was more than merely a copper interest at Tasu. The Queen Charlotte Fishing Company, with headquarters in Vancouver, built a small fishing station and boat building plant at Two Mountain Bay, on the east side of Tasu Sound. They set up a small steam powered mill and sawed yellow cedar lumber for two boats, each about 50 feet long. The boats were built but not yet outfitted when they were seized and sold in a sherrif's sale in January of 1913, and proceeds used to pay some of the back wages and other expenses.

One boat the *Dorothy Kalon* was used as a tug by the T. A. Kelley Logging Co. and Walter Dass was her first skipper. When Mr. Dass left to take over the larger *Nora Jane* for Kelley's Camp, the *Dorothy Kalon* under another captain was wrecked on Cumshewa Rocks and the engineer, Jimmy Clark, drowned. The other boat built by the Tasu company was the *Rennall* which was used in halibut fishing out of Prince Rupert for many years. She later sank in Wright Sound.

Although the mines at Tasu did not amount to a great deal, there was a recorded production between the years of 1914 and 1917 of 5,180 tons of ore from the number 3 zone, containing 94 oz. of gold, 1,408 oz. of silver and 165,566 lbs of copper. (1) When the area was reactivated it was pioneer staker

(1) Information contained in the 1961 and 1962 Report of the Minister of Mines.

Albert Jones of Skidegate who made the bonanza. The sale of his Tasu claims to Westfrob Mines in 1964 produced a cash settlement of $175,000.

Westfrob Mines Ltd. did extensive exploratory drilling in 1956 and 1957 and then abandoned work until 1961, when seventy more test drills were made and geological and magnetometer surveys were carried out. By 1962 a forty-man bunkhouse had been built with an access road a mile and a half long from the camp at sea level to the upper ore zone number 3 at 1,300 feet, and Tasu's development was officially sanctioned by the company's head office in Toronto. (1)

Over the hill and to the south-east of Tasu Sound lies Klum-Kwoi Bay which also had its share of activity in 1907. By the next year twenty-five men were living there in a small group of cabins and it soon became a port of call for steamers. When Captain Locke of the *Amur* began bringing his ship into the bay he thought the little settlement should have a good name and there was none better than the name of his hometown in Nova Scotia. The miners agreed, and Lockeport was officially adopted by the residents. (2)

It was a small community with a happy spirit of comradship and soon became the jumping-off point for the prospectors all around that area. At a meeting of the prospectors in the neighborhood, a Mr. Beresford was appointed to be their deputy mining recorder, and they notified the Jedway office of their decision — quite a switch from the usual way such appointments were made. They built a cabin for the Lockeport Club in 1908 with everyone pitching in. When it was finished they threw a big party for the people in the district — and it was an overwhelming success by all accounts.

W. H. Thompson opened a general store there and in July of 1908 ran a big advertisement in "Windy" Young's Queen Charlotte newspaper to say that he sold, "Groceries, boots, shoes, clothing, hardware and stationery." Captain Irving Wintermute brought his boat the *Maple Leaf* up and was in constant demand to transport supplies and parties going out, "to the hills."

Although there were a few cash buyers for some of the claims, one of which was millionaire Pierpont Morgan, there were also in Lockeport, as there had been in Jedway, many dreamers whose only prospect of cashing in on their claim was to find an unknowledgeable purchaser who liked to play the long shots in a gamble. The accepted pattern among the "boys" was to go out and made a little money, come back and work your claim as long as the rum lasted, then back out again to make some more money to tide you over another spell of "proving up."

One man who sold his claim for a good price was Jim Langell, and he took his money to the Nadu, on Masset Sound. Here he bought land out in the muskeg and used most of his fortune to prove that you could grow vegetables in muskeg if you went about it the right way. And he did just that. Some of the Langell cabbages were so huge it needed two arms to hold them. It was rumored that he used most of his money on lime and potash for his sour soil as he used to bring it home by the boatload.

One of the best known of all Lockeport people was William Morgan. Born in Wales, Mr. Morgan came to the Charlottes in 1908 or 1909 lured by the reported

(1) Westfrob is a subsidiary of Falconbridge Nickel, with head offices at 7 King Street, Toronto and 504, 1112 West Pender Street, Vancouver.
(2) Information from Mr. George McRae of Queen Charlotte City.

mining and prospecting activities in the Lockeport district. He opened (1) a store which one old timer says, ". . . carried groceries, tools, tobacco and a good supply of wet goods — as most of the prospectors were good drinkers." The store prospered even though his business methods and bookkeeping were something that no one but he could understand and it was doubtful if he did either. About the time the prospecting activity died, logging started up close to Lockeport. Later a salmon cannery was built there and Morgan kept the store going. As Mr. Hartie says, "He would give credit to anyone who came along and charge ridiculous prices. If someone complained about being charged three times what the article was worth, Morgan would admit it was a mistake and hand you something off the shelves that was more than the value of the overcharge."

About the time of the hungry thirties all activities around Lockeport closed and except for an occasional thirsty fisherman, Morgan had no customers. He got in debt with the wholesale people, closed his store and left the Islands, broke.

Later friends heard that he had hired out to a logging camp on Vancouver Island as a cook but was fired on the second day. It must have been the final straw in a series of reverses for he went into a deserted cabin and hanged himself. He was still at Lockeport in 1918 when Captain E. H. Simpson came in to put up the cannery. Captain Simpson had been in Sedgwick Bay, to the southeast of Lockeport, on Lyell Island, with his wife and young son Sam, where he had operated a fish buying camp for the two previous seasons. The dog salmon (chums) were the main fish bought, and they were packed south to Bellingham for processing.

In the spring of 1918 Mr. Simpson promoted the idea, with some Americans, of a cannery at Lockeport to can the salmon on the spot. They acquired the use of the ice-making and freezing plant at Pacofi (which had been inoperative since 1914) to run in conjunction with their cannery. The Lockeport cannery had put up a huge pack of salmon by October 1918 and, with the American Army taking everything possible in this line, the market was assured. Then came the embargo. After November 11th and the end of the war, sales to the States were nil.

In recalling those days, Capt. Simpson's son, Sam, who also has been a cannery man all his life says, "For some reason dog salmon are a jinx in a cannery man's life — they always seem to spell disaster." The Lockeport operation of 1918 was no exception. With a huge pack of salmon on their hands and no market, the whole thing went "belly-up." Capt. Simpson took what little he could salvage from the venture and went to Langara Island to open a small one-line cannery there with Captain H. Babington.

The boat Mr. Simpson owned then was named the *Chaos* recalls Sam, who adds ". . . apparently it had received its name from a former owner, a minister who had had a lot of trouble with his wife — and after its part in the Lockeport disaster, it looked as though it was still well-named."

William Morgan, whose name was known up and down the whole region by then, stayed on to operate his store and post office and to be the general factotum in Lockeport. In 1923 he came into the news as a result of his cat. She had mated with a wild marten, producing unique kittens, which were so highly prized by visiting tourists that some were stolen.

(1) He may have taken over W.H. Thompson's store, but this is not substantiated.

The Canadian Fishing Company took over and ran the Lockeport Cannery for the years 1926, 1927 and 1928 then abandoned it to centre their activities in the Lagoon Inlet cannery to the north, behind Louise Island. Col. MacMillan of Vancouver built the modern little cannery in Lagoon Bay the same year that Capt. Simpson built the one in Lockeport. The Canadian Fishing Company bought it in 1922 and ran it until it was destroyed by fire in 1941.

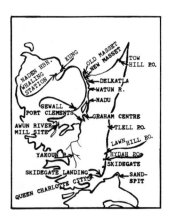

CHAPTER TWENTY-THREE

LET THE BUYER BEWARE

The financial panic which swept over Canada and the United States in the winter of 1907 seemed to hit with full fury in 1908. Railroads, banks and businesses of every size and description were forced to close their doors, and thousands of men all across the land walked the streets, hungry and desperate as they hopelessly searched for jobs, which by now were almost non-existent.

This depression which displaced so many people into insecurity, created a tremendous urge to own a piece of land — any kind of land — and to satisfy the hunger for a place of their own people would undergo incredible hardships.

The booklets put out by the B.C. Government at this time telling of the good land available on the Charlottes were avidly poured over. Their radiant offer of good farming land at give-away pre-emption prices was like manna from heaven. The regulations for pre-empting in those days stated that anyone over eighteen who was a British subject, or had made application to become a British subject, could stake a pre-emption in unsurveyed territory. Describe it — and you would be entitled to stake 160 acres. You must live on the claim for two years, (1) do $400 worth of improvements — most cabins would cover this — pay $1 per acre to the government plus the cost of surveying, then with a $10 Crown Grant fee the land was yours.

It was an irresistible opportunity which lost nothing in the telling in government bulletins.

However, the fine print in this seeming benevolence was that "unsurveyed" bit — to which should also have been added "unmapped." For as they advertised the land to encourage settlers the B.C. government also, with an almost gay abandon, issued coal, petroleum and timber licences covering vast acreages to all who applied. There were no maps, other than the very few old 1887 blueprints, and no attempt whatsoever was made to organize the best use of the land to benefit everyone.

It seems incredible that any responsible government could have been so blind

---

(1) Later extended to three years.

to the inevitable confusion and unnecessary hardship such an irresponsible lack of planning would create. With no maps to find out whether the land wanted was available and transportation to a government office not only expensive and time-consuming, but also fairly hazardous before the larger boats began scheduled crossings, one disgruntled Islander contributed this poem to Jimmy Campbell's *Queen Charlotte Islander:* –

The Lament of the Graham Islanders

What is our Island coming to, we ask the passer-by,
Since coal and timber cruisers got their finger in the pie?
You'll find their stakes from shore to shore, no matter where you go.
And when the farmer comes along he finds his cake's all dough.

When you write down to Victoria about this Island shore,
They send you books and papers and pamphlets by the score;
They tell you farming land is good – but they forget to say
That as for getting it's concerned, you'd better stay away.

These books tell all about the vast amount of farming land
And paint a glowing picture of a future near at hand,
When steamboats come and railroads run, of canneries galore,
Where you can sell your products, all you raise and then some more.

But when the people get here and start to look it o'er,
They find that timber limits run a mile back from every shore,
They find the whole blam'd country staked for coal and oil and tree,
And if they want to get a farm they'll have to stake the sea!

And the sea, as far as that's concerned, is staked for fish and clam
And submarine and Lord knows what – it's just as bad as land.
Oh, take a tip, you land-seekers, and do not wend your way
To Graham Isle to pre-empt; you'll find it does not pay.

The thing that bothers us the most, what we can't understand,
Is why the Gov'ment advertises to settle up the land?
It's like the treacherous lion who'd lure the deer into his lair.
Are they in league with steamboat lines for a rake-off on the fare?

I could name men among us who have travell'd many a mile
On the strength of pamphlets they've got regarding Graham Isle.
And if you don't believe me, come and see; you'll find it so.
For they're still awaiting records on land staked a year ago.

Now it may be just and legal to play this title game,
But to those who come and those right here, it's a dirty shame
To encourage people to find land, as I've already said,
With trees stak'd o'er and coal below, they'd better far be dead!

All east of Masset Inlet was reserved six years ago.
From purchase lease lend and timber then we thought we'd a show;
But now it's covered up with coal and oil lease as well,
And a pre-emptor couldn't get a spoonful if he were to go to h . . l!

134

Oh, yes! the prospects here, my lands, for farms are a fake,
You may as well stay where you are and dream about our stake.
We who are here will linger on and try to live in peace
Until some cruiser comes along and stakes the ducks and geese! (1)

As the government officials continued to send out pamphlets urging more and more settlers, and also continued in their amazingly unrealistic understanding of conditions, discontent increased very greatly among the victims of the scheme. The plunking of people on the land was as far as official responsibility seemed to extend. One M.P., with such a huge territory to cover and with transportation facilities almost non-existent, could hardly begin to visit the localities he represented let alone do anything concrete about the many grave problems.

The whole situation was so impossible that in 1910 several attempts were made to have an M.P. appointed to represent the Islands alone, a local man who would understand the problems peculiar to the isolated location. It didn't even get off the ground.

In 1913 the mounting frustration at continued Government indifference made two Islanders attempt to *do* something about the predicament. William J. Leary, the progressively minded J.P. from Miller (2) Creek, and Frank Rice, an equally concerned surveyor, went all over Graham Island circulating a petition to have the Charlottes, especially Graham Island, made into a municipality. Leary who earlier had been a Reeve in the Ladner municipality knew the effect properly organized territory had upon the government as opposed to the piecemeal efforts of unorganized areas. He was particularly incensed over the enormous revenues the B.C. Government was absorbing from the Islands in timber leases, coal claims and so on (3) — of which only an infinitesimal amount was being returned to the Charlottes. Leary and Rice felt that Islanders could, and should, be in control of all revenues originating from their Islands' natural resources.

The two men were very much in earnest and, with packs on their backs they covered most of Graham Island, securing signatures. Practically everyone signed — well into the hundreds. (4) One of the main difficulties was the lack of registered voters — the principal item in such a political issue. So many were not yet naturalized and even more did not yet have their names on the voter's list. There was influential opposition from Charles Harrison of Masset, who was doing extremely well under the existing set-up. Nothing came of Mr. Leary's and Mr. Rice's efforts ... but it is interesting to speculate about the course of history on the Islands had their plan come about. As one old pioneer said "They should have made our Islands a separate *province*, completely divorced from B.C., then maybe we might have got somewhere."

The way settlers poured on to the Charlottes from 1908 to 1914 is hard to believe today, and they came from everywhere. The four main contributing regions were the Northwestern United States, the Winnipeg area of the Prairies,

(1) "Queen Charlotte Islander" — Feb. 5, 1912
(2) Spelled either Millar or Miller, the name is a corruption of Muller.
(3) $125,000 each year for the timber lease along Masset Inlet alone.
(4) From diary of T. L. Williams, J.P. on Masset Inlet, one of the
    signers of this petition.

the British Isles and the Yukon-Alaska gold fields. Many of them were complete greenhorns about making a living off the land and much of the land they took up was almost worthless agriculturally. But they settled on every available patch — some going back in from the water's edge for miles, lugging everything on their backs along the rough forest trail.

Cabins were dotted everywhere and the atmosphere of optimism which prevailed among the occupants created a comradship which would make these years of great testing remembered with poignancy and nostalgia — even though bitterness at the unnecessary hopelessness of it all might remain. For most, it seems to have been a time of great personal truth and few were found wanting. Even those who did not rise as high as they might have hoped seemed to have achieved a measure of satisfaction that makes them recall the pioneering years as some of the best of their lives. Very few pioneers have not revisited, sentimentally, in later years "for one more look."

1910 to 1913 were the peak years for settlers. Dozens of little settlements sprang up, and between 1908 and 1914 a total of eight townsites were surveyed into streets, lots and blocks. Three did not survive — and it seemed as though it were just a twist of fate that determined the destiny of those which would make it and those which would not.

The most energetic and vocal of the townsite promotors were Charles Harrison and D. R. "Windy" Young, who advertised their towns as "Cities" when they were still in the virgin timber state. The most inventive advertiser was Charles Wilson, who even on his townsite's blueprint urged the early birds to come out and get the worm — "don't be just a canary waiting for the seed," he chided. The site of a bridge may have been the deciding factor in the demise of Graham Centre, and transportation difficulties would undoubtedly account for the reason Sewall did not survive. But for overwhelming persistance in the face of uphill odds, in his townsiting venture, the prize must go to Eli Tingley's Port Clements dream.

Taking the townsites in order of registration we would find that:
1. *July 22, 1908* saw the registration of the western portion of Windy Young's *Queen Charlotte City* from 1st Street, west to 11th. This took in the old mill site and was surveyed by T. S. Gore.
2. *November 3, 1908* saw the survey completed of *Jedway*. (1) Although it is today the site of the present town of Jedway, it is a company-owned village and not an open townsite in the usual manner of speaking. The original townsite died at birth.
3. *July 30, 1909* saw the registration of *Masset*, which had been surveyed in April of that year by Frank D. Rice and was put on the market at first as *Graham City*, but by the time of registration the name had been changed to Masset.
4. *March 4, 1910, Skidegate Landing* was surveyed by Arthur H. Holland for the Queen Charlotte Oil and Packing Company and was put on the market as *Graham City*, but this name was never put into use. Although fourth in order

(1) *As far as can be learned, Jedway was never actually registered, but it is included as it was an official governmental survey. The survey was done by John Elliott, B.C.L.S.*

136

of being laid out as a townsite, this is the *oldest* white settlement on the Islands, since it has had residents continuously, ever since William Sterling built his first dog-fish oil plant in the late 1870's.

1. (b) July 18, 1911 the eastern half of *Queen Charlotte City* was registered after having been surveyed by Noel Humphries in May, 1909.

5. *April 12, 1913, Sewall* was registered for S. Dart Sewall, of the Star Realty Company, after having been surveyed in December, 1912 by Fred Nash — who in eight months laid out four separate townsites on the northern part of Graham Island.

6. *April 25, 1913, Delkatlah* was registered for its owner Charles M. Wilson a few weeks after Fred Nash completed the survey of the townsite.

7. *September 12, 1913*, was the date that Charles M. Adam's townsite of *Graham Centre* was officially registered. Fred Nash had completed its survey some months before and Charlie was able to sell outlying acreages — however, the statutes required conveyance to the Crown, one quarter of all lots which were an acre or less of a townsite proper — and these were chosen by a Government official. When this was duly accomplished the townsite could be registered.

It was the placing of the Kumdis bridge that may have been the difference as to whether this town would live or die. Had the bridge been built nearer the more logical Kumdis Narrows location, instead of a mile away on the river, it would have made Graham Centre the natural headquarters for people living all up and down the Kumdis area. Travellers going along the beach trail from Masset to link up with the Mexican Tom trail — or into Mayer Lake — would have come by way of the bridge at the Narrows, just a stone's throw from the Graham Centre village proper. But when it was built up river, the long-awaited bridge instead, drained off all the traffic and created new routes of travel which by-passed Graham Centre completely. And the unexpected success of Eli Tingley's apparently doomed townsite after six years of battle with the timber company, was the final kiss of death.

8. *March 19, 1914*, finally Elias James Tingley's *Port Clements* was registered. Before laying out this townsite (his fourth) early in 1913, surveyor Fred Nash took time out from his busy schedule to marry Josephine, Henry Edenshaw's beautiful eldest daughter. Then bringing his bride to live in the newly built Yakoun hotel, Mr. Nash laid out the most complicated townsite of his career. Crescent-shaped and triangular streets, as well as the more orthodox type fit this imaginatively designed townsite to its peninsula location in a most interesting manner.

At the time of survey it was still known as Queenstown and Eli was not able to get a clear title to his property until 1914, at which time he registered his townsite renaming it Port Clements. This last townsite to be registered was actually the first one to have a shelter built on it with the idea of someday making the site into a townsite, since this was Eli's intention when he first pitched his tent there early in 1907. It was the following spring when he filed his pre-emption claim and put up his log cabin, unaware of a blueprint error which was to cost him dearly.

In addition to the registered townsites there were other recognized settlements with their own post offices, such as Tow Hill, Watun River, Nadu River, Tlell, Hydah (at Miller Creek), Lawn Hill, and Sandspit (on Moresby Island), as well as the canneries and the two whaling stations, one at Naden Harbor and the other at Rose Harbor.

Then there were those townsites which never got past the dreaming stage. A. S. Christie, a boot manufacturer, said he was going to make one on his "mile" at Tow Hill, Rev. W. E. Collison bought, and was Crown Granted, a lot just south of Kung at the mouth of Naden Harbor, which he planned to develop into a townsite. The coal company (1) held a site in fee simple on Rennell Sound with a view to making this into a port townsite and it was also proposed by them to put in a mill-town at the mouth of Awun River.

However, the mooted mill at the mouth of Awun River by the coal company was directly responsible for pressure being brought to have Masset Inlet charted long before it otherwise would have been (2) — and for this reason played its part in Island history.

(1) *Graham Steamship, Coal and Lumber Company.*
(2) *Charted in summer of 1910.*

CHAPTER TWENTY-FOUR

TENDERFOOT

Like many of his contemporaries, Trevor Williams came to the Charlottes for the sheer adventure of it — and almost by complete chance. Born in 1880 in Swansea, young Williams had felt stifled in the class-conscious life of Britain. As soon as he had finished his schooling he kissed his sweetheart, Meta Taylor, good-bye and set out to find a place in the world where a man could really flex his muscles and breathe. For over six years he covered most of the globe looking for his idea of "Shangri-La." In the spring of 1908 he checked into the Vancouver hotel where Charlie Copp and Jack Davies were registered.

Copp and Davies had prospected all around Moresby Island in the 1907 excitement without finding much to stake — and although they knew about the coal in the Yakoun Valley, they had a real hankering to get a look at the relatively unknown Masset Inlet region. Copp had enough for a grubstake, but Davies was in dire straits that winter, with barely enough to pay the $8 per month for a room in Vancouver. It was said that the prayer of all speculators in those lean times was, "Oh, Lord, give us this day our daily bread — send a rich, green Englishman!"

Young Williams was almost an answer to this prayer. Fresh from a good job in Montreal, he actually did have some money. Ready for any interesting adventure, at Davies' urging he listened to Copp's plans for a prospecting trip to Graham Island. Mr. Williams was somewhat sceptical about the "fortune" to be made but the opportunity to go along on such a trip with experienced men intrigued him — even though it meant he would have to foot most of the bill. "Sure, I'll grubstake Davies as well as my own share," he told Copp. This new B.C. arrival knew nothing whatsoever about prospecting but he had knocked around the world long enough to spot a "pro" — and if he was going to have a try at this new field he might as well be initiated by the best.

When they arrived in Port Simpson on the *Amur* with their tent, boat and six months supplies, Copp, Davies and Williams found that they were in luck. Henry Edenshaw of Masset had just brought over a group of Indians in his schooner *Josephine,* and would take the three prospectors back with him. As the *Amur*

139

only went to Skidegate, this opportunity to go back with Edenshaw would save them a long sail up the coast of Graham Island.

They were waiting in Port Simpson for the *Josephine* to sail when a giant of a man wearing a clerical collar came striding down onto the wharf and in a broad Irish brogue fell into conversation with them. This was the six-foot-four 300 pound "Father" Hogan. When he later bade them godspeed they each felt the crushing grasp of his warm handshake. *"What* a parson!" thought young Williams in admiration as he nursed his numbed hand.

On May 8, 1908 Henry Edenshaw loaded his boat which by now had twelve passengers — six white men and six Indians — all battened down in the hold of the small schooner as she fought her way across the stormy Straits towing the prospectors' sixteen-foot clinker-built boat. It was four in the afternoon when they landed at Masset Indian village, put up in the surprisingly good quarters of the village hotel and learned that their capable skipper Edenshaw was also the hotel keeper, school teacher and storekeeper.

After spending a few days in the Edenshaw hotel to arrange with Chief Weah for permission to use the Indian smoke-houses and camping spots up the Inlet, the three men loaded their double-ended boat and sailed down the long Masset Sound.

"Copp and Davies were artists in making camp," recalls Mr. Williams. "I couldn't have had better teachers. Jack Davies was an especially marvellous woodsman and completely fearless in his ability to survive anywhere in the bush. He could carry on his back everything he needed to make a home — tarpaulin, axe, pots, flour and dried fruit. Using material from the forest he would have a comfortable camp set up in no time at all, boughs for beds, dinner of bannock, stewed dried fruit and a few fish to round out the meal, or perhaps a duck of some sort. He could hike for miles every day and Copp and I were hard put to keep up with him.

"But in a small boat he was a quavering mass of jelly. We had a terrific time with him. Most of the shoreline had to be skirted so closely on his account that the bottom of the boat almost dragged. On an island off what is now Buckley Bay we went ashore to have a look at some stains on the rocks. Poor Davies had been in such a state of panic crossing that short strip of water that, once ashore, he completely refused to get back into the boat to make the return trip."

It was only when the other two men pointed out that with no water or game of any sort on the small island he couldn't possibly survive that he at long last got in, to sit pale and trembling as he clung grimly all the way back across the short channel.

However, if Davies had no love for the boat, to Charlie Copp, on the other hand, it represented the ultimate in prospecting luxury enabling them to carry a good tent, collapsible stove, heavy potatoes and even eggs, not possible when one had to cover the territory on foot. They found that the Indian smoke-houses made excellent shelters and the smoke from the central fireplace went straight up through the roof opening — at least as long as the door was kept shut. Davies would set up the cooking arrangement on an ingeniously notched branch for the pails over the fire.

For three months, without seeing another solitary soul, they travelled practically the whole region of Masset Inlet — going up the rivers, valleys and mountainsides. Except for copper stain in Juskatla and one isolated panning in Watun River which gave them a few flecks of gold, they saw nothing of value. Copp and Davies now decided to call it quits and leave. But for young T. L. Williams . . . *this was the land!*

The life in the bush under the capable guidance of Copp and Davies had been stimulating and extremely satisfying and three months had taught him a lot. At last he had found room to stretch and breathe deeply — and in that soft evergreen-scented air a man's very soul felt cleansed and energized. Most of his money was gone, but he had the good boat, tent, stove and plenty of ambition. He would stay, as it turned out, for the rest of his life — leaving only long enough to do his bit in the 1914-18 war — and is today one of the few pioneers who did remain with the land he found so attractive those fifty-eight years ago.

He took his partners to Masset to catch one of the Indian schooners going to the mainland. It was August and those schooners had apparently been doing a brisk business that summer bringing in land seekers who had read the B.C. Government bulletins. The steamer *Coquitlam* had arrived on a chartered trip July 10th with a party of seventeen Americans from Washington State who had taken up land on the west side of the Sound opposite Masset. Included in this group were Mr. and Mrs. Bert Millard; Mr. and Mrs. Frank Millard and their children Laulee (Spud), William, Lucy and Budd; and the Dow family with their little girl, Pansy. They were experienced people in opening up new land, having previously homesteaded in Washington State. It was their enthusiasm plus the interest mainlanders appeared to have in Graham Island that led Charles Copp to retrace his steps to Masset Inlet a few months later. In the Mayer Lake region he staked out a large section of land against the possibility of future sale to other interested people from afar.

When he had delivered his prospecting companions to Masset in August of 1908, Mr. Williams set up his tent on a grassy spot near a water hole on the south side of Delkatla Slough. His nearest neighbor was Charles Harrison up at the head of the Slough. Harrison, who owned all of lot 7, (which adjoined the Masset Indian Reserve) had sold a section of his land to the Anchor Investment Company of Winnipeg for a townsite. As part of the deal it was agreed that he was to have a well-built frame house on the location of his choice in the new townsite — courtesy of the company. Mr. Harrison expected to do very well with this company in its new venture and endeavored to direct all newcomers to locations that would be tributary to the new townsite. As the only government official, everyone had to go to him to file their claims and he possessed one of the few blueprints of the area, so if you were suspicious of his integrity and mistrusted his statements it meant the difficult trip to the mainland.

In an effort to prevent people from going up the Inlet to look for land Harrison told them that a bar across Masset Sound at Cub Island blocked navigation for anything but rowboats (1) — and if that didn't work, he would point out that timber claims covered most of the region to the south of Masset and he had sketched their approximate areas on his map.

The myth about the navigational obstruction at Cub Island was soon disproved when Eli Tingley's big sailboat with a 20-foot mast capsized one day when going

---

(1) T. L. Williams was one who was told about the blockage.

up the Sound. The strong tide caught it and as the two occupants clambered up on the inverted keel, the current took the boat, with its mast hanging straight down, right past Cub Island and into the big expanse of Masset Inlet without touching bottom at any point. At the entrance to the Inlet the occupants were able to beach the boat and, righting it, continued their journey in a more orthodox manner — but a red-faced Mr. Harrison had to discontinue the story that only canoes could get past Cub Island even at high tide.

However, stories about the timber claims were another matter — and only too true. For twenty-one years these timber licences effectively tied up almost every available strip of waterfront property for most of Masset Sound, Masset Inlet, Juskatla region and all around Kumdis Island. With water the only effective means of transportation, the loss of frontage created a formidable handicap to prospective settlers who had enough problems in trying to wrest the land from its wilderness state. It meant that they had to go inland up to a mile — and much more in many places — lugging everything on their backs, while land along the shoreline lay unused and untouchable.

The company holding the waterfront leases was the five million dollar Graham Steamship, Coal and Lumber Company whose president was Benjamin F. Graham. They were affiliated with the Anchor Investment Company which was buying Harrison's land; in fact the townsite being promoted by the company was named *Graham City* for Mr. Graham.

Born in Texas, Benjamin Graham had been a poverty-stricken man of twenty-two when he contracted tuberculosis in 1890 — a time when this was a no-recovery illness. But in four years he had miraculously defeated his "bugs" and by the time he was thirty had acquired a fortune as a result of lucky mining speculations. He became interested in timber on the south end of Vancouver Island and obtained title to 32,000 acres lying back of Port Renfrew and Port San Juan (1) and organizing the B. F. Graham Lumber Company he arranged for manufacture. One small mill was built on the timber site and a second mill for local trade was built in the city of Victoria. In addition a mill site was established in Esquimalt Harbor where plans were being laid to build a large mill, when Graham heard about the Wilson-Robertson coal lands up on the Charlottes. Not only was good coal supposed to be there, but the timber on the Islands was so magnificent it would have to be seen to be believed, he was told.

Calling a meeting of his board of directors, Graham told them, "Send John Young up there to cruise out the place and if it's as good as they tell me, I think he'd better stake everything else he can find before someone else jumps the gun!"

Young's report was inspiring and Ben Graham went immediately to Vancouver to talk with William Shannon, who had already acquired 51,500 acres of coal and timber leases on the Charlottes. He and his associate, a Mr. Martin, had bought part of this from the three men who had staked the first sixteen timber limits on Masset Inlet, W. E. Collison, Henry Edenshaw and Charles Harrison. Shannon and Martin had paid 20¢ an acre for the leases and now just six months later they were able to resell for $2.50 an acre to Graham.

In April of 1907, Mr. Graham and his vice-president, Charles M. Shannon of Los Angeles, took a party of lumbermen, engineers and business men to have a

(1) *American Lumberman, June 1907.*

look at the company's holdings which now amounted to 20,000 acres of Crown Granted land (purchased from Wilson and Robertson) plus 200 square miles of timber leases.

Arriving on the Islands, the Graham Steamship, Coal and Lumber group were met by the *Eurus* which had been chartered to take them all around the region. They liked what they saw. Grandiose plans were formulated to utilize either a site at the mouth of the Awun River, (just west of Shannon Bay) where water was readily available, or an alternative site — really more favored — at the mouth of the Yakoun River. Water was not quite so accessible here, but it was ideally suited for a railroad to come right down to tidewater from their coal lands.

It was proposed to build a small mill which would be in operation by October of that year (1907) with a larger mill to be completed the following year, and this would have a 500,000 feet per day capacity. It was decided to expand from lumber and coal into shingle and box manufacture and also to get out poles. A good-sized townsite with wharves and dockyards would accompany the building of the mill.

Another townsite could be developed later on in Rennell Sound (where Jimmy Shields had staked it out so many years earlier) and here they would run a rail spur out through the pass from the Yakoun River. Money was not the problem, according to the report, but securing the right manager to operate such a complex operation was going to be difficult, it was felt. Combining all phases of coal, timber and manufacture and utilizing economically the properties on such a remote location would require someone of unusual skill. It was planned to use Oriental labor for the most part, with skilled labor being provided by whites. Good houses would be built and it was pointed out that, using Mr. Harrison's excellent garden as an example, much of the produce needed for food could easily be grown right on the Islands, and any domestic animals needed could be brought in as there were no predators to harm them. (1)

But these plans were all that came of this trip — plus the report in the June 1907 *American Lumberman,* which devoted a complete issue to the subject. Many conjectures have been advanced as to why the company did not proceed with operations, although they hung onto the land for so many years — and topping the list is the fact of the big depression which swept over the land that winter.

As timber and mining would attract speculators, it was inevitable that land would also. Among the earliest of these was A. S. Christie, the genial boot manufacturer from Vancouver. Mr. Christie had met Charles Harrison in Port Simpson and although Harrison painted a rosy picture of residence on the Islands, Christie was too much of a city man to try pioneering, but his business instincts were aroused by the news of all that cheap land and the increasing interest being shown in it.

With local guidance Mr. Christie staked out six square miles near the Sangan River, then another section adjoining Delkatla and one square mile at Tow Hill. It was at Tow Hill he proposed to make a townsite and planned to have the mouth of the Hi-Ellen River dredged to accommodate large ships. His dream was to have his own house right on the top of Tow Hill itself.

(1) There are no wolves, cougars or snakes on the Charlottes.

He engaged Fred Nash, B.C.L.S., to survey his property in the summer of 1908. As mentioned earlier, Trevor Williams was camping in Delkatla at that time. He was joined a few weeks later by Captain Francis, a former Great Lakes sailor who had taken a fancy to life on the Charlottes and sailed up on his small boat to put into a creek beside Williams' tent. Nash hired both Williams and Francis to work for him as chainmen.

When Nash was surveying the square mile at Tow Hill for Mr. Christie (mostly muskeg and known today as "Christie's Mile") he tried to find some evidence of the old post marking the edge of the Indian Reservation there, which had been surveyed in 1887. If they could find the post it would save having to retrace their steps through the jungle-like undergrowth several miles back to their bearing post at the Sangan. As they searched, one of the party noticed a tree with an odd-shaped marking in its bark — and he remembered having seen something like this once before on another survey. Carefully with his knife he cut all around the edge of the mark, then lifted off a large section to reveal an old blaze with the "B.T." (Bearing Tree) mark on it and all the degrees and angles which had been carved there many years previously. They were as distinct as the day they had been put in.

Working with Nash, the men found that there was an error in the blueprints regarding the Delkatla region (1) and there was an unstaked area still available. Captain Francis lost no time in taking advantage of this and staked out his pre-emption here. But Williams wanted to go up into the Masset Inlet region. Noticing that a portion of the east side was free of a "T.L." (Timber Licence) claim — he decided this was for him and staked out his pre-emption on a piece of land almost adjoining the only other cabin to be seen on the Inlet — Eli Tingley's. There were, however a total of three cabins in the region at that time, for around the point from Eli — up in the Kumdis Bay — George Mayer had also put up a snug cabin, and at the north end of Kumdis Slough, Freeman Tingley, Senior, had established his Pioneer Ranch.

Mr. Tingley, a distant relative of Eli's, had arrived on the Islands from Pitt Meadows on June 1st, 1906, and in short order had a ranch in operation with pigs, horses, cows, chickens and enough produce to sell whenever there was a need. In this he had the very competent help of his third wife, Bertha, whose capable adaption to life on a pioneer farm made Mr. Tingley's way much easier.

As a result of three marriages, Mr. Tingley had a large family. He was proud of each one of his children and let the world know it. His eldest son, also called Freeman, had come over with George Mayer in 1907 ". . . just for the heck of it," he recalls today — and with two Freeman's in the area, it took another old timer to come up with a solution to avoid confusing the two. This was "Mexican" Tom Hodges. Tom, a salty old character, who had listened to Freeman, Senior, talk about his children often — perhaps too often — decided that the appropriate name for Mr. Tingley, Senior, was "Stud", and evidently its owner received the new nickname with a huge gale of laughter, to have it stick like glue.

All the old timers who knew him refer to him as "Stud" Tingley, and remember what a good neighbor he was. Many a greenhorn felt his helping hand

(1) Not a surveyors error, but an error in the later recording of an
  approximate location of claims in the unsurveyed parts of Graham Island.

144

during their difficult first days, and his never failing sense of humor eased out the rough spots of having to ask for help. He was a lively man, full of fun and always ready to get out his accordian for a dance or just to raise a bit of life. At any of the dances in what later became New Masset, ". . . if Stud Tingley was the M.C. you could count on a good time," remembers one old pioneer who added, "I can still see him stomping his feet and yelling out the whoo-oo-pee's — and boy, could he dance!" she said.

Around the end of the first world war the Tingleys left Kumdis Island and the Charlottes, to enable their younger children to have more opportunity for a good education. They settled near Quesnel. Here Mr. Tingley worked at freighting with his horses until he died. Mrs. Bertha Tingley is still there, and one of her sons was acting mayor of Quesnel in 1963. Steve Tingley, the well-known Cariboo pioneer, was a cousin of Mr. Tingley's father, John Tingley. When John Tingley brought his family around the Horn from the family home in Sackville, New Brunswick, in the old *Constitution,* Steve Tingley had come with them. Freeman, Senior, was a mere lad at the time.

The Kumdis Bay pioneer, Arkansas-born George Mayer, who had fought in the Spanish-American war and then gone prospecting up the coast as far as Nome, was helping to clear the townsite for the new city of Prince Rupert when he met Freeman Tingley, Junior — and he gave the same reason for going over to the Charlottes as Freeman, Junior, "I just wanted to see what they were like!" They looked good, so George got a job with some surveyors and during the survey was the first person to see and map out the large lake that bears his name. Like his neighbor, T. L. Williams, Mr. Mayer knew that he had found his "Shangri-La" in life on the Queen Charlotte Islands, and in 1910 he became a naturalized British subject.

The patch of soil that he chose to pre-empt in Kumdis Bay was particularly rich and required no fertilizing to produce the most wonderful vegetables. With so many of the other Islanders, he went overseas with the Canadian Expeditionary Force. Mr. Mayer was severely wounded in action at Ypres in 1916, but his subsequent hospitalization had a happy ending for it was there he met Miss Lucy Hardy. As soon as he was able to get his sea legs after being invalided out of the war, and back to Canada, he sent for the little nurse he had met in France to come and be his bride. The Mayers operated their farm until 1955 and sold much of their produce locally — then moved to Surrey to be nearer their married children.

CHAPTER TWENTY-FIVE

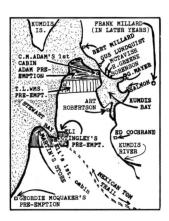

TO MAKE A TOWNSITE

Everyone had a few stars in his eyes and Eli Tingley, whose pre-emption practically adjoined that of Mr. Williams, had more than his fair share.

Born in 1880 in Albert County, New Brunswick, Elias James Tingley was seven years old when his family (1) moved to B.C. via Washington State. They lived variously in Ladner, Mission City and Vancouver before settling down in Victoria. In '98 the big Klondike Gold Rush drew the eighteen-year-old Eli like a magnet and for the next nine years he worked in the mining camps and at freighting along the Yukon and its tributaries from Atlin to Nome. With his elder brother, Brydone L. (Bert), Eli built and ran a roadhouse near Paxson Junction, on the Valdez trail to Fairbanks, for a year or so. It was there that he met Allan Stewart, who had been trying his hand in the mining game at the same time.

When Eli and his friend Allan left the north in 1907 to join Bert at the Tingley home in Victoria they found everyone there pouring over the B.C. Government's bulletins about the wonderful agricultural possibilities on Graham Island. Seventy-year-old John Calhoun and his son, Emerson, were visiting the Tingleys when Eli and Allan arrived. The Calhouns were from Alberta and having seen these same booklets, were so interested that they were now on their way up to the Charlottes to stake out a location for a farm.

McBride was premier of B.C. at that time and his secretary, Edward Gosnell, was a frequent visitor in the Tingley home. "Yes," he assured them, "it is the coming place. Farmland, timber, mining – this place is sure to boom." Getting out a map, he showed them the Masset Inlet region. "There's the place. I've just been talking to people who have been up there recently. It's a wonderful country and practically yours for the taking. In fact it would be the ideal place to set up a new townsite and get right in on the start of things." (2)

(1) *His family were distant relatives of Freeman Tingley, as they were both descended from Josiah and Levina Tingley who had come from Attleboro, Mass., in 1763 to settle in Sackville, New Brunswick.*
(2) *All information about the Tingley family contributed by Mr. Brydone L. (Bert) Tingley, Victoria, B.C.*

Townsite! The idea intrigued Eli irresistibly. And Allan Stewart liked the sound of the land — so the two young men decided to accompany the Calhouns to Graham Island. They caught the monthly boat to Skidegate and set about walking up the coast to Tlell and thence overland to Masset Inlet. Old John Calhoun found the travelling by foot along the beach much too hard for his years, so he returned to Skidegate after a few miles to wait for the others.

Eli, Emerson Calhoun and Allan Stewart walked along the beach to Tlell then crossed overland on the Mexican Tom trail — which was little more than a succession of blazes. At Masset Inlet the trail came out at a small bay near a good stream and as they prepared to set up camp there Allan Stewart cut his foot badly with his axe. Eli and Emerson made him as comfortable as they could in the canvas shelter facing the fire, left him a good supply of wood and water, and then set off along the shoreline to the north, going up into Kumdis Slough. At the north end of the Slough on Kumdis Island, they found Freeman Tingley, Senior, on his Pioneer Ranch. He loaned them a boat to bring Allan back to the ranch to recuperate under Bertha's capable care, while Emerson and Eli explored the adjacent lands.

By the time Allan's foot was well enough to travel once more, Eli and Emerson had staked several pre-emptions on Kumdis Slough, and when they returned to Skidegate by way of the "Trail", Eli named the bay where the accident had happened, Stewart Bay.

Excited by the good reports of this 1907 cruise, a group of seventeen people had assembled in Victoria by February of 1908 to go to Graham Island and settle. John Calhoun had his two sons, Emerson and Jack, and his daughter Anna, with her husband James Johnston and their five young children. The Calhoun's brought with them complete farming equipment including horses, and Johnston had a 16 foot boat. Allan Stewart had a 14 foot boat and Eli with his brother Bert had a big 30 foot sailboat. From Alberta to join the Calhouns had come Mr. J. Mason, Mr. S. Peterson and his sister Anna, and to complete the party was Ross Rumball, a miner from Alaska, who had decided to throw his lot in with the pioneers.

A huge stock of provisions, lumber and other essentials for setting up housekeeping were loaded on board the steamer *Vadso*, in addition to the boats and farming equipment, and with keen anticipation the group sailed for a new life on Graham Island. The first day out, when only as far as Cape Lazo, the *Vadso* was wrecked and quickly filled with water. However, enthusiasm was too great to be daunted by this. They put all their effects ashore at Union Bay to dry and sent volunteers to return to Victoria to arrange for the *Amur* to take them by special charter to Masset Inlet.

Captain Locke, skipper of the *Amur*, was so sympathetic to the party's transportation problems that he took his ship inside Masset Bar and up the uncharted waters of the Sound as far as the Nadu. Here, using the boats and a makeshift raft, everything was gradually ferried ashore and camp set up near an Indian cabin on Nadu point. Then the men built a snug cabin on the previously staked land (1) across the Slough from Freeman Tingley's ranch. Soon Mrs. Johnston and her five children were comfortably settled there whilst

(1) By Eli Tingley and Emerson Calhoun in 1907.

everyone else fanned out in small parties to decide which was the best land for farming.

The descriptions of land which had been furnished by the government bulletins plus the glowing reports of Graham Island from the two ex-miners — together with the sheer adventuring possibilities young Emerson Calhoun had enjoyed — had led the prospective settlers to expect that they could farm almost immediately with no extra effort. Now they found there was much timber and muskeg — and what little grass land could be seen would require extensive drainage and other work to make it profitable to cultivate. One by one the members of the group returned to the Johnston cabin, discouraged and downcast about the whole venture.

When a vote was taken it showed an unanimous decision to abandon the whole plan — with one exception. Eli had fallen in love with the land. He would stay — the only one of the party to remain. He was still irresistibly drawn to the idea of becoming a townsiter, and had chosen for his site the land on the south side of the little bay where they had made their first camp the year before, Stewart Bay.

While Eli set out his pre-emption stakes to take in 160 acres on the heavily wooded point lying between Stewart Bay and the mouth of the Yakoun River, the rest of the pioneering party took their belongings down to Masset on a raft. Luckily they found a ready market for everything — even the horses — and in a short while were on their way to the mainland in a chartered Indian schooner.

However, Allan Stewart, Emerson Calhoun and Bert Tingley stayed behind to help Eli build the first cabin for his proposed townsite. Eli had moored his 30 foot sailboat in the creek now known as Rennie Creek and on the bank of the creek pitched his tent to begin construction of a 16 x 16 foot log cabin with a large protective front verandah. It was May 1908 and his nearest resident neighbor was George Mayer in Kumdis Bay.

By the fall more and more people were flocking into this region; many of them came by way of steamer to Skidegate and walked northward along the east coast with everything they owned on their backs, seeking out a spot to pre-empt. The faintly-blazed Mexican Tom trail across the fourteen miles of mostly soggy muskeg that lay at the latter part of the journey to Masset Inlet made the sight of Eli's snug cabin — plus the enthusiastic warm welcome given to each traveller as he reached the western side of the "trail" — feel he had found the pot of gold at the end of the rainbow. In short order Eli had more guests than he could accommodate.

One of these was Gus Lundquist, a Swedish sailor, who had sailed all over the world before finding his safe harbor and "swallowing the anchor" to go ashore and become a pre-emptor. Eli and Gus built a small log cabin on another small creek which adjoined the one Eli's original cabin was on, and it was hoped that this would accommodate the overflow guests. But it was completely inadequate to the task. Anxious to keep as many people in the neighborhood as he could, and as Allan Stewart, Emerson Calhoun and his brother Bert were still camping with him, Eli enlisted their help to put up a good sized log cabin to serve as a shelter to visitors. This cabin was 18 x 30 and was built out on the point (slightly to the east of the site of the present government breakwater). In addition to help from Gus, Allan, Emerson and Bert in the building of this big log house, Eli also had plenty of assistance from his neighbors residing in the area — and by this time they ammounted to quite a few.

Three miles to the south, just inside the entrance to the Yakoun River, there was the big bluff Irishman, Frank Meldon. In 1908, "Muldoon" as he was commonly called, had come with a man named Stronach to the Adams River (1) across from Masset to represent the Patterson Lumber Company in staking out a site. According to his neighbor John Locker, who knew him well, Muldoon was left high and dry when the lumber company changed its mind. Stronach seems to have faded out of the picture, but Muldoon grew lonesome, bought a canoe, and when he learned through a survey party that there was an open spot on the Yakoun, he filed his pre-emption there. A year later, in 1909, John Locker filed on the other open spot adjoining Muldoon on the bank of the Yakoun.

A mile along the shore to the north of Eli was T. L. Williams and beyond him, in the Kumdis, were several pre-emptors. Up-stream in the Kumdis River was Ed Cochrane on the east side. At the mouth of the Kumdis, near the site of the present bridge, Arthur Robertson had put up a small cabin on the west bank of the river. Mr. Robertson, a former Shetland Islander who had been in the '98 Klondike excitement, later operated a mill in New Masset.

North along Kumdis Bay, across from Mr. Robertson and about a quarter of a mile away, were two New Zealanders, a Mr. Salmon and his friend. Mr. Salmon, who like Jack Davies, was so petrified in a small boat that he would rather walk the thirty miles along the beach to Masset than take a chance on the much easier water journey. (Budd Millard took over this place when it was vacated.) To the north of Mr. Salmon was pioneer George Mayer. As the bay curved westward, a country-man of Mr. Salmon's had a small section of land near the Kumdis Narrows. This was the six-foot-two-inch, one-eyed charmer, entrepreneur Alex McTavish, who even today brings an amused smile to the faces of those who knew him. "Ah, yes . . . McTavish!" they'll say, "He was quite a lad. Always making mysterious trips out to the mainland, and then when he returned he would be flush with money as he made halfhearted attempts to locate land for his "stakers" who kept him supplied with the necessary financing to live with a bit of a flourish."

On the south side of the Narrows Charles M. Adam was putting up a cabin, although his sizeable pre-emption took in the whole of the point north of T. L. Williams. Charlie later promoted a townsite on the other side of his pre-emption (near Mr. Williams) which was a direct rival to Eli's venture. All these men had found their waterfront land when engaged on survey parties and noticed that it was free from the stranglehold of a timber claim.

When the big log house on the point of Eli's pre-emption was completed, Stewart, Calhoun and Bert Tingley said their good-byes and hiked to Skidegate to catch the *Amur* on her monthly trip from the mainland. Eli was left alone with his vision of creating a townsite on the southeastern shores of a beautiful salt water lake — and with his location at the end of the much-used Mexican Tom trail, he felt he couldn't miss.

But two log cabins and a vest-pocket size guest house do not a townsite

(1) Shown on today's map as Otun River.

150

make — so it was off to Vancouver to drum up some interest. Here he met James Martin, who had just disposed of his store on the prairies. The infectiousness of Eli's faith in the future of his town must have passed on in full force to Mr. Martin, as Mr. Tingley was able to persuade this extremely shrewd business-man to go up, sight unseen, with a complete stock and material to build and operate a fair-sized store in that wilderness location.

On December 13th, 1908, T. L. Williams wrote in his diary:—

"Yesterday a flotilla of boats anchored off Tingley's pre-emption, two large Indian schooners and Eli's big sailboat, all loaded to capacity, plus a gas-boat (Martin's *Kathleen*) towing a raft of lumber. When I went over to greet the new arrivals, I learned that all the materials were for James Martin, who is going to build and run a store on Tingley's townsite. Martin had with him Frank and "Ole" (Louis) Van Valkenburg and Alfred Carse, a white-headed lawyer. (1) Everything was unloaded into the big log house on the point.

Today Henry White's schooner, *King George*, brought more lumber and goods for Martin and also my mail, which included my pre-emption record from William Manson, Government Agent in Prince Rupert — they must have moved from Port Simpson where I had sent my application. It is surprising how often and safely all sorts of mail keeps arriving, handled by so many before reaching its destination. No postal department on the northern part of Graham Island, so the mail is left in an Indian store, where it will be collected by the owner or anyone who knows the addressee and is going his way.

December 25, 1908 — Today Martin the storekeeper told me that he had christened the townsite (with Tingley's blessing) *Queenstown,* for his original home in Ireland. Tingley named his big sailboat the *Queen* to compliment the idea. Queenstown consists now of the Tingley log cabins and Martin's frame store building and they have applied for a post office. We had a cheerful Christmas dinner in Tingley's cabin with Eli, Charlie Adam, Gus Lundquist, Martin, Carse, Ole and Frank Van Valkenburg and Frank Meldon — whom everyone calls "Muldoon."

We all help one another with the heavy work on our cabins and have a number of good bridge games on the wet days. In January Bert Millard and his wife came up to pre-empt on the point across from Charlie's land at the Kumdis. Eli persuaded them to run a hotel in the big log house at Queenstown while they wait for their records to come through. So many people coming through here now, this will be a boon.

In February the first church service was held here in Martin's store when Rev. W. E. Collison and Bishop du Vernet rowed all the way from Masset in an open boat in freezing sleet and snow. My house is the highest log cabin in these parts now, eleven feet high — Gus and Eli helped me put up the final logs and on March 19th I moved into my first home. Also cleared and dug ground for potato patch.

In March of 1909 the timber surveyors arrived to lay out the boundaries on the ground that had been staked by their cruisers in 1907. The cruisers had done a fine job considering their lack of equipment and the rough terrain — most of the claims had been staked out by compass and pacing out the length

(1) Alfred Carse later played an important role in Prince Rupert's early days.

of the boundaries. But now the inaccuracies that showed up were serious news for some of us. Claims which had been staked by C. L. Copp, H. Gilmark, Gus Lundquist because they had been shown as free of timber licences were now found to be covered. Twenty acres of my one hundred and sixty are also affected. But for Eli Tingley the news is a stunning blow. His whole townsite is covered! It has one of the thickest stands of timber on the Inlet and the timber company had advised that they will vigorously protest any attempt to cut trees on any of their claims. Carse, the lawyer, held a meeting to get all involved persons to sign a petition which he will take to Victoria."

Possibly the only good thing to come out of this was for Gus Lundquist who learned that there was a choice site available at the Kumdis Narrows directly opposite Charlie Adam's cabin, so he shed few tears over the loss of his first chosen site near Eli, and filed on the new location at the Narrows.

With no subsequent word from Carse and rumors flying wildly, Mr. Williams began to do some writing on behalf of his own and his neighbors' interests. In the course of the endless correspondence about the timber licences it seemed inevitable that the T. L. part of his name would result in his acquiring the nickname of "Timber Limits Williams". "Oh, more than half the time I answered to 'Tim' . . . it was less of a mouthful than Trevor anyhow," he recalls.

With most of the huge area of Graham Island still not properly surveyed and with applications for land steadily arriving in Victoria the B.C. Government finally decided to act. There had been surveyors brought in by the purchasers of land to survey their claims at their own expense, such as the Christie claim on the north beach and Charles Copp's at Mayer Lake, and of course the coal and timber companies had surveys done by their own men. In the spring of 1909 the Government started gangs of surveyors to run their lines everywhere. The Island was laid out in townships, each township consisting of 160 acres where possible.

The work was done by contract. It went on steadily for four or five more years and was one of the chief sources of employment for the settlers (besides the very few trails and wagon roads put in at government expense). Every survey gang had several packers to keep it in supplies and top wages were 6¢ a pound for a six mile pack. It was hard, backbreaking work, but there were very few settlers who did not have at least one stint at it. In addition to the packers, gangs of men were needed to slash out lines and other attendent duties. Old-timers remember the surveying outfits of Humphries, Tupper and Rice and C. de B. Green, who was known as "Cedar Green" despite his firm admonitions to employees that he was to be addressed as *Mr.* Green at all times. Other surveyors were Fred Nash, J.C.A. Long, Allan Jessup and O.B.M. Wilkie to mention a few. Both Mr. Long and Mr. Jessup succumbed to the lure of homesteading on Graham Island and Mr. Long built a fine frame home on the west side of Masset Harbor, near Striae Island. Allan Jessup, who originally was one of the timber licence surveyors, took over Charles Harrison's piece of land at the Blue Jackets, a few miles south of New Masset, for his homesite.

Carse, the lawyer who had taken the petition to Victoria had been gone several weeks but there was still no word from him. Undoubtedly his negotiations with government officials were extremely difficult for they were anxious not to offend the big timber company in any way, as it was contributing to the provincial kitty in such handsome proportions, and yet they were also most anxious to have the land settled – and Eli Tingley's townsite plan had received strong support from a member of McBride's own staff. About this time, Charles Harrison, who was a salaried agent of the timber company, came up to see the settlers who had been affected by the new survey information, to warn them that they must not cut down a single tree on his company's licence. He was hard put to conceal his delight that Tingley's rival townsite was doomed – especially as it had been Tingley's capsized boat which had compelled him to back down earlier, about Masset Sound being blocked by a bar at Cub Island.

Harrison had a long talk with Jim Martin and the next day, April 29th, 1909, when Mr. Williams went into the store, Martin told him that he had decided to close his store in Queenstown as there appeared to be no chance of a future there. He was going to move down to the new townsite of Graham City which was being laid out about three miles south of Masset Indian village.

And to make the third link in the chain of disappointments for Eli, his application for a post office was turned down "if the name of Queenstown is to be used" – as there were other post offices by this name already. James Martin, who had chosen the name, was appalled at any idea of changing it and as he was very undecided as to whether or not he would operate a branch store in Queenstown when he made Graham City his headquarters, Eli was anxious to humor him – and for the time being agreed to let the original name stay. Martin put Frank Van Valkenburg in charge of the branch Queenstown store and Frank used the *Kathleen* to keep it supplied from Graham City.

It was April 6, 1909 – a few weeks before Jim Martin's decision to leave Queenstown – that Frank D. Rice, B.C.L.S. (classmate of Fred Nash) arrived on the *Capilano* to lay out the townsite of Graham City for the Anchor Investment Company.

"They only had accommodation on the *Capilano* for six passengers," recalls Mr. Rice, "and there were twenty-two of us altogether, so sixteen men had to sleep in the hold of the ship.

She also carried a full cargo of freight, including a team of horses, timbers and piling for a wharf, ten tons of hay and oats, and a quantity of groceries, all belonging to the Company. We arrived at the mouth of Masset Sound just a dusk and with no lights to guide us in, the skipper decided to sail a triangular course through that night arriving back at this spot by daybreak. The weather had been excellent – but when we got to the corner of Prince of Wales Island in Alaska, a gale sprang up and rolled the boat over on her side. On the second roll the engines stopped. It was a nasty situation.

However, the crew finally got a three-cornered sail rigged up and we were able to make headway. For twenty-four hours with the decks of the ship awash most of the time, the men and horses were battened down in the dark hold of the ship, until we were able to get back to the Rose Spit region and anchor off the east coast. Although it was getting dark, the skipper ordered off the hatch covers to let the men who had been the hold go ashore on the beach. Some of them raised their arms and solemnly vowed that they would never leave Graham Island again until a bridge was built!

It took a full day for the engineers to get the engines going once more on the *Capilano,* and after riding out another lesser storm, she was finally able to proceed to her destination and we anchored off Delkatla Slough to unload

153

the cargo."

With Frank Rice and his crew at work laying out the townsite, the promotion of Graham City could get under way now in earnest. Jack and Bill Cook, representing the Anchor Investment Company, hired a gang to clear the townsite — and all suitable timber was made into ties for sale to the Grand Trunk Pacific for the railroad which was inching its way into Prince Rupert. Great were the expectations for the future of the Charlottes once this railroad into the nearby mainland port was completed. It would provide an avenue for the coal, timber and farming produce of the Islands and would supply the anticipated stream of settlers from the east to raise the population of the Charlottes to the peak it had reached in the Haida heyday.

Charles Harrison, as mentioned earlier, was avidly promoting the new townsite and was a capable adviser to the Anchor Investment Company's representatives. With Eli Tingley's Queenstown townsite doomed, few settlers would be likely to go up the Inlet. The main opposition now lay in the fact that the Indian village of Masset was the hub of activity for the north end of Graham Island — activity which Harrison wanted to centre on the townsite he had such an interest in. Persuading James Martin to make Graham City headquarters for his store was only the beginning — but it was an important one. Martin had to use a tent to begin with, still it was not long before a proper frame building was erected.

"You've got to put up a hotel," he urged the Cook brothers. Without further ado they built a flimsy boxlike structure — and in the flat roofs of both Martin's new store and the hotel the prairie influence could be seen. The promised house for Mr. Harrison was being built to his specifications and a small wharf was under construction, but Harrison knew a post-office was an absolute necessity for any town hoping to attract residents.

However, by this time a post-office had been established at Masset with Rev. W. E. Collison in charge. With a population of over four hundred in that village, it would take some conniving to obtain another for the half-dozen people in the white settlement of Graham City, only three miles away. Then via some mysterious grape-vine, Harrison learned that Post Master Collison had applied for a transfer.

Remembering Bob Tennant's successful effort in obtaining his Skidegate post-office by capitalizing on the number of residents in the adjacent Skidegate Indian village and making his application under that name, Harrison persuaded the Cooks to change the name of their townsite from Graham City to Masset. When Collison left, they would immediately apply for the post-office and take advantage of the number of people now getting mail at the Masset address. They could be quite certain that the far-off uninformed government offices would have no knowledge of — or interest in — the subterfuge.

On June 7, 1909, the name of Graham City was dropped and the new townsite to which it had been applied was called Masset. The wave of local protests about this fell on deaf ears and in order to avoid the inevitable confusion, the two Massets were differentiated by calling the Indian village *Old Masset* and the new white settlement *New Masset*. (1) When in due course Rev.

(1) *In the beginning Masset had two T's (Massett) but when mail for Merritt and Massett became confused fairly often the Postmaster General requested the dropping of one of the Masset T's.*

154

Collison was transferred to Stewart, the post-office was installed in Martin's store in New Masset.

The Anglican Church had been pressing for a doctor to care for the Haida people for some time. In the spring of 1909 Bishop du Vernet announced that he had been able to secure the services of Dr. A. Ross Fraser, a medical missionary who had served in South Africa. The government agreed to assume the bill for his small stipend to aid the Haidas. Dr. Fraser and his wife, who was a trained nurse, brought with them Mrs. Fraser's sister, Miss Diane Outram, to help in the care of the five young Fraser children, Betty, Aileen, Douglas, Tom and Don, and teach Sunday School.

They arrived on the *Coquitlam* at seven one May morning, and everything was put onto the beach by the ship's boats at Old Masset. With a sixth sense about the young unmarried lady in the party, who should arrive with a flourish to gallantly assist them but the huge bearded New Zealand charmer, Alex McTavish, to be followed soon by some of the Haidas and Mr. Collison. Housing eight people was going to be a problem, but Henry White, with true Old Masset hospitality, let the Frasers have the use of his new house until suitable quarters could be found.

A log house which had been used as a bunkhouse by a crew of men cutting ties on the townsite was empty by September so Mr. Harrison offered the Frasers this accommodation, adding that it would be more advantageous for the whole district if Dr. Fraser was in New Masset, as it was a more central position to render his invaluable aid to everyone, settlers and Indian alike. That fall with five young Frasers and four Millards there seemed to be a nucleus for a school. The tiny cubicle of a building which served as a church on Sunday was used during the week for the schoolhouse. When the teacher who had been engaged to open the school suddenly cancelled the arrangements, it was Diane Outram who filled in for the first month and was paid the teacher's $65 salary.

In October of 1909 Miss Jessie Peck, a United Loyalist from New Brunswick arrived to take over officially. Betty Fraser (now Mrs. R. C. Robertson of Vancouver) says that every day they were sure to sing "God Save the King", "The Maple Leaf" and "Rule Britannia." Miss Peck later married Bill McLeod — Bill worked on the new townsite that summer with his friend George McDonald and the two young men put up a smokehouse near the wharf where they processed some very good smoked fish. Miss Peck, as teacher, was followed by Lillian Nichols, sister of Marsh English's wife (who financed the Jedway Hotel); and then by Miss Robertson, who also found romance in this little outpost school. She married Fred de Lisle, brother of Walter de Lisle who designed and built the big residence for James Martin and many others. Walter lost his life in the battlefields of the first World War, to lie beside so many other young Islanders who had hastened to give their services.

The townsite hotel had been advertised for sale as a "going concern" and was purchased by Arthur Ives who had worked in the Vancouver Hotel for years. He sank his life savings into the deal and brought his wife and their five children, Sam, Charlie, Arthur Junior, Nellie and young Fred up in the fall of 1909. His heart sank when he saw the jerry-built, leaky affair he had been sold — but he had no choice except to make the best of things. Old timers all remark on warm hospitality and comfortable atmosphere Mr. Ives and his wife created under the most adverse conditions a hotelman could encounter. He put in a bar the next year which was well patronized.

When Bert Millard and his wife had moved to Queenstown early in 1909, his brother Frank took his family to live on the Delkatla side of New Masset. Like so many others they lived in a tent for awhile — even the hospital was a tent — and with the Millards was their wonderful ninety-year-old father. Early in the spring of 1910 he slipped away in his sleep. The same Union Jack which was used to cover the coffin of Grandpa Millard, a Civil War soldier, was used later to cover the coffin of Mr. Bourke, an Imperial Army man, and the two old soldiers were laid to rest in a little plot near the Blue Jackets (1) that Mr. Harrison, who had a small pre-emption there, had donated for a cemetery.

The Dow family who had come in with the Millards in 1908, were still living on the west side of the Sound and had the most wonderful vegetable garden there. They often rowed across to visit in New Masset to exchange their produce for meat or fish.

Bill Wallace was the cook for the townsite clearing gang, and young Betty Fraser was fascinated to see him take a knife one day and cut holes in his boots to cool his feet, then calmly use the same knife to finish slicing meat for the men's supper. She remembers Mrs. Wallace as a sad little lady who took too many pills in an attempt to commit suicide, and then to her husband's dismay, recovered.

Cecil Pallant, whose tall slender form earned him the nickname of "Slim" Pallant, lived with the Wallaces for awhile in Masset and when Ethel Wallace left her husband, Mr. Pallant and Mr. Wallace batched together all one winter, ". . . and it only cost us $25 for groceries," remembers Mr. Pallant, "as we had all the fish and game we could possibly eat right at our door."

Living beside the Wallaces were Mr. and Mrs. Leslie who had two children for the school Mr. Harrison was trying to get under way — Edith and Jimmy. The next year the Leslies had the first baby to be born in New Masset and he was named Graham for the Island.

The Harrisons moved into their new home on the townsite in the fall of 1909 and Betty Fraser remembers how quickly Mrs. Harrison had a garden in full bloom. Since it was on, or very near, the site of Alexander McKenzie's first garden, this may have explained the comparative ease with which the Harrison garden was established. The Harrison home became the centre of hospitality and the understanding sympathy of Mrs. Harrison was long remembered by many of the early day brides. As they knew her help sprang from a personal knowledge of even more lonely and harrowing times, her advice was greatly valued as she sought to ease their transition into the new and strange pioneering life. When the Harrisons moved out of the big farmhouse, with its four fireplaces, on Delkatla Flats their houseguest, Mrs. Allan Jessup, left also and went to Vancouver. In 1912 she returned with two-year-old Allan to the land at the Blue Jackets which her husband had acquired from Mr. Harrison. Percy Harrison did not go into the new townsite house with his parents, instead he stayed in a small tent on the beach — a strange and silent lad much more at home in the woods than with people.

(1) This site became known as the Blue Jackets after a party from the EGERIA camped there during the 1907 survey.

156

Allan Orr gave up his job of working on the townsite to open a blacksmith shop and brought his family to live in New Masset in 1909. His daughters, Clara and her young seventeen-year-old sister Flo, were very nice girls who were greatly appreciated in that largely batchelor population. The five younger Orrs helped to swell the school class.

A man named Harris from Mission City started a sawmill that first summer but did not stay long and it was taken over by Earl Wanless. It was located near the wharf which, incidentally, was too short and resulted in several steamers being grounded.

The first Christmas in New Masset in 1909 was a happy one with entertainments, dinners and exchange of visits with friends from Old Masset and the whole Inlet region. A general feeling of optimism and good fellowship pervaded. One of the most welcome of new residents was Rev. Hogan — the big Irish parson from Port Simpson who had been sent to take Rev. Collison's place. From the first day his strong personality was in evidence, and Mrs. Hogan organized the first Women's Auxiliary for the ladies.

On April 10, 1910 Thomas Deasy was recommended by the Liberal Executive for the position of Indian Agent, replacing Charles Perry the first Agent who had been appointed in December 1909. Deasy's duties were the care of all the Haida (1) problems — as they related to the government — but he had his official headquarters in Old Masset. He and Mrs. Deasy arrived in June, 1910. That same month it was announced that the Anchor Investment Company had not been able to adhere to its financial part of the bargain with Mr. Harrison, so the land reverted to him and he resold it to the Natural Resources Company of Vancouver who were to "put in a little life into it."

The tiny shack which had served as a school and church was replaced by more suitable buildings which were erected side by side midway along Collison. Avenue. Although that school in turn has been superseded by the big modern Elementary-Junior-Senior High School, the church built in 1912 is still in use. In 1914 a joint community-government effort resulted in a comfortable hospital to take the place of the log building that had been commandeered by Dr. Fraser for his patients — after the first tent hospital was demolished by a falling tree during a storm.

When Arthur Ives, the genial hotelkeeper, passed away with shocking suddenness at Christmas-time in 1911, his eldest son Sam took over and ran the overflowing Ives Hotel. Before long Mr. and Mrs. Hudson opened their Hotel Masset, a few doors up from the Ives, with beds from 35¢ to 50¢ a night. The exterior of their hotel was built of the very modern cement block — and was the object of admiring comments. Their pretty daughter married Henry Holland, a skilled carpenter who was in constant demand to build houses, which were being put up so fast the sawmill had difficulty in meeting the demand for lumber.

Real estate and insurance offices were opened by Allan Jessup, Bob Entwistle and Alex McTavish. Martin's store was doing a brisk trade and James Martin was appointed agent for Albert Dollenmayer in connection with the townsite — among his other duties — but still found time to take an active part in community affairs. Hicks and Cauthers built a pool hall between the two hotels, and three

(1) Skidegate and Masset

newspapers ran at various times cashing in on the lucrative mining and land applications as well as the rash of local business advertising. Regular steamship service was perhaps the greatest boon of all to the community with weekly trips scheduled for the summer months, and fortnightly trips during the winter when late in 1909 the G.T.P. was awarded the mail contract for the Charlottes. Boats of every size were calling frequently by 1911. Wallace Fisheries had built a cannery at the entrance to Naden Harbor, on the east side, and the Pacific Whaling Company was constructing a whaling station on Germania Creek on the west side of Naden Harbor. Among the supply ships for these ventures was the *Henriette,* after she was taken off the first G.T.P. mail contract and replaced in summer of 1910 by the *Bruno* (soon to be renamed the *Prince Albert*) under the command of Captain Cecil Wearmouth.

Captain Wearmouth had replaced Captain Buckholtz (1) who had "got soused up" at Port Simpson once too often before crossing Hecate Straits and ended in Ketchikan, Alaska instead of the Charlottes. Wearmouth took over command of the *Henriette* first, and then was transferred to "the *Albert*". He was so entranced with the Islands that he persuaded his two brothers Bert and Ernest to go there. Bert went in May of 1910 to work on the *Finn* collecting fish for the Wallace Fisheries cannery in Naden Harbor and Ernest followed in October and went to work for J. C. A. Long's survey gang. As soon as they had some cash the two brothers went into business for themselves and bought the *Bernie.*

"She was too small, really, and not much of a success," recalls Bert Wearmouth, "but Ernest and I were always the live ones to buy the boys a drink in Masset." These two very popular "live ones" stayed to take part in all phases of that pioneering life until the Big Call came in 1914. Then with Allan Jessup, Jack Dodson and Frank Batchelor they joined the Muskeg Scouts in Prince Rupert, transferring next to the 30th and then the 16th Canadian Scottish. Ernest was killed in battle the next year and Bert, after the war, went to live, with his wife Margaret, on an island in Prince Rupert Harbor which still bears his name locally. The farm they built up and their hospitality made it a real asset to the region — but when the second World War cost them the life of their only son they decided to leave the familiar associations and move to Sidney on Vancouver Island.

Although Masset never boomed in the same way as its neighbor Port Clements down the Inlet did in the latter war years — yet it never recessed in the same way either, but maintained steady growth. So Charles Harrison lived to see his dream fulfilled before he and his wife retired to England in 1919.

New Masset was on its way never to look back.

(1) Rumored to be the original of Jack London's "Sea Wolf"

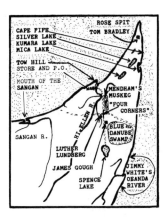

CHAPTER TWENTY-SIX

THE NORTH BEACH

According to Haida legend, the first settler who came to live on the North Beach was Tow of Juskatla Inlet. In this big south arm of Masset Inlet, Tow had lived by the side of his twin brother, known as Tow-us-tas-in (brother of Tow), who was an even-tempered, agreeable fellow.

But old Tow was forever grumbling and finding fault because the Chief of the Sea would not allow him to have his brother's share of the salmon, halibut and dogfish, as well as his own. He thought he was very unfairly treated. Tow-us-tas-in stood this everlasting, unreasonable complaining of Tow's as long as he could, then one day as Tow napped in the warm sun, Tow-us-tas-in decided that he had had enough. He would give old Tow something to squawk about. There was an unusually heavy run of fish that afternoon and Tow-us-tas-in set to and ate up every one — not leaving as much as a fin or scale for his brother.

Tow was livid with rage when he awoke and learned what had happened. Never, he decided, could he tolerate such treatment. In a furious temper he made up his mind to leave his brother's side in Juskatla forever.

As the moon rose full and bright that evening, Tow began to storm down the Inlet, making such a fearfully hideous noise in his anger as he passed that all the people were terrified. When he approached Masset on his way to the open sea, the moon went behind a cloud and Tow was caught halfway across the peninsula and quite unable to force his way through to the sea. In his displeasure at having to retrace his steps he stomped around so much that he made what is known today as Delkatla Slough, then finally changing direction he moved eastward to the Chown, leaving behind huge rocks which can be seen in Delkatla Slough to this day.

Pausing to rest at the Chown, he stayed a few months, but decided grumpily that he didn't like it there either. More frustrated stomping produced another slough and as he moved out towards Yakan Point, he left more big rocks straggled behind him at the Chown. It was much better at Yakan and he settled down. There was excellent fishing in the area and he could have all the food he wanted without having to share one bit of it. Yes, he thought, he would remain in this region and began to cast about for a good site — one that would be suitable for

159

a hill of his proportions. The west bank of the lovely Hi-Ellen River seemed ideal and so Tow ponderously and untidily moved from Yakan Point to remain by the Hi-Ellen forever. Facing out to sea there, he makes the best landmark for miles around.

Tow-us-tas-in remained in Juskatla Inlet and now at last there is peace and harmony in that family.

Centuries later, when the white settlers began to crowd into the north end of Graham Island and found there were no roads, they streamed down the same magnificent thirty-mile stretch of sand along the North Beach. The fact that no waterfront property on Masset Inlet was available made the beach land look even more attractive.

It was this complete dearth of transportation facilities everywhere that made the settlers lives so incredibly difficult. The hardship of having to pack every item on one's back over trails, as well as lack of communication caused by the difficulty of travel, brought inevitable isolation and aggravated the impractibility of families joining the men as they established residence and proved up on their pre-emptions.

Many of the people whose names were well-known along the North Beach were actually located in the Cape Fife region on the East Coast where the possibility of placer gold in the black sands had first been the attraction — rather than the land. Victor Vigelous (1) and Charlie Spence were the first to recover paying amounts of gold from the Cape Fife sands when they collected $300 worth of dust, but when they returned from their subsequent celebration on the mainland it was to find that extremely high tides had destroyed all signs of their claims. Shortly after this Arthur Pearson tried to mine the sands on a more elaborate basis, as did many others after Pearson gave it up — but it was always an elusive proposition.

Victor Vigelous, reported to be a Count from Scandinavia, had come to the Islands from Alaska, and previously had lived in South America for many years. Vigelous's name could be found in connection with speculations on the West Coast and he is credited with being the first man to blaze a trail from Naden Harbor to Otard Bay. About 1911 he became unbalanced and a religious fanatic. Old-timers still tell of the time he made an altar in Masset, then armed with a gun he marched round and round the town raving that the walls of Jericho were about to fall. To keep him happy half the town marched with him, but when he said he would shoot the first person he met on the third time round, to sacrifice on his altar, things looked to be getting out of hand.

Charles Harrison came along at this stage and stepping into the path, stood straight in front of Vigelous and said firmly, "Do you know who I am, Vigelous?" "No," was the reply. At which, Harrison in a loud clear voice told him, "I am the Prophet of the Lord ... don't stand in the way of the Prophet." Turning from him, he commanded the demented man, "Follow in my footsteps! Left, right, left, right ..." and led him safely into the local pokey.

Charlie Spence liked the black sands region so much that he pre-empted at Kumara Lake. Today the comfortable cabin that Mr. Spence built there and much of his land is now under the ocean as that part of the shoreline recedes

---

(1) *This name has a variety of spellings, i.e.; Vergalious, Vigaleous, Virgalias.*

160

Where it all began. Langara Lighthouse stands on the headland sighted July 17, 1774 by Juan Perez, when he gave British Columbia the first name to be recorded—Cape Santa Margarita.

THE QUEEN CHARLOTTE ISLANDS 1774-1966

At the other end of the Queen Charlottes Cape St. James Lightstation keeps her lonely vigil.

Forest of totem poles at Old Masset before 1880.

Old Masset in 1909.

*Amos Russ, the first Haida to
converted to Christianity (Ch
18), and his wife, Agnes.*

*Jatice "Nani" of Sandspit who was
so beloved by all the children.*

Haida craftsman at work: Alfred Davidson, who with his brother, Robert, built this canoe for the Seattle Exposition. (One of the few pictures of it in existence.)

First Church and Rectory built in Skidegate. The churches built later in New Kloo and Haina (Maude Island) were exact replicas of this one.

Constable Condon stands beside the much-photographed Edenshaw Memorial Pole. Monument on right honors Chief Albert Edenshaw for his part in the "Susan Sturgis" highjacking, 1852.

Right: Early Skidegate.

Above: "Waiting for the boat" at Henry Edenshaw's home in Old Masset, this group includes (left to right): Wes Singer the young man who came in 1909 to see if the sand on the shore of Mayer Lake was really as white as he had heard; Mr. and Mrs. Orland P. Merrill from the coal drill at the Nadu; Henry Edenshaw, skipper of the Josephine; *George Mayer, who discovered and first mapped Mayer Lake; and Fred Nash, B.C.L.S., who laid out four Graham Island townsites in addition to all the other surveying he was engaged to do.*

Returning home from fishing to Old Masset—1911.

Above: Supplies were freighted up the Yakoun by canoe (Louis "Ole" Van Valkenburg, dark shirt with pole, and Wes Singer lifting box).

Or they were carried on the sturdy backs of packers. Left to right: Jim McLay, seated, Bud Millard, Willie Millard and Jim Allison.

Surveyors came in to restore order in the unsurveyed chaos. William J. Leary, the progressively minded J.P. from Miller Creek, goes out on a party with Sam Lassiter, C. de B. "Cedar" Green, B.C.L.S., and Mr. Green's son.

Bridges were built. Walter de Lisle stands on the first Sangan River bridge.

The twelve-mile plank road from Port Clements to Tlell. It took steady nerves to drive this thoroughfare. Later, six-inch planks were laid on each side of the wheel tracks.

THE PEOPLE . . . *came from every walk of life* . . .

To ranch—Mexican Tom, W. T. Hodges, with his mail-order bride who was deeply honored to be part of pioneering, stand on the bank of the Tlell.

PHOTO—MRS. FRANCIS RICHARDSON

To evangelise—Rev. William "Father" Hogan, the six-foot-four, three hundred pound Irish parson who said, "This is my land, bhoys. When I die bury me beside my Haida braves," and his wife, Margaret, who always called him Willie.

PHOTO—MRS. J. TICEHURST

To homestead—T. L. Williams who built his log cabin on Masset Inlet in 1909, and Mrs. Williams who came to live in it the next spring.

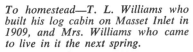

PHOTO—T. L. WILLIAMS

And to build a town—Elias James "Eli" Tingley came first in 1907 to select his site. Returning with a party of would-be settlers in 1908, he was the only one of the group to remain. The others left in a few months, but Eli's vision of a townsite on the point of land near the mouth of the Yakoun River was too strong to be denied. Because of a timber claim on his chosen site he was to be six years in a long drawn-out battle before he could finally obtain a clear title and register his townsite under its second name, Port Clements, which replaced the original Queenstown chosen by the town's first merchant, James Martin.

Charlie Adam's Graham Centre.

SETTLEMENTS GREW INTO TOWNSITES

Windy Young's Queen Charlotte City, *and the mill which was the reason for its existence.*

INFORMATION AND PHOTO —MRS. ROY FIELD (FORMER LOTTIE LEARY)

The "hub city" of the Charlottes for years was Skidegate Landing, which probably had more names in the course of its history than any other Island point; Gontha, Sterling Bay, Oil Works, Skidegate, Graham City and is today known locally as Skidegate Landing.

This is how it looked March, 1908 when the W. J. Leary family arrived. From left to right: (Wharf and oilery not seen were at the extreme left) in the picture was the boat shed, then the can-making building, with a bunkhouse on the second floor. Nicknamed "Bachelor's Hall", this was where Ed Wiggans, George McRae, Al Daise, Jim Omand, Dick Husband, Bob Kitson, Jim Mullock and Bert Porter batched in 1908.

The house, called the "Company House" where the Leary family lived had a wonderful garden which had been established by the first owners, Mr. and Mrs. Bob Tennant in 1885 or 1886.

Next house was built by John Mathers and was later A. J. Gordon's. In front of this is the Company store and the buildings beside it were lived in by employees of the Oil Works. The building from which the smoke is issuing is Smith's Hotel, the three small buildings in front are the deluxe bedrooms. At the back of the hotel is Captain Haan's home; one of the houses on the hill became the Skidegate school later.

Charles Wilson takes Clement Carter, left, to choose a lot in his embryo townsite of Delkatla.

"Buy one of my lots for your Town House," Mr. Wilson urged pre-emptors and many took his advice. From left to right: Nigel Sherwood, Mr. Wilson (later Dr. Graves home), Roscoe Rupe, Harry Lamb and Woody Prosser's home.

The grandest house in Delkatla belonged to Dave Ruttan and his wife, "Dutch Annie", popular pioneers from the Oeanda River on the East Coast.

W. J. "Hotel" Smith in white shirt (right) stands with guests on verandah of his new Premier Hotel.

The modern exterior of the Hotel Masset drew many admiring comments. The proprietors were Mr. and Mrs. W. Hudson.

Bert Tingley added a store (right) to his Yakoun Hotel in Port Clements.

Newspaper and Land Sales offices were soon in evidence. This was one in Masset.
Jimmy Campbell, shirt sleeves, editor of The Islander, stands beside Allan Jessup (right). Sign above window "Allan Jessup Lands."

Outlying stores also had Post Offices. Jim Anderson's Tow Hill store on right, was across the road from the coffee shop and overnight stopping place run by Jim and Nellie Hammond. Standing on the Hi-Ellen bridge left to right: Jim Anderson, Mr. Taylor, Bert Swain, George Wyman, and Charlie Spence.

Mrs. W. J. Leary stands in the doorway of the Hydah Post Office and store at Miller Creek, which was a wing of their large home.

PHOTO—T. L. WILLIAMS

The non-denominational church services of early years were well attended. The 16 x 20 St. Luke's Anglican Church at Graham Centre was strained to capacity when nearly everyone in the settlement turned out for the christening of Dorothy Rennie. From the left: John Boyes, Grandpa Godwin, Sid Wormald, James Thomas O'Flynn, Charlie Adam, Captain Hart Jenkins, Mr. W. J. Rennie with baby, Felix Graham, Anne Adam, Jim Allison, F. C. Wright, Mabel Godwin, her father, Mrs. T. L. Williams and son, Jack, Mrs. W. J. Rennie, Bert Millard, Mrs. F. C. Wright, Mrs. Bert Millard, Mrs. John Boyes, holding Ailo; doorway: T. L. Williams, Rev. Heber Greene, Mrs. Greene, Bishop du Vernet, James McLay and Mr. Peters.

St. Mary's Spring which has a legend — whoever drinks from its pure cold water must return to the Islands.

(Picture taken Xmas week 1909 in Masset by Jim Anderson)

1. Douglas Fraser	22. Charles Harrison
2. Allan Orr	23. Laurie Hughes
3. Dr. A. Ross Fraser	24. Wilfred Hughes
4. Harold Orr	25. Betty Fraser
5. James Martin	26. Mrs. Harrison
6. Bill Cook (Townsite Representative)	27. Walter de Lisle
7. Gus Lundquist	28. Robert Cross
8. Jack Cook (Townsite Representative)	29. George Mayer
9. Alex McTavish	30. Mrs. Ives
10. Mrs. Bill Cook	31. Geordie McQuaker
11. (not known)	32. Arthur Pearson
12. Frank Millard	33. Reggie Orr
13. Bert Millard	34. Laurel (Spud) Millard
14. Mrs. Frank Millard	35. Fritz Rampmaer
15. Frank Van Valkenburg	36. Cap. Francis
16. Arthur Ives (Senior)	37. Bob Entwistle
17. Lucy Millard	38. Mr. Larson
18. Louis (Ole) Van Valkenburg	39. Bill Millard
19. (not known)	40. Bud Millard
20. Charlie Adam	41. Arthur Ives
21. Mrs. Bert Millard	42. Tom Fraser
	43. Donald Fraser

PHOTO—BERT ROBERTS

Some Islanders hunted bears—and wonderful were the stories told. Ed Wiggans (left) and Roger Roberts pose with one they got at Tlell.

Right: Most Islanders played tennis. This court belonged to Captain Gillatt and his family in Sandspit. Today it is the driveway of the Islander Hotel.

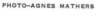

PHOTO—AGNES MATHERS

PHOTO—MRS. A. S. WARD

Left: Sooner or later all communities built a Community Hall, complete with benches and a wind-up gramophone (extreme left). This hall in Port Clements was built by invitation on church property—and became the center of a heated controversy.

PHOTO—MRS. FRED LA SETTE

Above: Gradually, a town began to take shape—this is the business section of Queen Charlotte City. The buildings from the left: Lauder Hotel, Sach's Grocery, Windy Young's house (in distance at back), the newspaper office, Donald Cochrane's store, and George Beattie's Dry Goods and Drug Store.

The people from the left are: Dorothy Barge; Marie de Pape; Alice Barge; Juliet Girard; Mrs. Molitor; Asseline Girard who married the man she stands beside— George Beattie; Walter Dass; Cochrane with their first baby; Clarence Johnson (with rake); Sammy Scowcroft; Tom Reid; Howard Fairbairn and Havigal Atkins, (the teacher 1911-12).

ISLANDERS FARMED . . .

Fine barn belonging to Francis Evans, on his ranch at the Divide, on Kumdis Slough.

AND DRILLED FOR COAL . . .

Brent Lea (left) and George Richardson with Barton's drill at Camp Wilson.
The boiler is the first boiler the Vancouver Fire Department used. It had five hundred copper tubes. The two-cylinder engine shown at the back of the cable drum is from a Stanley Steamer automobile.

The first Haan seine boat. It had no mast. Nick Shug, Ed Anderson, Captain John Haan, Eddie Moore and Ed Stevens (senior), haul the net in by hand.

Above: They worked in canneries like this one at Alliford Bay.
The steamer Famous *shown loaded with canned salmon, was the* Amur *so well-known to all early travellers. This picture taken 1925.*

Below: The war years 1917 to 1918 were the mill years, creating a "boom" as the world learned about the superlative spruce native to the Queen Charlottes, unequalled in quality anywhere else in the world. This is Buckley Bay mill which operated until the early twenties and had a population of four hundred and fifty people during its peak period.

PHOTO—B.C. GOVERNMENT

Spruce trees of this proportion are commonplace on the Charlottes, where butts on some trees have been seventeen and one-half feet in diameter. *This one is just under* ten feet.

Early logging camps were miniature villages on rafts. This is the J. R. Morgan Logging camp, 1935, in Sedgwick Bay.

PHOTO—MRS. ELMER PALMER

The J. R. Morgan, *formerly* Prince Albert *and the smaller* Mary Roberta *tow Morgan's Camp from Sedgwick Bay to Thurston Harbour in 1936.*

As logging methods have changed, shown by this picture of the MacMillan, Bloedel and Powell River logging truck and road in Juskatla . . .

So have the main streets of the settlements. This is New Masset in 1963 with its avenues "the size of baseball diamonds" wrote one reporter.

Some cemeteries are sad places, and most are stereotyped. The one at Masset is almost like a fairyland with its soft carpet of moss which keeps out weeds. The ocean is only a stone's throw from here, its roar is muted and softened by the trees which are also moss-hung.

Hudson's Bay Company store and residence at Old Masset taken about 1890.

"The Golden Spruce" on the west bank of the Yakoun River, Graham Island.

H.M.S. Egeria.

If ever a vessel was truly the Islands' own, it was the veteran Prince John, *shown here at the Masset wharf.*

Mr. W. A. Robertson, (Robertson Coal Mine) on left, with Mr. Arichika Ikeda of Ikeda Mines, and three students from Japan. Taken in 1907.

PHOTO—PROVINCIAL ARCHIVES

PHOTO—PROVINCIAL ARCHIVES

Lockeport began as a miner's base; later a cannery was built to the right of beach shown here.

PHOTO—PAUL BASTIAN

Naden Harbor Whaling Station, 1912.

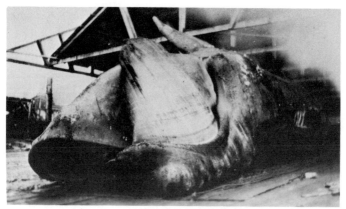

Some of the whales were so huge, the head had to be removed before processing.

Commodious house built by William Demerald Cood at Sandspit. Department of Transport homes now occupy this site, which is adjacent to the Sandspit airport.

Miss M. I. Lett, sister of Chief Justice Lett, and her class at Sandspit. Pupils were: Simon Woods, Belle Gillatt, Elizabeth Lundfield, Charlie Haan, Myrtle Cole, Kathleen Mathers, Bernice Cole, Elizabeth Mathers, Harvey Cole, Sidney Cole, Peggy Gillatt, Agnes Mathers, Jack Haan, Jean Haan, Peter Haan and Alpha Cole. Taken in 1915.

PHOTO—BOB MALLORY

Mah Wing and Billy, well-remembered personalities from Port Clements.

PHOTO—AGNES MATHERS

Right: Captain William Oliver, the pioneer Methodist missionary.

Below: The west coasts of the Charlotte group offer a variety of rock formations, such as this huge basalt hill in Tana Bay. It is known locally as "Pipe Organ Rock", and the cove it is in is called "Cathedral Bay"

PHOTO—CAPTAIN G. GRAY HILL

Pinnacle rocks near the south entrance to Hippa Passage are called "Hippa Fangs".

Left: The remains of the old oil drill at Tian Point.

Right: And the more tragic remains of the wrecked "Clarksdale Victory", which was wrecked on Hippa Island in 1947, with a heavy loss of life.

Bodies of important Haidas were placed in a coffin above the ground so that their spirits might roam free. This grave is at Tian.

The B.C. Government arranged to have some of the better remaining totems removed for care and subsequent display in Victoria—apparently feeling this could be more adequately done away from the natural habitat. Which seems strange, since Haida creativity has never waned, as illustrated by one of the many carvers, Henry Moody (left) who is shown working on argillite in his Skidegate home.

Right: Farmer's Institute building at Lawn Hill. Built originally as a private residence for F. C. Wright in connection with coal drilling, it was used for a period by Mr. and Mrs. Jory (lady on left), when Mr. Jory, a geologist was making tests for an oil company. Purchased by the Farmer's Institute, it was utilized as a school for the first Lawn Hill class.

Left: First Queen Charlotte City school. Classes were held, temporarily, above Moore's Poolroom in September, 1909. Mrs. Butler filled in until the regular teacher, Donald Cochrane arrived. Back rows Edith Fraser, Keo Katsura, Azeline Girard, Mrs. Butler, Carrie Barge and John Kitson. Front row: Fosie Fraser, Charlotte Young, Dorothy Barge, Theoline Girard, Nola Young, Bertha Girard and Juliet Girard. Missing from picture is Alice Barge.

Right: First Masset school classes were held in a converted boathouse, donated by Charles Harrison. It doubled as a church on Sunday. School opened here September, 1909 with Miss Outram as a temporary teacher, until Miss Jessie Peck shown in picture, arrived. Front row: Laulee (Spud) Millard, Donald Fraser (white shirt), Bill Millard, Freddy Ives, Douglas Fraser (white pants), Aileen Fraser, Lucy Millard (polka dot dress), Betty Fraser behind Lucy. Standing, back row, is Budd Millard, with Tom Fraser and Harold Orr sitting on fence. Missing from picture: Edwin Orr, Reggie Orr, Jimmy Leslie, Edith Leslie and Nellie Ives.

Above: The Haida village of Cumshewa in 1878, photo taken by G. M. Dawson.

The Haidas were not tepee dwellers. Their huge lodges aroused the admiration of all. This was the home of Chief Henry Weah (Weha) in Old Masset. Left to right: Wm. Harding, Joshua Collison, Mathew Skil-tling (father of Wm. Matthews, Chief Weah today), Wm. Matthews (boy), Mr. R. Dodd (H.B.C.), A. McKenzie retired H.B.C., Henry Edenshaw and Rueben Thompson. Lady seated to right of door was Mr. Wm. Matthews' mother. Lady in white scarf was the first wife of Chief Henry Weah.

PHOTO—C. M. ADAM

Pillar Rock, near Langara Island, is 95 feet high.

Interior of the A-Frame type church built in Queen Charlotte City by the United Church.

Crab pots await repair outside Simpson's cannery in Masset.

Above: The only permanent residents in the pioneer settlement of Sewall, today, are Mr. and Mrs. Stanley Unsworth and their three children, and Mrs. Julius Grewe, who makes her home with the Unsworths. Mrs. Unsworth, shown here, was born and brought up in this tranquil place.

The post office is still in the house John Mathers built in Sandspit in 1907.

Right: Water Taxi awaits passengers at Alliford Bay landing.

Left: Pole railroad built by the J. H. Baxter Pole Company, to transport poles from Mayer Lake to Kumdis Bay. Note old wagon road on left.

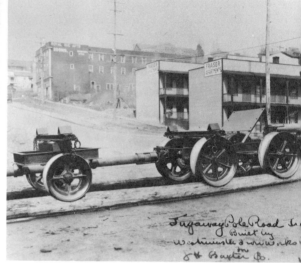

Right: Jugaway Pole Road tractor, built especially for use on Graham Island by the J. H. Baxter Company in the 1920's and early 1930's.

Davis Raft with 2,500,000 feet of spruce from the J. R. Morgan Logging Company.

into the Hecate Strait. Spence was well-known around Tow Hill where he freighted, and then in Delkatla where he built some of the early houses. For many years he was the Masset road foreman, in the days when politics mattered for this job.

Down the East Coast, to the south of Spence's place was the beloved little talker – Jimmy White of the Oeanda. Jimmy and his brother Bill had come first in 1909 to work on the survey gangs – and that winter they set out traps near the Oeanda River and caught ten beautiful otter. Knowing that they could get $200 each for them the Whites decided to settle there. But from that time on they were never able to trap another. However, Bill sent for his wife and daughter, Ione. They lived at the Oeanda for several years until the isolation proved too much for Mrs. White and Ione and they prevailed upon Bill to leave the Islands.

Jimmy lived there for the rest of his days, hunting, trapping and panning a little black sand once in awhile. One of the most tender-hearted of men, he built a big barn for his horses from beachcombed lumber – lugging every stick of timber on his own back for, he said, he just hated to have his fine horses do such heavy work. Jimmy was renowned for his stories – and how he could tell them! Many a visitor to his cabin remembers going to sleep late at night with Jimmy's voice droning away, to awaken the next morning and find he was still yarning – apparently with no stops or pauses for breath during the interim hours of the night.

He loved to make trails and thought nothing of starting one on the East Coast and blazing right through to Masset Inlet, and he had a cabin about halfway from the Oeanda to the Nadu which he frequently used. He had trails everywhere through that part of the country. Jimmy was one of the very few men to have gone through the white water of the Grand Canyon in the U.S.A. and live. To prove his story, he went ashore in one place and carved his name, James Sterling White, on a tree. Years later this was discovered by an expedition and a newspaper article was written about it. (1)

His counterpart in story-telling was the little Londoner, Alf Charles, who came to live on the North Beach about 1920, naming his cabin "Bishop's Court." One night the two met in a hotel in Masset and it was not long before wagers were being laid as to which would outtalk the other. For hours and hours the conversation went on, each man talking at once, engrossed in his own tale – neither listening to the other. Next morning when the other guests came downstairs Alf Charles had fallen asleep and Jimmy, the master talker was still regaling him with stories – oblivious that he was talking for his own ears only.

Both men were very well-liked and their idiosyncrasy had the affectionate acceptance of everyone. Alf Charles lived alone in his "Bishop's Court" cabin until 1964, when at the age of 87 he was persuaded to take things easier in an old people's home in Vancouver – and the North Beach doesn't seem the same without his cheery greetings.

Jimmy White was popular with all his neighbors, except the one next door, Caesar Verhyden. Caesar was a later comer to the Oeanda, having spent his early pioneering days at Sewall. The stories about Caesar are many – especially about

(1) Information from Bert Roberts, Queen Charlotte City.

his diet. Once he invited a group of neighbors to have dinner with him and when the meal was over someone said, "By gosh, Caesar, that was a fine roast you fed us." And Caesar replied with a sigh, "Vell, it's goot you enjoyed it. That vas my old bitch, Nellie."

Just north of the Oeanda is the Blue Danube area — a marshy piece of land to which came Mr. and Mrs. Dave Ruttan of Holland. They hoped to establish a colony from their homeland there, but it never materialized. They ranched for some years then moved into a big house in Delkatla. Mrs. Ruttan was much better known by her nickname of "Dutch Annie", and had a heart as big as they come, although how she made her money was usually a subject for interesting local speculation. It was Dave Ruttan, Caesar Verhyden and Neil Walsh from Tlell, who dug the huge ditch 10 feet wide and 600 feet long. In that flat country of meandering streams it had the unexpected effect of changing the mouth of the Oeanda River.

There were few women among the early pioneers, but they were greatly appreciated in that preponderantly male population and are well remembered. Some had young children who always seemed to be the especial pets for the kind-hearted batchelors. One such family was Mr. and Mrs. Tom Bradley. They had been enticed by the B.C. Government pamphlets to sell out in Manitoba and in Victoria had been helped to select land which was "just waiting for the plough." It took all their money to do it, but they arrived in Masset in 1911 with complete farming equipment, their four children, Lucy, Edith, Herb and Jessie, and Mrs. Bradley's parents, Mr. and Mrs. Wilkes.

Tom Bradley had chosen for his site the legendary Rose Point, close to the old Haida Point-Town-Village location. It was a lovely spot, but lonely for Mrs. Bradley although Mrs. Bill White and Ione came up to visit occasionally. To the west of the Bradleys were the Carpenter family. Howard Carpenter had first come to Graham Island in 1910 — a big man, known to all as "Carp", he was one of the most amiable of men and it was always said that if you couldn't get along with Carp, you were impossible for anyone to get along with. The Carpenters moved into Masset after some years and Mrs. Carpenter ran the telegraph office. Of their four children — Charlie, Mary, Josephine and John — it was Charlie who decided to follow his father's footsteps and ran the ranch near the Spit for many years before moving with his wife, the former Kathleen Dunn, to Vanderhoof to farm under more equitable conditions.

Tom Bailey came with a team of horses and brought his wife and six children to ranch on the North Beach. So did Jack Parks. In 1912 Mr. and Mrs. Hanson and their family came from Denmark to live on the shore of Mica Lake, which lies about three miles east of Tow Hill. Bill Champion had his aunt and uncle, the Johnsons, living beside him. They were an energetic family who built two large cabins on the banks of the Hi-Ellen about two miles from the mouth. They cleaned out all the logs and debris and were able to carry all their supplies in a dug-out from the Swan Creek junction right up to their cabins. In 1913 Mrs. La Farge, a registered nurse, came to join her husband on the shores of Spence Lake seven miles south of Tow Hill.

By 1911 almost the whole of the North Beach from Masset to Rose Spit was solidly pre-empted. With a particularly heavy concentration in the Tow Hill region, Jim Anderson, who had been in Masset since 1909, decided to set up a

162

store on the west bank of the Hi-Ellen. This whole region back into Spence Lake and out to the East Coast was sprouting cabins, so that when Mr. Anderson was appointed to take the census in 1911 he had great difficulty in locating all the legion of scattered settlers. The Federal Election was held in September of 1911, but there were only twenty-seven votes cast in Masset. It was too difficult and too time-consuming for people to go all the way into Masset to register and then in again later to vote — although there were scores of eligible voters in the area. It took four hours to walk along the beach from Tow Hill to Masset and when the difficult trek from inland to the beach is added, reluctance to make the trip is understandable.

For those coming along the beach by wagon from the east side of Tow Hill it was necessary to take a wagon apart and carry it piece by piece over the rocks at this spot and reassemble it on the other side. After much petitioning, the government finally built a rough wagon road behind Tow Hill. Today, it is no longer necessary to go via the beach from Masset to Tow Hill, for the road runs inside the tree line all the way.

Jim Anderson's became the logical place for people travelling along the beach to break their journey and he soon found he had more than he could handle with overnight guests, breakfasts and other meals to prepare. So when Jim Hammond walked the beach from Skidegate in late 1911 with a view to settling somewhere on the Islands, Mr. Anderson suggested that Jim bring his bride and they start an overnight stopping place and serve meals to travellers.

Nellie Hammond knew nothing about cooking, but being very much in love and realizing that her husband wanted to try pioneering at Tow Hill, she agreed. It was January 3, 1912 when she and her husband arrived on the Masset wharf to be met by Jim Anderson. "Never will I forget that ride out along that beach," she recalls today, "the majesty of those big trees and the huge breakers rolling in along the shore — I felt as though God were very near, and it seemed to be the loveliest place in all the world."

Charlie Smith was keeping store with Anderson when the Hammonds arrived and the next day he helped divide the big tent that Anderson had put up for passers-by to stay in, so that one half could be used for the Hammond's bedroom and the other half for a kitchen-dining room. For the overnight guests a smaller tent was put up with bunks and fragrant fresh boughs for mattresses.

Jim Hammond worked hard and in three months had built a trim three roomed cabin for his bride, directly across the path from Anderson's store, which gave them much more room. "The men who came were all so kind and friendly," remembers Mrs. Hammond, "and I really loved the life." Mr. Anderson had to show her how to make bread, pies and cakes, and to use the tinned goods that formed their staple supplies. "I had the proverbial beginner's luck," she says, "most of my baking was amazingly successful — to my great surprise and joy."

On December 12, 1912 the first christening took place at Tow Hill when "Father" William Hogan and Bishop du Vernet walked out from Masset to baptise Harold Alfred Hammond, who had been born the month before in Masset. Jim Anderson was invited to be godfather, and all the nearby settlers attended the ceremony.

At the outbreak of the 1914 war Jim Hammond enlisted and they left the Islands for good. Reluctantly, Nellie Hammond bid farewell to Tow Hill

163

forever. "They were the never-to-be-forgotten days for me," says Mrs. Hammond, now living in Vancouver, "and if I were younger I would like to do it all over again. It was a healthy thrilling life and now that I am older, the memories of it are priceless."

In the spring of 1912 when the twenty-two-year-old Luther Lundberg came to B.C. from Tacoma to strike out on his own he was persuaded by the Victoria Land Office to go to Graham Island. He arrived in Masset to learn that all available waterfront land was gone, but in the Ives Hotel he met James Gough, who was living behind Tow Hill. "I've got a fine place just three and a half miles south of Tow Hill," Gough told the young American "and there's lots more around me. Good neighbors, cheap land — if you pre-empt it — wild geese, grouse and ducks. There are even wild cattle free for the taking whenever you want a roast of beef." And when he told Luther that there was an unoccupied quarter section of land adjoining him which had a good stream, ". . . it all sounded like Utopia," says Mr. Lundberg, "and I could hardly wait to see it."

By this time Jim Anderson was running a gas boat between Masset and Tow Hill, carrying supplies and passengers. "The fare was one dollar from Masset to Tow Hill, so Gough and I went out with him," recalls Mr. Lundberg. "We had a good lunch at the Hammonds' place then loaded up with supplies from Anderson's store to take into our land." By then survey lines had been run in and a well-trodden path led down past Mendham's Muskeg (1) and through Four Corners as it became known, then down to Spence Lake. At Four Corners there was an intersection and another trail led to the East Coast above the Blue Danube. A wagon road was built there in later years — but it is overgrown today.

When Luther Lundberg saw his land, he never doubted that it would be productive after the wonderful assurances in Victoria. True, there was quite a muskeg, but he also had a fair amount of good timber. In just seven days he had built a 10 x 10 cabin using logs from the timber on his own land, and had beachcombed the lumber needed for a door and window frame. It was a good life for a young man, he thought, and he got along well with his neighbors. His site was on the southwest side of Four Corners, which he shared with Frank Jamott to the north, and John Graham to the east. Bert Swain was nearby, Richard Levin on Luther's south and his friend Jim Gough was southeast of him. Joe Cobb, Fred Yarborough, (2) and George Wyman (Charlie Smith's good friend) were to the north. Pete Keay had his cabin opposite Mendham's. They were a good group to share life with for Lundberg.

In the fall of 1912 the government announced it would finance two months of work for seventeen men to build a road — using hand tools. Joe Gibbs was appointed foreman, and top pay was three dollars a day. With saws, axes, wheelbarrows and shovel they dug out a ditch, and struck sand eighteen inches down. (3) This made a fine bedding for the small trees that were laid end to end to form the pathway. Joe Cobb had one of the few teams in the region and he

(1) Named for a 1910 pre-emptor who built a cabin there and then left.
(2) Fred had formerly been doing the diamond drilling on test holes at the Chown for McIntosh, the former New Westminster police chief.
(3) When Mr. Lundberg returned to visit 52 years later, this old ditch was still working and draining effectively (1964).

164

was engaged to haul beach sand to surface the roadway. Cobb had also built quite a good road into his own place using his team – at his own expense.

In the fall of 1913, a year and a half after he had come to the Islands, young Luther Lundberg suddenly became homesick – a feeling intensified by the fact that his land had not produced the crop that he had expected. So he packed up his few effects and left the Islands. Like so many of his contemporaries, he found that the year spent in pitting himself against the challenge of a new land had left such an indelible mark he was irresistibly drawn, fifty years later, to return to visit the site of such vivid memories. The man-made things were gone – back to the nature they had come from. The more enduring landmarks that Nature had created were almost unchanged. A scraggly jackpine which he had nicknamed "Joshua Tree" was still there, perhaps a little taller and fuller but otherwise just as it had been so many years before.

Charlie Smith's friend, George Wyman, was an interesting young man. He was the son of the Governor of the Island of Celebes and had rebelled at the pattern of life which would have been his role had he remained in the land of his birth. To own a ranch in Canada was his dream. In the Fraser Valley he worked in a B.C. Electric Co. camp for awhile and met Charlie Smith. "I think visions of his wonderful ranch occupied his every waking moment," says Mr. Smith, "and when he got hold of the Victoria literature about the farmlands on Graham Island he knew he was nearing his goal." Learning that Charlie had previously farmed on the prairies, George Wyman cajoled him into accompanying him to Graham Island.

"I had been to the Islands aboard a freighter in 1909 to look them over and had not cared for them too much," says Mr. Smith "but George was very persuasive. So in the spring of 1910 we went to Masset. We walked all over the place trying to find a free pre-emptable place. We'd stake out a place – then find we couldn't have it. And then another – and it would be already taken. But finally we found one just behind Tow Hill, so George took it and I went to work in Anderson's store."

As things turned out, it was Charlie who remained to love and grow up with the land. He worked with Anderson in the store for some years, then saw a chance to pre-empt a good piece of land in the Silver Lake region. His property adjoined that of Ronald Currie and his niece Miss Alice Harling, and the three decided to join forces which gave them a 1500-acre ranch. Miss Harling, who had been an esteemed stenographer in the Victoria Parliament Buildings before going to stay with her uncle at Silver Lake, was a remarkable woman and held her own with the men in every way in the running of that ranch. For awhile they ran a good sized herd of Jerseys, made butter and used the ranch brand of CH & S on their wrappers. Then they went into white-faced Herefords with a pure-bred Shorthorn bull to build an excellent herd.

After his stint in the Navy during the 1914-18 war, Charlie came back to the Silver Lake ranch to rejoin his partners. Romance was in the air and in 1921 Alice Harling became the bride of her longtime admirer, Charlie Smith. During the Second World War Charlie was also connected with ships, for in 1942 – when he was sixty years old – he was appointed lightkeeper of Cape St. James. The Smiths were very popular with the personel of the R.C.A.F., who had a wartime base on this isolated post, and entered wholeheartedly into the joke which was played on newcomers to the station, when one lad was dressed very convincingly in stylish lady's clothing and introduced as the "lightkeeper's daughter." He played the part well, says Mr. Smith, to the chagrin of any airman so duped.

Also in the Silver Lake area was Leonard Siples, a hard-working neighbor of the Smith and Currie ranch, who spent a number of years working his ranch before moving to North Vancouver to go into the real estate business. When he died his widow became the second wife of another early ex-Islander, Rev. James Gillette, who as Anglican parson ran the *Western Hope* there for many years and then became an Indian Agent after leaving the ministry.

About 1914 Jim Anderson sold out to J. C. Frizzell and moved in to open a branch store for a short time in Masset — but then he, too, joined up and left the Islands for good. Frizzell had problems running the Tow Hill store and particularly so when it came to selling coal oil. Everyone had a different sized container to be filled and he had great difficulty in trying to measure the coal oil with any degree of accuracy — so he weighed it. Customers still recall going to Frizzell's for two pounds of coal oil.

A. S. Christie who did so much talking about his proposed townsite at Tow Hill never got beyond that. His hoped-for house on the top of the Hill itself never materialized because the Government commandeered the site for their navigational marker, and as the war and following depression drained the population away Christie, too, abandoned his dream.

Today Tow Hill is a deserted settlement. But for many seasons it was headquarters for a razor clam cannery, and Norah Stewart-Burton (whose father, Frank Ward, built the unique Sangan Grange) remembers well the first time the cannery ran in Tow Hill.

"It was in 1923," she says, "and we used Jim Anderson's old store for the bunkhouse and office, and made an improvised cannery in his big barn. I made the pulley, used to mince the first clams, out of a five-inch slice from a hemlock log. Jep and Frank Edney came up from a clam cannery on Capalis Beach in Washington to set up the operation and help us run it.

The clams were dug every time the tide went out, and were hauled off the beach by horse and wagon, driven by Dave Ruttan and Cecil Baker. (1) There were only a few workers, but we'd all go out and dig — even the Edneys — and then come back and can. The Bradley girls, Lucy and Edith, were there, along with my brother Fred, sister Eva and me. Katy Brown (now Katy Collison) and Nellie Harding (now Yeomans) from Old Masset and Cyril Harrison and his wife Mabel worked there too. Mabel cooked for us. We had wonderful fun that first year," recalled Norah and added "it was Frank Edney who later married my sister, Eva."

The Tow Hill cannery was a Babington and Simpson sponsored venture. When Captains Eugene Simpson and Hume Babington were operating their crab cannery in Naden Harbor, they learned from their Haida employees of the presence of razor clams on the North Beach. Captain Simpson, having come from the mouth of the Columbia River where there were other such beds, knew their value. He and Babington staked out great sections of the beaches, in much the same way as one would stake out placer gold sand areas. In 1924, when the first

<hr />

(1) *Brother of Ed Baker, who lived a mile east of Tow Hill.*

small pilot operation had proved the feasibility of a commercial cannery the main Tow Hill cannery was built, on the other side of the Hi-Ellen, about a quarter of a mile east of Anderson's old store. In addition to the cannery there was a store and some fifty Indian dwellings.

"They bought five model T trucks," remembers Sam, Captain Simpson's son, "and it was really a wild existence. Those darn' trucks were used for everything — and were forever getting stuck in the sand, especially at the mouth of the Sangan River, and it would take two or three of the others to pull one out. We used the beaches, entirely, for transportation then. But the Tow Hill cannery ran steadily every season until 1930 when everything seemed to go belly-up in this line."

The Simpson family still hold those same clam beach leases that Captain Simpson staked forty-five years ago, and the beaches are still being dug for razor clams, which are now canned in the Masset cannery under the managership of Gene Simpson, grandson of Captain Simpson.

Sangan Grange, the lovely log mansion which was designed and built by architect Frank Ward, stood for years as an example of what could be accomplished in the way of a log house, when one used imagination and had some strong young arms to help in the building. It had a large central hall with all bedrooms leading off the balcony. Mr. Ward had come from Alaska in 1918, walking the beach from Skidegate around to Masset — and it was the picturesque Sangan area that took his eye. So in 1921 he brought his youthful family over and set about building the Grange. Of his children — Kathleen, Pat, Eva, Norah and Fred — both Norah and Fred have remained on the Charlottes, and as grandparents, are watching still another generation of Wards grow up on their favorite Islands.

We cannot leave the Sangan region without mention of the Sangan Holiday Resort which ran for many years. Transportation problems made its operation difficult and after two changes in managership, it was forced to close. Dr. and Mrs. J. C. Dunn and their lively family — Kathleen, Eileen, Doreen and John — began the venture by building small cabins beside their own home near the mouth of the Sangan River, then sold out to the Limberlost Company of Prince Rupert.

Dr. Dunn and his wife had come to Masset in 1922 as part of a group of fourteen adults and nine children from England who had been irresistibly attracted to Masset by the elaborate statements and brochures put out in London by the Queen Charlotte Islands Natural Resources Limited. The managing director of this company was Dr. E. H. Lawson, who had spent nine months on the Islands during the War, and two of the other directors were Charles Harrison and Bob Entwistle. Originally there were sixty people in the group of prospective settlers — but warnings from the Agent-General for B.C. that the colonization scheme was to sell land and that the immigrants should therefore be aware that the facts presented by the vendors of the land were not necessarily accurate — caused the rest of the party to change their minds. Dr. Dunn soon learned that the medical practice he was to take over in Masset would not support a family, so he and Mrs. Dunn ran the Queen's Hotel there to supplement their income until he retired and went out to live at the Sangan.

In the 1920s Karl Kirmis, who had come to Masset about the same time as

167

Dave Ruttan, began a cranberry farm on the McIntosh Meadows near the Sangan. He conceived the idea of crossing a hardy strain of berry with the wild ones which grew so well there and had a good business for a few years.

Probably the best known residents in this section of the North Beach were the Carey brothers, Austin and Len, who ran a farm at the Chown for years. Len played the guitar unusually well and also turned his hand to painting the big glass balls that drifted on to the beach, with the deft hand of an instinctive artist. Austin Carey's amiable nature seemed to give him an especial way with animals. The brothers had come originally from Somerset to live on the Charlottes.

Today, except for the seasonal clam digging and a brief flurry of activity when a few test holes were drilled by an oil company recently, all that wonderful stretch of beach is practically uninhabited and unused from the mouth of the Tlell River to Masset. The two exceptions are the cattle which still do well on their own out there, but today they all carry brands on their flanks. And the one lone settler is Harry Crooks who lives about fourteen miles from Masset, near White Creek. Mr. Crooks, in his late seventies now, is an old soldier who spent considerable time in India and took an active part in both World Wars. He liked the idea of pioneering and came to Masset in the mid-1930s and picked this site. Building a good log cabin, he cleared more land and put in a fine garden. At the time he came there were still a number of people living on the North Beach, but the fact that he is alone there now bothers him little — he would not think of leaving.

CHAPTER TWENTY-SEVEN

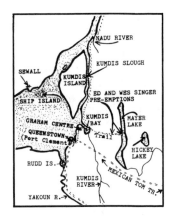

MAYER LAKE'S
FIRST SETTLERS

The fledgling town of New Masset was still a tent town on October 10, 1909, when the *Henriette* nosed into the outer harbor with a diamond drill on board. It belonged to the B.C. Amalgamated Coal Company, whose headquarters were in Portland, Oregon at that time, and under the direction of Orland P. Merrill, one of the directors, they were going to put down a test hole at the mouth of the Nadu River. The company was basing its hopes on the 1906 report of Dr. R. W. Ells, plus a good showing of lignite coal along the shoreline.

The drill was set up about a stone's throw in from the shore near the Nadu River and drilling went on steadily until February of 1910 — then abruptly shut down. O. P. Merrill and his wife stayed on as caretakers of the site for a few years, but no reports were issued by the company as to the results of their test holes, and no further drilling was ever done there. Local "reports" flew with wild abandon, at least for awhile. But it was the arrival of settlers which was the main interest.

And how they streamed in! The trickle began in 1909 — gaining momentum with every passing month and spreading in all directions — from the East Coast to the northwest tip on Cape Knox, where Herman, Lake and Plumer applied for pre-emptions in 1914, then down the long Masset Sound to take up land back of the timber claims on both sides, into Masset Inlet, the Kumdis and Yakoun and into Mayer Lake. The basic thing they had in common was youth, otherwise they were diverse in every way.

"I guess we were exiles by choice," says Wesley Singer, one of the earliest. He and his younger brother, Eddie, were at the Swanson Bay mine when they met Frank Rice, B.C.L.S., who had completed the New Masset townsite survey. Rice thought Graham Island was one of the finest places he had ever set eyes on and his enthusiasm for it infected young Wes. In particular, Mr. Rice's description of the nine-mile-long Mayer Lake with a beach of pure white sand caught his interest. He had to go and see for himself.

It was September, 1909, when he left Port Simpson on Henry Edenshaw's *Josephine* with his friend Denny Allen (1) and the two Hughes brothers, Larry

(1) Denny Allen was later well-known in Prince Rupert and is now retired in Victoria.

169

and Wildfred. Larry, who had been on the Islands previously, wanted to be let off at Rose Spit where he had taken out a pre-emption, but a gale was blowing up making it too rough for Henry to risk a landing. And it got rougher.

With the huge swells came the paralyzing seasickness that to this day is so vivid to Mr. Singer. "Boy! I could never forget it!" he says. "Regularly all four heads would hit that bucket ... then an agonizing breather when we prayed we could just die then and there and get it over with ... then, oops, the bucket! It was awful." Up on deck Henry and his deckhand for that trip, Roger Weah, were doing their best to control the boat in the huge waves.

Suddenly a tight-lipped Henry broke the news that he was out of gas. Yes, he said, he did have a spare can — but it was too rough to be able to use it so he was going to try and make a run for the shelter of Tow Hill. "It's going to have to be every man for himself from now on," Captain Edenshaw told them, "I won't be able to help you."

The seas were terrible. But the ghastly prostrating seasickness stopped immediately, as of that moment. "Completely cured by fright, I guess," says Wes.

After a nightmare trip, they were finally able to get in behind Tow Hill and up into the Hi-Ellen River, where they lashed the boat upright. It was several days before the storm subsided enough for them to go into Old Masset. "Gosh, I'll never forget young Roger Weah's hands after that trip," Mr. Singer added, "they were cut right to the bone trying to control that tiller — he was some brave boy."

After exploring Graham Island, Wes decided Frank Rice had not exaggerated the beauty of Mayer Lake one whit and sent for Eddie to join him. The two brothers staked their pre-emptions midway up the west side of the lake. That winter they built their cabins, Wes on the lake and Eddie about half a mile inland. Laboriously whip-sawing the lumber, they also built a 16-foot boat for use on the lake, although they still had their serviceable sail-boat moored down in Kumdis Bay for use along the Inlet. Later they planted fruit trees, some of which are still growing, according to Ed Singer who with his wife, the former Edith Bradley of Rose Spit, now lives in Masset.

"It was a great life," he reminisces today, "lots of activity. Plenty of game for food, and when we needed cash there was always work to be had on the survey gangs. We had some big skating parties in the winter when everyone would come out from Queenstown, hiking along the survey trail which ran in from Kumdis Bay. If we wanted a holiday we'd go down to Masset for a month or so — usually George Mayer would come with us. There we'd meet the Vans, (1) the Hughes, Bob Cross, Fred and Walter de Lisle and the rest — all single chaps."

Within a few years the shores of beautiful Mayer Lake were solidly occupied. The two Singers, two de Lisles, Bob and Walter Cross and their brother-in-law, Bill Hastie, Jim McLay, Jim Allison (cousin of the Cross brothers), John McDougal, A. J. Grimshaw, Bill Toop and the McLellan's, two brothers and their sister, Mary, (2) and many others.

(1) The Van Valkenburgs were always known only as Frank Van, Ole Van and Jack Van.
(2) Bill Toop later married Mary McLellan and went to live in Port Clements across the road from Dave and Mrs. Crocker. One McLellan brother returned to the prairies but the other, John, took up a pre-emption at the south end of Mayer Lake, near Gold Creek bridge. There he lived for the rest of his life, working on the Port to Tlell road when it replaced the old Mexican Tom trail, then moved into Port Clements in his last years to keep his widowed sister company.

170

The first big land sale was made in October of 1912 when the Winnipeg promotor, James McCrea sold 40,000 acres in the Mayer Lake region. Jim's company, the Queen Charlotte Land Company Limited, had its office in the Confederation Life Building in Winnipeg, and he escorted his first Mayer Lake clients on the train to Vancouver.

In Vancouver, he and his brother Andy purchased the big launch *Westover* to transport everyone to Masset Inlet. Included in the party besides the McCreas, who were both ex-C.P.R. engineers, was another former C.P.R. engineer, James Love, and T. E. Femby who had been a storekeeper in Watrous, Saskatchewan, as well as T. M. Funnell, Mr. and Mrs. William J. Rennie, Miss Olive Jones, Miss Freda Johnson and Captain Patterson. The party liked the land so well they bought 41,187 acres between them, all except Miss Jones — she bought Ship Island. There is no record of her having lived there but the McCreas cleared land and put up a few cabins on Ship Island shortly after.

Only Andy McCrea and Mr. and Mrs. Rennie stayed behind on this trip to build cabins on their Mayer Lake land. In March of the following year (1913) Jim McCrea brought in seventeen more prospective buyers from the prairies. By now the *Westover* was in such constant demand for local transportation that it took both McCreas to operate her and keep up with the rush. Jim McCrea, after leaving the Islands, went to Vancouver to live and died suddenly there in 1928, just as he was preparing to go to the Cocos Islands to dive for reported treasure.

But Andy brought his family to live on the Islands, first of all in Woden (1) River and then for years in Port Clements. He left to live in Prince Rupert later moving to Georgetown, about twenty miles from Prince Rupert. Like so many other ex-pioneers, he was drawn back again to Graham Island by happy memories of earlier times and he returned to spend his last years in Port Clements accompanied by his daughter, Alice, who is now the settlement's capable postmistress.

After Mayer Lake was abandoned by the settlers, it lay quiet and serene until the late 1920s when the J. H. Baxter Pole Camp took out poles from there. A unique logging road (2) was built for four and a half miles, and much of it followed the same route as the old pioneer wagon road. In the past few years this region has been reactivated as the same pole company, some forty years later, has come back to cut for poles, trees that were mere saplings during that earlier operation.

This time the poles are transported by modern logging trucks along a different route — to be boomed in the same place in Kumdis Bay as forty years ago. Headquarters for the company this time, however, are not at the lake, but in the old Bert Tingley Hotel which lies down the hill from Alice McCrea's post office.

---

(1) *Anglicized version of Indian name Watun*
(2) *Baxter Pole Company operated first at Ferguson Bay, then in
Mayer Lake and lastly on Kumdis Island — using the same type
of road in each place. (See Chapter 46)*

CHAPTER TWENTY-EIGHT

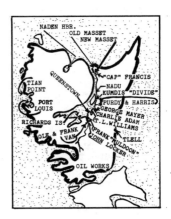

A PIONEER TAKES A WIFE

The usually cocky T. L. Williams had a terrific case of butterflies in his stomach which was becoming more turbulent by the moment – in fact the whole trip down from Masset in James Martin's *Kathleen* had been an agony of increasing apprehension.

It was April 18th, 1910 and by his side sat his bride of a few weeks – the former Meta Taylor who had come from Swansea to Vancouver to marry him – despite all the advice and pleading from her family to "just wait a little bit longer." She felt that she had waited long enough and, now that her beloved had found the one place he could be happy in, it was ridiculous to wait any longer. They had the same background and if he liked it she knew she would.

Holding her hand tightly, the young bridegroom remembered his moment of utter panic when he had received her letter the previous November to say that she was coming out to marry him and join in the pioneering of a new land. He thought of how his newly completed cabin, which shortly before had been his pride and joy. It became a rude, rough shelter as he tried to see it through the eyes of the daughter of a prosperous chartered accountant living in the city of Swansea. He recalled his frenzied papering, enlarging and so on, to try to make the place more adequate in some way. Then those difficult letters to Meta and her father – trying to be honestly realistic about life in the wilderness.

Samuel Taylor shared his prospective son-in-law's apprehension completely – in fact topped it – for he had even more anxiety about the wisdom of his daughter's decision. All he knew about far-off Canada was that it was populated by wild – very wild according to some stories – Indians, a few renegade Frenchmen, and that brash Williams boy with the itchy feet, who used to be around the Taylor home so much in earlier years. "Life in a primitive log cabin. . .Meta, why you haven't even a remote idea of what it will be like. At least wait until he is more established financially ... until the country builds up a bit more and is somewhat civilized," he pleaded with her. But the diminutive Meta was adamant and all entreaties fell on deaf ears. "Trevor is there," she would reply and it was the end of any discussion.

173

Now as the little launch chugged its way up the long Masset Sound, she sat quietly, realizing that she was nearing the end of her long journey — and had burned a lot of bridges behind her. Canada was so vast, so huge, so tremendous. Those Rockies! She had never visualized anything of such stature. There was nothing like them in Wales to have prepared her. And that strange boat they had come over from Prince Rupert to Masset in, the *Henriette,* which everyone called "the old Hen" with her colorful skipper Captain Buckholtz. To Meta it was as though she were living a scene from an adventure book, interesting and exciting, but at the same time unreal. Only the down-to-earth company of Mrs. James Martin and her six children going to join Mr. Martin in Masset for the first time, had reassured her that normal people and normal things did indeed occur at what seemed like the end of the earth.

If she had any doubts as to this, that wonderful reception by such kind and understanding strangers when the boat docked in Masset dispelled every vestige of fears. It had been overwhelming. She felt at home with the people immediately and knew she had made the right decision.

"We're rounding the point of Kumdis Island now," Trevor told her, and then, "That's it. . ." he began anxiously, but she knew without being told. It looked exactly like the picture he had sent. As the dingy made innumerable trips to the launch to unload the many items she had brought to set up housekeeping, the city-bred bride took a long look at her isolated log home in its wilderness setting — and loved it. So now there were two women on Masset Inlet, Mrs. Bert Millard and the new Mrs. T. L. Williams.

The Bert Millards had moved over from Queenstown to their pre-emption on the point, west of the Narrows, and having built a large log house there, were operating their hotel from this new site. It was when Mrs. Millard came over to meet the new arrival that the Williams learned of Mr. Purdy's death.

Purdy, Rice and Harris were living in retirement in Nova Scotia when they read the B.C. Government pamphlets about the, "acres and acres of virgin land waiting for the plough on Graham Island" and, urged on by the young Rice boy and his chum Ridge Purdy, the older men had thought it might be a good idea to go out there and stake homesteads on some of that fine land. They could work the land and then turn it all over to the boys when they came of age — to give the lads a good start in life.

They came to B.C., going first of all to the Land Office in Victoria to pick out their sites, "Masset Inlet is the place," they were told, and were shown a likely site about a half mile inland — just beyond the timber limits on Kumdis Slough. But when they came up on the boat to Skidegate and saw the rain, it looked so depressing the Rices wanted no part of it. They left immediately on the same boat to return to civilization.

For young Ridge Purdy, there was so much excitement and adventure in the air, he could hardly take it all in. It was wonderful! No small part of this was engendered by his first sight of "Mexican" Tom Hodges on the wharf. Standing just under six feet, a well-built man with a stetson hat, similar to the ones worn by the R.C.M.P., and long black shoulder length hair, Tom was one of the most legendary men to have come to the Islands. It was a matter of minutes before Ridge fell under his spell. The feeling of friendship was mutual.

"Come on up to my ranch with me, boy," he said to the lad. The words were

174

music in Ridge's ears. As the main purpose in coming to the Charlottes was to get Ridge established on a place of his own, Mr. Purdy was not keen on the idea. However, he did agree to let the boy ride up the coast with Tom to Tlell on one of Tom's horses. Mr. Purdy and Mr. Harris would go by boat with Johnnie Mathers to Tlell.

Leaving Mr. Mathers to take their effects around to Masset when weather permitted, Purdy, Harris and Ridge planned to hike across the "trail" to Masset Inlet. When the packs were being set up, Mexican Tom persuaded Mr. Purdy to give Ridge only a thirty-five pound one. The strapping lad was insulted — he could twirl that much with one finger. But Tom knew his man. By the time the party had crossed the stretch of muskeg, that thirty-five pound pack felt like two tons to those young unaccustomed muscles.

At Queenstown Bert Millard took them across the bay to see their land and after staking it out, the three went down to Masset to, "get acquainted." They learned that the Dow family, living on the west side of the Inlet, behind the island of Maast, were very anxious to sell out. A bargain was struck on the spot, making the newcomers the owners of a boat, cattle, chickens and dozens of jars of Mrs. Dow's preserves. Harris, who was an expert carpenter, built a good raft to take the purchases up to the pre-emption via Kumdis Slough.

At certain stages of the tide there is an enormous eddy near the Nadu and the Purdy party went too close. Round and round they went. Jim Langell saw their plight and with his two guests, John Locker and Fritz Rampmaer, came out to try to extricate them. By using the three boats this was finally accomplished — but they had missed the tide needed to get them over the Divide (1) with their raft. It was beached by Stud Tingley's and young Ridge was sent on ahead with the cattle to walk the shoreline to Purdy Creek eight miles south, leaving his father and uncle to come with the raft on the next high tide.

Up Purdy Creek at what they called the "Corners" Harris and Purdy built a huge house — big enough for all three to use in qualifying for their eventual pre-emptions. It had a large woodshed, workshop and big verandah to connect all the buildings so that one could go about freely, rain or shine. They had a magnificent stand of cedar on the property and could whipsaw lumber for floors, window and door frames. Uncle Harris introduced Ridge to the art of whipsawing.

"You're good and big," he told the boy, "I think you'd be all right on top." Ridge quickly found out that this was where the work was. The man in the pit simply had to guide the saw and try to keep the sawdust out of his eyes, whilst the man on top pulled it back and forth, using every muscle he had.

The house was soon built and they had a comfortable winter in it — then early in the spring Mr. Purdy became ill. With an omen of impending death, he called his son in one afternoon and told him gently, and then said, ". . .as soon as I go, I want you to go down to Masset. Tell Jim Martin and "Cap" Francis — they will know what to do." It was not long before the end came and, true to his promise, Ridge delivered the message to Martin and Francis who seemed to know what was behind it all. They told Ridge they would see to everything.

The boy returned to find his uncle building a coffin and Ridge was put to

(1) The shallow region midway along Kumdis Slough.

work digging the grave. It was a difficult job as a few feet down he ran into the hardpan which underlies the soil in that location, and had only just completed his sad task when everyone arrived for the funeral. Mr. Purdy was a Mason and his fellow lodge members, Martin and Francis, knew that he had greatly desired a Masonic funeral. So in 1910, in the centre of Graham Island, the first Q.C.I. Masonic funeral was held with full rites, conducted by James Martin and "Cap" Francis.

Ridge stayed on with his uncle to clear and improve the land, but it was lonely now without his father. George Mayer and Charlie Adam had promised to go up for a visit ". . . maybe tomorrow." As Ridge Purdy says, "Up there when anyone tells you he is coming the next day — it may mean next week, or even next month . . . but it seldom means tomorrow."

The two went out to work on their slashing as usual, when suddenly they heard a shot. "There's the boys — let's go Ridge," called Uncle Harris. Then there were more shots in quick succession, culminating in a regular fuselaide. "Something's wrong!" he shouted now. "Hurry! I think the house must be on fire . . . that's all our ammunition going off!" They sped up the trail only to find the whole house a mass of flames. Besides their fine house, six months supply of food and ammunition — everything they owned was lost in a matter of minutes.

This was the final straw for Mr. Harris. He made arrangements to leave, to seek a more peaceful retirement on the Hawaiian Islands. But Ridge stayed on. Jim Martin found the boy a job with Ed and Wes Singer packing for the survey outfits near Naden Harbor. He plunged into adulthood at seventeen, doing a man's work and getting a man's wages — $60 a month for ten hours of heavy packing every day, rain or shine.

On May 10th, 1910, three weeks after the newly-wed Williams had come home, they looked out to see the first ocean-going steamer to enter Masset Inlet, anchored off Ship Island. This was the *CGS Lillooet* which had been detailed to survey the uncharted waters of the region. The *Egeria* had previously surveyed and charted as far as Delkatla Slough, beyond which no large vessel would proceed.

Now "the *Lil*," sending her sounding launches before her, would be occupied for the next two or three months. Captain Musgrave her skipper — a fine old R.N. type, without any humor — came over to the Williams' cabin. He was going to set up a tide gauge on Richards Island, at the entrance to Juskatla, and wanted to know if Mr. Williams would look after it when the ship left. Musgrave was full of indignation at being sent into Masset Inlet, because he felt there was much more important work waiting for his ship outside. But political pressures from the timber and coal interests to open up the Inlet waters took priority.

It was with great reluctance that Mr. Williams agreed to look after the gauge, for it would be a tiresome chore to row there and back every five days — a seven mile row each way. There was, however, no one else available to take on the job, and the records would be of inestimable value to everyone in the region.

"On June 19th," he wrote in his diary, "two surveyors, Parker and Davis, from "the *Lil*" took me in their launch to the tide gauge. A brass plate, called a bench mark, had been set in the rock at lowest tide. All records were based on this mark, over which, above highest tide, was erected a contrivance, very clever, with a ball, which rose and fell with the tides, recording its movements on paper, with a clock, giving times. My job was to wind this every five days, remove the recorded papers and insert fresh rolls.

This last chore was often hard to accomplish, with strong head winds and rough sea. Once I had to hire a man to help me row over. Another time I would not have arrived in time if Martin's launch had not luckily arrived at the store and towed me over. Meta often went with me. And the trip we made on September 7th was memorable. We had sailed to Juskatla in the morning and going directly to the gauge set it for the next five days. We landed in a little cove back of Richards Island, in the deep water entrance, sheltered from the heavy seas outside, and after returning from the gauge to the boat, thought to avoid part of those rough seas by going round the back of Shannon Island to the other entrance, Canoe Pass. Tide was boiling out past us — impossible to row against. So we started to tow the boat through the deep entrance, Meta on top with the rope and me at the water's edge fending boat off the rocks. We were nearly through the worst part, when one of those powerful eddies swung boat out of my reach. We both grabbed the rope, which parted and off went the boat into the tide rips and out of sight. It was a terrible moment.

There we were on an island, with no food or water or coats — everything was in the boat. The Inlet was empty, no people nearer than the Yakoun, out of sight. We started at once for the Indian cabin on Canoe Pass, having a hard struggle through the salal brush which grew thickly to the water's high tide mark. Reached the cabin and wondered how to ever cross Canoe Pass. The current was too strong and water too deep to wade. Hunting around for a few logs to make a raft — or anything to float us over I found an old dugout canoe in the brush, with many large cracks. What luck! Using a piece of old board for a paddle we got across safely in a few minutes with the canoe full of water when we landed. We pulled that old life saver up to the woods with our grateful thanks for getting us off that island.

Then we started to walk to the Yakoun. In and out of bays, over stony beaches for three hours to the Cooper Johnny Point (1) — where to our unbelievable delight we saw Henry Edenshaw's schooner anchored in the Yakoun channel, waiting for the tide to be able to go up to the Indian village where he was delivering supplies for the crew clearing the river.

I might mention that my footwear for that never-to-be-forgotten walk were fishermens' ALL LEATHER HIP boots — about ten pounds apiece. Don't think they were ever worn again," added Mr. Williams as he recalled the episode many years later. "The pay for looking after that gauge was thirty dollars a month."

Subsequent tide-tables for those parts have been based on records resulting from this first gauge.

Pleased to have any excuse to cut down the amount of surveying in the Inlet, Captain Musgrove went only as far as the mouth of McLinton and Dinan Bays, using for his excuse the big rock at the entrance to the latter. The presence of the reef at the entrance to Juskatla Inlet provided his legitimate excuse to omit this big inlet also. The real purpose behind the survey was the proposed sawmill at the mouth of the Awun River by the Graham Steamship, Coal and

(1) Point on the west side of entrance to the Yakoun River.

177

Lumber Company, and he had covered the needed waterway for that.

Biting in T. L. Williams's time in addition to the tide-gauge, was the office of secretary-treasurer with the Masset Inlet Settlers' Association. In an effort to get backing for the requests to be sent to the government for much needed assistance, the pioneers had formed this organization in January of 1910. Mr. McIntosh, the ex-New Westminster Police Chief, was the chairman. Initially the organization had as its goal the curbing of indiscriminate granting of coal licences which, at that time, not only gave the holder the right to underground resources, but also gave surface control of hundreds of acres.

These licences, which interested speculators only, were a sore point with land seekers — now arriving in a steady stream. When coal rights were granted no one was allowed to pre-empt within their boundaries and, except for the drill at the Nadu, no legitimate prospecting was being done on any of the licences — yet they alienated land desired by settlers. In addition to attacking this problem, the Settlers' Association was pressing for roads and bridges. It was gratifying, therefore, to have a letter from Mr. Jennings in June of that year (1910) saying he would put gangs to work on trails to Mayer Lake, and at the Nadu and Woden Rivers.

A request had gone in for assistance to clear some of the log jams in the Yakoun River to help the handful of settlers there. The reply that came back staggered everyone.

Hon. William Templeton advised the Association that $10,000 had been appropriated for this work and an engineer, Mr. Trodden, would arrive in July to take charge. Pre-emptors up the Yakoun at that time were Geordie McQuaker, Frank Meldon, John Locker, Frank and Ole Van, Mr. Davis and Mr. and Mrs. Dave Crocker, who with Dave's brother, Bob, had dragged their canoe twelve miles up-river to build a cabin on the rich bottomland of the Yakoun Valley. Of these, only the Crockers, Mr. Davis and the two Vans would benefit from this unusually generous government help. It was almost beyond belief.

There was no one in Queenstown now. Even the Martin store was closed and the key left with the Williams in case anyone needed supplies. Eli, with no satisfaction about his pre-emption, was only keeping token residence to comply with regulations, but every spare moment saw him out on the west coast.

There was excitement about the oil drill which was working at Tian Point at this time so Eli, with his brother Bert and John Coates, went to Port Louis to do some prospecting. He built a cabin in one of the coves which was frequently used by the surveyors from the *Lillooet* who were charting out there, and Captain Musgrave invited Eli to supply names for some of the rivers and bays in the area.(1)

When the Tingleys went to the Port Louis area, Eli sold his big sailboat *Queen* to Charlie Adam and Geordie McQuaker who used it freighting supplies to earn some extra cash. The Tingleys bought another, the epic *Little Johnnie* (named for John Coates.)

In mid 1910 the only occupied cabin visible from Masset Inlet was that of the newly-wed Williams. However, there were many cabins out of sight in the region, for Kumdis Bay was ringed and there were from fifteen to twenty out at Mayer Lake, with several up Kumdis Slough and the Yakoun. But still only the two

(1) See Appendix 3.

178

women — Mrs. Bert Millard and Mrs. T. L. Williams.

When it became known that a baby was due in the Williams home, the solicitous neighbors all agreed with the prospective parents that no unnecessary chances should be taken and that they should go to live in Masset for the event that winter. Housing was at a premium in Masset at this time, so Mrs. Harrison took Meta and Trevor Williams in to stay with her until Jackie Williams howled his way into the world in January of 1911, to be taken home a few months later — the first white baby for Masset Inlet.

CHAPTER TWENTY-NINE

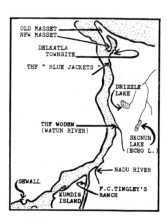

DELKATLA

Masset was growing steadily from the tent town of 1909 to a promising little community by 1911, when there came a challenge to the thriving town from an upstart across the slough. This was Charles Wilson's Delkatla.

Wilson had been in the real estate business in Prince Rupert when land on Graham Island began to look like the pot of gold. He lost not one moment in getting there, and when he was able to buy out Cap Francis he went into the townsiting business. Always a believer in the power of the press, Wilson used it to full advantage from the beginning. In March, 1911, the *Prince Rupert Optimist* ran his advertisement in bold type.

"ONE OF MY ACRES NEAR MASSET WILL MAKE YOU A FORTUNE. THE ONLY COURAGE WORTH ANYTHING TODAY IS MONEY COURAGE. SEE CHARLES WILSON, ROOM 14, IN THE ALDER BLOCK IN PRINCE RUPERT."

Absentee ownership was not for a man as energetic as Mr. Wilson. He had a home built on his proposed townsite — almost directly across the Slough from Charles Harrison's fine new Masset home and taking his wife and daughter to live there, set about promoting and developing his town with typical gusto.

"Delkatla is the LIVE WIRE of Graham Island," flashed out his advertisements. And, "Masset Inlet will see many fine towns in a few years, but the GOLDEN KEY to them all will be Delkatla. The rush will soon be on us. For just as soon as the G.T.P. railroad is through to Prince Rupert, the people will be swarming in on us from the zero blizzard region, the sun stroke and tornado belts, in huge numbers. You won't be able to get lots on Main Street in Delkatla for $100 much longer."

For a change of pace, he urged all pre-emptors to buy one of his lots for their "town house" — this idea did attract many customers. T. L. Williams bought one from him as did C. S. "Sid" Wormald. (1) Sid was on his way to his Kumdis Slough pre-emption that first year and took Charles Wilson's suggestion. Although

---

(1) Now living in retirement in Victoria.

Mr. Wormald changed his mind and built his "town house" in Charlie Adam's Centre, he still owns his Delkatla property.

Both Nigel Sherwood and Roscoe Rupe built homes in Delkatla as did Harry Lamb, who used this residence for his "town house" when not proving up on his pre-emption behind the Blue Jackets. When Woody Prosser came in 1912 to stake a pre-emption behind Delkatla he built a house to the west of Roscoe Rupe. Here he left his wife, Annie, and their five children as he went out each week to prove up on his land in behind the settlement. A favorite visitor to the Prosser home was Perce Downey, a kindly man, who had his pre-emption next to Mr. Prosser's. When another Prosser family, Mr. and Mrs. Arthur Prosser, came to live in Masset, Woody and Arthur were surprised to learn that they were related — although they had lost touch with each other for years.

Woody's eldest son, Ivan, was twelve when the family first came to Delkatla in 1912 and has many memories of those early years — one of the most vivid was the time he helped Mr. Rupe to put the goats on an island west of Masset, an island which to this day is often referred to as Goat Island locally. Ivan's sister, Pearl, now Mrs. Monahan of Burnaby says she remembers the daily boat trips across the slough to go to school in Masset — as Charles Wilson kept prodding the government to put in a bridge between the two townsites. By the time Clement Carter came with his wife and daughter, Ruth, Wilson was waging an intensive campaign to get this badly-needed bridge to his growing townsite.

In August of 1913 his efforts were rewarded and a bridge was built across the Delkatla Slough connecting the foot of Collison Avenue in Masset to the foot of Wilson Street in Delkatla. Fred Nash had been hard at work laying out the streets and lots for Wilson and, in April of 1913, Delkatla became a registered townsite. For a bonus Wilson announced that in selecting its customary quarter portion of the townsite lots, the government had agreed to donate one of them for the proposed Delkatla Town Hall.

Never one to rest on his laurels, Mr. Wilson had in mind an even more ambitious scheme. This was to dyke a large portion of the Slough and reclaim land covered by tide flats. A great deal of time and money was expended on this dyking project. Then a raging storm came at the peak of a very high tide and washed the whole thing out in a matter of hours.

Delkatla continued to grow. Frank Millard bought the little building which was used for Masset's first school, moved it to Delkatla and set up a butcher shop. He owned few cattle himself, but with the wild herd running on the North Beach who needed a private herd? If there was a cow within shooting range, it was said, Millards had fresh meat.

Albert Goulet, retired from the prospecting and land locating, opened a store which he called the Delkatla Cash Store and promised, "A trial order will convince you. On Parle Francais Ici." Harry Lamb ran his advertisement in the local Masset paper to let people know, "Boot repairing done while you wait Harnesses, holsters, saddles etc. neatly repaired. Open every Thursday and Friday at the log cabin in Delkatla."

James Blades says he was working at the old Vancouver Hotel as a tool sharpener in 1911 when the Star Realty, who promoted the town of Sewall, opened an office on Hastings Street. Their offer of 40-acre tracts for $15 an acre sounded good to Mr. Blades, so he made a down payment. In August of 1912 he went to see what he was buying. It didn't appeal to him. He abandoned that idea, and filed instead on a pre-emption in the Drizzle Lake region, inland north of the Woden River.

Taking Charles Wilson's suggestion about the "town house", Jim Blades bought two lots in Delkatla, built a comfortable cabin on one of them and sent for Mrs. Blades. Tragedy struck this little family a short time later when their adored baby, Grace, died suddenly. But in 1913, with the birth of their second baby, Margaret, they found new happiness in the pioneering village of Delkatla.

"It was a very pleasant life, indeed," recalls Mr. Blades today, "lots of work in the survey gangs, and in the winter when all the men were home, there was a great deal of visiting and dancing." Mr. Blades played the accordian well and was always in demand. When war broke out he tried to enlist, but was turned down so he came back to the pre-emption until 1916. With many of those they had known now gone things weren't the same, and in 1916 Mr. and Mrs. Blades left the Islands to settle permanently in Alberta.

It was the spring of 1913 when Jesse Bridden returned from a trip to England bringing with him his beautiful bride. "One of the loveliest," remembers Mr. Blades who knew them well. The Briddens lived on their pre-emption at the Blue Jackets, beside Mr. and Mrs. Allan Jessup for a short time. When they learned that there was an heir on the way, Mr. Bridden rushed down to build a house in Delkatla for his family. Mrs. Bridden still smiles at her young husband's panic. "It was months before our baby was due . . . but my husband was taking no chances at all that we would be on the pre-emption when things began to happen," she says fondly.

The Briddens were one of the best known of the pioneer Delkatla families and lived there for many years to bring up their six children. The eldest, Eli, was the first baby to be baptised in the Masset area by a Roman Catholic priest. Father McDonald of the Woden River conducted the baptisimal service on May 9, 1914 in the Masset schoolhouse when he christened Eli Charles Bridden. The second son of Mr. and Mrs. Bridden, Bernie, who was born in 1916, built Masset's first Catholic Church in 1938, with Cyril Harrison (1) to assist him.

Mr. Jesse Bridden was one of the most conscientious road foremen that the government ever employed on the Islands. When a road to Tow Hill was being planned, it was his suggestion to use planks laid end to end on stringers in the sand — and to be sure that the whole operation in this experiment was done exactly as he felt it should, he nailed every spike that went into them. After this epic feat, he had huge calluses running the full length of the palm of his hand.

His idea for an economical, yet practical, road along the North Beach timber line was so successful that a few years later when a road across the muskeg to Tlell from Port Clements was put through, Mr. Bridden's plans were adapted for use there.

The little town of Delkatla has maintained a steady population. Its wonderfully fertile soil produces many fine gardens. The old wooden bridge, rebuilt several times, has now been succeeded by a gravelled causeway and the townsite of Delkatla itself has been incorporated as a part of the Village of Masset — to better serve both communities with services they can both share and not duplicate.

(1) Charles Harrison's younger son.

All the pre-emptions behind Delkatla have been abandoned for many years and most of the cabins built on them so long ago have returned again to the soil. But there was an exceptionally fine one which was a source of admiration for all who saw it. This was about four miles in from the Blue Jackets and was built entirely of whip-sawn yellow cedar timbers. Those heroes had somehow packed the heavy logs to their pit, then painstakingly whip-sawed each of them by hand — and left a huge pile of yellow cedar shavings and sawdust as mute testimony to the undertaking.

CHAPTER THIRTY

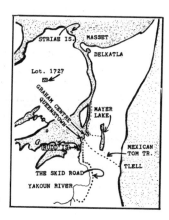

INCOMERS

Across from Delkatla on the west side of Masset Sound, land seekers were flocking in with a similar zeal and passion for a "place of their own." A winding trail led in six to eight miles at one place and cabins were dotted all along it. One of these cabins had a four hundred pound iron range in it, six miles from the beach, proof of the serious intent of that pre-emptor.

Not only pre-emptors acquired land. As soon as the surveys were made, some private purchasers bought directly from the government as was the case of barrister Eli Harrison of Victoria. In 1912 he bought and was Crown Granted, lot 1727. Almost in the centre of the peninsula lying between Masset Sound and Naden Harbor, it cost him $1605, and contained 642 acres of inaccessibility. Two months later he sold the northwest quarter section for $640 to brother barrister Victor B. Harrison of Nanaimo. This piece of property did not revert to the government until 1925 when it became part of the Soldier's Homestead Land — which meant that some returned man could buy this extremely isolated hunk of land on, "easy terms and conditions." There were no takers.

Land speculators were interested in this west side region too, and one of the most vigorous was Mr. McIntosh, the chairman of the Settlers Association. He and G. W. Cramer, another speculator, brought in teams of horses and equipment to improve their holdings in 1914 and boost sales. J. C. A. Long, B.C.L.S., who had done most of the surveying in that region, bought land behind Striae Island. He named this fertile spot, (once an ancient Haida encampment) West Side Ranch, and built a large frame home there. On August 8, 1914, Mrs. Long gave birth to their son at the ranch and Jimmy Campbell ran an announcement of the event in his *Queen Charlotte Islander.*

To return to 1911; the aggressive Masset Inlet Settlers Association was short-lived. When the second meeting was held to elect officers, it was not well attended owing to inclement weather — a major factor in travel in those early days. As a result the officers elected were too representative of the unpopular coal and timber interests. A very stormy meeting followed and resulted in the whole thing being dissolved, but several good things came from its brief existence. The Government, in response to the repeated urgings, agreed not to issue any more coal licences on the east side of Masset Inlet. From then on, also, coal people could use only as much of the surface as was required for their operation – and not tie up 640 acres as before. Survey fees for pre-emptors to the government were to be reduced from 50¢ to 25¢ per acre.

One of the first "pre-emption jumping" incidents took place early in 1911 when Ed O'Brian took over Arthur Robertson's Kumdis River site. Mr. Robertson, far more interested in prospecting than in becoming a settler, had neglected to put in the required amount of residence on his location. With waterfront land at a premium, O'Brian filed claim for the land, stating that Robertson was not fulfilling the pre-emption requirements. He was granted the site and Robertson's application was cancelled. O'Brian soon had the same "pre-emption jump" tried on him.

When Sid Wormald (1) came in 1911, with him were Albert Clark and Bob Currie. They came on a scouting trip and Wormald found a free site next to the Purdy place so he filed on it. Mr. Clark could find nothing available that appealed to him, but Bob Currie liked O'Brian's Kumdis River site – and believing that O'Brian was not living up to the pre-emption requirements – he tried, unsuccessfully, to take it over. Ed O'Brian lost no time in moving up from Masset to this suddenly popular river site, built a cabin, and sent for his wife to join him there – he was taking no chances after that.

In May of 1911, it became apparent why the government had appropriated $10,000 to clear the Yakoun River the summer before. Generosity to settlers be hanged! The parties who were interested in the coal licences up the Yakoun had arrived and went back and forth frequently with gangs of men and a gas boat. They bought most of the machinery from the old Nadu drill (2) and took it up the Yakoun. On September 8th, Mr. F. C. Wright and his wife arrived. He was the manager for the prospecting company.

It was announced that they were going to build a thirty-mile road overland into the Yakoun Valley.

There was a great deal of activity around the previously abandoned Queenstown now. Mr. and Mrs. Wright took up residence in the big log cabin on the point and a Mr. and Mrs. Danbrier moved in with them. The Martin store was taken over by the company and run by the English timekeeper, Mr. Kerr, who kept a small stock of goods there. Mr. Green, the superintendent, set up camp by Eli Tingley's first cabin which was now used as a bunkhouse. A gang of men were making sleds on the beach to transport the machinery on the overland road to begin test drilling for coal in the Wilson Creek region of the Yakoun.

Launches were coming and going across the Inlet daily, and on October 24th, 1911 the first big ocean-going steamer (after the CGS survey ship *Lillooet*) brought in a load of machinery and supplies for the coal company and stayed four days unloading it onto scows in front of Queenstown. This was the Northern Steamship's freighter *British Empire*.

On November 4th, the sleds were finished and loaded to start down the fabulous Skid Road, a name usually synonymous with degradation and lack of

(1) Chapter 29
(2) Chapter 27

186

drive, but in this case it represented a Herculean effort. It was proposed to move 83 tons of equipment on sleds through trees and over muskeg, uphill and down dale for thirty miles into the heart of the Yakoun Valley. The word "road" was purely a courtesy title.

The train consisted of four sleds, each constructed of two logs, four feet in diameter and sixty feet long, with the necessary cross pieces and fastenings. The first sled contained the "muscular," a 74 H.P. logging donkey with three or more cable drums. An impressive machine. The second sled was the bunkhouse, followed by the third and fourth with cookhouse and fuel sheds. Supplies to keep this train functioning were transported by river boat up the Yakoun (subject to water conditions) and the balance on the backs of packers. (1)

Harry Scott was foreman. John Locker remembered him well. "I ought to," he said "I guess I packed supplies into him for almost every step of the way." John had left his native Austria at an early age to go to sea. A letter from his brother, Louis, who had found work in the Louisiana oil-fields around the turn of the century, caused him to change his mind and go there instead. He met and worked with Bill White as well as with his brother Louis, and in later years met Bill White again at the Oeanda, when Bill went there to live with Jimmy.

Louis and John worked in the oil-fields for four or five years until the big 1906 San Francisco earthquake and fire offered a bonanza in high wages for labor. Then attracted to Canada, and the Charlottes in particular, Louis, John and another friend, Fritz Rampmaer, came up. Louis remained in the Prince Rupert area, but in 1909 Fritz and John went to the Islands and became permanent residents. Hardly had they arrived, however, when John learned that he had acquired a heritage from his sojourn in Louisiana — malaria — which plagued him for years.

The influx of people to the head of Masset Inlet in the fall of 1911, in connection with the coal interest, brought to the fore the real need for an established town in the region. Hearing that T. L. Williams had obtained his Crown Grant, although he was forbidden to touch any timber on the twenty acres covered by the Timber Licence, Eli Tingley now went after his own Crown Grant in earnest and succeeded in getting it in 1912. He was still faced with that frustrating Timber Licence covering his proposed townsite.

When the Martin store shut down in Queenstown, Charlie Adam, in partnership with Geordie McQuaker, built and was running a store on the west side of Charlie's pre-emption, near to the Williams' cabin. And when Eli had been refused a post office for his Queenstown, Mr. Adam, supported by a local petition in 1911, applied for a post office.

"Got any good ideas for a name for the place?" he asked the Williams.

"Well it's almost in the centre of Graham Island," said T. L., "what about Graham Centre?" And so it was named. On May 5th, 1912, Charlie Adam received a letter from Ottawa appointing him Post Master for this first Masset Inlet post office, and Geordie McQuaker was appointed to carry the mails from Masset at $200 per annum — weekly trips of 30 miles each way. This gave him $3.85 for a round trip of sixty miles in all weathers.

The store in Graham Centre was doing so well the two Scots began building

---

(1) *More about this road in Chapter 36.*

a larger two-story building to expand their business. This second structure was 20 by 30 feet, built of squared logs with carefully dovetailed corners — a masterpiece of the woodsman's art. The two Swedes, Ole Anderson and Alec Johnson of the Nadu, were the craftsmen — but many volunteers helped in hauling, by hand, those long logs out of the woods and putting them up. Mr. Williams had been commissioned in January 1912 as a Notary Public and Commissioner for taking affidavits. This was a boon to many, who otherwise had to go all the way to Masset to Charles Harrison, the only other official on the north end of the Islands.

Using the rough Skid Road and another survey trail, known locally as the Centre Meridian, the vanguard of settlers had gone inland south of Queenstown. Among them were the well-known Mr. and Mrs. Fred Chapman with their young family; Dave Tuft, the beloved philosopher; D. E. "Maxie" Maxwell; Harry Ross; Bill Spiers; William Mesner, who set to and cleared four acres as well as building a good cabin; and G. Daniels and D. Merrans who each had two places proved up on by 1914. Eastward along the Mexican Tom Trail were Partridge, Dodgson and others.

Available sites along the Yakoun were being taken with James Martin and Geordie McQuaker on the east side of the Yakoun entrance, although they used their lots spasmodically they did both build houses on the sites. Next to Geordie was Frank Meldon, then John Locker, and Bryon Inions of Chilliwack adjoined Mr. Locker. On the opposite side of the river, just above John Locker, Mr. Davis had his family on a pre-emption. Frank and Ole Van were farther upriver on the south side of the Indian Reserve (No. 4), with the three Crockers twelve miles upstream. The Crockers had come from Alaska, where Mrs. Dave Crocker had taken part in most phases of the gold rush, from driving her own dog team to running a roadhouse, and Dave always like to say that he had actually won her in a card game. If you believed it, they let you. A woman of tremendous energy, she would hear of a dance in Queenstown, walk along the 12-mile trail, dance all night — and how she could dance, remembers Bert Tingley, — then after the dance, would put on her boots to walk home the next day, and think nothing of it.

It was in 1911 that the big island just inside the mouth of the Yakoun River, caught the interest of red-headed Quaker, Bob Rudd. Mr. Rudd had been on a trip to Vancouver, from his home in Lethbridge, when he heard about Graham Island and went there. He was so impressed that he pre-empted the island which still bears his name and sent for his wife and their two younger daughters, Hilda and Mary.

"He was so enthusiastic about it all," says his son Jack, "that I quit my job to go up and help him. They were all living in Masset when I got there, but Dad was itching to get up onto his island. So Ralph Stafford, Harvey Lamb and I all went up to help him build a cabin. The soil was very fertile and we soon had a good garden in." The coal rush was just beginning, so there were few days when the Rudds didn't have visitors on their way up the river. They fully intended to make it their permanent home — leaving only long enough to go out and earn necessary cash once in awhile.

The 1914 war changed their plans. Jack Rudd enlisted early in 1915 with James McLay and Jim Allison, his good friends from Mayer Lake. Bob Rudd joined the Artillery in 1916. The two Jims lost their lives overseas and when the

Rudds came back to take up life once more, the Charlottes were not the same for young Jack with so many of his friends gone; however, the Islands still held an irresistible pull for his father. Upon his return, Mr. Rudd, senior, went to work in the big Buckley Bay mill and bringing his wife with him, made his home in Buckley until he was killed by a line thrown from a steamer coming in to tie up. Mrs. Rudd moved to Port Clements near her daughter, Hilda, who had married and was making her home there. Mrs. Rudd was a fine old lady and one of Port Clements' most devout Roman Catholics. She did not, as was usual with that faith, insist on her children following her beliefs, but left them to make up their own minds. She accomplished this and still kept in good standing with her priest.

Jack Rudd did not come back to the Islands to live, but has come back repeatedly for visits, "they have always held a fascination for me," he says, "as some of the best years of my life were spent there."

CHAPTER THIRTY-ONE

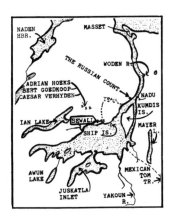

THE STORY OF SEWALL

With all the activity coming into Masset Inlet and with Eli Tingley's townsite plan paralysed by the refusal of the timber company to come to terms, it was inevitable that other locations would begin to vie for the honor of being the "town" on the Inlet.

The story of Sewall begins in January of 1910 when the Graham Island Settlement Company was incorporated with a capital of $50,000. They bought a large tract of land in the Ship Island region, on the northwest side of Masset Inlet, at the government price of $2.50 an acre, had it surveyed and laid out into "farms" of 40, 80, 160, 320 and 640 acres, which they planned to resell at $15 an acre. To handle this the Star Realty Company was formed, and its officials, Mr. J. Maben, Nicholas Monjo, William Fuller and Samuel Dart Sewall, opened an office in the Dominion Trust Building on Hastings Street in Vancouver in 1911.

But it was James McCrea of Winnipeg, Dart Sewall's old home town, who promoted the first attempt to settle this site. In the spring of 1911 he brought a group of Icelandic people from Winnipeg to form a colony at Sewall. Mrs. Snidal of Prince Rupert was one of this group. She and her husband brought their year-and-a-half old son, Sam, and began to build a cabin on the plot of land they selected.

However, the prospects of earning a living looked slim so they left to go fishing at North Island in the summer and went to live in Skidegate that fall. But Masset Inlet drew them too strongly. After the sailboat they hired brought them from Skidegate to Tlell, the three Snidals hiked across the Mexican Tom trail to take up residence in Eli's proposed townsite. "What a trip it was," recalls Mrs. Snidal, "my husband carried Sammy on his shoulders and I carried just what we might need on the trail. Up one hill, and down, then another, and another — I thought it would never ever end. Some places we had to wade creeks up to our waist. Then at the other side we finally came to Mr. Tingley's little cabin . . . it just looked like heaven!"

The Snidals built a home, which later became the well-known Dyson place, at

191

the east end of Port Clements (Queenstown at that time) and lived there for several years during which time another son, Edgar, and a daughter, Gina, were born.

Although the Icelandic colony at Sewall was of brief existence, the challenging and candid advertisements of the Star Realty for ". . . people who are willing to put their shoulder to the wheel and not expect to find ready-made farms . . ." aroused interest in other colonization schemes.

The first of these was by the Seventh Day Adventist whose leader, Rev. Tom Watson, came to locate a site for his group to set up a self-sufficient agricultural community. The gently sloping land at Sewall which faced southward and had an abundance of good timber looked like the perfect location. A mill could be easily established which would not only be able to cut the lumber they needed for their own buildings but would leave plenty to sell locally for needed cash.

The Star Realty promoters were delighted at the prospect of having an industry established to boost the attractiveness of their land on the real estate market and co-operated fully with the leaders of the group in getting the mill in operation (and peddling all the land the traffic would bear to the prospective mill-workers). With George Crane of Vancouver in charge, the first little Sewall mill was built with great speed and on December 12, 1912, the first lumber cant was manufactured and presented to Magistrate Charles Harrison of New Masset, with appropriate ceremony.

About this time Archbishop McNeil of the Roman Catholic Church in Vancouver sent up scouts to enquire about making a colony for his church's adherents in the, by now, widely advertised farm lands on Graham Island. It was Father J. B. McDonald who came to Sewall on behalf of his superior. He stayed at Sewall long enough to open and run a post office — then like the leader of the Adventists' group, he decided that he preferred Woden River. So both religious groups made their headquarters at the mouth of the Woden River — although the Adventists' mill continued to operate for a few more years at Sewall.

By the end of 1912 land near Sewall was being sold in fairly large acreages and people were going as much as six or more miles inland for their sites. In the Ian Lake region L. K. Ruddick settled six miles inland and Caesar Verhyden built a cabin on his 160 acres and had to cut a three mile trail to reach it. The two Hollanders, Adrian Hoeks and Bert Goedkoop also settled near there. They had come to Canada to work for Ignace Van der Bom in his New Westminster nursery and when he was unable to pay their wages, he gave them, in lieu, the deed to land he had previously bought from the Star Realty. They discovered that Mr. Hoeks' land was four miles inland and Goedkoops adjoined it. The two friends built a joint cabin on Mr. Hoeks' land, then decided to put up another cabin on the edge of a small lake nearby.

They were putting the finishing touches to this cabin when they heard a faint calling far back in the woods. Mr. Goedkoop fired his gun to guide the traveller, and says they were amazed to see one of the officials of the Star Realty stagger out a short time later. He had been lost in the woods for several hours and in his panic had thrown away both compass and gun. It was sheer chance which led him to that spot in the late evening. In his exhausted and frenzied condition it might not have gone well with him had he spent a night in the woods.

The Star Realty partners had come to investigate the feasibility of developing

192

a townsite, to boost land sales, and had chosen a little bay to the west of Ship Island. Late in 1912, Fred Nash was engaged to plan the townsite for "Star City." However, by the time the plan was ready for registration in April of 1913, it had been unanimously agreed to name the new town after the popular member of the Star Realty company, Samuel Dart *Sewall*. (1)

Every town must have a "hotel" so one of the first structures to go up on the new townsite was "Hotel de Bum" — a log cabin which sheltered many a wayfarer. The little town of Sewall went ahead by leaps and bounds — as did the surrounding area. A seven mile trail leading north four miles from Sewall, then east three miles and emerging near the present Blinker site was lined with cabins. Among the settlers on this trail was the well-known Beebe family with their many boys and one daughter, Mrs. Serl, and their wonderful Grandfather Beebe. The Serls lived at Sewall until 1919 and their two youngsters loved the free and easy life. Mr. and Mrs. Sewall and William Fuller had homes there, but the first woman resident may have been Mrs. Jim Hogarth, who with her husband, was there before 1912. Another Sewall arrival, Count de Catilineaux, had a wife who "was very proud and didn't speak to the other settlers," (as proof of her nobility, the Count told Paul Bastian.) The Count bought four acres at Sewall in 1912 and built a cabin for his wife and baby.

With a post office officially opened and a much needed wharf built at the mill, James Martin thought things looked prosperous enough to open another branch store — and put Bert Goedkoop in charge. When in August of 1913 the large Donroe family moved onto one of the acreages behind Sewall, it looked as though even a school might be a possibility. Not only was Mr. Donroe a licenced teacher, but he had enough children in his own family to warrant requesting the government to establish a school at Sewall. The rejoicing was short-lived. Within a month Donroe decided he wanted no part in Sewall's development and engaged Charlie Adam to move his brood over to Kumdis Bay.

The idea of those children going into the woods with no shelter of any sort was appalling to Charlie, so he offered the Donroes the use of his original Kumdis Narrows cabin. It was a tight squeeze for a family of twelve, but it was a roof. With the notion of going into the townsiting business himself, Mr. Adam thought it would be a good idea to establish a liason with this bonafide teacher, who came complete with a ready-made class in his own family. An arrangement might be worked out that would benefit everyone.

But the irascible Frank Lennie Le Tonturier Donroe had no desire to help anyone but himself. He used Charlie's cabin and hospitality freely as he set about acquiring land by pre-emption farther up in Kumdis Bay and sent his elder sons to build a cabin (the eldest was barely eighteen at the time). With the required number of children in his family and being the only licenced teacher available, the wily Donroe sought, and obtained, a government stipend to hold classes in his own home and taught only his own children. It was a unique situation.

By the end of 1913 seventy families had settled at Sewall. On the Donroe location was the Stockford family — and immediately Mrs. Stockford set about planting a garden. The gooseberry and white currant bushes she planted in those early years were used by others for many, many years. It was typical of

(1) Current maps (1966) show this townsite incorrectly spelled as Sewell.

Mrs. Stockford that she also grew a few flowers to brighten her home. In an old Royal Yeast box, on a stump, this little pioneer planted forget-me-nots. As the years passed the little box fell apart and the seeds spread. Today in every wet spot in Sewall the blue forget-me-nots grow — a legacy from Mrs. Stockford.

In 1914 two men brought brides to share the new life. First to arrive was Mrs. Bert Goedkoop, and Bert brought her straight from Holland. Their little girl, Bertha, was the first baby born in Sewall. Also in 1914 a man, whose name seems almost to mean the town of Sewall, Paul Bastian, brought his bride out from Germany.

To give Mr. Bastian his correct title of Marquis de Bastian, is to bring to light that he comes from an old and distinguished family. The de Bastians were Hugenots who fled from France in 1692 to settle in the Rhine valley where the family estate has remained intact. Paul like so many of his contemporaries from Europe, yearned to see the world, and the best way was to go to sea. Few are the places open to shipping that young Paul did not visit during this period of his life — and he sailed on almost as many vessels. Perhaps the most memorable was the period on the Kaiser's yacht, *Hohenzollern*, when he was appointed a personal bodyguard to the Kaiser.

Then it was back to the roving sea life for this vigorous, handsome young man, until 1912 when he decided to, "come ashore." In Vancouver he met the partners of the Star Realty Company, bought shares, and came to see what his impulse had brought him. He liked it. In 1914 on a trip to Vancouver, he was about to buy his ticket back to the Islands, when he learned that the *Prince Albert* had been wrecked and it was uncertain when transportation to the Islands would be resumed. Wondering what to do next, he became intrigued by the travel posters, once again acted on impulse, and bought a ticket to Germany. To meet a very beautiful girl, as it turned out, who agreed to become his bride and come to the pioneering life of the Queen Charlotte Islands.

The newly-wed Paul Bastian had only recently returned to Sewall, when in a panic that there might be some official secrets that he could divulge about the isolated community of Sewall, he was stripped of his guns, and told not to leave Sewall — except once a month when he had to report to Charles Harrison in Masset, and give an account of his actions. The officials couldn't realize that Sewall was the one place in the world that Bastian wanted to be — and would stay for long, long after his internship was over. "But the loss of my guns really was a hardship," says Mr. Bastian, "for it meant that I couldn't hunt, and had to depend on the goodness of my neighbors for meat on many occasions."

When the outbreak of the 1914 war brought a cessation to all development, Eli Tingley bought the equipment of the Adventists' Mill at Sewall, and towed it on a raft to his townsite where he built what was later known as the Lewis Mill. When the big rush came for aeroplane spruce during the latter part of the war, another mill was established at Sewall by the Vancouver Trading Company. This little mill, under the competent supervision of Bill Aiken, then Bill Strip, and finally Mr. Foss, was credited with turning out the highest quality spruce lumber on the North American continent.

After the war, Sewall fell into a general decline and Mr. Bastian purchased most of the townsite, for which he obtained a Crown Grant. Julius Grewe came to live there too. He had come to the Islands in 1912, but as a single man did not settle in any spot for long — until he met and married the shy young girl, Hilde, who had come from Germany in the nineteen-twenties to help in the care of the two Bastian children, Frieda and Paul. For many years the Bastians and the Grewes constituted the sole population of this little townsite. The vegetables they grew were the envy of everyone.

In later years Paul Bastian, junior, left Sewall to marry and make his home on the lower mainland. His parents retired from farming and logging their land in this sunny place, to live among friends in New Masset. Willie, the only son of Julius and Hilde Grewe, opened a repair shop in Masset. His parents loved Sewall too much to leave until the marvelous Julius, actively farming until his 90th year, in 1965, was felled by a stroke and, much against his will went into a chronic care home in Vancouver.

Frieda Bastian, who was born and brought up in the lovely quiet place — where every spring hundreds of geese come and sit tamely, whilst dogs, children and cattle move freely among them — married a man who shares her love for this life. He is Stanley Unsworth, who like most resident Islanders, has seen much of the world, but says he likes the unique Island way of life best of all. In Sewall, the Unsworths have built their home and are raising their own three youngsters, David, Elaine and Betty to have the same appreciation of their natural surroundings and heritage. It is a sign of the changing times that whenever Stan goes on a business trip to the mainland, the plane drops him off at his own front door. Modern methods of travel and communication have dispelled the feeling of isolation that was so much a part of earlier days.

The Russian family who lived across the Inlet from the Nadu were frequent visitors to Sewall. The man, who was known only as "the Count", built his house there — ten feet by ten feet, and three stories high, one room to a story, with a tarpaulin on top for a roof. It was generally felt that it was the "tarp" which had dictated the unusual size of the house. When a cupboard was needed, the Count simply nailed a box on the outside. Two spruce trees were braced against the structure to keep it from falling, and additional guy wires were lashed around it after some gale winds gave him a few scares.

The Count had barely finished the house when their baby arrived — to be named Alphonse, which his father invariably pronounced as "Elephant". He had a government pension for shell-shock received during the war, and before coming to the Islands in 1928, had been a beekeeper in Michigan. Not much of a hunter, if he was unable to find a goose for the larder, the Count often shot a cormorant — and forever after these birds were known locally as Russian Geese. When it was cold, he wore his wife's coat, fur collar and all, with complete aplomb.

He was cruel to his wife and beat her severely whenever she failed to please his particular wishes — as a religious fanatic he had some peculiar ones. As for the baby — Mrs. Bastian says she will never forget the parents attempting to feed the two-month-old infant on salt herring. Whenever the Count picked up his son, he was as likely to be carried upside down as the right way — it made no difference. Paul Bastian recalls seeing the poor baby being carried wrong way up one day when the Count was going upstairs. When the infant Alphonse slipped from his father's arms, he bounced all the way down the steps on his head. The Count picked him up, brushed him off and continued on his way as though it were all routine. And somehow little Alphonse survived.

The child was about six years old when a letter came from the Count's former wife. She had finally learned his whereabouts and was demanding some of his pension to help support their two children. In a panic, the Count made haste to quit Graham Island. He loaded his family's few possessions onto a raft to catch the steamer at Masset. On the way the raft began to come apart — they were only just able to land at the wharf and take off their belongings before it separated completely. Not long after this the Count was committed to an asylum.

Perhaps the Count is best remembered for his cement boat. He bought an old double-ender, turned it over and applied ten sacks of cement to the outside. Scrounging empty milk cans from neighbors all up and down the Inlet he plugged the holes then placed them along the sides to provide air-space and then covered the whole thing with more cement. "He was so proud of his wonderful boat," recalls Francis Evans, whose parents ran the post office at the Nadu, "every time he came for mail he would tell us of what a fine boat he was building. When the great day came for launching, everyone was invited to bring their cameras and record the event. But the craft was so heavy it couldn't be turned over and for years it lay face down on the beach, an object of much curiosity, until the tides and weather finally disintegrated it."

CHAPTER THIRTY-TWO

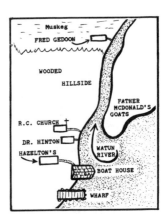

THE WODEN

Some call the place by its Indian name of Watun and others use the anglicized Woden — but when two church groups, the Seventh Day Adventists and Roman Catholics, made this site their headquarters in 1912 it acquired a third name — "the Holy City". Even the Anglican parson, William Hogan, found this spot so attractive he applied to pre-empt on the south bank of the river.

Father Hogan built his cabin there, but soon found his Mission at Masset was a full-time job and he was unable to live on his pre-emption as much as was required to hold it. Although it was cancelled as a result, his friends had taken up a collection and, when he died so unexpectedly, the money was presented to Mrs. Hogan, who bought the land outright in the summer of 1914 and held it for some years.

William Hogan's counterpart, Rev. J. B. McDonald, the energetic Catholic priest from Sewall, came down to the Woden late in 1912. By early March of 1913 he had a snug log cabin church built near the mouth of the river, on its north bank — the first Roman Catholic Church to be built on the Islands and the only one to ever have a resident priest.

Popular with everyone, regardless of their leanings, Father McDonald soon had a store and post office there and in 1914 managed to get a school going in the little community, persuading Mrs. A. R. Mallory, a staunch Presbyterian, to come from Queenstown to be its first teacher.

Mrs. Grange came to be the priest's housekeeper and her son took over the operation of the store in addition to running a launch, the *Rosemary*, back and forth to Masset on the many trips for supplies and to transport settlers. In all communities a hotel is needed to accommodate travellers, and the Haines opened one in Woden, offering, "Clean beds, Meals and a Bakery."

By the time Father McDonald arrived in the Woden, Rev. Tom Watson's group were already actively settling in this region and two men from this Adventist group, Roy and Don Hazelton, brothers who had married sisters, built a boatyard immediately south of the little wharf. Many excellent boats were built there. The first Anglican mission boat on the Island, the 22 foot *Ione* was built and launched with much ceremony from this Adventist boat shop in 1914.

In gradual stages, from 1911 to 1920, a wagon road was built inland towards the East Coast for two miles, with a good pack trail leading off the end of this for a considerable distance. Settlers cabins lines it all the way. People flocked to this area in the same steady stream as elsewhere, and it would be difficult to list the many families who came to make their homes there just prior to the 1914 war.

Among the well-remembered ones were Mr. and Mrs. Gedoon who lived beyond the rise of the first hill along the river. Fred Gedoon had brought his family from the prairies. He was a husky, popular man who was an accepted leader among the "backpackers" on the survey trails, and his son Rex was one of Woden's schoolchildren. Rose and Gordon Campbell had their pre-emption on the edge of Echo Lake, just back of Woden, they sent their two young boys to the little Woden school also.

In isolated areas it was always difficult to get enough children in one spot to qualify for a school, and Ruby Hazelton, (now Mrs. Adams of California) remembers her mother — Mrs. Don Hazelton, who took over the school from Mrs. Mallory — saying how delighted the community was when Dr. Hinton, his wife and five children moved into a cabin just below the Catholic church. Not only would Dr. Hinton's professional skill be a great asset to the region, but, what a boon those five children would be for the school.

Woden was well supplied with medical knowledge for a pioneering place, as this is where Jimmy Hoar made his first home. He was training to be an M.D. before he came to try the pioneering life. Julius Grewe, that grand old man of Sewall, (see Chapter 31) lived at the Woden for awhile when he first arrived on the Islands. He says that Fritz Rampmaer was ensconced on his pre-emption on the north bank of Woden River then. It was this land which Fritz pre-empted in 1911 that the Wallace Fisheries bought to begin building a cannery on in 1919. Fritz bought the old Frank Meldon place from John Locker (which John had purchased when Meldon left to live in the States in 1917), and moved up to ranch on the Yakoun.

"A Mr. Berg came to live at Woden for awhile, then changed his mind and took up land on the west side of the Inlet," recalled Mr. Grewe, who also remembered George Vaughn and his chicken ranch, Frank Patmore, William Hudson and Mr. Whitehall. Reese Dill and his family were there and also Lester Wren. Settler George Hewitt was known as the "Woden Philosopher", but he must have had a kindred spirit in his fellow pre-emptor, Arthur Hitt. Mr. Hitt was backfiring on his land when a spark fell on his cabin and burned it to the ground. "Oh, well. . ." he is supposed to have said, "at least it will save me from worrying about a fire burning me out this winter."

Roscoe Rupe of Delkatla staked a pre-emption at the Woden and in 1914 opened a blacksmith shop. Martin S. MacDougal known as "Black MacDougal" was there, as was the skilled carpenter, Henry Holland. Henry's son, Arthur (now living in Masset) went to school in Woden and says he remembers that Father McDonald's goats were the bane of the community. The day they got into Mrs. Andy McCrea's garden and created havoc was just too much — Mrs. McCrea took after them with a broom, telling the good Father later that she only wished she'd had a twenty-two handy. And the rest of the community secretly agreed with her feelings.

198

Ed Moe had a pre-emption on the edge of the muskeg, but in 1914 he moved his family to live in the Woden settlement and opened a shoe repair shop. The Moes had three little girls, Ethel, Bessie and Alice. Some years after Mr. Moe died, his widow married the well-known Ole Ormbrak and two more children arrived — Harold and Esther.

As the years passed, one by one the people left until only the Ormbrak family and Mr. and Mrs. Adrian Hoeks and their daughter Betty, were left to enjoy Woden's peace and quiet. Except during the cannery season, and then the population would swell enormously for a few months. Cannery works was not well-paid and the hours could be very long when there was a good run of fish — but there was so much fun and good fellowship during the season that it was looked upon as the ideal way to spend the summer by most of the younger people.

The Wallace Fisheries sold their interest in the Woden cannery in 1926 to the B.C. Fishing and Packing Company and when the big amalgamation of fish companies took place in 1928, Woden cannery (among others) became the property of B.C. Packers. In 1930 when they closed it down to use the more modern six-line cannery at Shannon Bay, this marked the end of Woden as a settlement.

Today (1966) there is only one family living at Woden River — Mr. and Mrs. Glen Clarke — who both commute to work in Masset. The Clarkes have built a modern home near the site of the Hazelton Brothers' boatshop (long since disappeared) on the ten acres they own on the north side of Woden River.

Nature has reclaimed much of her own on the dozens of little pre-emptions, but when Ruby Hazelton (Adams) and her cousin Eva Hazelton (Crites) returned for a visit in 1966 to the pioneer home of their parents, one thing remained unchanged. This was the big rock with a white top which always had an eagle perched on it. "We thought Woden was as beautiful as ever," said Mrs. Crites. "There was even an eagle sitting on Old Eagle Rock just as when I was a little girl there."

CHAPTER THIRTY-THREE

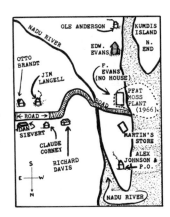

NADU AND KUMDIS
SLOUGH NEIGHBORS

Six miles south of Woden, lies the mouth of the Nadu River. It was to this region that one of the few real farmers came in all that stream of hopefuls – Mr. Edward Evans. He arrived at Masset in March, 1911, with his two sons, Francis and David, to look over the Graham Island farmland about which they had read such glowing accounts. Mr. Evans liked the grasslands bordering the north end of Kumdis Slough and staked his site almost directly across from the Pioneer Ranch of "Stud" Tingley. Then he engaged those two master axe men from the Nadu, Ole Anderson and Alec Johnson, to build the house for his family – which was so admired by Charlie Adam that he promptly hired them to build a duplicate building for his store in Graham Centre.

Francis, Mr. Evans's elder son, pre-empted the lot adjoining his father on the north, but when the government forbade him to build on it, claiming that it was timber land – he went southward along Kumdis Slough to the grasslands of the Divide and staked another pre-emption on Kumdis Island. David Evans bought the Purdy and Harris place, but his heart wasn't really in farming at that time, (1) and he was soon off to the more exciting life with other young men on the pack trails.

The Evans home was completed when Mrs. Edward Evans and her two daughters, Agnes and Gladys, arrived – to learn about tidal ebb and flow the hard way. Their belongings had been landed on the beach and carefully piled a good distance from the water and they rushed up the beach to look at their new home. When they came out again what a sight met their eyes! All their possessions were lying in disorder, covered with seaweed and debris in the waters of the incoming tide which was now well up the beach.

"Poor mother!" recalls Agnes who was thirteen at the time, "what an awful mess it was to dry out." Agnes, who needs to stand on her tip toes to reach five feet, later married Brent Lea, the tall debonair supervisor of the building of the Buckley Bay mill, and her sister Gladys married Frank Van, who with his

---

(1) David was later a successful turkey farmer in Courtenay, B.C.

brothers Ole and Jack, was among the best known of early Island arrivals.

There were several settlers already in the Nadu region by the time the Evans arrived in 1911 — the senior Freeman Tingley, Bill Vyse, Jim Langell, Mr. and Mrs. O. P. Merrill, Alec Johnson, Ole Anderson, Mr. and Mrs. Dan Sievert, Richard Davis and his family, and Claude Corney, a relative of the Davis's.

Bill Vyse went to the Nadu in 1910 and tried unsuccessfully to make a farm in the muskeg, about two miles inland — the same muskeg which today is highly prized by the operators of the new peat moss plant being built at the Nadu. Mr. Vyse cleared a measured five square acres but after wrestling in vain for ten years with his land at the Nadu, he bought an acreage from T. L. Williams about one mile from Port Clements, where he made his home. Occasionally engaged as foreman when a new road was being put in, Bill's roads were recognized by their straightness — like arrows — in those early days of twisting and winding paths when most of them looked as though they had "followed the old cow." It was said of Mr. Vyse that " . . .he built better roads with a pick and shovel than they do now with all their machinery."

Everyone who knew him was delighted in the nineteen-thirties when this cheerful man, with a quiet unassuming manner, married his childhood sweetheart from the prairies. The Vyses were not young so when in less than a year they learned that they were to have a baby it seemed like a miracle of unexpected happiness. A stunned community stood aghast a few months later, when the eagerly awaited baby arrived stillborn — and within hours Mrs. Vyse was also dead.

In an effort to live with his grief, Bill turned to the work he knew best, building roads — and for this road he chose incredible terrain. Down an impassable gully he built, entirely by hand, a road that would take cars from his house to the beach a quarter of a mile away. When his wife had to be buried in the cemetery at Queen Charlotte City Mr. Vyse, feeling that it might be comforting to others in the Port Clements area who were similarly afflicted, to have a cemetery nearer, donated a section of land for this purpose — deeding it to the Anglican Church in Port Clements to administer.

One of Bill Vyse's earliest neighbors at the Nadu was Jim Langell, a Dane who made his money when he sold a mining claim at Lockeport. Mr. Langell bought land about a half mile inland and set out to prove that you could grow garden produce on muskeg soil. He had begun to savor the fruits of his battle when the Evans family arrived in 1911 and had an excellent crop from his big vegetable garden that year. "One of the things I remember best about Jim," says Francis Evans, "was the time he became imprisoned in his own cabin for three days by a big buck deer which had gone beserk — similar to a bull moose in mating season. Jim had no rifle shells at the time so had to stay put. But he had lots of kidding about his "romance" after that incident." Mr. Langell died about 1915 on the land he loved so well — and his big garden has not, as is usual, been taken over by the forest. Instead it is today a large, grassy park-like clearing, set in dense forest and can be easily seen from the Nadu road.

Of Mr. Langell another favorite story is often told. He ordered $150 worth of groceries from a Vancouver store and purchased the money-order to pay for it from the post office in James Martin's Masset store — and from Martin himself. Mr. Martin realized that this huge sum of money was going for purchases from an outside store and was furious that Langell had not given him the order.

Whenever Martin was irate he would break out into a tuneless whistle. It tickled Langell's sense of humor to hear Martin suck in his breath and begin this as he made out the money-order and for a long time after he would brag about, "going down to make Martin whistle."

Richard Davis and his family had the first house on the north side of the road after climbing the steep hill from the mouth of the Nadu. Mr. Davis was forced to divide his time living half on his pre-emption and half in Masset, so as to send his children to school, and do freighting with his team to support his family. This meant walking his horses back and forth along the beach each time to make the transfer. His relative, Claude Corney, was on the section of land next to Mr. Davis.

Adjoining Mr. Cornie's land was the pre-emption of Danny Sievert. Mr. Sievert brought his bride to the Nadu in 1910 and, like the Davis family, found that when their children began to arrive, they had to compromise. When their first baby, Dorothy was born in April, 1911, they went to live in Masset, with subsequent trips in the next few years to live in Delkatla for the births of Eleanor, Edith and Max, but one daughter, Margaret, was born on the beloved pre-emption. With five children to support Danny Sievert could be found cooking in some of the many camps or working wherever he could in the next few years, until with reluctance he had to abandon his land at the Nadu as unprofitable and moved to the booming little mill town of Port Clements during later years. Here they lived until the twenties and finally moved into Prince Rupert where widowed Mrs. Sievert, still bright and active, keeps house for her two seafaring sons, Captains Max and Norman Sievert — well-known Prince Rupert skippers.

Mrs. Sievert remembers the fine story-and-a-half frame house (in contrast to the usual log cabin) that Otto Brandt built for his wife and her mother, Mrs. Armstrong, on the other side of the Nadu road from the Sievert home. James Love, who had originally come from Winnipeg with Jim and Andy McCrea, took out a pre-emption near the intersection of today's Nadu road and the Port Clements-Masset highway. Mr. Love built a cabin and sent for his parents, but taking Charles Wilson's suggestion about a "town house" he soon built a more permanent house in Delkatla. Isobel Love came to join her parents and brother there and met Dr. Allen Graves of Masset and they were later married.

Lithuania had a representative at the Nadu in Enoch Rice, who after coal mining and textile working in his native land, came to the United States and thence to the Nadu about 1910 or 1911. To provide an income, whilst he proved up on his land, Mr. Rice opened a shoemaking and repair shop. A creative man, his hobby was woodcarving, using the special tools which he made. During the booming aeroplane spruce years Mr. Rice moved into Port Clements and the home he established there gave him scope for his hobbies.

By 1913 there were eighteen homes along the Nadu road with six more in the vicinity of the north end of Kumdis Island, and in response to a petition from the settlers, the government agreed to establish a post office. Alec Johnson was asked to take on the job of post master, ". . .which he did very well. In later years he asked my mother to take it on — so it was moved to our house," says Francis Evans. "That year Jim Martin built a store — his fourth — a little to the west of Alec's. I had worked for awhile in Martin's Queenstown store and later in his Masset store, so he got me to open and run the Nadu establishment on a short day basis, before and after boat days."

Even the government came into action and authorized the building of a floating wharf for unloading supplies and, during the years 1911 to 1920, built a road wide enough for wagon traffic for about two miles inland, with a good pack trail leading from it for several miles more. The road built in connection with the peat moss plant, today overlies the old wagon road. Jimmy Campbell delegated pre-emptor Fred Howes to supply Nadu news for his *Queen Charlotte Islander,* and Mr. Howes special brand of humor was introduced into each item to the delight of Campbell's readers. (1)

In December 1911, Ole Anderson and Alec Johnson canvassed the whole Masset Sound, Kumdis and Graham Centre region gathering names to form a Farmers Institute, which was organized in early 1912 with Francis Evans as secretary. This Institute enabled settlers to purchase stumping powder, lime, fertilizer, feeds and so on at reduced prices. It was through the Institute that the Evans were able to build up a first class herd of Aberdeen Angus cattle, since they were able to purchase a pure-bred male calf every two years from the Livestock Branch in the Department of Agriculture.

Kumdis Slough was being settled all the way along. On the east side, beyond the group of settlers on waterfront property near the Nadu, there were a number of pre-emptions behind the timber limits which tied up all the shoreline the rest of the way south. Walter Purkis was behind the limits at the Divide, with several more settlers, J. C. Brosh, F. S. Taylor, Hugh Watt and William Bert, farther in behind him. Among the rest of the settlers to the east, along the timber claim, were Edward Brust, Sid Wormald, Mr. Minaker, Mr. Godwin and David Evans, who was on the Purdy-Harris land.

On the west side of the Slough was Kumdis Island and a considerable portion of its southern end had shoreline free of timber claims. Felix Graham, bookkeeper for Wright and Green in Queenstown, had his "town house" in Charlie Adam's Graham Centre, but had a pre-emption on Kumdis Island about two miles from the south end of the island. He built a lean-to shack near his adjoining neighbors, Mr. and Mrs. Jim Shaw. The Shaw's had a large, well-built log cabin which was used for many years after they left, and south of them, the Burtons also had a well-built home which was of squared timbers. Mr. Burton ran cattle which Francis Evans bought when they left. Gus Johnson bought the house. He sold it to Jack Hewison about the time the Baxter Pole Company began to operate on Kumdis Island. (2) All these homesites were on waterfront land, but a timber licence blanketed the shore for the next section and the rest of the settlers had to go inland behind it.

Many well-known men took out land there, J. McKay, W. Hall, Mr. Monk, Ralph Stafford, Ray Willans and L. (Bob) Dyson. When Mr. Dyson brought his bride from England to live on the Charlottes in 1923, he did not return to his pre-emption on Kumdis Island, but bought the little cottage which Mr. Snidal

---

(1) Other Nadu pre-emptors:— J. Engblum, L. C. Turcotte, Eleis Stein, F. J. Tingley, Herman Jeska, Ed Mesner, H. T. Weber, Jr., Harry Weber, Sr., and John Brickbealer.
(2) In the late twenties and early thirties, at which time there was a small settlement between the original Shaw and Burton homes, on Kumdis Slough, in connection with the pole camp.

built on the east side of Port Clements. In addition to operating a taxi for years, Mr. Dyson, with his wife, created a garden that was one of the beauty spots of the area.

The best known farm of Kumdis Slough was on the Divide land of Francis Evans. Evans beef was known far and wide for its excellence. In April of 1930 Francis paid a visit to his father's home at the Nadu to learn that there was a guest from Surrey, England visiting the elder Evans — Miss Daisy Geater. For the next two months Francis had an inordinate number of reasons for visiting his father's home. On June 26th Francis and Daisy were married. The young Evans set up housekeeping at the Divide and had a most successful farm — run entirely by themselves. Their big barn was equipped with every labor-saving device available; steel track and hay carrier for unloading hay from wagons, using horsepower instead of pitching hay by hand. It also had a steel track and manure truck to facilitate cleaning the stalls and sheds. The hay mowers, tedders, rakes and hay storing arrangements were ultra modern for that time.

Three daughters were born to this farming couple. Only the desire to provide a more balanced environment for them than was possible in their isolated location, made Francis Evans and his wife decide to sell their farm (1) and move to Richmond, B.C. They both say that part of their hearts are still at the Divide in memories of the satisfying days of pioneer farming.

(1) Sold for the timber on it — and never used as a farm after the Evans left.

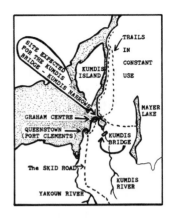

CHAPTER THIRTY-FOUR

FROM CROWN GRANTS
TO TOWNSITES

In 1912 the news that Eli was going to receive a Crown Grant for his Queenstown property galvanized the rest of the Tingley family. They knew that he couldn't touch any of the timber on that portion covered by the Graham Steamship, Coal and Timber Company's claim — but with a clear title to the rest ... even hard-headed brother Bert took an interest.

The Wright and Green Skid Road operation and the W. L. Barton outfit were both making Queenstown the base for their Yakoun coal operations. Perhaps Eli's townsite dream wasn't so silly after all. There was enough promise to make Bert decide to build a good hotel and say, "By golly, if Jim Martin doesn't reopen that store of his in Queenstown, I'll add one of those to the project as well."

Laura, (Eli's sister) and her two friends, May and Ruth Woods, had been to visit Eli's dream site in August of 1909, crossing Hecate Straits each way in Eli's open sailboat. They begged to be included in the 1912 plans. They were so lively the boys welcomed their company — but this time the girls went with Captain Nowell on the *Vadso* which, when it sailed up to Queenstown on May 17, 1912, was the second ocean-going vessel to enter the big inlet after the *Lillooet's* survey.

It took three days to put ashore the big load of lumber, supplies and crew that Bert had taken to build his hotel and open up Eli's townsite. As the men set to work, the three young ladies, joined by a fourth, Florence Woods, — all ardent tennis players — soon recruited volunteers from the bachelors to build a tennis court on a patch of clay near the edge of the beach to the east of the hotel.

Scraping, clearing and rolling as they went, willing hands soon had a fast court ready for play, surrounded by a high netting. With a big spruce block as a roller, the well-patronized court was kept in tip-top condition. When a group of visitors from the Masset end of the inlet came to pay their respects, Charles Wilson was so impressed with Queenstown's tennis court that he immediately promoted a similar one for the grass flats at Delkatla — and soon inter-community tennis matches were being held regularly, extending into well-attended picnics and dances.

Bert's hotel had progressed so well under the capable foremanship of Charles "Matey" Clayton that in four months it was ready. Bert sent for his mother to come and live with them and then to her horror applied for a liquor licence. Mrs. Tingley, who was a leading member of a Victoria temperance organization, was appalled at her son's action — so much so that Bert cancelled his application. In his advertisements he stressed that there was "NO BAR IN CONNECTION" with his Yakoun Hotel.

A gala evening was planned for the opening of Bert's hotel, with entertainment and dancing until the early hours, and guests came from afar. The first signature on the new hotel register was that of H. S. Clements, M.P. from Ottawa, who had come with four Prince Rupert men, Alfred Carse (of Eli's early Queenstown days), J. G. Scott, E. D. Tite and M. M. Stephens. Bert and Eli intimated to Mr. Clements that they would like to use his name for their developing town. For even though it meant going against Jim Martin's strongly expressed wishes, the brothers knew they would have to change the name of Queenstown — it was unthinkable to go much longer without a post office if they hoped to promote their townsite. As Bert said later, "...in those days of tough townsiting competition, you had to do the best you could not to overlook any bets." M.P. Herb Clements looked like an excellent bet.

The Honorable Member was flattered at the suggestion of this promising town bearing his name and said he would try to get government action, especially on a wharf. The new blood being transfused into the Tingley townsite was attracting much interest — and perhaps the best barometer was Jim Martin's enlarging and reopening of his store and putting young Francis Evans in charge. Mr. and Mrs. Snidal were clearing more land around the cottage they owned, and when the Hastie and Cross families, who had been living in Masset whilst their men pre-empted at Mayer Lake, showed interest, Eli was elated. With six school-aged children among them there would be the nucleous of a school — a real asset in attracting more families. But Eli's besetting problem was that, except for a few acres, all his choice townsite land was tied up in that paralysing timber claim, and he could do nothing about it.

Across the bay the little community of Graham Centre was shaping up as a rival — and it had no timber problems to worry about. Charlie Adam and Geordie McQuaker ran a flourishing store, mail contract and post office — and when a travelling library was installed it became a natural hub. When McQuaker and Adam moved into the two-story building, Geordie's sister, Mrs. Rowan, with her husband and young son, Willie, came from Glasgow to live in the first cabin they had used for the store. The Rowans planned to open a boarding house. McQuaker and Adam were hard at work clearing more land when Frank Wright of the coal company came to buy two acres from Charlie, saying that after he had built his home in Graham Centre he intended to put up a big hotel there.

Jim McLay and Jim Allison had pre-emptions at Mayer Lake, as did John McDougal — but they wanted a small acreage to build a cabin on near Graham Centre for their "town house". T. L. Williams had 160 acres, more than he would ever use, so he offered the young men a free acre. The offer was accepted. McDougal built a small cabin on the ridge behind Mr. Williams and McLay and Allison built a two-story house beside McDougal on an adjoining acre. Mr. and Mrs. John Boyes came to live at the Centre and being friends of McLay and

Allison were invited by them to use the new two-story home. Mrs. Williams was delighted to have Mrs. Boyes for her neighbor, and more especially when she knew that the Boyes had a daughter, Ailo, who was the same age as young Jackie Williams.

With the demand for land in this locality increasing and with the Tingleys apparently blocked, hopelessly, by the adamant attitude of the timber company, Charlie Adam decided he might as well make a bona fide townsite out of his little settlement. On December 23, 1912 Fred Nash and his party came to make the survey which they completed on January 6th of 1913. It was September before the townsite was registered, but since the government did not take its usual quarter share of acreages, Mr. Adam could sell these at once — and did.

He and McQuaker finished building a forty-foot drydock in March and soon had several boats in for repairs. Several houses were being built. Frank Wright engaged Bill Rennie to build his, and the Rennies liked Graham Centre so well they abandoned their Mayer Lake site, bought one of Charlie's acreages and built their home next to the Wrights. Their baby, Dorothy, who arrived early in December of 1913, was the first baby to be born in Graham Centre. Felix Graham, accountant with Wright and Green, unable to buy land from Eli (because of timber claim) bought the two-story frame house that Sid Wormald had built near the Graham Centre store, and moved over with his wife and son, Charles. (Charlie Graham later married Jim Martin's daughter Aileen.)

Grandpa Godwin, who had been with his son and granddaughter, Mabel, first at Sewall and then on the Kumdis Slough pre-emption beside Sid Wormald, thought pre-emption life was too isolated for a young girl, so he bought an acreage from Mr. Adam near Kumdis Narrows and brought Mabel to live with him. "I never saw soil like that in my life," said Mabel, who married Charles Harrison's younger son, Cyril. "Grandad planted scarlet runner beans beside the house and they grew up over the roof and down the other side. Everything we grew there was huge — daisies as big as saucers. It was wonderful."

Arthur Richardson built his "town house" in Graham Centre, so did Thomas E. O'Callaghan, who like his countrymen, Mr. and Mrs. O'Flynn brought the Irish element into the community. The O'Flynn's took over the top part of the store and ran it as a hotel.

One day a tall, engaging man appeared at the Williams door — Captain Hart Jenkins, an army friend from the Boer War days. "An absolute prince of a fellow, but one of the most helpless chaps on his own you could ever meet," says Mr. Williams. "We didn't dare let him go out into the woods alone — he'd have been lost in five minutes, so we put up a small cabin close to us. His good company more than compensated for any inconvenience."

There was plenty of social activity in which people from both Graham Centre and Queenstown joined. Dances were held for the least excuse in the new Hastie dance hall and in the big dining room of the Yakoun Hotel. Eli Tingley cleared a natural depression near the site of the proposed government wharf and they had some good skating there one winter. As his sister Laura says, "Whenever things did get a bit slack, brother Bert would announce that it was his birthday and throw a big party with everyone invited. One year he had seven birthdays in as many months."

A lively debating group was organized, as well as a Literary Society, Settlers'

League, Conservative Association, Farmer's Institute, and the Queenstown Tennis Club.

Alex MacTavish, the big New Zealander who lived near the Kumdis Narrows, was so entranced when Charlie Adam's sister, Anne, came to live in Graham Centre to keep house for her hard-working brother, that he decided to make his home in Graham Centre. Mac acquired a cabin in Charlie's settlement, and a young man from Germany, Mr. Peters, moved in to batch with MacTavish soon after. Mac was an asset to the social part of any community for besides his gift of gab, he loved to sing and could play several musical instruments well. He came into the news with a flourish in 1912 in his newly appointed role of Fire Warden for the north end of Graham Island. In July the McLeod brothers had started a small fire to burn stumps on their land near Sewall. One brother went to visit in Masset leaving the other to guard the fire. That whispy bit of smoke didn't seem to need much guarding, so the second brother went off to do a little hunting. In his absence, their cabin caught fire and this in turn started a fire in a few surrounding trees. After the first flash, very little damage was done to timber, but the muskeg section smouldered for months afterwards.

In Graham Centre when Fire Warden MacTavish spotted the first puff of smoke in the trees, he flew into action. The O'Brian, Tingley, and Wearmouth launches were engaged with much dispatch to round up fifty men with a similar number of shovels, axes and great quantities of food from Martin's store in Queenstown and Charlie Adam's store in Graham Centre.

At the scene of action a tent was set up for the Fire Warden's headquarters. He marshalled his men by fives and detailed them around the edge of the burning muskeg. There was nothing anyone could do, or needed to, about the smouldering muskeg but the weather was gloriously warm so the fifty men had a relaxing time lolling around the whispy smoke and taking full advantage of the unexpected paid holiday. At the end of three days Mac emerged from his tent headquarters and announced that the fire was now under control and everyone could go home. The muskeg smouldered away unchanged.

"Boy, what a whopping bill the Forestry Department must have had," recalls T. L. Williams, "we were all paid for a full twenty-four hour day – and by the hour – from the time of leaving until our return home. Only Mac would have been able to emerge a hero from something like that. The Rupert papers really played up how he had saved the forest wealth of Graham Island – news which was undoubtedly supplied by the hero himself. But anyway, for once we settlers had an unexpected government bonus – and so our local celebrity had our blessings too, although for quite different reasons."

The government had put in a good trail along the survey line (for the timber limits) from Queenstown to Graham Centre and then on out to the Kumdis Point where it faced the trail on the opposite side from Masset, which ran along the east side of Kumdis Slough. Both these trails had branches to the Narrows where a third trail joined, the one from Mayer Lake. (1) Foot traffic had to wait for low tide and wade across at the Narrows. So when the government bulletins announced in 1912 that a contract had been let for the bridge at the Kumdis, local jubilation was high.

(1) See map.

210

Charlie Adam was drawing up his townsite plans and after sentimentally naming the streets in his town for his many brothers and sisters, he asked Fred Nash to sketch in the supposed location of the bridge at the Narrows on early blueprints. The contract for the bridge was awarded to Ed O'Brian, as had been expected, but when it was announced that the bridge was to be built up by O'Brian's house and not at the Narrows site – people were appalled. To put a bridge up the river, over a mile away from where it was needed was not only ridiculous, it was detrimental to the good of the whole area. There wasn't a trail or road anywhere near and it was completely out of the line of traffic.

James Martin had influential political ties which he didn't hesitate to use if anything threatened the welfare of his stores – although it was the only time he did use them. It was an accepted fact in the early days that if you wanted any government work, such as working on trails, roads or contracts, you bought your groceries from Martin.

Jim Martin had been watching the increasing amount of business being done at McQuaker and Adam's store with grave concern. He didn't need a crystal ball to know that a bridge at the Narrows would make Graham Centre flourish – drawing people from all around to do their business there. Especially with Tingley unable to develop his location normally. A petition was quietly circulated in Queenstown to have the bridge built well upstream in the Kumdis – using the argument that the Narrows site would block navigable waters. The strategy was successful; the government stipulated that the bridge must go in high enough up the river so as to avoid interferance with normal shipping. (Even though the Delkatla bridge was built in 1913 in a similar situation.)

In the ensuing uproar those who protested were told that no one would suffer, "since trails will be made to connect with all existing traffic and will lead down to Graham Centre and thence into Queenstown."

But it didn't work out that way!

Instead all Mayer Lake traffic was rerouted directly into Queenstown and entirely by-passed the Graham Centre region. Kumdis Slough travellers still had to ford the Narrows at low tide. There is no doubt in the minds of people who lived in that region then, that the site of the Kumdis bridge affected the future of Graham Centre and the rest of the Kumdis area adversely. Had it gone in at the Narrows site the road, which normally would have replaced the early government trail, running from Queenstown (via Graham Centre) to the Kumdis, would have been along the edge of settled acreages all along the route. The extension to Mayer Lake would have done the same for the Kumdis Bay people.

1913 was a memorable year for the two little settlements at the head of Masset Inlet, with steady development (1) and wonderful fun as people visited back and forth to take part in the various events and became hosts for visitors from other parts of the area. For Eli Tingley it was feast after famine. Miss Ruth Woods became his bride and they took up residence in their town. After years of frustrating attempts at negotiation with the timber company, Eli was advised

(1) By the end of 1913 both Graham Centre and Queenstown were connected
    with the rest of the Island by a telephone line which ran from Queen
    Charlotte to Cape Ball, thence to Mayer Lake, Queenstown, and Masset
    and out along the north beach to Tow Hill.

that they would sign a quit claim – if he bought, at their prices, all the timber involved. As Eli had no option in the matter, he agreed – and with one of the thickest stands of timber in the Inlet on his land, he had to pay heavily for the release, which became final on December 20, 1913.

At last he was home-free.

In anticipation of this final liberation Eli had sent for Fred Nash, in April of 1913 to lay out the fourth and last of the Nash townsite surveys. Nash had a fine new yacht for his use now, the *Polaris*, which Captain Ferguson ran for him. Ferguson, in the course of his work with Nash, learned that a section of waterfront land, in the sheltered bay to the east of Juskatla entrance was free of a timber claim and he homesteaded there – to have the bay bear his name. "Cap" Ferguson was drowned in a sudden storm in 1919 as he went in a small boat from Port Clements to his homesite, but the trees he planted by his cabin bore fruit for years, which was picked by visitors at every chance.

Eli was successful in attracting the Hastie and Cross families to his townsite from Masset, and they all helped to build a big log home on the acreage at the east end of town for the Cross family. Bill Hastie, with Walter de Lisle to help him, built a fine family home, and a pool and recreation hall near the Martin store. With enough children for a school and a capable teacher in Laura Tingley, the little cabin that Eli had first built in Queenstown was utilized for a classroom and the school was opened in June of 1913.

H. S. Clements was true to his promise and a 700 foot wharf was authorized for Queenstown in the summer of 1913, which meant that a new name for the settlement was coming into effect. In anticipation of Martin's ire at the jettisoning of the old Queenstown name, and possible retaliation by closing his store, Bert opened a store in an annex to his hotel. But business was too good for James Martin to close down. Both Martin and Bert built small wharves in front of their stores to handle their supplies. W. L. Barton had been drilling up the Yakoun, and as his contract ended he thought a good way to make money was in supplying lumber for the new government wharf and in the tremendous amount of building going on in Queenstown and Graham Centre. He opened a saw mill. And with all that shoreline to choose from Barton chose the edge of the popular tennis court for his mill site. In a few years the subsequent slab pile and sawdust covered the whole court. But they had had so many enjoyable hours from tennis that, in the twenties, a community effort spearheaded by D. E. "Maxie" Maxwell obtained donations of lumber and many willing hands built a planked court on the hill south of the original clay one. (1)

Jimmy Campbell, who had been running a newspaper in Windy Young's Queen Charlotte City, thought prospects in Queenstown looked better and as soon as Eli built a house for him in August 1913, Campbell published his *Queen Charlotte Islander* in Tingley's town. (He later moved to Masset to publish.) Charles Harrison, New Masset's booster, bought lots and ordered two houses to be built in Eli's town. Mr. and Mrs. Dave Crocker moved into one and Mr. and Mrs. A. R. Mallory, newly-weds, rented the other. Mr. Mallory had come to the Islands to visit his brother, Frank, government teamster at Lawn Hill, then hearing about the growing town of Queenstown hiked over the trail to investigate.

(1) On part of the site of the 1966 Mac-Blo housing development.

He fell in love with it on the spot, and made arrangements for his bride to come around from Queen Charlotte on the *Prince Albert* and join him.

Church services had been held in the Tingley hotel on the few occasions that William Hogan managed to come down from Masset. Mr. Mallory arranged with Rev. Len Bygraves, the Presbyterian minister in Queen Charlotte to come up and hold more regular services. Apparently Mr. Bygraves success aroused alarm in mainland Anglican headquarters. They regarded the north end of Graham as their territory and wanted no interlopers. The Bishop took immediate action and sent word that he had appointed Rev. H. H. K. Greene to be resident parson in Queenstown and hoped to be able to include Graham Centre in the plans as well. A church would be built at once, it was announced. In the summer of 1913 Heber Greene brought his bride, Jean, from Toronto to live in their first parish, and until the new church and rectory were ready they lived in the tiny one-roomed cabin that Gus Lundquist had helped Eli build for a guest house in 1908.

Eli donated the land for the Queenstown church and Charlie Adam did the same for the proposed one in Graham Centre. Charles Clayton built the 36 by 22 foot structure which became combined church and rectory and on January 25, 1914 the first service was held in St. Mark's Church, Queenstown, with Rev. H. H. K. Greene [1] to officiate at the opening service.

At Graham Centre, Sid Wormald, assisted for a time by Jim Shaw from Kumdis Island, built the 16 by 20 foot St. Luke's church where the opening service was conducted by Rev. Greene on November 5, 1914. Sid Wormald says, ". . .they had a very appropriate bell for a pioneer church, it was a shake splitter which was hit with an iron bar."

How Graham Centre acquired a Church Hall before the church is told with a chuckle today by Canon Greene. "MacTavish came to me," he says, "and wanted to know if they could have dances in the new church when it was built and I said, 'Oh, Mac, that would hardly do.' He flew into a temper and said, 'Parson, if you won't let us use your damn church, I'll build a hall.' But Mac, ever the promotor, never did any of the actual bull work himself. As soon as the building was completed, Mac took it over as his private residence – and to this day no one knows how he did it. But," added Canon Greene, "I think that MacTavish met his match in Charlie Adam. For when he was planning to leave, Mac went to Adam's store and paid his bill – a pretty big one – with a phoney cheque. Charlie said nothing, biding his time – and sure enough, in a few days MacTavish came back to ask Charlie if he would like to buy his house (the ex-church hall). Adam agreed that he would. When the transaction was duly witnessed and notarized, Adam paid MacTavish with the phoney cheque . . . leaving Mac for once in his life completely speechless, as he realized that Charlie had known it was phoney all along and had outsmarted him."

The first wedding to be held in Queenstown was conducted by Rev. Bygraves on February 13, 1914 when he united Freeman Tingley, junior, with Hilda, the auburn haired daughter of Bob Rudd. Their eldest daughter, Vera, was the first baby christened in the Port Clements church. Although Presbyterian Mr. Bygraves was still active, Heber Greene was the best emissary the Anglicans could have

[1] *Now Canon H. H. K. Greene.*

sent. Honest and forthright, he was more concerned with helping than whether those he helped were "ours" or "theirs". During his residence he made the Church the hub of the community, and everyone turned out to hear him each Sunday. "And", he says now, "I think sometimes I had just about every denomination except Anglican sitting in the pews."

He hiked over the rough Mexican Tom trail wading streams waist high to hold occasional services at the Turney's in Tlell. He became lost more than once but a Guiding Hand led him safely back to the trail, although he was forced to spend a night out occasionally. In the Mission boat *Ione* he went to Sewall to hold services in the mill bunkhouse and frequently went along the Yakoun packer's trails to hold them in the mining camps. When some of the Anglicans asked him to, he went to visit and hold services for them in Methodist territory — and walked both ways.

The townsite plan was completed and registered and the little town of Queenstown became officially *Port Clements* on March 19, 1914. The long awaited post office was granted under the new name and the first postmaster was Mr. A. R. Mallory. It seemed that nothing could halt the growth of Eli's townsite now. In fact, the doughty Frank "Muldoon" from the Yakoun used to say, "you can as soon hold back the tide with a pitchfork as stop Port Clements from being the biggest center on the Islands."

But they had not foreseen the 1914 war.

Around the end of July in 1914 the papers from the mainland began to hint about the tense world situation and possibility of a war — to which little attention was paid. The *Prince Albert* which brought over the papers at the end of July, ran on the rocks near the mainland on her return trip and was out of commission for the next six weeks — during which time there was little outside news.

In August, with the declaration of war and the rumor of a German cruiser somewhere in the vast Pacific, an unseemly panic swept down the coast. Suspension of all coastal steamers was mooted, since telegraph messages might give away information, coal on wharves might be used for refuelling and so on. The telegraph and telephone operators in Masset, Port Clements and Queen Charlotte City were told they were to suspend service indefinitely. Several people needed to get to the mainland on urgent business so a party of sixteen engaged Andy McCrea's *Westover* to take them. That was the only communication from Masset Inlet until the *Prince Albert* resumed her regular run near the end of September and brought newspapers with accounts of what had actually happened during the Islands' six weeks of virtual blackout.

"Things look dismal for the future on these Islands," Mr. Williams wrote in his diary, "the threat of another disruption of communications at any moment. Closure of all public works projects, wharves, roads, bridges and trails, as well as the private ones in surveying, drilling and building will leave our people with no means of subsistence for the future — as well as the possibility of isolation. I think we have all decided to enlist and get the war over with as soon as possible."

As the young men joined up, one of the first communities to feel the effect was Charlie Adam's Graham Centre. Leading the volunteers was Geordie McQuaker, a fiercely patriotic young lad, and when he was rejected, he became

214

despondent and brooded unnaturally — until it was obvious that he had become irrational. He was so well liked in the community, it was with great reluctance that steps were taken to have him committed to Essondale, where he lives to this day — remembered by all the pioneers with affection.

Losing Geordie was the final straw for Charlie Adam. His pioneer townsite which, earlier, had held such promise, now appeared to be inexorably doomed. When George Beattie, of Queen Charlotte City, agreed to buy what remained of his stock, Charlie closed his store and joined his neighbors as they streamed off the Islands to enlist. It was 1916.

After the war Felix Graham returned to sell war surplus materials for a brief period, using Mr. Adam's store as his headquarters. He was the last person ever to live in Graham Centre. The once happy little community has taken its place among the ghost towns of British Columbia.

Even Mr. and Mrs. T. L. Williams did not return to their beloved homesite adjoining Graham Centre when they came back to the Islands in 1919. The comfortable, furnished home they had left in 1914 had been ransacked so badly during their absence that they could not bear to live there again. They had a six-month-old baby daughter now, as well as Jackie, who was school age. Graham Centre was abandoned by this time. With a heavy heart they decided to begin Island life anew in the booming town of 1919 Port Clements. They were joined by other of their pioneering friends who were returning from overseas, Arthur Robertson, George Mayer, the Singers, Fred Chapman, Harry Ross, Bob Dyson, Bill Hastie and many others. The Cross family, however, went to Victoria to open a meat market, which they still operate.

CHAPTER THIRTY-FIVE

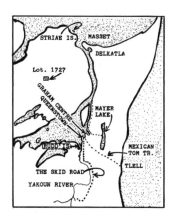

AFTERMATH

By mid 1918 Port Clements was a bawdy, free-living town with brothels, bootleggers, and saw mill gangs supplemented by 800 loggers from the fourteen logging camps operating in the inlet. At least a thousand people, by a conservative estimate, lived in Eli's town, but they were coming and going so often, it was difficult to keep count.

The early years of the war had been touch and go. The Barton mill had to close because of no market — and left men waiting for their pay. Eli Tingley had formed a company with McLory, Hewitt and Sipes to buy the equipment from the Adventist mill at Sewall. They moved it to Port Clements on a raft — taking twenty-four hours to cross the ten mile stretch of water when they encountered heavy winds. With this equipment they built and operated the Port Clements Mill, to the north of the government wharf. Times and marketing were difficult and Eli had to reorganize his company in 1916, this time with Charlie Caulson as his new partner. But timber was always to be a jinx for Eli. They were on the edge of the big aeroplane spruce boom when their engine blew up — and being over-extended in their credit, their creditor foreclosed. This was Leffeson, who was with the Mexican Consulate in Vancouver. Leffeson sold the mill to John Lewis and his brother in 1917, who ran it until 1922, doing well at first — then caught in the sudden collapse of the aeroplane spruce market at the end of the war, they too, eventually failed.

The Barton mill was taken over by a Vancouver group and Mr. Nadeau was put in charge. Early in 1917 Nadeau planked the whole of the main street of Port Clements from his mill to the government wharf. His lumber for shipping was hauled by using two-wheeled trailers with solid iron wheels, drawn by horses, until trucks were procured. The trucks were small Model T's, which had sharpened steel spikes riveted to rear wheels instead of rubber tires, as the planked road was often slippery. The spikes cut up the planks necessitating frequent replacement. In 1919 another company took over the old Barton mill, but caught in the slump of the early twenties, they operated only briefly. Frank Malloy bought it and ran the mill as a shingle mill for a few years. Its final owner

217

was Mr. H. R. Beaven of Queen Charlotte City who operated it for a short time about 1930 or 1931.

The big Lynch Mill on the south side of the government wharf — the remains of which could be seen for many years — was built in 1917 by Mr. W. P. Lynch, the New Brunswicker who had known Bert and Eli Tingley in the Klondike, where he had run a big store about fifty miles from Dawson. Bill Lynch had been in Prince Rupert, where he opened one of the first stores and in 1910 was a member of Prince Rupert's first City Council before going to Port Clements. Mr. Lynch also was caught when the market fell out of aeroplane spruce — and he left B.C. in the twenties to go to San Francisco where he died shortly after.

Frank Hicks, who had operated a pool hall in Port Essington before going to Masset to open one with his partner, Cauthers, moved up to cash in on the boom in reawakened Port Clements in 1917. Hicks built a pool hall which he later enlarged with rooms upstairs for a hotel. He sold out in 1926 to the well-remembered trio of Jimmy Ciccone, Herb Hampton and Tony Costillino, who put in the community's first beer parlour. Three of the regular patrons were Bill Hastie, John McLellan and Martin Newby who played solo in the pool hall every night for more years than could be counted. Mr. Newby (whose house, built by the Lynch Mill, had belonged to a lady of easy virtue during the boom years) and Bill Hastie had terrific arguments over each game — whilst McLellan sat silently waiting for them to finish, and then usually picked up the pot.

John Pyper ran the hotel for years after Mr. Ciccone and his partners left, and when he died his son Adam took it over. This historic old hotel at the head of the government wharf was lost in a fierce blaze on June 21, 1964 when the proprietors, Mr. and Mrs. Adam Pyper and their guests escaped with little more than they stood in.

The log cabin which was used for the first school house gave problems, as at each exceptionally high tide the floor became flooded. "Gosh, how we kids used to pray for the big winds to bring that tide up," recalls Fred Chapman, who with his sister, Louise, was one of the early class. "Because when the water got to the door, the teacher would declare a holiday." The Greenes left in 1915 and the church was empty so permission was given for temporary classes to be held there until the new school on the hill was ready in 1917.

When Mrs. Greene had become critically ill following the birth of a daughter in the combined Church-Rectory and as medical aid was almost non-existent, the Bishop arranged to have the young couple transferred to a less isolated parish. It was the last time Port Clements had a resident minister — as ever since then this parish has been administered by the incumbent at Masset, who goes down twice a month. There are no Leonard Bygraves around to threaten Anglican security today.

With the rectory empty, permission was given for the Sipes family to move there until they could find satisfactory housing. Mr. Sipes was in partnership with Eli Tingley in the Port Clements mill in 1914 to 1916 and was away on a trip in August 1916 when tragedy struck. His mother, Martha, wife, Lethe, daughter Rae and son Ian, all died within two days from eating improperly canned fish. Only the baby, a boy, too young to eat fish, survived.

During the war a Community Hall was needed and everyone donated material and work. Rev. A. E. Price, Anglican incumbent from Masset said the community

218

could use the vacant corner on the property Eli had donated to the Church, and the hall was built there as a community effort. Although in deference to its location it was called the Church Hall, it was regarded by everyone as community property and was a great asset to the village, being in constant use for every social, school and church gathering for years. During the flu epidemic of 1917 and 1918 it served as an emergency hospital.

In the nineteen-thirties an Anglican parson arrived whose regulations for the hall's use were so unreasonable that the situation became untenable. It was depression time and there wasn't twenty-five cents in the community kitty, but somehow the whole village rallied to the cause. Loggers hauled out logs, fishermen towed them to Masset where they were cut, with the sawmill operator, Arthur Robertson, taking half the resulting lumber in lieu of pay for cutting, and anyone who could use a hammer or hold a board lent a hand, and a new community hall was built. This time it was not put on any "free" property that could boomerang. The affair did not help the Anglican cause and was far from anything anticipated by Rev. Price.

As people had swarmed in for the boom, now in the post-war slump they swept out again just as rapidly, leaving the little community of Port Clements to struggle for existence. Not everyone left — Island magic held quite a few. One of these was the little Chinese, Mah Wing, who had been a foreman of the Chinese workers in the Lewis Mill. Mah Wing built and ran a restaurant, which he called the B.C. Cafe, at the end of the wharf, across the street from Harry Ross's store. For his companion had a big dog, of uncertain heritage, called Billy. Billy weighed a hundred and fifty pounds to his master's slight eighty-five, but there was never any doubt about who was boss. Should Billy stray, Mah would hold out a rolled newspaper and the huge dog would slink behind the counter. "Oh, he awfu' scared o' me," Mah would giggle. It was like a step into the Orient to enter his immaculately clean premises with its Chinese calendars, the abacus upon which he could reckon accounts with lightning speed, exotic labels on his spices and herbs — and the wonderful Chinese lillies scenting the air at Christmas time. With powerful binoculars to aid the bright bespectacled eyes, there was little that went on in the community that Mah didn't know — but except to a few intimates he kept his own counsel.

Well educated in his own country, he knew herbs and medicines that could cure illnesses miraculously quickly but he was extremely reticent about them. He was a victim of Canada's immigration policy when no Chinese were permitted to bring their wives and he died without ever being able to see his wife and sons after he had left to seek his fortune in the new land at the turn of the century.

When the men came home from the front in 1918 to the booming, prosperous Port Clements, they found that the Hicks and Hastie pool halls, the big dance hall above Hastie's as well as the Church Hall were in overflow usage with the local inhabitants plus the hundreds of loggers who came to swell the town on week-ends. The veterans decided to have a club room of their own. The idea, which started modestly, was enlarged to include a dance hall upstairs with club premises, dressing rooms and space for rent downstairs. A player piano was bought, lumber, fittings and material delivered, with promises to pay later, and the big building was constructed by the members themselves, without pay. (1) Money

(1) Building cost $4389.22 to finish. C.W.A.Drader, who was teaching in Port Clements in 1919-1920 was one of the prime promotors initially.

was borrowed, dances and entertainments held to raise money. Then the mills closed, population dwindled, money became scarce and creditors pressed.

"It looked as though all our good work would be lost," recalls T. L. Williams, "and our good name tarnished. This Great War Veterans' Association branch had no legal standing and could not own or dispose of property. I was elected secretary-treasurer, with authority to try to clear up the difficulties. With the help of some of the Vets, the United Services Society was formed, incorporated and registered. We sold the big building to Frank Pearce, (1) who gave us enough to pay off our principal creditors at once and the balance of $2000 later in the year. By January of 1930 everyone who had loaned money was paid off in full — a terrific satisfaction to us all," he added.

Pearce had a bargain, and moved in to start a store on the ground floor, later converting the big G.W.V.A. dance hall upstairs into bedrooms for a hotel. This large building is still in use, but today is the busy store of Ernie Chapman and his wife, Maureen, who have remodelled the old store of Frank Pearce into a modern self-service one.

With the coming of the slump in the twenties the Tingley family decided they had weathered enough storms in Port Clements and one by one they moved to Victoria — returning to their hard won townsite for only an occasional visit. Bert had closed his store in the annex of the hotel in 1917, just before the boom struck, and was too busy with other interests to reopen. His mother died in December, 1921, at eighty-two, in Port Clements Hotel, (which Bert had renamed Yakoun Hotel). Eli with his wife, Ruth, and daughter, Evemary, left in May 1923 as did his father-in-law, Mr. Woods, who with his two daughters, Forence and May Woods, had been living next door to Eli in Port Clements.

Bert shut down the hotel to go logging for awhile near Shannon Bay, then in 1924 left to go fishing. The big hotel stood empty for years until a private purchaser, Mr. Terricho, bought it and leased it to the Baxter Pole Company in the early 1960s as headquarters for their Mayer Lake pole operation.

All that remains to mark the distinct place of the Tingley family in Port Clements history is a street sign (2) outside the little house that Eli built for Jimmy Campbell's newspaper in 1913.

---

(1) Frank Pearce was running the White Lunch counter next door.
(2) The sign marking "Tingley Street," the first street sign in Port Clements, was put there by the Department of Highways in 1964 to commemorate the fiftieth year of the settlement as a registered townsite, and as a tribute to Eli, who died in January, 1964, at his home in Victoria.

220

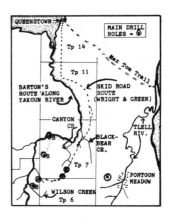

CHAPTER THIRTY-SIX

THE DRILLERS

It was the activity surrounding the Skid Road operation which motivated the development of Port Clements – and the idea for this road was the brainchild of F. C. Wright and E. Green. To them it represented the only feasible way of transporting the Graham Island Coal and Timber Company's drilling equipment into the coal fields of the Yakoun Valley. They had discussed the plan with Burke and Grey, directors of the English syndicate who had engaged them, and were given the go-ahead.

Moving eighty-three tons of equipment overland in that type of terrain was heavy going and the better part of a year had elapsed before they reached Mud Creek, behind Canyon Creek, to put down their first and main drill holes. Part of the delay was due to the necessity of building new sleds for the machinery on the way.

After the Mud Creek test holes were completed, they went on for about three miles to the Divide (1) where the second drilling took place. Wright and Green used the Davis "chilled shot" type of drill in contrast to Barton, who used a diamond drill. From the Divide, the Skid Road was continued for another three miles to Drill Creek, a tributary of the Yakoun, where the third drilling was done. Now backtracking over their established Skid Road, as far as practical, they left it to turn eastward to the region known locally as the Pontoons, and near this area put down their final borehole.

"All supplies up to this point were transported by being poled up the river to Canyon Creek and then backpacked the rest of the way," said Mr. John Locker, whose sturdy back was in daily use. "George Mayer, Ole and Frank Van, the Singers and de Lisle brothers were the principal boatmen. When the drilling equipment went into the Pontoons, the supply route changed and material was brought in from the East Coast along the road running inland from Lawn Hill, by horse or ox team and wagon, then packed the rest of the way along a trail."

(1) Name refers, here, to the high spot of this region between east and west. Not to be confused with the better known Kumdis Slough Divide.

John Locker remembered how he and Bill Hastie struggled to get the heavy steel casings to this last drill site, and when the operation was abandoned everything was left there — where it remains to this day.

When the supply base and headquarters for the last drill hole were transferred to Lawn Hill, the company built Frank Wright (1) a comfortable house for his home and office on land purchased from John Bray, a pioneer Lawn Hill settler, whose house was to the north of Wrights. Wright used it for only a brief period, however.

The Skid Road had begun on November 4th, 1911 and by the end of 1912 the whole operation was finished and local workers were told that the firm had run out of money. Mr. Green and his wife left, but Frank Wright stayed on to become associated with William Barton as a driller.

Barton had arrived in Queenstown in April of 1912 and that whole Skid Road operation had given him a wrinkled brow. He planned to take his outfit up the Yakoun to drill for the Graham Island Collieries. ". . .but why go overland when there's a big river to take you the best part of the way?" he wondered. He had recently been at Quatsino Sound on Vancouver Island, where he had been landed at a wharf with his equipment and found that the boat to take him to his destination might be months in arriving. "Give Bill Barton any kind of an engine and he can go anywhere in nothing flat," was the comment made of this ingenious man. Annoyed by the delay of the tow boat, Barton put his ingenuity to work in Quatsino. Loading all his stuff aboard a scow, he set his diamond drill over the stern of the scow, on an angle — and firing up the donkey engine he used for power at that time, was soon steaming away up the inlet to the beach where he was to drill.

When he was put off with his rig at Masset, it looked as though much the same situation might face him. He built a sixty-foot scow, cut a propeller from some boiler plate, then loaded his machinery and supplies. His engine this time was from an old Stanley Steamer automobile, and the boiler had been the first one in use by the Vancouver Fire Department. Several small launches were engaged to take surplus supplies and the strange looking flotilla got under way, landing at Queenstown to reorganize for the trip up the Yakoun.

Working his way up-river with his big scow and using a steam winch to get over the rough spots. Barton went several miles above Canyon Creek to Section 7 in Township 30 where he put down his first drill hole on the left bank of the Yakoun River. Using his diamond drill he went down 1,100 feet, and to keep his rig steady in the river he used an old-fashioned stock anchor. Fifty years later cruisers for the MacMillan, Bloedel and Powell River Company, who now log this region, discovered the old anchor still in its original location and moved it to the camp in Juskatla, where it holds a place of honor beside the company's bulletin board.

Barton's second drill hole was about two and a half miles southwest from the first, and for this he had to winch his rig inland. Evidently this was the end of his contract with the Graham Island Collieries — and with the chance to make

(1) *Wright's lived in Farvaque's house at first and when it burned, the new house was built for Wright — this later became the well-known Farmer's Institute building. (information — Mrs. Roy Field, Courtenay, B.C.)*

222

money with a mill cutting lumber for the new wharf and many frame buildings scheduled for Queenstown, he left the drilling for the time being. The steamer engine and historic boiler were brought down as far as Canyon Creek and cached.

In 1914 Professor Milnor Roberts of the New York Metropolitan Trust Company, upon examination of the results of Barton's last drill core, engaged him to work for them with his drilling rig. They were attempting to prove the existence of 350 million tons of available coal on the Wilson property, and were prepared to spend one and a quarter million dollars.

Brent Lea, who had just come from the extensive 1913-14 J. D. MacKenzie Geological Survey of Graham Island, joined Barton. Log jams had once again begun to build up in the Yakoun River, he says, and there were three particularly big ones, two miles long, that Barton would need to get past. Using more of his resourcefulness, Bill Barton applied to the Government for free powder to blast the jams out, saying that they were blocking the escapement of fish. He got his powder, hired a crew of twenty-one men and sent ten of them ahead to begin the demolition of the jams. The rest of the crew built a scow in Queenstown, then went as far as Canyon Creek where they picked up the equipment that had been cached.

Mr. Lea was fascinated by that old Fire Department's boiler which Barton had managed to acquire. "The blessed thing had 500 half inch copper tubes in it," he says, "and the way Barton had rigged up that old Stanley Steamer was really something."

Using the big diamond drill, which was capable of 4000 feet, and two small hand operated diamond drills, Barton worked for two or three years for the New York Trust Company and found several pockets of excellent quality anthracite. They used this coal to fire their big boiler and in the blacksmith's forge, as well as in the cookhouse and it burned well. There were from thirty-five to forty men engaged in the drilling project and there was no doubt that the coal was there, according to both Mr. Lea and Mr. Locker, who was still packing. However, it was badly faulted. "We would come across a seam thirty-five feet wide," says Mr. Lea, "then, putting down holes on either side of it, would find that it was only four or five feet there, and in less than half a mile it would have pinched out altogether."

Bill Hearn was engineer on the main drill, and with Danny Sievert cooking in one of the camps and Bill Toop in another, morale was excellent. Wes Singer recalls the efficient supply system which had been set up prior to his going overseas. He and one of the Vans would take up a boatload one day, and George Mayer and Dave Crocker would go on the alternate day, keeping things constantly on the move up to the camp. Boats were added as needed.

The years following the outbreak of war brought such an overall slump that even the New York Metropolitan Trust was adversely affected, and by 1916 abandoned the project. It marked the end of the drilling. The unique boiler, Stanley Steamer engine, and much of the other equipment was left at the main camp in Wilson Creek, never to be used again.

CHAPTER THIRTY-SEVEN

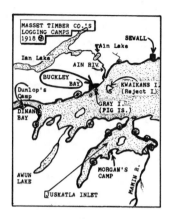

BUCKLEY BAY

In 1914 the only industries in the Masset Inlet region were the three struggling sawmills, one in Masset, one at Sewall and the Barton mill in Port Clements. The chief occupation of the population was land settlement. As the war developed and the outlook for the future on the Islands looked bleaker, people began to leave in as steady a stream as they had come. An indication of how lean times were in 1916 was shown when, in spite of his shrewdness, James Martin went broke. His creditors took over and attempted to run the Masset store, and Martin went to Ocean Falls. Then even the creditors began to lose ground. Martin was recalled to run his own store — for them. (1) It was rock-bottom economy.

Until 1917. That was the year the British Government discovered the superlative value of Queen Charlotte Islands spruce. In those days aeroplanes were constructed of wood, and nowhere in the world was there anything to equal the qualities of lightness and strength in the lumber from the large Sitka spruce on these Islands. The trees from which the "aeroplane spruce" was produced were magnificent specimens. They had to be large, completely free from knots, very fine grain and with no twists or defects.

The British Government went after them in spectacular fashion. They formed the Imperial Munitions Board, set up offices, with experts and unlimited funds, in Port Clements and Thurston Harbor (on Moresby Island). Buying up all the high grade spruce and helping individuals and concerns to produce the timbers required, the I.M.B. paid unheard of prices for everything which passed their inspectors. The famous Mosquito Fighter-bombers made from Queen Charlotte Island spruce were the most successful machine in the air and helped to end the war in 1945.

Thurston Harbor was the big collection center for the south end of the Islands.

---

*(1) It was clear to them, almost immediately, that if Martin was unable
to show a profit, no one could. Martin took over, to repay every cent
and recover his business. None of the branch stores were reopened,
but he operated the big Masset one until he died.*

Logs were brought there, from camps scattered all around, to be made into Davis Rafts (1) and shipped to the mainland for sawing. To supplement the facilities of mainland mills, the I.M.B. began the erection of three large sawmills at Thurston Harbor, however, these were not completed at the time of the armistice and were almost immediately dismantled.

Cooper Young was the I.M.B. representative in the Graham Island head office in Port Clements and he was no match for some of the tough logging representatives he had to deal with. With no limit to the funds he dispensed he obtained any amount of aeroplane spruce, not only from the local sawmills, but also in unsawn logs which were sent over to the mainland in the scores of Davis Rafts which were towed by the G.T.P. *Lorne.*

When the war ended and contracts expired, millions of feet of spruce could find no market. "The waste of those unique logs was something deplorable," recalls T. L. Williams, who went into the Forestry after his overseas service, "for instance, anchored in front of Buckley Bay, I saw three Davis Rafts of aeroplane spruce logs. Each time I went over they were sinking lower and lower with the teredos eating into them. Until they finally disappeared under the water. . . three to four million feet of Nature's finest product."

But it was a boom time while it lasted.

There were fourteen logging camps in Masset Inlet, and the Government issued permits for people to log anywhere, regardless of former timber claims, for this special quality spruce. A new sawmill was built in Sewall and three went into full production in Port Clements — but the fifth and perhaps best known, was built by the Masset Timber Company under the managership of Frank L. Buckley.

Having obtained lucrative contracts this company was organized in December 1917. In January, 1918 they went to Port Clements to put in a mill. Mr. George Higgins was put in charge of all woods operations and Brent Lea in charge of construction. Lea was in his element in this new role and built an office-residence on the hill for Cooper Young in less than a week. At the head of the wharf he put up warehouses and another office for the Masset Timber Company.

The idea of building the proposed mill in Port Clements, miles from the source of logs seemed impractical to Mr. Lea, so on his advice and with Buckley's concurrence, it was decided to move across to the west side of Masset Inlet and put the mill nearer the site of logging operations. A bay to the west of Ain River was selected and named for the manager of the firm, Buckley Bay. The first building on the new townsite of Buckley Bay was James Martin's Port Clements store, which was purchased and moved on a raft to the opposite side of the Inlet for the Masset Timber Company. Construction of docks and warehouses at the new location quickly followed.

Six months later, in mid 1918 the mill was in production, cutting from 100,000 to 150,000 feet a day, with some 400 men employed. Brent Lea took time from his amazing accomplishment to marry Agnes Evans, who had come from the Nadu to work in the office at Buckley Bay.

The first radial saw in Canada was used here in the initial stage of the mill operation. Its purpose was to get edge grain lumber. "It was two saws operating

(1) See Davis Rafts, page 320.

together, one on an angle," says Mr. Lea, "They cut out a section of the log, like a piece of pie. After the first cut was made, a six-inch saw went into the V opening and made another cut, paralleling the bark on the tree. It carried on until the log was cut, leaving a core of about fourteen inches. By cutting in this way edge grained lumber in the first degree was obtained, but it was so slow to operate it was soon abandoned as unprofitable. With timber so plentiful the waste of the standard saw method was unimportant."

The Masset Timber Company had eight camps getting out timber for them, and there were six independent operators selling to the highest bidder. One was John R. Morgan, who started with practically nothing and had parlayed his small outfit into one of the largest camps on the Charlottes by the mid 1930s.

Another well-known logging operator was Ed Crawford, the original inventor of the A-frame, who never got around to patenting his idea. He was the reverse of J. R. Morgan in business and ended up losing his shirt in the logging game. Free-spending, hail-fellow-well-met, Mr. Crawford was known far and wide as the biggest soft-touch in the world. He may have lost his logging camp, but his warm heart and inventiveness were evident always as he went first into fishing, where he had a leading part in the formation of the North Island Trollers Co-operative, and later when he ran a small sawmill in Sandspit.

Oscar Dunlop was foreman for the logging camp in Denan Bay, under contract to Buckley Bay. Oscar had the men lining up to work for him, even though Denan Bay was one of the most depressing places to work in, as it seemed to rain there continuously. However the wonderful cooking of Mrs. Dunlop, whose pleasant smiling face matched her superb pastry, made Oscar's camp the most sought after in the region. "Boy, those strawberry shortcakes. . ." remembers one old logger nostalgically today.

After the war, the Masset Timber Company reduced its scale of operation and reorganized several times to raise more capital, until in 1922 the Los Angeles Lumber Company took over the mill. The logs now were made into cants, which were shipped to Los Angeles for remanufacture into dressed lumber, box lumber and so on. To move the lumber cants they bought three vessel, *El Abeta, El Cedro* and *El Ciuta.*

El Abeto made the first trip and loaded 1,500,000 feet. Each ship going to Buckley Bay picked up a pilot at Masset for the tricky channel up into the Inlet. Their method of loading at Buckley Bay was out of the ordinary. Instead of tying to the dock, they anchored a short distance off-shore, with the bow headed into the bay and stern lines run out to "deadmen" on the beach. Tugs then towed the rafts of cants alongside. The rafts were made up of cross-laid timbers of large dimensions, 8 by 10, 10 by 10, 12 by 12, and were from 24 to 40 feet long, placed in tiers of six or seven and several layers to a tier. (1)

When the second trip to Buckley Bay was made it was *El Cedro's* turn, and not to be routine.

"As she was loading a fire, which started in the waste burner at the mill, spread to the lumber piles and then the town's water tank. Fanned by a stiff breeze it spread eastward, levelled the Japanese and Chinese bunkhouses, and jumped

(1) *"Los Angeles Lumber Products Steamship Company, 1922 - 27."*
Frank A. Clapp.

227

the gap to set fire to Otis Davis's (1) and Billy Mitchell's." remembers Mrs. Brent Lea. "They seemed to go in less than a minute and the roofs of dozens of other homes appeared to take fire now all at the same time. Just then thirty loggers from Ain River camp came and formed a bucket brigade with the mill men, and somehow managed to put the fire out — saving the rest of the houses.

During this time all the women and children were put aboard the *El Cedro*, and we had to climb a ladder from the beach on to the ship. Our baby was just an infant then, and I was in bed with bronchial asthma, when a strange man rushed in and help me put on some warm things and get out, as our house was right in line for the fire. I found out later that he was the Chief Engineer from the *El Cedro*.

Funny things always happen at times like these. As a young man was hurriedly collecting all the buckets available for the bucket brigade he saw one on the beach full of blue huckleberries — his favorite pie material. He couldn't bear to dump them out on the beach, so he opened the lid of a trunk nearby, saw there was an empty spot, and in went the berries. It must have been quite a surprise for the owner of the trunk. The anonymous donor was my husband, who still thinks you can't beat a blue huckleberry pie.

Our furniture was floated out in the water to save it and the *El Cedro* had to pull anchor and leave to go out into the Inlet as it was not safe at her first anchorage off the mill. As we pulled out we could see the whole town lit up by the trees blazing at the back of the houses. Hog Island (2), three quarters of a mile away caught on fire from sparks flying over, to give an idea of what a fire it was.

When we got back the next day, what a sight! Everything burned, sidewalk gone and ashes everywhere. The men were all hoarse from breathing the smoke. But the mill was saved as the wind blew the fire down to our end of town."

In July of 1924 the Masset Timber Co. embarked on a plan of expansion at Buckley Bay, under the Los Angeles Company. Additional machinery was installed in the mill, a box factory erected and a gravity system for the water supply was put in. A larger townsite area was cleared but the post war slump was setting in rapidly. When *El Cedro* went up in October of 1924 and took all the sawn lumber from the mill, it was the last export from Buckley Bay.

In April of the next year all construction at the mill site was halted and it was said that the company would have to undergo extensive financial reorganization before it could reopen its operation.

It never did.

For years there was only a watchman left in charge at Buckley Bay as the mill and machinery and many of the houses were sold at nominal prices. A five-roomed house could be bought for thirty dollars — the buyer had only to jack it down the hill onto a raft and it was his. Several houses were taken to Masset — one of

---

(1) *Otis Davis patented, but did not invent, the idea of the Davis Raft.*
(2) *Gray Island on the map, it was also known as Hog Island and as Pig Island, when the mill management kept pigs to provide fresh pork for the dining room, during the operation of the Buckley Bay mill.*

228

which was to be used for the Masset Community Club. (1)

There is nothing left of the once busy milltown, in fact, it is difficult to imagine what an active place it was — as Nature has inexorably claimed her own.

(1) Howard Carpenter used a horse and windlass to get it up from the beach to its location. It was found to be too small, however, so was torn down and a larger hall built in its stead.

CHAPTER THIRTY-EIGHT

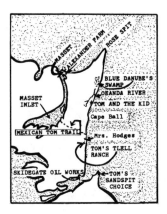

MEXICAN TOM

William Thomas Hodges, much better known as Mexican Tom, was one of the most colorful of all early pioneers.

He was about five-foot-ten, well-built, with a swarthy complexion and a heavy black mustache. The Stetson hat, with its carefully braided horsehair G string and band, and the revolver he was seldom without, would have been enough of a trade mark. But it was his long black hair, kept trimmed to clear his shoulders, which really made him stand out in a crowd. He was inordinately proud of his hair and combed it frequently with a large silver comb. When, during one of his drinking bouts in Skidegate, some misguided joker did a barbering job and cut off the raven tresses to scalp length, Tom nearly took the place apart when he came to and realized what had happened. If he could have found the prepetrator he would have committed mayhem then and there.

"I believe," says Charlie Hartie (now of Queen Charlotte City), "that his ambition was to be known as a bold western cowboy and he certainly played the role well. When he first met you, he would stand sideways with his right hand hanging above that big revolver he always carried, and size you up thoroughly. It left one wondering whether he intended to shoot or shake hands. You had the impression that he was not a man to be taken lightly. He could be very friendly and had a wonderful list of stories, some rather lurid — but never dull, and when the boys were having an evening session with a few drinks and stories, Tom always held the floor."

"He told several versions of where he acquired his nickname," says Charlie, "but the one that seemed to fit his role best was that in his younger days, hearding cattle close to the Mexican border, they had trouble with Mexican bandits who would raid across the border and run off with a herd of cattle. The way Tom told the rest of the story was," Charlie went on, "...'we didn't bother goin' to no lawmen about it. We jest went and got them cattle back ourselves, and just to teach them fellers better manners, we got a few Mexicans too. Before we learned them fellers to leave our stock alone, I had the pleasure of sending twenty-one Mexicans to hell. The ranch boys reckoned I was a hard man on Mexicans and

231

started calling me Mexican Tom'."

His early life can only be guessed at, although he seems to have spent a portion of it in Texas, and he had the genuine drawl characteristic of the Mexican border of that state. The first real knowledge of him was that he was running a pack train up in the Hazelton area of British Columbia, when one night he got into a heated argument over a poker game and drew his gun — meaning business. Constable Jim Kirby, standing nearby, was just as quick on the draw and disarmed Tom, telling him to leave the region — pronto!

So it was about 1901 that Tom arrived in Port Simpson, and being broke was persuaded to take a job as Wiggs O'Neill's boatman, to go out and repair the telegraph line. "He may have been a born horseman," recalled Wiggs later, "but he sure was no boatman. So it ended up by me doing all the rowing, and Tom sat in the stern to watch for line breaks." Then while Wiggs climbed the pole to make repairs — as Tom had an injured foot and couldn't wear the climbing spurs — Tom would make the coffee, ". . .strong, with lots of coffee and very light on water." But he was entertaining company on the trip, yarning for hours in his engaging drawl, his conversation liberally spiced with the Spanish idioms he had picked up in Mexico.

After the stint on the line, Tom worked as a handyman for George Rudge, who was the hotel-keeper at that time in Port Simpson — but this was pretty tame for the colorful Tom. When Mr. Rudge told him about the ill-fated attempt by Mr. Alexander to raise cattle on the Islands (Chapter 16) Tom's ears pricked up. A cattleman at heart, he talked Mr. Rudge into financing him to go to Masset to round up the abandoned cattle. The scheme was to hire a schooner and send it to Masset with a cargo of baled hay and grain. Tom was to build corrals and a series of fences, and in the winter when feed was scarce, lure the young cattle into the corrals, tame them and start a cattle empire.

The cattle were running wild on most of northeastern Graham Island, but they had a favorite haunt near Rose Point, so it was here that Tom built his corrals. He did eventually manage to get a few calves into a corral, but holding them was another matter. They broke out of every fence his long years of experience had taught him to build — and about this time he found he had other problems as well.

Charles Harrison, who had bought the land and some of the cattle connected with the Alexander venture, had run into financial difficulties and the government had taken over his land and stock for nonpayment of taxes. The chief of police in New Westminster, Mr. McIntosh, bought the Harrison land in a tax sale for $150 and sent a man up to begin rounding up the cattle. Harrison had two years to redeem his land, and was in the process of so doing when the McIntosh man arrived to begin work. Not only did he attempt to corral the cattle belonging to Harrison, but he also entered Tom's territory. Tom went to Masset to talk to Magistrate Harrison. Harrison, who had been seething with indignation over McIntosh's highhanded actions, must have thought this was the answer to his prayers. He gave Tom a writ ordering the McIntosh man, "to desist or be held liable for cattle stealing," and sizing up the calibre of the complainant, gave Tom the writ to serve on the McIntosh man, himself. According to Tom's later story he went to the McIntosh man, wearing his guns, delivered the warrant and then quietly informed him that where he came from in Texas they settled

232

their disputes about cattle out of court and if the agent didn't want trouble, he'd best do some travelling. The fellow left for the mainland the next day and Tom took over his horses and equipment. However a lawsuit followed about the cattle which tied things up for quite some time — so George Rudge told Tom he was calling the whole thing off.

Tom liked the wild free life on Graham Island and decided to stay and put down roots. Eddie Stevens, whose father had been the H.B.C. storeman in Masset, had worked with Tom a few times in the attempt to round up cattle. Tom invited the young lad to accompany him on a trip to find a suitable ranch site on the Islands. They went along the North Beach, then down the East Coast to Skidegate and crossed to Sandspit — but it was the lovely grassy spot (1) on the bank of the Tlell River that took Tom's practised eye as the place to set up his ranch.

Eddie went back to Masset and Tom settled in to build up his ranch. However, hardly had he put up his cabin when another stranger came to the Islands. This was William Demerald Cood — a wealthy Englishman from Cornwall.

Cood had come to Masset with a dream of founding a private empire on a suitable tract of land. Meeting the personable young Eddie just back from his Island tour with Tom, Mr. Cood listened to Eddie's description of the East Coast and liked what he heard. But he wanted to have a look at the big Masset Inlet first. Could Eddie guide him overland from there to Tlell? Eddie thought he could.

A canoe was engaged to take them around Masset Inlet and land them in what later became Stewart Bay. It was 1904 and the two men set their course overland to the East Coast, blazing a rough trail as they went — the first people known to have used this route. At Tlell, Cood liked Tom's location so well he offered to buy it on the spot. The price was very good and Tom liked an area at Sandspit almost as much, so a sale was made. When Tom moved to Sandspit, near the site of the present airport, Cood and Eddie Stevens built a new house beside the Tlell River and settled in for the winter. They had a visitor one day, H. A. Collison, second son of Archdeacon Collison, who was on his way up the coast to visit his brother, Will, in Masset.

"Here in very pleasant surroundings, an Englishman has built a commodious and substantial log house," wrote Mr. Collison later, "and it was strange to find a cultured man in such unwonted surroundings. He made us thoroughly comfortable and the horses were cared for, but with the single exception of this Englishman at Tlell and his handyman, we did not see another soul until we arrived at Tow Hill where my brother was waiting."

That winter there were terrific storms, which caused the high tides to come into a depression to the southeast of Cood's house, and they swirled well inland, and at the same time the Tlell River, swollen with heavy rainfall, overflooded its banks. Cood feared that he and Stevens were in danger of being completely engulfed by the waters. He liked not his bargain now. Taking what they could carry on horseback, he and Eddie left in a hurry.

The place at Sandspit was supposed to be as good as this — from what Eddie had told him. Perhaps Tom would like to make another sale. Tom, meanwhile had built a small cabin at Sandspit, but he missed his first choice location on the

(1) Today this location is the Richardson Ranch.

broad banks of the Tlell. So when Cood offered him $1000 cash, plus the return of his old Tlell land, it didn't take Tom a minute to agree to the deal.

With a good ranch site and a thousand bucks in his pocket, the old chap thought his luck was in. To add a little more to the situation, it was about this time that L. T. "Lucky" Watson came from Masset Inlet on his way to Skidegate to catch the boat to Jedway during the copper boom. He had followed much the same route as Cood and Stevens, adding a few more blazes to the trees along the way. "It was some journey," he told Tom as they shared supper at Tom's that night, "they told me in Masset it was a trail. . ." he snorted. Tom began to tease Watson about having it called Watson's New Trail. "No, by gosh, you don't, Tom," responded the colored man, "because I'm giving it to you. From now on its going to be the Mexican Tom Trail." (1) And like so many things said in jest those days, this name stuck. Although the trail became widely known and used, no one ever heard of Tom using it himself. He preferred the beach.

Tom's days of hard living and his many accidents were beginning to demand a reckoning and he became increasingly crippled with rheumatism. He needed a younger man to help him and on a trip outside to buy stock he met Benny Cromp. It didn't take long for Tom's tales of adventure to capture Benny's interest and they became very friendly. Benny was just the man for Tom, easygoing, hardworking and able to take slug for slug with Tom in the bar — no mean accomplishment. He liked the idea of going back to Tlell with Tom and it was agreed that wages and shares would be worked out as soon as the ranch became productive.

Every aspiring rancher should have a wife, thought Tom. As he could neither read or write he enlisted help from his friends at the Skidegate Oilery to put an advertisement in a lonely hearts' column. It caught the interest of a Mrs. Flora Burns who was a widow with a problem.

Mrs. Burns knew all about ranching as she had grown up on one. She was an excellent cook, and in her late forties living in Seattle with her two sons. One was an industrious lad, but the younger one, Byron, had an inborn trait for getting into trouble. After a series of escapades, the police told Mrs. Burns that unless "you get that young scalywag out of town, we'll run him out. In fact," they told her, "if you don't get him onto a ranch or somewhere like that, he's going to end up in jail for sure."

Tom's advertisement was just what she needed. She liked the idea of pioneering in a new land. The Queen Charlotte Islands were far enough from the bright lights to keep young Byron out of trouble. . . she hoped, so she answered Tom's advertisement with her fingers crossed. Tom enlisted the help of his Oilery friends to write the ensuing love-letters for him — and they must have done a persuasive job.

"The news got around like wildfire," remembers Charlie Adam, "and everyone who could get there was on the wharf to meet the prospective bride when she arrived in Skidegate on the *Amur*. Captain Locke was quite a teaser, and he was making the most of this situation when someone suddenly said, 'well, how are they going to get married — there's no minister here now?' 'Oh, come on,' said Locke, 'I'll take you out on the *Amur*.' So the whole gang piled on board," says

(1) This version told to Charlie Adam by Tom himself.

234

Mr. Adam, "The bar was opened and they had a merry old time. Locke performed the ceremony and acted as MC for the party afterwards – and it was some party!"

Two more contrasting natures would have been hard to find – the tough-talking, hard-living, illiterate Tom and the aesthetic ex-Mrs. Burns, but things might have worked out, for they both knew ranch life and wanted to make this marriage a success. Byron, however, was another story. Musical and entertaining, but completely irresponsible, Byron got into almost as much trouble on the Islands as he had in the city.

Tom decided that it was his duty to cure Byron of this habit and tried to beat some sense into him with a harness belt – so vigorously that Byron was in bed for a week. To his mother this was inhuman. She moved out then and there, taking Byron with her, to the place down the road which had been abandoned by Perry Parker, who had decided he wasn't cut out to be a farmer. (1) Calling her place the "Do Drop Inn", Mrs. Hodges sold meals to travellers, when she wasn't out cooking in survey camps or road camps, to make enough money for Byron and herself.

She loved to dance and walked the twenty-six miles to Skidegate for dances, frequently. "She would be the first one on the floor and the last to leave," according to Bert Tingley who remembered her well. "She often told us what a great privilege it was to be a pioneer in the shaping of a new country and seemed to be conscious of this all the time. I thought she was a wonderful person," he added.

For the last few years of her life she ran a branch store in her home at Tlell for Donald Cochrane of Queen Charlotte City. "No big sales," says Charlie Hartie, Cochrane's brother-in-law, "but enough to keep them in groceries. I used to take the supplies up each month in my boat." In 1915 Mrs. Hodges became ill and died within a few months – requesting that she be buried on her own land. Her wish was fulfilled and among the pall bearers to carry this early Islander to her last resting place were her neighbors from the mouth of the Tlell, Bert and Roger Roberts. After his mother's death, Byron sold the place to Joe Rajeau and left the Charlottes for good. Mrs. Hodges' grave, unmarked, and little known, is only a few hundred feet to the west of the luxurious private lodge which today stands on her former land.

After his marriage Tom went in for farming in style and acquired some well-bred cattle and farm machinery, borrowing the money for most of it from Simon Leiser, one of the partners in the Skidegate Oilery. Leiser demanded, and got, Tom's farm and stock as security for the loan. Trying, on a small income, to live the life of a wealthy rancher, with drinking binges, poker games and high life, got Tom into trouble from the start. Benny Cromp began to wonder when, or even if, he would see any cash returns. He was having to work on the government road to get what little money he had, and Mrs. Hodges, even before the breakup had begun to wonder about her share.

Tired of the constant haggling and with a feeling that the handwriting was on the wall as far as Benny Cromp was concerned, Tom was standing on the Skidegate wharf sizing up the disembarking passengers that day in 1909 when

(1) Site later occupied by the well-known Dunes Hotel, which burned down in 1965. The land is owned now by an American Syndicate.

the Purdy family arrived. Ridge, big and strapping, was a tonic to his eyes. He took a great liking to the boy and persuaded Mr. Purdy to let young Ridge ride back up the coast with him and spend a few days on the Tlell ranch. "There was no sign of Byron," recalls Ridge Purdy of this visit, "but Benny was still there. It was plain that things were not going very well. Tom seemed to think that Mrs. Hodges and Benny were in cahoots to try and get his money from him — evidently they were pestering him to make some sort of agreement or will. Mrs. Hodges was at the door when we arrived though, and soon had a good meal for us. And, boy, what wonderful hotcakes she cooked for breakfast the next morning."

The big split came shortly after this. Both Benny and Mrs. Hodges left, and Leiser needing his money told Tom to repay the long overdue loan, or he would have to foreclose. Which Leiser did, selling the ranch immediately to recover his money. Tom at first threatened to keep his beloved ranch by force, but when the new owners, Jake and Neil Walsh arrived, both of them old-time Montana men who talked Tom's language, he tamed down and finally left with a team of six horses, a wagon, his other shirt and a beautiful young filly.

Below Jimmy White's place at the Oeanda, Tom pitched his tent to begin life anew, and decided that the first thing on the agenda would be to ride to Masset and go on a big drunk to get the taste of the past year out of his system. As he was sobering up — or trying to — who should he meet but the "Kid" — young Ridge Purdy. Mr. Purdy, senior had died and Harris, the Kid's uncle, was getting ready to leave. It looked as though they were both at loose ends.

"Well," he asked the Kid, "are you ready to come out and ranch with me now?" But Ridge had a job with the surveyors and wasn't keen to give up $60 a month so soon. He hedged and made excuses. Tom played his trump. "Well, I tell you, Kid," he drawled, "you go down in behind Allen Orr's blacksmith shop and you'll see a young filly. If you come out with me, she's yours today." One look at that young horse and Mexican Tom had a new partner. The Kid was never to regret it. He had an education from a master in every phase of horsemanship from breaking, riding and training, to the making by hand of every piece of equipment they would use. For Tom had a plan to go into freighting up and down the north and east coast — and with Ridge to take over the active part, the old cowboy Tom would patiently guide and instruct. It was Adventure, with all the trimmings thought Ridge — always "the Kid" to Tom.

They built cabins along the coast to use in the course of their business. Everything was beachcombed. "That beach was a veritable treasure chest after every storm," remembers Mr. Purdy, "with a host of things scattered there just for the taking. After one gale, we found the beach covered with lumber when a vessel towing a scow past our tent location, had to cut the towline to save itself. We had all the lumber from that episode we could use for our fences, houses and took load after load into Masset, where we sold it for a good price."

Tom was using his six-horse team to do what little freighting he could to raise cash for his big venture. It was instinctive for him to be always the showman. Edith Bradley (now Mrs. Eddie Singer of Masset) says, "How he used to wheel into our yard at the Spit with a great flourish and all his horses stepping in time! I can see him yet. We kids just lived for his visits."

The Kid was in the process of breaking in a particularly spirited set of horses that Tom had brought back with him from a buying trip to the lower mainland, when Tom came out from Masset one day with some entertainment for them to enjoy. It was an old Edison gramophone with a fine big horn and several roll records. As the Kid worked, Tom played the records for him and every time "The Blue Danube Waltz" was put on, one of the big bulls came to the top of hill and began to bellow. Both Tom and the Kid had seen this big bull frequently and referred to him as the "King". Now as the great beast lumbered out for the fourth or fifth time to roar as the familiar waltz floated out into the still of the evening, Tom called out, "There's old Blue Danube, Kid — listen to him bawl!" From that time on that swampy piece of land in behind the hill in that region was known as Blue Danube's Swamp.

Tom was itching to take the new team the Kid was breaking in, to Masset to show it off. "No, Tom, they're not quite broke yet," Ridge told him, "if they ever got away from you. . ." But Tom pleaded and assured Ridge that he'd driven horses far less broke than that, many a time — and long before Ridge was even born. Eventually, against the Kid's better judgment, he gave in and helped the old man to harness up. "Don't let them get away from you. . ." but his words were lost in the rattle of the wagon as Tom triumphantly slapped the reins and the spirited horses responded. They were off!

Nearly two weeks passed and there was no sign of Tom. The Kid was worried. Tom must have gone on a spree. Knowing that those horses were too skittish to let anyone else near them the Kid wondered if he should go in to Masset and see how things were. As he stood making up his mind he heard a horse galloping — and rushed out to see an Indian boy coming into the yard. He had brought a message from Tom who had said, "Tell the Kid to come right away. Tell him I've got a broken leg and I need him bad."

It was getting dark, but the urgency in the message made Ridge decide to set out then and there. Taking Tom's own personal horse, Big Jim, the Kid left on the double. Big Jim was a one-man horse and allowed no one but Tom to ride or even touch him — until the Kid came along — and then he sensed that his master would approve another rider in an emergency. He was a fitting horse for Tom, afraid of nothing on earth, not even bears. Ridge Purdy will long remember that moonlight ride along the beach into Masset. They had just rounded the Bradley place and were on the first leg of the North Beach stretch, when Big Jim began to edge up to the timber, ears erect. The Kid let him have his way. There, near the timber's edge was a huge whale cast upon the shore, with a bear on top gnawing away furiously at the blubber. Most horses are very nervous, if not terrified, of bears — but not Jim. He was curious. When the Kid returned a few days later the whale was partly covered by sand and beginning to decompose. For several months it lay there creating an awesome smell until another high tide mercifully washed it out to sea.

That night as he left the big beast, Ridge remembered the old Haida superstition that when a whale was cast ashore it was an omen of impending death.

When he arrived in Masset, the Kid found that, as he had suspected, Tom had decided to go on a binge. Then, in the back of his bleary mind, must have realized that the Kid would be anxious about him with that new team. Staggering out of the bar he had met Allen Orr. "Gotta get back out . . . Kid's gonna be worried," he told Mr. Orr.

237

The team had been tethered to graze for Tom's visit into town. Still half groggy the old cowboy attempted to hitch them to the wagon, and had stumbled, slipping under the wagon. Alarmed, the spirited horses bolted — running the wagon wheels over his leg and breaking it. Remembering Ridge's, "Don't let them get away from you, Tom. . .", the old fellow tried to hobble around on his broken leg to get things under control. He was found lying unconscious on the ground, hours later.

Perhaps the wheel of fate had come full circle for Tom. The accident happened at the old Alexander farmhouse — and it was the Alexander cattle that had first brought him to the Islands. He was taken to the Ives Hotel in Masset and Dr. Fraser tried to set the broken limb and make sure that Tom kept off it until it had a chance to mend. But Tom nearly went out of his mind cooped up in that hotel room and got the "boys" to bring him up some whisky to ease things. It was no place for a man like Mexican Tom to heal a badly broken leg — at one time he even took the hated splints off. Gangrene set in, and Dr. Fraser made arrangements for Henry Edenshaw to take his patient to Prince Rupert. The boat had just left when Ridge got in — too late to say goodbye. But Tom had left his big revolver, his stetson hat with its braided bands made from 32 long black horsehairs, for the Kid, in care of Allen Orr.

On November 23, 1912, six weeks after he was admitted to the Prince Rupert General Hospital, William Thomas Hodges died. He was buried two days later on Garden Island, in the harbor of Prince Rupert, under a marker long since lost to the weather. He was fifty-five years old.

Charlie Hartie says of this unique man, "I suppose Tom would appear to most people as just a rough creature who wasted his life and ended up a failure. But to me he was the last example I ever expect to see of the old time cowboy — the genuine article."

Tom must have had a premonition of the end, because before he left on Henry's boat he called Allen Orr to his bedside. Laboriously this almost illiterate man wrote on a piece of paper, "Everything I have goes to the Kid," and signed it with Mr. Orr as witness. He left the paper with Orr, "just in case. . ." Tom still nursed a great grievance against his mail-order family.

When he died there was a commotion over who would get the stock and so on the old man had left. When things got to the threatening stage, Mr. Orr went to Prince Rupert to seek legal advice on Ridge's behalf. Showing the scrap of paper to his lawyer, he was told, "That's one of the best wills I've ever seen, and everything he had *will* go to the Kid, make no mistake about that."

Ridge Purdy stayed out at the East Coast site for another eight or nine months, but it could never be the same on the Islands for him without the old man who had taught him so much and who put so much meaning into the life there. He left Graham Island for good in mid 1913. Well, not quite for good. For like so many of his contemporaries he made a return trip to have one more look at the places he knew and which hold such a host of memories. In July of 1966 as Rev. Ridge H. Purdy of Wabasco, Alberta — the Kid took his wife, Helen, and made his pilgrimage.

CHAPTER THIRTY-NINE

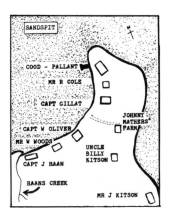

SANDSPIT

On the curving scimitar of Shingle Bay, slightly to the west of Spit Point, William Cood began to build his private empire.

Choosing Eddie Stevens and a young Frenchman, George Shabot, as his right-hand men, Cood recruited additional help from Skidegate Mission to assist in the project.

A wharf was built — entirely by hand labor — which was big enough for steamers to tie to. An old pile-driver hammer had been located and, using a hand-winch, the big hammer was laboriously hauled to a height then released for the free fall on top of a piling. This was repeated over and over until ninety pilings were securely driven in to support the decking of the small dock.

A well-designed home, with gabled windows, comfortable fireplace and a large verandah was constructed according to Mr. Cood's instructions, with equally good outbuildings and barns. Landscaping the region appropriately, he had an attractive and functional headquarters for his estate. To begin the ranching part of his dream, Cood ordered a good saddle pony and imported thirty-five head of cattle from Chilliwack, with three properly trained dogs to round them up when needed.

This estate in the wilds was being created with one major purpose — to win the admiration and approval of his fiancee in England. He wrote describing the enchantment of life on the Charlottes in the surroundings he had been at such pains to create, only to receive a letter saying the lady wanted no part of the wilds of Canada. Not then or ever. He was scarcely able to digest this stunning news when a boat arrived by special charter from the mainland with an urgent cable from his mother. His father had died and Cood was needed at home immediately to help settle affairs in the wealthy family. Leaving with little more than the clothes he was wearing, Cood went back with the chartered boat.

As he bid farewell to the two men he had become so fond of, and realized that there was no hope of his betrothed ever coming to join him at Sandspit, he impulsively gave the whole estate jointly to Eddie Stevens and George Shabot. But his "I'll send over the money to pay off the workmen later," was received

239

with black looks and scepticism by most of the workers. He was as good as his word, however, and the money arrived very shortly afterwards.

George Shabot had come up by the school of hard knocks and thought there was "somet'ing feeshy about the whole deal — you don't get a fine house and all for free," as he and Eddie had done. He wanted to take his share and move on immediately before anything happened, so he propositioned Eddie, "How about you take the house and land, and I take all the cattle — and we call it square?"

This arrangement suited Eddie fine. Amos Russ's eldest daughter, Grace, had returned to live in Skidegate after completing her education on the mainland, and Eddie was greatly attracted. With a good house and ranch land behind him, he was in a position to do some serious courting. "It's a deal," he told the Frenchman. The big Cood house was to have a bride after all, for when the wedding celebrations were over the newly-wed Mr. and Mrs. E. C. Stevens made their home there.

Shabot moved his cattle south along the coast to Dogfish Bay, built a cabin and began ranching on his own. Before long other settlers came to join him and the remains of several cabins and a dam may still be found there. More pioneers settled along the coast to the north of Dogfish Bay as well. Captain and Mrs. Sheldon went to the bay which bears their name, and Mr. and Mrs. Norman Fraser (always called Ma and Pa Fraser) settled on the edge of the lagoon at the head of Sheldon Bay. The lagoon was known as Fraser Lagoon at that time but is called the Salt Marsh today. Copper Bay, to the north of Sheldon Bay, also had several cabins. Joe Molitor brought his wife and family to live there briefly and their daughter, Rose, was born at Copper Bay.

In 1907 Walter Rudge brought his wife and family from Port Essington, and they, too, lived at Copper Bay — later moving to Sandspit. 'Walter was a soft-spoken, easy-going sort of a chap," remembers an old-timer. "I always thought of him as Rip Van Winkle. The children all around here adored him as he was never too busy for a story. He would help anyone out, but could never seem to see all that there was for him to do at home," which meant that his wife, Irene, did practically all of the caring and providing for the ten girls and one son born to them. When Mr. and Mrs. Rudge arrived on the Islands their two eldest daughters, Maggie and Rose, twins who were four years old at the time, were the object of much admiration with their long ringlets and bright eyes.

In 1908 twin girls were born to Mrs. Rudge's brother, Eddie Stevens, and his wife. With a family to support, Mr. Stevens, who was not really cut out to be a rancher, thought he would be able to provide more adequately for his family if they moved to Skidegate Landing, the hub of the Charlottes at that time. He decided to try to sell the big Cood place.

About this time Dr. Pallant, a doctor from Harley Street in London, had become fascinated by all that he had heard from his son, Cecil, about the Islands, and nothing would do but that he and Mrs. Pallant must pay their son a visit. Cecil had staked out a small section of land adjoining Tom and Mrs. Hodges in Tlell, and the doctor liked it so much that he looked for a place to buy on the Islands. The big Cood house at Sandspit was exactly right. In the autumn of 1909 he bought it from Eddie Stevens. It would be difficult to mention the Pallants at Sandspit without the often-told story of Dr. Pallant's bear hunt.

In the early days there were a tremendous number of bears on the Islands

240

and in order to bring the bear population down, the early settlers used to hunt the animals steadily. Wonderful were some of the stories told about bear hunting. These tales had reached Dr. Pallant via his son's letters, and if there was one thing the doctor longed to do above all else, it was to go on a bear hunt. He offered twenty dollars to anyone who could lead him to a bear.

William Woods could use that money. He set a bear trap and two days later knocked on the Pallant door to announce, "Well, Dr. Pallant, I've got a bear for you."

"Oh, have you, my boy — splendid! Just a minute and I'll be with you," was the doctor's delighted reply.

Whilst Mr. Woods waited, Dr. Pallant raced upstairs to put on the complete hunting suit brought especially from England for this moment. On top of the suit he put the big cartridge belt, and another belt, with spare cartridges, was placed diagonally over that then, lastly, his wide brimmed hunting hat. Taking his big gun from the rack he came downstairs calling to Woods, "I'm ready now, Mr. Woods." "Okay," said Woods, "now follow me."

Down the forest trail they went, Woods walking lightly and Pallant in hunting stance, sneaking along. After a short time, Woods caught the doctor's arm, "See, there . . ." he pointed.

Taking his time to get properly ready, the doctor took aim — then in horror lowered his gun. "Mr. Woods, he's in a trap!" he exclaimed in anguish. "Well, of course," replied Woods, "go ahead, shoot!"

"Shoot!" exclaimed the doctor, "I couldn't shoot a bear in a trap. It would be most unsportsmanlike. Please let him out!" Mr. Woods' reply has been lost to posterity, but that tale has been savored and told ever since.

Dr. Pallant had not had nearly enough of Island life when it was time for him to resume his London practice. Fully intending to return to Sandspit, he engaged Mr. R. H. Cole of Port Simpson to care for the property in his absence. Mr. Cole brought his wife and six children to live in the big house.

Cecil Pallant had staked his land at Tlell using the rough estimating and pacing out that was customary before the surveyors arrived. But when the government survey was made he learned that the small section he had chosen was part of someone else's land and, according to the new lines, his described land lay out in Hecate Straits. "Well, my boy, why don't you go on down to the Sandspit place?" urged his father when he heard the news. As there was no comparable land available by then, Cecil decided to accept his father's invitation.

Robert Cole, who had been wanting to go into a sheep-raising venture with John Mathers, had moved out of the big Cood house to the small cottage he had built close by. He would still be able to help on the Pallant place if needed, as well as share in the care of the four hundred sheep he and Mathers were planning to pasture.

Dr. Pallant was never to return to Sandspit — he died suddenly in London. But Mrs. Pallant, who had loved the Spit as much as her husband, sent Cecil a cable to say she planned to make her home on the Islands with him. Her daughter, Mrs. Ryder, accompanied her for an extended visit with Cecil.

He chuckles at his memory of a young Chinese boy his mother engaged to do the cooking in the Sandspit house. "Mother had to show him pretty well everything, and one of the recipes she taught him to make was brandy sauce.

He really liked that idea and for some time we had brandy in everything — cakes, puddings, and so on — until he got over the novelty of it."

During the war Mr. Pallant left the Islands for several years. He joined the police force in Alberni and it was here he met his future wife. After their marriage they returned to live in the big house at Sandspit and a daughter and five sons were born to them. The youngest was still a baby when one afternoon a mysterious fire swept through the house and left only the brick fireplace and a few charred timbers to mark the location of Sandspit's first frame home. Today the Department of Transport houses are on this site. After the fire the Pallants lived in a cottage at Sandspit before moving to Queen Charlotte where they made their home for many years.

The first wedding to take place in Sandspit was in 1908, when Catherine Boyd became the bride of George Carmichael. "One of the finest men I ever knew," as Charlie Hartie describes him. Mr. Carmichael had come from Nova Scotia to the Islands in 1905. During the clearing of Prince Rupert's townsite he lived on the mainland for awhile, helping to clear and then, with another pioneer of Prince Rupert, John Vierick, built several of the town's first houses. Miss Boyd, who was a cousin of the two sisters, Mrs. Mathers and Mrs. Haan, had come to visit Captain and Mrs. Oliver, her aunt and uncle, in Sandspit. George Carmichael soon lost his heart to the pretty blonde girl from Scotland and began a serious campaign to persuade her to stay and become his wife.

Their wedding was a full dress affair in the best pioneer tradition, complete with white gown and veil. "There were no flowers around at that time," recalls Mrs. Carmichael, "so I had to make up my mind that I wouldn't be able to have that final touch. When someone brought a bouquet of dainty flowers — real ones — I couldn't believe my eyes. It was so pretty. After the service I learned that I carried a mixture of geraniums, potato flowers and wild ferns."

The Carmichaels lived first in Skidegate Landing, then like the Haans, moved to Queen Charlotte City. Unlike the Haan family, however, they built their home and remained to raise a family of eight children, whereas about 1911 or 1912, Captain John Haan moved his family to Sandspit. "It was such a lovely place to live in," recalls Mrs. Wes Singer, now of Parksville, who was the former Jean Haan, "my brothers were particularly delighted with the big creek (1) which ran through our place.

In September 1911 another well-remembered family went to live at the Spit. Captain William Oliver, always an Island booster, had met Captain Gillatt in Port Simpson and drew such an attractive picture of Island possibilities that Captain Gillatt decided to take his wife and two daughters, Belle and Peggy, to the Spit and go in for chicken ranching. "Dad," says Belle (now Mrs. Brandon of Victoria) "always did things in a big way. If it was to be a ranch, then in addition to the flocks of chickens, we also had to have riding ponies, cattle ... the works." He built a large home, where the present Islander Hotel now stands. It equalled the Cood home in landscaping with picturesque shrubbery and trees. In addition it had an excellent lawn tennis court in front of the house with an equally good badminton court on the side lawn.

"It was a wonderful life to grow up in," says Mrs. Brandon. "There was so

(1) *Haan's Creek.*

242

much freedom to roam about in, ride our horses and, with the big families at the Spit, the constant going and coming of survey ships and so on, we always had a gang of young people around." Like all good things, however, it did come to an end, but by the time the Gillatt family moved nearer civilization, a son had been added to their family. Perhaps he is the truest Islander of all, as he was born on board the old *Prince John* half-way across Hecate Straits to Prince Rupert. In honor of his birthplace he was given the name of the ship, John — but was dubbed "Jock" by his friends.

In 1910 Jonathan Kitson, who had come to the Charlottes in 1905, built his home on the east side of the Spit, at Cape Chroustcheff, and moved his family there from Queen Charlotte City. Some time later, Mr. Kitson's brother, William, came to live near them. A batchelor, "Uncle Billy" Kitson raised bees and had the first radio in Sandspit. He was appointed to the first school board at the Spit and took his responsibilities very seriously — often going to sit in school all day to be sure that everything was in order.

Another of Sandspit's early residents was Jatice (in Haida "The-Lady-that-lies-down"). Very old and popular with the children who would search for the elderberries she loved. They called her "Nani" and she had Haida names for each of them which they valued very highly. Believed to be Mrs. Oliver's grandmother, she wore a large labret in her lip — and had a fund of tales of the days of her girlhood. The Olivers let her live in her old way and did not try to force her into theirs, so she lived in a tiny hut on the beach with an outside fire. When she died in March, 1912, it was estimated that she was at least one hundred years old, as people who were old then, said she seemed to be an old woman when they were children.

In 1910 Sandspit acquired its first industry with the building and operation of a dogfish oilery. The machinery was purchased from the Skidegate Mission plant, moved and installed in the large shed built for this purpose near the end of the Cood wharf. William Woods was one of the supervisors and Mr. Moulton of New Westminster was manager. He brought his wife and family and they lived in the big Cood house. "Mr. Moulton was a great hand in extolling the wonders of his product," remembers Agnes Mathers, "and would advise everyone to do as he did, drink a large glassful everyday for the health. Ugh! I can still remember how we would shudder as he downed it. . ." The Oilery at Sandspit ran for five or six years and the remains of the plant could be seen long after.

William Woods built his home next to Captain Haan. His daughter, Louise, (Mrs. John Dover) whose home is on this site today, says "I think the most treasured possession my mother had was her sewing machine. She was able to buy it before she was married — and it had taken a lot of savings. Coming back to the Islands with it on the *Sardonyx,* (1) they were off Cape Ball when the ship was wrecked and everyone was ordered off with only what they wore. But no one could part Mother from her sewing machine, and she clung onto it for dear life, carrying it in her arms as they waded ashore from the lifeboats, and for

(1) Canadian Pacific Navigations Sardonyx was wrecked June 13, 1888 on White Cliff Shoal, near Cape Ball. At four in the morning Captain Smith felt her position on the rocks was dangerous and ordered the ship abandoned. It was one and a half miles off-shore.

miles along the beach."

There were enough children in Sandspit to warrant a school, but when no teacher appeared to be forthcoming, temporary arrangements were made. Captain Gillatt volunteered to teach, the big Pallant living room was made available as a class-room, and all the fathers built desks for the children. That first Hallowe'en, Captain Gillatt went to a great deal of trouble to obtain fireworks to put on a big display for his class. When he made the announcement of the fireworks he had arranged for the end of October, he was puzzled by the lack of enthusiasm. "Perhaps none of you know what fireworks are. . ." he began. But in a flash little Maggie Rudge's hand shot up. She did, she said emphatically. "It's carrying the wood."

When Dr. Spencer built the little Methodist church at the Spit, classes were held there and occasionally in Captain Oliver's home, with a succession of men as teachers. In the 1914 to 1915 term Sandspit had its first qualified teacher, Miss I. Lett (sister of Chief Justice Sherwood Lett of B.C. who died in 1964). "She was a terrific person, and I know it was her example that inspired both my cousin Jean and me to become teachers," says Agnes Mathers, who has taught school for more years than she cares to remember. Miss Lett married Scotty Fraser who had come with his brother, Duncan, to build the big wing onto Captain Oliver's home. The story of their romance was that Scotty had been ardently courting Miss Lett for some time, and worried that he was not going to get his answer before she left, he arranged for them to be marooned on Grassy Island (1) one evening by letting his boat become high and dry on a falling tide. (And as one old timer remarked, "Scotty knew the tides like the back of his hand.") It achieved the desired end and Miss Lett married Scotty shortly after. He was killed overseas during the war and sometime later she married the the other Fraser brother, Duncan.

The Hall family of Scotland came frequently to visit their married daughters at the Spit, Mrs. Haan and Mrs. Mathers. In 1914, Peter Hall, their brother, opened the first store there and also ran the settlement's first post office. John Mathers' parents, Mr. and Mrs. Adam Mathers came to live with him in 1920. As Johnny Mathers had been only fourteen when he left his home in Ireland, this was a special reunion. To make it easier for his wife to get around, grandfather Mathers bought a spanking new brougham to drive her where she wished. Mr. Kitson bought one for his wife as well, and these two ladies were the envy of all Sandspit — for early day wagon travel did leave something to be desired as one got on in years.

Agnes Mathers remembers seeing large excavations in many places on her father's land when she was a small girl, and was told that the holes had been made by people searching for old bones. Before the Mathers went to live at the Spit, two men, Abe Johnson and Ed Hewitt, former prospectors from Rossland and Nelson, had learned of the existence of very large bones in the Sandspit area. They had an idea.

Taking great care in the excavation of the bones, they packed quite an assortment of them into crates, and with some well-placed publicity (2) had

(1) Recently renamed Gillatt Island by Canadian Permanent Names Committee.
(2) Vancouver Province, July 12, 1907 — "Rancher at Skidegate discovered
    mammoth rib of the Proboscides Ungulata";
    Victoria Times, July 13, 1907 — ". . .found relics of a primeval age."

them shipped to Vancouver on the *Princess Beatrice* in August, 1907."

"One tusk," according to a newspaper account, "measures eighteen feet, six inches and is twenty-five inches in diameter at the large end. It is nearly straight, having two feet curvature. The bones so far recovered show that the mastodon from which it came was sixteen to seventeen feet across the rump and seven feet between the eyes." It was this last item which received the headline.

"SEVEN FEET BETWEEN THE EYES – THIS MASTODON MUST HAVE BEEN FORTY FEET HIGH – AND THE BONES ARE IN A GOOD STATE OF PRESERVATION"

was the caption in a Vancouver paper which heralded the arrival of the bones.

Engaging a good location on Hastings Street, Hewitt and Johnson put their find on display for thirty cents a look, and drew large crowds with their "PRE-HISTORIC MASTODON BONES FROM THE QUEEN CHARLOTTE ISLANDS" sign.

The resulting publicity from Hewitt and Johnson's venture sent a rash of "bone-hunters" to the region to dig for more specimens. "We only managed to save part of a rib and vertebrae before they were all carted away," says Agnes Mathers as she points to the specimens lying in the shade of a tree in the vegetable garden today.

The first World War affected Sandspit relatively little, but the second one was a different matter. The R.C.A.F. purchased the Pallant property at Spit Point and in 1943 built an airstrip, which was the forerunner of the busy airport it has become today. In 1945 the airport property was turned over to the Department of Transport and is still under this jurisdiction. It handled in the neighborhood of forty-eight thousand passengers in 1966. Complete and up-to-date navigational aids are maintained to assist the many commercial and private aircraft which use this base.

In 1940 a division of the Crown Zellerbach Company opened an operation at the Spit; its Northern Pulpwood Limited engaging fifty men. This pilot operation has grown to over one hundred and fifty men who, with their wives and families, have swelled the settlement's population to five hundred and necessitated a school which engages four teachers. A paved road runs from the airport to the old Kitson property, with a branch line to Alliford Bay.

Only one of the original Sandspit homes is in use – the Mathers home – where the post office is now. Next to this house which John Mathers built in 1907, live his son Bill, and his wife, Margaret, who operate the only self-supporting ranch on the Islands, the feature of which is milk from their immaculate Glenn Dairy.

Sandspit's "suburb" is in front of Uncle Billy Kitson's old place, on land that was formerly occupied by Dick Husband and his family from Miller Creek and the Japanese family of Mr. Oshawa. The north end has a D.O.T. signals installation, but the southern part is owned by Mr. Howard Harding, Government Agent in Prince Rupert, who has built a number of rental units on his property – resulting in the local nickname of "Hardingsville."

CHAPTER FORTY

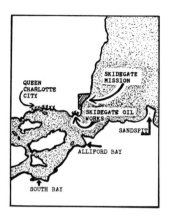

ALLIFORD BAY

Ten miles west of Sandspit is the snug harbor of Alliford Bay. Captain D. Pender, master of the H.B.C.'s *Beaver,* which had been engaged for the survey of Skidegate Inlet, named it in 1866 to honor William Alliford, A.B., quartermaster of the *Beaver,* who was coxswain of the boat engaged in the sounding of of this bay. (1)

Lot number 4, which takes in the land at the head of Alliford Bay, was among the earliest lots to be registered for the Charlottes. William Sterling had it surveyed and registered in 1879, along with Torrens Island and Skidegate Landing. (See Chapter Nineteen)

Although these properties (lots 2, 3, and 4) changed hands several times — whenever the Oil Works at Skidegate Landing was sold — Alliford Bay was never developed. Its moment of recognition came in 1911 when it was selected by Sir George Doughty, the Grimsby fish merchant from England, who headed the B.C. Fisheries, to be the site of a model cannery city. He announced that no expense would be spared in its development, electric light, running water and all the latest amenities were scheduled.

By the spring of 1912 the B.C. Fisheries had bought two hundred acres of virgin Crown Land, as well as the Oil Works at Skidegate Landing, from Simon Leiser and his partners. It was planned to enlarge and modernize the old Oil Works at Skidegate and run it in conjunction with the big cold storage plant, cannery and reduction plant at the Alliford Bay operation.

In March 1912 one hundred men were engaged to work on the extensive building, and the mill in Queen Charlotte City ran at full capacity to try to supply all the lumber needed. To ensure a stable population for his new town, Sir George said that he was making it conditional when he engaged men in Britain that, "each shall promise to bring out his wife and children at the earliest opportunity and," he added "this is only one of the many such fishing stations my company proposes to build."

(1) "B.C. Coast Names" J. T. Walbran.

With so many of the men from Skidegate Mission engaged in construction at Alliford Bay, wives and families went to keep them company, and as a result a temporary school was set up that spring. Mr. B. J. Russell, a student missionary, and Mrs. Solomon Wilson volunteered to teach the forty pupils. At the close of school in June a big party was held for the children, parents and friends, with Messrs. Rhineheart, Carter, Pearson and Curry supplying the music as everyone pitched in to make the event a success. It was announced that the big dance on Dominion Day which was usually held in Skidegate would, that summer, be held in Alliford Bay.

Two steam trawlers, the *Triumph* and the *Canada* were brought from Grimsby, under their own power, to fish for the new enterprise, and the *Edrie* (1) plus another smaller tug were purchased to serve as the nucleous for the fleet of fishing vessels planned.

In June the *Vadso* brought a huge supply of materials as well as a number of small boats to Alliford and it was hoped to put the cannery into limited production that year — 1912. By September they had completed two good-sized wharves, a large cannery building, curing houses for the fish and fifty residences for the workmen. High on a hill overlooking his dream town Sir George had his own home built. He and Lady Doughty, an Australian-born writer of some note, furnished the house with the best of everything — including a fine piano. For years this house was known as "Doughty's Castle."

On November 5th, 1912 the Prince Rupert papers ran big write-ups about the immense load of machinery — reported to be worth one million dollars — which had been loaded aboard the *Princess Ena* for shipment to Alliford Bay. One paper noted that, ". . .the Doughty cannery, one of the largest on the coast has gone into production this summer with the processing of 25,000 cases of fish — operating on a limited basis."

Less than a year later, in September 1913 the whole thing was in the hands of the receivers. On July 10th, 1914 the assets of the company were offered for public sale and included the land at Alliford Bay, Torrens Island, and Skidegate Landing, plus the Skidegate Oil Works, together with the fertilizer plant, cannery, vat house, cold storage plant, office buildings, houses, wharves, and storehouses in Alliford Bay. In addition there were five steam trawlers, four gas launches, seventeen fish boats and twenty-six Columbia river boats. Local feelings about the disaster were that an inexperienced company had gone too far too fast.

On paper the company's assets were shown to be $1,500,000, but when they brought only $300,000 at the receiver's sale, there was a hue and cry. As the sale had been in England it meant that B.C. creditors fared very badly. Sir George's premature death shortly before the collapse mercifully spared his witnessing this inglorious end of his dreams.

Mrs. Helen Wilson of Prince Rupert remembers the Doughty venture only too well, as it was the spark which drew her husband, Bill, to the idea of coming to Canada. "Doughty had great big ads in the Aberdeen papers for help in this model plant," she says, "and especially good offers were being made for coopers. Well, my husband, Bill, was a good cooper and things were not too

---

(1) Now the GRYHME of Francis Millerd and Company, Vancouver.

248

flush in Scotland at that time — so when he heard he would get his fare and all found to come out to this new job — it wasn't long before he talked me into things too."

Mr. Wilson came to Skidegate in the fall of 1911 and, as soon as he found a place for them to live, sent for his wife and small daughter, Nellie. "We had a tiny house in Skidegate," says Mrs. Wilson, "and although we were only there a year until it all folded up ... I remember so many things about the life there. Especially the dances — they were so much fun. Charlie Strachan and his wife and their daughter, Jean, were there at the time too. Young Jean worked in Fraser's Boarding house at Skidegate and later married Tom Young."

There were two big weddings in Skidegate Mission during the time the Wilsons were in Skidegate, these were the weddings of Mr. and Mrs. Solomon Wilson and Mr. and Mrs. Moody. Invitations were extended to everyone for both events. "They were awfully kind to us — such wonderful hospitality," recalls Mrs. Wilson, "Nellie was pretty small at the time and I wondered what to do, until Mrs. Amos Russ took me under her wing and put my little girl to sleep in their big home in the Village." When the big Doughty plan collapsed the Wilsons left to make their home in Prince Rupert.

The Alliford Bay project was a calamity to the principals of the B.C. Fisheries, but was not a loss to the region, for it was taken over by Maritime Fisheries Limited and operated as a cannery on a more appropriate scale until the late 1920s. "It was really a wonderful cannery," says Mrs. R. C. Robertson, (1) "as it had been built properly and no expense spared in its construction." The Robertson family were at Alliford in 1925, 1926 and 1927 as was Alec Reid, the engineer, and remember that the cold storage plant was beginning to fall down at that time.

"The big house on the hill, Doughty's Castle, was used by Tom Sanderson, the manager, and was still stocked with the wonderful furniture — including the piano," says Betty Robertson. "My husband was the bookkeeper and we lived in another good-sized house at the other end of the cannery village. There was a large store, many Indian, Japanese and Chinese homes, as well as several small houses and a big bunkhouse. Our pack of fish was all sold to Crosse and Blackwell." (2)

Marsh English was the manager of the B.C. Packer's cannery at South Bay, five miles to the west of Alliford Bay, and Betty Robertson was pleased to meet his wife — for Mrs. English's sister, Miss Nichols, had been Mrs. Robertson's second teacher in the early days at Masset, and she had met the English's several times when they had visited Miss Nichols there.

The Maritime Fisheries closed their operation in Alliford Bay after the 1927 season, as they felt there were not enough fish in the area to keep two canneries fully occupied. Canadian Fishing Company took it over, but only for a brief period as, during the next big run, a combination of the heavy load of canned fish awaiting export, plus teredo-eaten pilings, caused the ignominious collapse of the main section of the cannery into the "salt chuck" below. This marked the end of Alliford Bay's cannery days.

(1) The former Betty Fraser, eldest daughter of Masset's first doctor.
(2) A British firm.

In 1937 it sprang into public interest again when the rumor spread that the Dominion Government had purchased one hundred and sixty acres at Alliford Bay to establish a seaplane base. The international situation was becoming increasingly threatening and, realizing that Canada had only one R.C.A.F. station (in Vancouver) for the whole of its western seaboard, the government decided to establish an advanced base on the Charlottes.

The work of building up the base had barely begun when, as had been feared, the second world war broke out. Officially opened as a Detachment on September 4th, 1939, it did not become operational as a seaplane base until May 13, 1940. On that date Number 6, Bomber Reconnaissance Squadron — flying Shark aircraft — was transferred from Jericho Beach in Vancouver to Alliford Bay. (1) With replacements of twin-engine flying boats in 1941 and long-range Canso's in 1943, routine work continued there until the end of the war. This consisted of anti-submarine patrols, transporting personnel and supplies to many spots on the coast and photographing vital areas. Also at the base was a half-battalion of infantry and a field artillery battery, placed there immediately after Pearl Harbor. At the peak of the station's activities, personnel strength numbered approximately seven hundred. For five years this base was considered to be a key point in the Dominion's West Coast defences. With the cessation of hostilities the station was closed in September, 1945 and later dismantled.

Alliford Bay today is the Moresby Island terminus for the barge and water taxies which operate between Graham and Moresby Island.

(1) Information from Wing Commander R. V. Manning, Chief of Defence Staff, Canadian Forces Headquarters, Ottawa, 1965.

CHAPTER FORTY-ONE

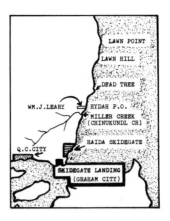

SKIDEGATE LANDING

The Graham Island terminus — and headquarters — for the water taxi and barge service is at Skidegate Landing. This little settlement was hub of the Islands when Simon Leiser appointed William J. Leary to be manager of the Oil Works in March, 1908. (1) The mining town of Jedway had been becoming increasingly important since 1907 — but it was too far away in those days of poor communication to be a challenge to the prestige of Skidegate.

In addition to the supervision of the Oilery operation, Mr. Leary assumed storekeeping duties and, although he was most co-operative in assisting his customers at all times including the delivery of orders by boat to settlers up the coast, there was one thing he did not do. This was to duplicate the situation which had earned his predecessor the nickname of "Coal Oil Johnny." John Mathers had acquired his affectionate name because of the fuel he used in the engine of his boat, the *Skidegate*. "Pheww! you could smell the stuff a mile away," recalled one old-timer. "No one had to tell you Johnny Mathers was on his way."

The *Amur* brought in four other passengers the day she came in with the Leary family — all destined to stay and settle on the Islands. In addition to George McRae of Nova Scotia, there were Pete Adams, Bill Jardine and Ed Wiggans. George McRae had been working on the clearing of Prince Rupert's townsite when he met a couple of men who had just come back from the Islands. "By golly, I think I'll go over and take a look at the place too," he decided impulsively — and remembers his first night in Skidegate only too well.

"We put up at Smith's Hotel," he says. "Accommodation was a bit limited so I slept on the table and Pete Adams slept under it. The others went upstairs — called the "Ram's Pasture" — and that's where I first met Walter Dass," (2) and

(1) Skidegate Landing's earlier history Chapter 19.
(2) Chapter 20, Dass at Jedway, Walter Dass married Flora Cook
who came to visit Mrs. Donald Cocrane in Queen Charlotte City.
Several years after Flora died, Walter married her sister, Dora Cook.
Walter, in his nineties, lives in Toronto with a relative today.

he chuckles as he recalls, "they were calling him the 'Bald-headed Wanderer' in those days."

Nicknames were the order of the day, even houses had names, such as the Pest House and the Dirty Dozen, according to Mr. McRae. "They seemed to be a real good bunch of men," he says, ". . .until they found out they had a wood stealer among them." This was the lowest of the low. A plan was laid by some of those who had been victimized and it was not long before the culprit was caught ". . .red-faced and almost hairless," says George. They had picked out some of their choicest dry wood as bait, then packed the centers with stumping powder.

With accommodations being what they were at the hotel, Mr. McRae soon moved into the bunkhouse on the upper floor of the can-making shed. There for the spring and summer of 1908 he, Ed Wiggans, Al Daise, Jim Oman, Dick Husband, Bob Kitson, Jim Mullock and Bert Porter batched together in what inevitably became the "Batchelor's Hall."

Mr. McRae got hold of a dory to try dogfishing for the Oilery up and down the coast from Skidegate to Tlell. "Handline fishing," he says, "mostly at night as it was generally calmer then." Bait was salt herring, furnished by the Oilery. They got fifteen cents a gallon for the livers and this price soon dropped to twelve and a half cents. "It took about nine fish to make a gallon of livers," says Mr. McRae, "so I could see I wasn't going to get wealthy in a hurry with the fishing. Tom Anderson and a chap named Miller were going up to try panning gold from the black sands at the Oeanda. I went along with them to try my luck too." The gold was just as elusive for the Nova Scotian as it had been for others.

Several of Mr. McRae's friends had become pre-emptors and he followed suit – choosing his land near Clay Hill, to the south of Tlell. He did enough work on it to qualify for his Crown Grant then sold it to Mr. George Pitt-Turner for the fabulous sum of $600. "Real wealth in those days. But now," he adds, "the place belongs to them sporty fellows – millionares from the States."

Mr. McRae bought Tom Sanderson's house in Skidegate Landing, and as he had a steam ticket went to work in the logging camps running the donkeys, then after a short stay in Anyox, returned to Prince Rupert to work on the railway. But the lure of the Charlottes was irresistible – he came back to stay. Today he lives on his waterfront property at the west end of Queen Charlotte City, and his quick step and sharp come-back to questions belie his calendar age of eighty-six. One is conscious of his many years in the realization that so many of those good friends he speaks about, of earlier days, have now, "gone across the bay."

The Leary family liked their new home at Skidegate – in fact Mr. Leary liked everything about the Islands so much that he began to look at a section of land near Miller Creek with the idea of becoming a serious homesteader instead of a fishing plant manager.

He was deeply aroused by the indifferent treatment being accorded to the Islands by the government and began almost immediately to see what could be done to force the government to return to the Islands some part of the enormous revenues being collected at the time in coal and timber licences. He knew there were many others who felt the same way, but it just needed someone to get an organization started.

On Thanksgiving night, eight months after his arrival, Mr. Leary invited

252

everyone in the area to a big dinner, meeting and dance, Mr. W. J. Smith, proprietor of the hotel was engaged to serve dinners from six to nine that evening to accommodate the one hundred and seventy-five people who arrived, mothers, fathers and children — youngsters were always packed up and taken to social events.

After dinner everyone went to the spacious net loft for the meeting which was chaired by Mr. Corlett, foreman of the mill in Queen Charlotte City. By unanimous consent the Graham Island Settler's Association was formed, with A. J. Gordon as its first president and N. McGillivary, the secretary. Forty enthusiastic members signed up with escalating hopes that they might at last get some government action.

After the highly successful meeting, the benches were pushed back for dancing, with Messrs. Swiller and Rhineheart supplying the music. The Skidegate Indian Band, in their new uniforms, came to play several selections for the delighted crowd during an intermission. Captain John Haan put his big *Ranger* at the disposal of the guests who had come from a distance to take part in the first organization of this kind on the Islands.

A few months later, in March 1909, the annual meeting was held, once again taking the form of a dinner and dance in Skidegate, and it was learned that the membership had increased to sixty-two. There were representatives from Lawn Hill, Skidegate, Queen Charlotte City, Gold Harbor, (1) and Tasu as well as mining, fishing and other occupations. It was the results which were obtained by this Association which motivated the organization of the Masset Inlet Settler's Association in 1910.

In the fall of 1909 it appeared that the Oil Works at Skidegate Landing might change management when a Vancouver syndicate applied to lease it from the Simon Leiser company on a trial basis. The market for dogfish oil was poor at that time, so Leiser and his partners were happy at the chance to unload. The Vancouver syndicate announced that they had ambitious plans for the site. Leon Melekov, Manager of Standard Trust and Industrial Company of Vancouver, was managing director, with J. G. Allen of Allen Brother, Charles Hooper, M. G. Waddell and Dr. C. B. Mansell also on the board. Mrs. Fanny Artaud and Olier Besner of Prince Rupert indicated serious interest in the firm. Mrs. Artaud announced that she was going to build a three-story hotel, and Ole Besner was applying for a liquor licence for it and would be the manager.

"They will develop fishing and its by-products," ran a news item in October 9, 1909 issue of a Prince Rupert paper, "and the harbor of Skidegate will be the port of the lower section of Graham Island. The coalfields of the interior of the Islands are expected to pour out thousands of tons of freight over their wharves annually. The town is now being surveyed and as soon as the work is completed, lots will be put on the market. A site will be given to each denomination for a church, and in addition, lots will be set aside for a hospital. The name of the new townsite will be GRAHAM CITY."

---

(1) John McLellan, a former B.C. Assayer, operated a gold mine in Gold Harbor at that time, on land adjoining the old H.B.C. find of 1852. He put in a stamp mill and did well in a small way for several years.

On January 1, 1910, Windy Young came out with headlines in his paper,

"POOR OLD SKIDEGATE IS DEAD! Nothing remains to great the eye except a few dilapidated empty buildings, an ancient wharf, store and P.O. — *and* the odor from the empty oil works situated on the side of a mountain. Wonders will never cease. We are told that after struggling for over 20 years the old name was an utter failure and that the sidehills are to come out with a brand new name — Graham City."

When the Prince Rupert papers reprinted the item they added their own caption of "Queen Charlotte City takes a fling at Neighbor."

Arthur Holland, B.C.L.S., laid out the new townsite and on March 24, 1910, Graham City, Skidegate Harbor, was officially registered. This was less than a year from the time that Charles Harrison had persuaded the Cook brothers to abandon this name for their townsite in favor of New Masset. The second Graham City designation was to be used for even less time than the first — and undoubtedly the post office was the prime reason for the decision to retain the old name of Skidegate after all.

By this time Mr. Leary had succumbed to the lure of Miller Creek and taking up land, bought the house which had been built there earlier by Norman Fraser. (1) Archie J. Gordon, his neighbor of Skidegate, was appointed to be the storekeeper-manager at the Oilery in his place. Rumors were flying as to the big changes to be made by the new company taking over the Oilery — but all the plans came to little more than an idea. However, Mr. Clement de Pape, who had been trying unsuccessfully to operate a hotel at Lawn Hill, made Leroux an offer for his hotel in Skidegate. (Leroux had bought it from Mr. Smith, who had moved to Windy's city of Queen Charlotte.) Leroux was only too glad to sell out. No doubt he was not a hotel man at heart, for under his management the establishment had acquired the nickname of "the Stomach Robber." Clement de Pape's advertisement in Windy's *Queen Charlotte Islander* on August 24, 1911 said:

"SKIDEGATE HOTEL UNDER NEW MANAGEMENT, C. de Pape — Beds from 25¢ up.

To augment his hotel earnings, Mr. de Pape planned to keep the contract to deliver mail between Skidegate and Lawn Hill.

With the big Doughty splash in 1912 things looked so promising in Skidegate that Mrs. "Ma" Fraser bought de Pape's hotel and expanded it to a twenty-room hotel-boarding house. Former hotel man, Leroux, went back into business and opened a store near the Oil Works. For a short and glorious time it looked as though Skidegate Landing was going to come into her own again — despite Windy's snide remarks. The harbor was crowded with boats on June 14, 1912, with the *Albert, Vadso, British Columbian,* and *Edrie* all there. Mr. Sherman was engaged by the government to take charge of a road gang to begin rock work for a wagon road between the two Skidegates.

But the big Doughty collapse marked the end of this pioneer community as the most important settlement of the region, and her position in this respect was gradually and inexorably usurped by her neighbor to the west — Queen Charlotte City. There were several loyal Skidegaters who never considered making their

(1) Information Mrs. Roy Field, Courtenay, B.C.

254

home anywhere else — the longest residency is that of Mrs. E. C. Stevens who, with her husband, came to live there in 1909. Many other names will be remembered by old-timers — and among them would be Al Beebe. Mr. Beebe came to the Islands in 1910 and ranched on one end of Sandilands Island before moving to Skidegate.

He had been raised in the United States in what he called "Indian Country" when raids and scalpings were a daily possibility. His parents had come by covered wagon to claim their land from the wilds, and defence of it by gun was a frequent necessity. Mr. Beebe and his brother were sent to the nearest school — several miles away — until too many close calls from unfriendly Indians made his parents decide it was better to have uneducated, but live children. His use of language as a result had an unusual twist, and Beebe-isms are remembered with affection; he would talk about "going into the Pontoons to find my two-year old heifer, which I ain't seen for four years;" and about getting his "conscription for the *Daily Province*," of "the Sam-hill cranes and the Saw-mill ducks," and he was pleased when he entered hospital to find out that "the nurses are all granulated — no greenhorns."

He was a slender, handsome young man when he met and married a Spanish girl in Mexico, greatly against her parents wishes. The young couple had to flee in the night when her family made it clear that they would murder Beebe to get their daughter back. Very much in love, the Beebes would settle in one town until the girl's family discovered them — then to avoid bloodshed they would flee again. A daughter was born and was about four years old when both Mrs. Beebe and the little girl were killed in a train wreck.

Al Beebe came to the Charlottes then. Several years later he visited Miller Creek. Dick Husband's daughter, Dorothy, was playing in the garden when Mr. Beebe reined his horse in to visit. Beebe stopped dead in his tracks, almost transfixed as he looked at the little girl — but said nothing. He took an especial interest in the Husband family from that moment on, with particular affection for Dorothy. Just before he died, he told her the story of his early days, saying that when he had first seen her that day, she was the exact image and age of his daughter, and in his close relationship with the Husband family, he felt he had something of his own family back with him.

Mr. Beebe was a fine dancer and knew all the steps of his day. He was in great demand as a square dance caller, "...there were few to equal him," recalls Mrs. Sybil de Bucy. Buried in the Tlell cemetery, his tombstone wears the fitting epitaph, "The Last of the Old West."

CHAPTER FORTY-TWO

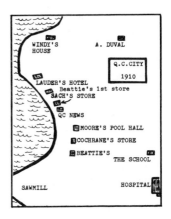

QUEEN CHARLOTTE CITY

The first activity at what was to be Queen Charlotte City began when the North American Timber Holding Company, with headquarters in Seattle, began to build a mill there in early 1908.

The B.C. Government in its desire to capitalize on the natural resources wealth of the Charlottes was advertising that they would grant a long term lease on the rich timber lands of the Islands to anyone who would start a sawmill or a pulpmill there. By building a small mill which even in peak production could only put out 30,000 feet a day — and which averaged less than half this as a rule — the American company secured a thirty-year lease on ninety square miles of virgin timber land around Skidegate Inlet.

This was the era of the big land boom — when people would invest their money in anything that remotely resembled land. It didn't take long for an interested, on-the-spot group of men to recognize that the establishment of a mill was a heaven-sent real estate opportunity. Early in 1908 several of the mill owners, together with members of the Gore and McGregor Surveying and Cruising outfit, got together to form the "Townsite Company." Buying a strip of land lying to the east and west of the mill, they laid out the western section into streets, lanes and lots — being careful to reserve a section of land for the railway station. This was for the mooted trans-Graham Island Railway which would have one of its terminals on Skidegate Inlet. For the time being the place was known merely as "the townsite" in lieu of a better name while the directors looked around for a good promotor.

They couldn't have found a more enthusiastic or imaginative salesman for their wares than Daniel R. "Windy" Young. Windy had lost a leg in a mine accident which finished his mining career, but he soon found an even better niche for his talents. With his persuasive spiel and effervescent energy for any product he promoted (regardless of its chance of success) he was able to earn a better than average living for his wife and family. He had a prosperous career in the Okanagan Lake district boosting fruit lands and mining shares. When business became slack in that line he went to the Queen Charlotte Islands which were

257

being widely heralded as, "The Last Great West."

One of the first things Windy did upon being appointed as sales manager for the Townsite was to give it a fitting name — Queen Charlotte City. A newspaper was the perfect vehicle for his type of sales pitch. Windy got hold of a printing press and proceeded to go all out in the boosting of his "City". On April 4, 1908 the Islands' first newspaper, Windy's *Queen Charlotte News,* made its debut — temporarily published in Victoria, since the town he was advertising was still covered by trees.

When George McRae arrived in March 1908 they were just beginning to peel the spruce rafters for the mill. However, under the capable supervision of Mr. P. Foster, a crew of twenty-five Indians and fourteen white men had the mill in running condition by early fall. Although located on Graham Island it was given the name of Moresby Island Lumber Mill.

The townsite plan was officially registered on July 22, 1908, making it the first registered townsite on the Islands. By now Windy had established his news office in its rightful setting. Engaging Jimmy Campbell to attend to the actual printing, Young was free for full time campaigning. "Want ads" were listed prominently for:

"20 good men, with families only, at once; steady work — Apply P. Foster, Foreman, Moresby Island Lumber Co."

"A Barber; come at once and bring a chair with you; money in sight,"

"Druggist and Doctor, with small stock; can do well here."

"Jeweller with small stock; can make some money."

"A Laundry; people here too busy to wash; bring utensils; can have our cash."

Early in 1909 he arranged to charter a special excursion trip of the *Princess Beatrice* to bring a group of possible investors to see his townsite.

Selling Queen Charlotte City to the world was not enough to take up the talents of this energetic salesman and he soon expanded to the boosting of dozens of other possibilities. James Faulkener was appointed to be townsite agent during his frequent absences and Windy started several companies on his own. They sounded wonderful on paper. One was the Queen Charlotte Cold Storage and Fishing Company which made headlines for awhile. Windy did actually have some cod caught, processed and sold on the mainland — but the actual fishing fleet was never more than one man in a power dory.

Perhaps his most audacious action was when he fast-talked a coal drilling outfit, on its way to drill at the Chown for Mr. McIntosh, into coming ashore en route and putting down a 1500 foot drill right on the Queen Charlotte townsite. On the strength of this he instigated the formation of the Northern Anthracite Collieries Limited, with T. S. Gore as president. 1,500,000 shares were offered for sale at 15¢ each; terms were 5¢ down, 5¢ in 30 days and the final 5¢ at the end of 60 days. H. F. McRae and Co. on Second Avenue were the Prince Rupert agents. Not only did Windy hope to make something on his sales commissions, but it would also aid real estate sales for the Townsite.

Thomas S. Gore's name could be found on most of the larger schemes connected with making money in Queen Charlotte, but it was Windy who believed enough in the future of the town to establish residence there — building the biggest home and bringing his wife and six children to join him. Because of his volubility on its behalf, Queen Charlotte was as well-known as "Windy's City" as it was by its right name.

Jimmy Campbell stayed with him to do the printing until August 1911, when he left to found his own paper. His editorials contained pointed remarks about his former boss's "wind". (With the Yakoun coal rush of 1913, Queenstown began to boom and the alcoholic Scot moved his plant to Eli Tingley's town.) Windy made little mention of Campbell's quitting except to say "there isn't room for two newspapers in this town and it will be a fight to the finish". He added that he was going after his share of the advertising revenue "regardless of costs", and hired Clifford Irwin to do his printing for him for awhile. But the slump was setting in. The paper was closed down before too long and the Youngs moved away. Windy died soon after, and later on Clifford Irwin married Mrs. Young. As one old-timer said, "Whether it was for good or otherwise, it was Windy who advertised this part of the Islands more than anyone else and who really got it going. But for him I don't think Charlotte would have got the jump on Skidegate like it did."

Trying to bridge the gap between Windy's glib statements and the harsh facts of reality set a dizzy pace for the embryo town. In 1909 the mill was operating, with the newspaper office to the west of it and, west of the newspaper, Mark Lauder of Seattle built a hotel — for which he had the foresight to secure a club licence to sell liquor. As Charlie Hartie remembers, "All that was needed to qualify as a member of the club was a thirst and the price of a bottle."

Windy's newspaper announcements attracted John L. Barge, a carpenter in Victoria. It sounded like a good opportunity to get into a business of his own. Kissing his wife goodbye, he left her and their four young girls in Victoria and he arrived in Charlotte in May 1908. "He had to clear a spot to pitch his tent the forest grew so close to the beach," says his youngest daughter, Dorothy, who recalls those early years.

"On August 3rd, we arrived at Queen Charlotte to join him. There was no wharf and we climbed down a ladder into a row boat bobbing up and down so far below us. I was carried down. Our furniture, including a piano, was slung over the side onto a raft and shoreward we went.

Dad knew about tides from books of course, but he had no practical knowledge of such things. He neglected to tie up the raft and soon it was floating out in the Inlet, furniture and all! I think he was just too busy getting his brood on dry land and stationed in the hotel, that he hadn't time to bother with lesser things. Luckily it was a summer's day and the weather kind, so it was not too long before the drifting raft was retrieved and safely moored. Our first few days were spent in Lauder's hotel," Dorothy went on, "Dad and Mother had a room with a bed in it — the only one, I believe. We children slept on mattresses on the floor. How thrilled I was to be staying in a hotel!

Our first home was nothing but a shack, one big room really. The one bedroom had a curtain for one wall and the packing case for the piano for the other wall. That case made a good clothes closet. The corner behind the packing case was the kitchen and the rest was the living-dining room. Such fun we had! Taffy pulls, parties, church — many services were held in our little shack. At first the four of us girls slept in tents, but one night there was such a terrific storm that Dad came out and took his terrified daughters inside while Mother made up beds on the floor. Thereafter we stayed inside and Dad built a lean-to with bunks in it. The wall was papered with Happy Hooligan and Katzenjammer Kids.

We must have had some good storms in those early days, for one morning we got up to find that thirteen trees had fallen during the night on Dad's two newly cleared lots.

I thought it was a most fascinating town to live in," she goes on, "and I remember in particular the "bark" cabin which Mr. Kitson built for his family. He had selected slabs of wood from the mill, with bark still attached, and fitted them together so carefully that the cabin appeared to have been built entirely of bark."

James Faulkener brought his bride to live in Queen Charlotte soon after John Barge had settled his family so Windy gave Faulkener *his* permission to use the Barge raft to unload their supplies, and had a good log home built for them. Their son was born the following September (1909), the first baby to be born on the townsite and was named Graham after the Islands.

"Mrs. Faulkener's mother and sister came to visit her for a few months," recalls Dorothy Barge, "and one day the sister, Miss McDougall, asked my sister, Carrie, and young Johnnie Kitson to go with her to Skidegate. Johnnie's dad had a boat so the three of them went down to the Oil Works. Once there, Miss McDougall left Carrie and Johnnie on the pretext that she wished to go to the store. In reality she had a rendevous with her young man, and together they set out for Prince Rupert on his small gas boat. She had used Johnnie and Carrie as a cover-up so she could get to Skidegate without too much questioning by her mother and sister. However, the elopement was a success and word was sent back that they were happily married in Prince Rupert."

Mr. and Mrs. Sanderson, who lived at the Oil Works, will always stay in my memory because of the way Mrs. Sanderson could go along a trail, knitting away like fury as she walked," says Dorothy.

Community spirits were good in the region right from the start — for the mill had not begun to operate when the people of the whole area got together to make a much needed hospital a reality. The Townsite Company donated the lot, a group from Skidegate Mission came down and cleared it, then another group of volunteers, led by Ed Wiggans, built the foundations. As soon as the mill went into production the Moresby Island Lumber Company donated the lumber and company carpenters, assisted by George Carmichael, completed the actual building. The Provincial Government was prodded into providing $1000 for equipment, plus $300 a year subsidy to encourage a doctor to become resident in the town. In August of 1908, Dr. J. W. Cross arrived and using temporary headquarters, engaged his first nurse, Miss Lauder ("Honeybunch"). With the able assistance of the newly formed Hospital Association the formal opening of the hospital took place in the summer of 1909. Dr. Cross was still in charge, but his regular staff now consisted of Miss Carey as superintendent and Mrs. Rogers as her assistant, both of whom were from Seattle.

260

It was the little nurse from Winnipeg who joined the staff that year who is remembered for her long outstanding service to the community. She resigned to marry Archie Duval the next year, but was always called upon whenever there was a serious illness or accident. "As we often had no doctor, or sometimes elderly men who couldn't hold a practice anywhere else, Lottie Duval had to do many things in emergencies that were considered far beyond a nurse's duty," says Charlie Hartie, "and many were the lives she saved in the forty years she unstintingly gave her service to this community."

Archie Duval was born in Ontario in 1878, spent his early years in eastern B.C., working as a carpenter in Revelstoke, Nelson and Vernon. He came to the Islands in 1908 with a party that did considerable work on the mining claims in Gold Harbor owned by John McLellan. He left the Islands that fall, but came back in 1909 to live on the Charlottes for the rest of his life. "He married Lottie in 1910 and built a home in Queen Charlotte," says Mr. Hartie, "and was an active man — could give a good account of himself at any kind of work such as carpentry, blacksmith or logging."

By 1909 families had begun to arrive as lumber was made available for houses and a row of false-fronted business establishments made the shoreline to the west of the mill look crowded. The steady influx of newcomers were attracted by the mill, and the mining possibilities, as well as the land that lay up the east coast. The eastern half of Queen Charlotte City was surveyed into lots by Noel Humphries in May, 1909, although this section was not registered until July 1911.

Remembered among the early mill people's names are the Emmanuel Girard family. Mr. Girard was the manager of the mill, and had originally come from Quebec. He had four daughters at home and another was married to young Dagneault who worked as a millwright. Then there were the Butlers, Mr. Butler was the bookkeeper at the mill. Norman Fraser was the engineer, had two daughters, and was known as "Dad" or "Pa" Fraser. His wife, "Ma" Fraser, ran the mill boarding-house before going to Skidegate during the Doughty regime to take over de Pape's hotel there. The Frasers went to live in Prince Rupert afterwards and ran the Queen Charlotte Rooms there for some time. And there was Andy Dickson, the old-time Highlander, who was the first mill machinist and blacksmith. (1) The yard crew were mostly Japanese and the sawyer and planermen changed so often that few names can be recalled. Of the Japanese, Mr. Katsura was destined to be remembered in a most tragic way.

(2)   "The Katsuras with their daughter, Keo, were a highly respected family who had come to Queen Charlotte early in 1909. About the time the Katsuras had arrived, a young Chinese, A. Gong, came and was employed by the mill as a cook, later going to work in the kitchen of the newly-built Premier Hotel.

Keo Katsura was fifteen years old in 1911 when Gong began to pay court to her, visiting the girl always in her parents' home and always behaving within the bounds of propriety. One day, however, he accosted Keo on her way home from school and chucked her affectionately under the chin. She was alarmed by this advance and told her father, whereupon Mr. Katsura went

(1) Information from Mr. C. Hartie
(2) Condensed from an account sent by the Islander to the Prince Rupert
Journal, January 3, 1912.

immediately to Gong and told him that he was never to do this again.

A few days after, Mr. Katsura went hunting for the day, leaving Keo and her mother at home. Gong, having seen him go, felt that it would be an opportune time to pay his beloved a visit. As nothing had been said to Mrs. Katsura about the accosting incident, she welcomed the young man — as had been the custom for the past year.

He stayed for some time but it was clear that Keo was not receptive to his friendliness. Suddenly he announced he had to leave to see about the next meal at the hotel. At the hotel he told the kitchen help to keep a good fire as he would be back shortly, then going to his room he emerged with what appeared to be a roll of soiled aprons for Mrs. Katsura to launder.

Mrs. Katsura was surprised to see him back again, but she liked the young man and was about to take his aprons from him when he asked her if she would just make sure his help had put the fire on — and he would lay out his laundry for her and prepare to settle his account. She was puzzled by this request, but as he had asked her so politely, she nodded agreement — and was barely out of the house when she heard shooting.

Benny Cromp was approaching the Katsura home to pick up his laundry when he heard the shots. Cautiously opening the door he saw two bodies lying on the floor and Mrs. Katsura rushed at him crying urgently "Policeman! Policeman!" Benny raised the alarm but it was too late. By the time help arrived, Dr. Winters (Charlotte's third doctor) had pronounced both Keo and her would-be suitor dead. The Chinese had fired two bullets into the girl and then turned the gun on himself."

The horrifying news swept through Queen Charlotte. "Several men grabbed a rope and there is no question but that there would have been a lynching," recalls Charlie Hartie who remembers that day vividly, "but the murderer was dead, too. Several men kicked the body to be sure he was really dead, though." At the Post Mortem conducted by William J. Leary, evidence showed that Gong had bought the gun from Cochrane's store shortly beforehand for fifty cents.

Keo's murder was the first of three tragic deaths to shock the small community that year, 1912. In July, Edwin, the two-year old son of Mr. and Mrs. Fairbairn was drowned. Two months later Dr. Winters died unexpectedly — he had come to take charge of the Queen Charlotte hospital the year before. To offset sadness there was rejoicing in August when Clarence Johnson married Ida Graham, Mrs. Fairbairn's sister. Johnson had come with Howard Fairbairn in 1911 to hand-log on the Islands and soon after the two men acquired the well-known tugs *Aimee* and *Edwin*. There were few people who knew the coastline of the Queen Charlottes as well as Mr. Fairbairn, who in later years was engaged as a Fisheries Protection officer for the south end of the Islands. Mr. Johnson was killed in a mining accident when his children were quite young, and as his wife had pre-deceased him, the Fairbairns brought up the two Johnson girls with their own four daughters in Queen Charlotte.

In September 1909 school classes were first held in Queen Charlotte, the same month as New Masset's school began. Like Masset, Charlotte had also to make do with temporary quarters and a substitute teacher. Mrs. Butler took over the teaching for the first month until Donald Cochrane arrived in October — and classes were held above Moore's Pool Hall until a proper school could be built that year. This school is still standing and is now used as an office for the school secretary.

When Mr. and Mrs. Cochrane arrived they decided to open a small store which Mrs. Cochrane would run. The business prospered and it was not long before Cochrane had to resign his teaching position to assist in the store and make the deliveries — by launch in those roadless days. In the summer of 1911 he persuaded his wife's young brother, Charlie Hartie, to take over the running of the boat. "I just came up to run a boat for my summer holidays," says Charlie today when people ask him why he came and why he stays. "Well, I'm still on my holidays and still running a boat." Then he goes on, "I've tried to leave here several times, for good — but its no use. I like it too well, and always come back."

As well as Cochrane's store (which was later purchased by Mr. and Mrs. Gordon Jolliffe), the Lauder Hotel, Moore's Pool Hall, and Windy's News Office, there was also the pioneer drug and clothing store of George Beattie. Mr. Beattie was appointed Charlotte's first postmaster. He built the first store — a small one — next door to Lauder's Hotel, then engaged Barge and Kitson to build his second and permanent store on the corner adjoining Cochrane's. (In recent years it was the Government Liquor store.) To the east of Beattie's first store was Robert Scharfee's general store. Mr. and Mrs. Scharfee sold their store to John Sachs in 1910 and they moved to Lawn Hill. Sachs ran his store in Charlotte until about 1924 and the Scharfees ran their store in Lawn Hill also until 1924, when they moved to the big rambling building in Skidegate Landing to operate a store for the rest of their years. John Barge had a carpentry business, and was persuaded to take on the duties of undertaker — he bought Moore's Pool Hall to use as his headquarters. Barge was later variously, the Government Agent, Mining Recorder, and Road Superintendent until he left the Islands with his family in 1928. He died in 1960 at the age of ninety-five years — and was active to the end.

W. J. Smith, who ran the first hotel in Skidegate, built the Premier Hotel in Queen Charlotte in 1910. Known as "Hotel" Smith, he and his wife had a liquor licence and, in addition to meals and rooms they had a barber shop on the premises run by Fred Mattock. This pioneer hotel is still standing, greatly modernized, and operates today as the Haida Hotel.

The Scowcroft Boarding-House in Queen Charlotte began in 1911 as a second choice venture. Originally Mr. and Mrs. Scowcroft, who were from Saskatchewan, had intended to farm near the mouth of the Tlell River. They sent part of their farming equipment, a big selfbinder, by scow to be set ashore at the place they had selected (opposite Bob Beitush's), and loading another larger scow with their remaining possessions, they prepared to follow by boat. The binder was landed safely but the second scow overturned in a sudden storm and everything went to the bottom. The farming venture was abandoned and they opened a boarding-house which did well in the thriving town of Queen Charlotte. The Scowcrofts had with them their own four children and Christina Goodall. Chrissie Goodall had come with her parents from Edinburgh when she was sixteen to live on a farm. The Saskatchewan climate was too rigorous for the young girl and it was arranged for her to accompany the Scowcroft family to the milder climate of B.C.

Miss Goodall became friendly with Charlotte Laughlin, who worked in the Queen Charlotte hospital. It was not long before these two young ladies were being courted by two friends from Tlell — Ed Wiggans and Antoine (Benny) Cromp. The Islands' first double wedding took place in Skidegate Landing in 1912 and was an "everybody welcome" affair in the best Island tradition. "Ma" and "Pa" Fraser handled the arrangements. Juliet Girard was Charlotte Laughlin's bridesmaid and George Beattie acted as best man for her groom, Ed Wiggans. Fosey Fraser was Chrissie's bridesmaid and Pete Adams supported Benny for the ceremony which was performed by Dr. Spencer from Skidegate Mission. Speeches were given by Dr. Winters, Jimmy Campbell and "Cap" Davey. Benny Cromp built a house for his bride in Skidegate where they lived until 1917, then with their three-year old son, Louis, moved to Prince Rupert. Although the Cromp's marriage was a happy one, the Wiggans was not. "Ed had been a batchelor for too many years to be able to adjust to double harness," said one of his friends. After a few years Charlotte divorced him to marry another Islander, Jack Cook, and Ed went back to his first love — hunting bears.

Another early Queen Charlotte business was "Cap" Davey's Land Office. He had come from Cornwall, England, and his title was purely honorary. As well as running the Land Office he was a Notary Public and ranched on Maude Island. His beet-colored nose was his famous feature and because of it, for fifty years or more the scarlet beaked Oyster Snipe have been known locally as "Cap Daveys".

Other business names are more recent. "Pot Roast Hansen", the nickname given to Armund Hansen Fotland, the popular Norwegian cook, who ran a cafe next door to Charlie Miller's barber shop. Mr. Miller, a veteran barber from Prince Rupert had gone to Buckley Bay during its heyday, and had come to Charlotte in 1925 to buy Moore's Pool Hall from John Barge. Using the downstairs for his barber-shop, the upstairs was utilized as a dance hall — and was in great demand for many years. One of Mr. Miller's proud memories was that he had cut Lloyd George's hair. Mr. and Mrs. Roy McKenzie came in the late 1920s to buy the Premier Hotel from "Hotel" Smith. The store part of the Premier Hotel was sold in 1927 to H. R. Beaven by Mr. Smith. Mr. Beaven was working in Prince George when a travelling salesman told him about the Charlottes. The mill was still operating when Mr. Beaven arrived in Queen Charlotte and he liked the community so much he sent for his wife, Sylvia, and their two children, Francis (Harry Jr.) and Edna.

As Howard Phillips of Masset says, ' They just don't make storekeepers like Harry any more. I remember so well one occasion when I went into the store, Harry was serving old Paddy Dwyer. He just dropped everything, parked his rear end on the back counter, feet on the front and settled down to discuss the local topics of the day. Paddy didn't mind waiting for his groceries and joined in the conversation as well."

Dr. Size, the Islands' first resident dentist came with his wife and their two younger daughters, Hayden and Frances, to live in Charlotte in 1923. With five foot Mrs. Size as his nurse, the tall, slightly stooped dentist would cover the whole of the Islands periodically, and on foot. Carrying all their dental instruments — including a portable wheel — on their backs they stayed a few days at each place along the way. They had a home in Masset as well as in Queen Charlotte to recuperate after the journeys. Dr. Size, practicing until his death in 1938, was one of the gentlest dentists to practice in those pre-anesthetic days — you got a "shot" only for an extraction — but few patients ever suffered under his deft hands. Mrs. Size was a talented artist who lived to be ninety-one years of age and played bridge to within two days of her death, ". . .mad as a hatter when everyone wanted to quit and go to bed, when it was only 2 a.m.," says her daughter Frances, now Mrs. Barney Munro.

"About half the ground on Graham Island was staked for coal," recalls Charlie Hartie, "and one hundred thousand dollars was spent at the Slate Chuck (near Cowgitz) in 1911 and 1912 just to prove that coal from there wouldn't burn. I worked at that "mine" packing imported coal in from the beach for them to use in sharpening the drills while their prospectus advertised that they had five seams of the best anthracite coal, all ready to ship."

In May 1912 the government office of Gold Commissioner was moved from Jedway to Queen Charlotte City, naming Windy's town as the unofficial capital of the Islands. Speculative mining was the talk of the day, but the man who had tangible results was John McLellan in his operation of the gold mine in Gold Harbor. When Mr. McLellan married Leslie Barraclough, a Queen Charlotte school-teacher he bought a site on Lena Island which had been an ancient Haida village. Appreciative of the totem poles near the site of his proposed home, he constructed his house appropriately of carefully matched logs with the upper section sheathed in red cedar shingles. No expense was spared. Lawns with attractive shrubbery, a tennis court and a badminton court, surrounded the large dwelling which was the object of admiration.

Gold Commissioner E. M. Sandilands was also Government Agent and Superintendent of road for the Islands (he took over this job from C. J. Gillingham who was transferred to Stewart, B.C. in 1912), which made him a busy man. He appointed Mr. Jacks to be his deputy and put him in charge of the group he called out on rescue parties. Charlie Hartie was one of the rescue group and remembers the time they were called to search for Jimmy Bell, a batchelor of about forty-five years of age who had been missing for several days. Mr. Bell had a ranch on Maude Island so the party began the search there. Jacks, who was a slim, nervous man had come armed with a huge revolver, and lining his men up on the beach told them, ". . .now don't take any chances, the fellow may be crazy," then staying out on the beach himself, sent his group into the woods to search. It was Mr. Hartie who found poor Bell. He had committed suicide by using dynamite. "I called out to Jacks, 'Here he is. . .'," recalls Mr. Hartie, "and I'll never forget his reaction. He lept into the air, big revolver pointed up to the sky, then with his legs going to beat the band — but not moving an inch forward, he called to me, 'All right, Charlie, stay where you are. I'm coming, I'm coming!'" But he was careful to wait until Charlie came out to him.

Arthur Solomon had had a musical career before he came to live in Queen Charlotte and was a talented conductor. With the good neighborliness which existed between the two Skidegates and Queen Charlotte there was much visiting back and forth, so it was inevitable that Mr. Solomon would hear of the struggling Skidegate Mission band and, with his love of music and skill in direction, it was just as inevitable that they would come together. Under his guidance they perfected their technique to such a degree that when they came to take part in mainland band competitions they won the top award for three years running — and were entitled to keep it permanently. There was, however, one snag. The competitions were confined to Native participants only — race was a factor for

265

the first time in Island arts. Sadly, "Professor" Solomon had to designate someone else to stand on his podium. Arthur Moody, the coronet soloist, was chosen to lead the band. In September 1912 they came home for the third time with the coveted cup. It stands in an honored place in the Village (1) Hall today.

In June 1912 it looked as though the much talked about trans-Graham Island railway was actually going to come. A surveyor named Riley was sent in that month to survey a route from Wilson Creek Mine to Rennell Sound. By June of any year all the men worth hiring were already employed, so Riley had to hire the town bums. He did manage to run his survey lines but had great difficulties. Every time the surveyor let any of his men out of his sight they would try to sneak back to town. That survey was all that was ever done about the proposed railway.

Not all the women who came to live in Queen Charlotte were received with open arms. This was particularly true of a strumpet named Bertha. The good Dr. Spencer, supervising his Methodist flock (2) from his headquarters in Skidegate Mission, was worried that she might encourage others of her profession to take up business there. He began a crusade urging the townspeople to get her to leave and "...rid the town of evil." Charlie Beck found the idea of a persecution campaign so ridiculous that he took old Bertha up the Inlet to live with him.

Shortly after this Rev. R. M. Reid, agent for the Canadian Bible Society paid Queen Charlotte a visit. The two young resident ministers, John Murdoch for the Presbyterian church and Alfred Kaley, Dr. Spencer's Methodist assistant, borrowed a boat to take the visitor for a sail in the Inlet. As they turned to come home a sudden southeast squall caught them, upsetting the boat. Clinging to the upturned craft, they were swept along until the boat grounded near Charlie Beck's cabin.

Charlie had gone to town that day but when Bertha saw the three half-frozen, dripping young men, she took them to the cabin to dry out. As she made hot drinks and hung up their wet clothing, Kaley and Murdoch realized where they were. With Spencer's recent denouncement of their hostess they felt they'd better leave — in a hurry. Somehow they managed to make their way back along the beach to Charlotte, although Alfred Kaley was almost exhausted from exposure.

When Charlie Beck returned from town, Bertha told him about her visitors. The opportunity was simply too much for Beck to resist. He immediately went back to Charlotte and with a look of outrage he strode up to the ministers' house and denounced the men. "Why a man can't leave his home for an hour but someone comes and tries to steal his woman. . ." If they ever came back and tried that trick again, he'd have the shotgun waiting for them. In vain they tried

(1) Skidegate Mission is commonly called "The Village" on the south end as similarly, Old Masset is called "The Village" on the north end of Graham Island.

(2) Methodist Church was the main church for the south end of the Islands, despite a serious attempt by a few Presbyterians to gain a foothold. Several Seventh Day Adventists and one Salvation Army family kept to their own faiths. The latter were Mr. and Mrs. Thomas Smith, and Mr. Smith was always known as "Salvation Smith".

266

to explain. It was futile. Beck was in his element. Savoring their discomfort he left them sputtering and proceeded up town telling his story to everyone he met. Each time he told it, the story grew worse and worse, until by the time he was uptown it was a sizzler. The next week became an agony for the ministers. Everyone they saw put on a broad grin. When Dr. Spencer gave Alfred Kaley a dressing down for having allowed himself to be put in such a position, it was the final straw for Kaley. He quit his job then and there. Charlie Beck had a glorious time over the whole affair.

After Bertha left he became very friendly with Sam Larsen. Mr. Larsen, who had a stake from a mining claim he had sold in his native Idaho, bought a fishing boat and was well-known on both the mainland and Island side of the straits. It was Sam Larsen, who with two Prince Rupert men, George Ness (1) and Con Michaloff, successfully salvaged a large amount of copper one from the *Kennecott,* which was wrecked near Hunter Point (2) on October, 1923, when southbound from Cordova, Alaska, to a Tacoma smelter. Con Michaloff had enough from his share to start a machine-shop in Prince Rupert.

The saw-mill which was the basic reason for Queen Charlotte City's existence ran steadily from 1908 until the end of 1912. It was put into operation again towards the latter part of the first world war to saw clear spruce for aeroplane lumber then shut down when that market closed. In 1925 it reopened to run for about eighteen months then failed. The Forestry Department seized the machinery for debt owed them for stumpage and sent a scow and tug to take the machinery away. The scow upset in the middle of Hecate Strait and the mill history ended. Shortly before the seizure, before it was known that the mill was in dire financial straights — although it had ceased to operate — a skeleton crew was told to prepare things for an extended closure. "They had been burning trash from the office one morning," recalls Mrs. Edward Moore, whose husband — a nephew of John Barge — was Inspector of Fisheries, "and I thought there was rather an excessive amount of smoke, so before I left home that afternoon to go to the store, I took in my washing. By the time I came home a few hours later the whole office was a roaring mass of flames and the fire was spreading rapidly to the rest of the mill. The men were called out to fight it, but there was such a strong suspicion that the fire had been deliberately set, they refused to endanger their lives by fighting it. Instead they protected the lumber pile — as they were all still waiting for their pay when the mill had closed down so unexpectedly."

In 1946 the community found that financing the hospital — which had been built at almost the same time as the mill — was becoming an insurmountable problem and the United Church of Canada was asked to assume the responsibility for its administration. However, the years were catching up with this pioneer building and in 1952 it was condemned as unsafe for a hospital. A tremendous drive was started which covered industries and citizens from one end of the Queen Charlotte Islands to the other. One Tuesday, November 15, 1955, a modern hospital costing a quarter of a million dollars was opened as a result of that drive. It is still under the administration of the United Church.

(1) Mr. Ness came to Prince Rupert in 1909. Went to live on the Islands
    in 1926, where he is now caretaker at Aero camp.
(2) On the west coast of Graham Island, south of Kano Inlet.

Queen Charlotte benefitted from the aeroplane spruce boom in 1918 as Thurston Harbor, on Moresby Island, became headquarters for the Imperial Munitions Board. This was followed by the same slumps and recoveries that other Island communities had but, perhaps as a legacy from Windy Young, she still contends that she is the capital city of the Islands — an assumption which has been viewed with amused tolerance by other Island communities. Surpassed in population by Haida (Old Masset), Masset and Tasu, and barely even with Sandspit in the number of residents, it is, nevertheless, a hub city today. Headquarters for several government agencies, the only hospital, (1) the only bank, the only community with two hotels, as well as being headquarters for the MacMillan, Bloedel and Powell River booming grounds, all help to make Queen Charlotte City one of the Islands' busiest communities. When Masset and Port Clements became organized communities, (2) progressively minded citizens in Queen Charlotte City attempted to have their village follow suit — but the idea was voted out. When one resident was asked why he had voted against it he was quick to reply, "Look, the whole reason I came here was that I was fed up with having people tell me how I should live, what my house had to be made of . . . the more unorganized a place is, the better I like it. A man can do as he pleases then."

Windy's ghost must have covered his face in dismay at the rejected plebiscite, for as Queen Charlotte City gained her individual independence by the negative vote — there is no question but that as a community it lost status as the unofficial capital to the incorporated Village of Masset.

(1) *There is a Red Cross Outpost hospital in Masset for emergency cases only, and they are then transported to either Prince Rupert or Queen Charlotte City.*

(2) *Masset is an incorporated Village. Port Clements is an Improvement District, organized under the Water Resources Board. Both communities are legally empowered to levy and collect taxes and have elected officials at their head.*

CHAPTER FORTY-THREE

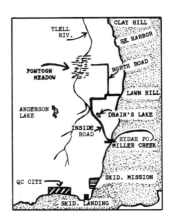

EAST COAST SETTLERS

East Coast settlers did not have the handicap of timber claims along their waterfrontage to the extent the Masset Inlet people had. There was a small section between Skidegate Mission and Miller Creek which was encumbered but northward from Miller Creek all the way up to Rose Spit the land was available.

The primary motive for pre-empting land in the Rose Spit to Cape Fife region was interest in the placer gold possibilities of the black sands. Charlie Spence reported that in the spring of 1909 there were thirteen settlers near him at Kumara Lake, and by the summer twenty men had settled in the Cape Fife region, working the sands whenever conditions were favorable. They were using a new method to recover the fine gold dust, he said. Instead of the customary sluice box, they had adapted a woollen blanket as a sieve and were having fair success with it. (1)

It was farming possibilities which attracted settlers south along the rest of the coast. Many of the settlers in the Oeanda tried a bit of panning to augment their incomes, but the lush grasslands there made the running of cattle more profitable. A few placer claims had been staked on the beach near Lawn Point in 1905, but Bob Switzer who had come to Lawn Hill in 1907 and built the first white settler's (2) home in that area was not interested. William Duncan, however, who followed him the next year, took up land a few miles to the north of Switzer at Lawn Point and obtained enough gold from the beach to supplement his income for years.

Mr. Duncan had come from Scotland as a boy and was one of the original settlers at Okanagan Lake. He owned the place known as Duncan's Landing, but in the big stampede to the Klondyke he practically gave this land away to join in the rush. After spending a few years in Atlin he moved to the Queen Charlottes where news of mining was making headlines. Attracted by the possibility of having a steady income right on his doorstep in addition to a panoramic view,

(1) Taken from the Prince Rupert Empire, August 1909.
(2) Information from Mrs. Roy Fields, Courtenay, B.C.

Mr. Duncan chose the site at Lawn Point overlooking the waters of Hecate Strait. After clearing his land and building his home and outbuildings, he constructed a 750-foot sluice box along the edge of the beach. In April 1910 with a companion he processed his first placer sand, recovering $30 worth of gold in three hours of washing. But, like the black sands farther north, this Graham Island beach gold was there only in enough quantity for one man to use as a supplementary income. Later attempts entailing much time and labor to make it produce more profitably have been discouraging.

Near the mouth of the Chinukundl Creek Frank Edwards staked out a pre-emption in 1908. Mr. Edwards had been prospecting on the Islands since early spring and liked the region so well he changed his vocation from prospector to rancher. It was another early-day pre-emptor for whom the place was named — Mr. Müller. Müller had lived there for a few years when he became unbalanced and was sent south for treatment. The story is told that William Leary met Müller in Vancouver several years later and Müller announced, "I'm not crazy anymore, Mr. Leary." "Oh, that's fine — when are you coming back to the Islands?" was Leary's reply. "I told you, Mr. Leary, I'm not crazy any more." Over the years the name of Müller's Creek has been corrupted to Miller Creek, and is never called anything else locally.

William J. Leary moved his family to Miller Creek in 1909 and applied for a post office. The application was denied under the Miller Creek name, as it was a duplication (of another post office elsewhere), so Leary made his next application using a variance of the spelling of Haida, and the Post Office was granted for Hydah. (1) Later the Hydah Post Office and store were attached to the big Leary home. "The old house had five bedrooms and a huge living room where overnight visitors could put their blankets on the floor," says Mr. Leary's granddaughter, Dorothy (now Mrs. Francis Richardson), "Grandma would never let anyone past her house without feeding them and giving them a bed if needed. My mother used to tell me though, of how Grandma would shudder when Jake Walsh came down from Tlell, wearing his silo-smelling clothes — but he always got the same welcome as the rest."

The supplies for the store at Miller Creek came from Skidegate by boat and after packing all the orders, Mr. Leary would send his son, George, and nephew, Charlie Helmer, to deliver them. The two young men would go to the settlers' homes along the coast, then at Lawn Hill turned the horses inland to service cabins along the Inside Road. This was the name given to the road which ran in a large semi-circle inland from Lawn Hill to emerge at the Miller Creek store. From Lawn Hill the road followed the survey line to Al Daise's (see map section) and here there was a branch road called simply North Road, which ran north for a few miles to serve settlers along that route. At the southwest corner of Austin Richardson's (Lot 574) it turned to go west to the Pontoon (2) Meadows. This was the road used by the packers for the Wright and Green drill camp when they put down their last bore hole. (3) A trail ran east from the

(1) Mrs. Roy Fields, the former Lottie Leary.
(2) The marshy area of the Tlell River behind Lawn Hill. Pontoon is a name given by Louisiana people to that type of terrain and someone from that region coined the expression for this land behind Lawn Hill.
(3) Information from Mr. John Locker who packed on this trail for Wright and Green.

North Road (at its north end) emerging at Pott's Purchase (1) on the coast.

The successful petitioning for this road was entirely due to the efforts of the Settlers' Association which had been formed in November 1908 at Skidegate, and it was characteristic of William Leary to call a meeting at his store as soon as word had come that $400 had been allotted for this road. Mr. Jennings, the newly-appointed road superintendent was invited to attend and forty-one settlers of the immediate area turned up for the meeting which was held in May, 1910. All present were aware of the part political favoritism could play, so with Jenning's consent a secret ballot was held resulting in Nick Schug and Nick Schaeffer being elected as the foremen for the project. It was agreed that all settlers were to have equal chance for employment at $3.50 a day.

William Leary's Hydah store at Miller Creek prospered and he was able to provide a comfortable living for his wife, Susan, and their seven children, Lena, Edna, Ada, George, Edith, Eddie and Charlotte who ranged from pre-school to late teens, as well as his nephew, Charlie Helmer who lived with the Leary family. It was not long before one of his brood left the fold. Lena, his eldest daughter, dark-haired and vivacious, married Dick Husband. Miller Creek's first newly-weds built their cabin near the big Leary home and it was there that their first baby, Dorothy, was born.

Mr. Husband had come from England with his friend, Bob Kitson, to live on the prairies, before going to the Islands in 1908. They were among the group who lived in "Batchelor's Hall" in Skidegate Landing in 1908. For a time they had a carpentry and joinery shop in the can-making shed at the Oil Works and built a house for John Mathers (which became Archie Gordon's home when Mathers moved to Sandspit). Bob Kitson married Ada Leary. Mr. Leary's fourth daughter, Edith, married Charlie Helmer.

Perhaps it was because Mr. Leary was secure financially that he could afford to take a leading role in public affairs, although it did not make him popular in some quarters as a result. When it was obvious that the long promised redistribution of seats (which would result in the Islands having their own M.P.) was not making progress, Mr. Leary decided to take action. In April 1912, with Frank Rice, who was an ardent supporter of the idea, Mr. Leary drafted a well-thought out petition to have the Islands formed into a municipality. "A separate province would be a better idea," urged some of their friends — however it was felt that this might be unrealistic.

With packs on their backs these two public-spirited men walked to every settler's cabin they could locate on Graham Island, explaining what the petition was hoping to accomplish and obtaining hundreds of signatures. This was a big political issue but those who signed had been so busy with getting the bare necessities for daily living that they had neglected to get on the voter's list and the signatures were, as a result, considered invalid. The petition supporting a plea to control their own revenues was tossed out. Discouraged by the overwhelming obstacles to the Islands coming into their own and about the enormous amount of money from the coal and timber licences — money which could do so much

---

(1) In 1909 Arthur G. Potts bought this land instead of the usual method of pre-empting, as a result early residents dubbed it "Pott's Purchase." He sold it 3 months later to J. Savannah and J. I. L. Meyer for a profit of $300.

to develop the Islands for people interested in becoming resident Islanders — being drained away and in control of, greedy off-Islands principals, the two men wearily returned home. Mr. Rice to his home at Tlell, across the road from Mrs. Tom Hodges "Do Drop Inn," and Mr. Leary to his busy life as J. P., storekeeper, postmaster and father of a lively family at Miller Creek.

Judging by the number of Crown Grants issued to that East Coast region there were plenty of serious settlers. Some of the people lived in Charlotte or Skidegate and took out pre-emptions in the Miller Creek–Lawn Hill area as a sideline with a view to settling eventually or perhaps selling to latecomers. Then there were the carefree loggers from the camp which supplied the Queen Charlotte mill. The mill was inactive usually through the winter, so these men took up land near Miller Creek and each winter went ostensibly to "prove up", but as one old-timer says, ". . most of the time they could be found hard at work sampling each others home brew."

It takes all kinds to make a new country, as Captain Edward Mabbs learned a few years later. He was taking his ship *Prince John* to Skidegate from Masset on her usual course — which is well off-shore in these shallow waters — when he was surprised to see a small boat rowing into his path off Lawn Hill. One of the two occupants was vigorously flagging him down.

Knowing it must be an emergency of some sort, the Captain ordered his ship to come to a stop and hailed the men to ask what he could do for them. "Can you tell us the right time, Captain, please?" came the unexpected request. It was the Hyder brothers, Ed and Henry, who lived about three miles behind Lawn Hill, and their clock had stopped that morning. They didn't get along too well, and were not really brothers. They had been brought up together in an orphanage and having no one else in the world, had adopted one another as kin, using one boy's surname for both. Wanting to live near, but not with each other, they built their cabins on either side of the property line separating their pre-emptions. "Ed's was quite distinguished," recalls George McRae, who took out another pre-emption in the area after he sold his first to Mr. Pitt-Turner, "it was twelve feet high, six feet square — and had two stories. He went upstairs by way of a ladder on the outside."

Mr. and Mrs. George Pitt-Turner came to the Islands in 1912. They had met Dr. Spencer from Skidegate Mission during one of his ecclesiastical visits to the mainland and his descriptions of the Charlottes had intrigued Mr. Pitt-Turner, and when Dr. Spencer learned that Mrs. Pitt-Turner was a graduate nurse he used every persuasion to induce them to come to his region of the Charlottes where her skill would be of inestimable value.

"We came over on the *Vadso*," says Mrs. Pitt-Turner, (now living in Victoria) "and landed first at Sandspit." Anxious to make her welcome, Dr. Spencer took her to meet Captain and Mrs. Oliver. "The tide was high at that time," says Mrs. Turner, "so the gangplank was level from the boat to the wharf. But when we came back to go aboard again the tide had gone out and the gangplank was on almost perpendicular angle. I was very apprehensive about slipping but after much cajoling and help finally managed to get on board again." This was just the beginning, for when they got to Skidegate Mission there was no wharf. She would have to go down the side of the steamer by a rope ladder and get into the small boat at the bottom. "I just can't do it," she told them. In vain did

Mr. Pitt-Turner and Dr. Spencer try to explain that people did it all the time. After listening to the futile persuasion for quite some time the captain of the *Vadso* walked over to her and said, "This is enough. There is no other way. Here, take these. . ." he handed her two big safety pins. "Pin your skirts between your knees and down you go." "Somehow I did," she recalls, "but I'll never know how – it seemed miles down."

They were to stay with Dr. Spencer until they got their bearings. ". . .and the first night I was needed to help deliver a baby," says Mrs. Turner who lost count of how many she brought into the world after that memorable day. Like nurses Mrs. Archie Duval of Queen Charlotte, Mrs. Ernie Gladstone of Skidegate Mission and Mrs. Harry Frosst of New Masset, Mrs. George Pitt-Turner went far beyond the call of duty. As one man says of these exceptional women, "They were truly the Florence Nightingales of the Islands." ". . .oh, sometimes I would get a dozen eggs to deliver a baby," says Mrs. Pitt-Turner, "but it didn't really matter, we went whenever we were needed." Over the course of the years she thought she had encountered every sort of situation but she still chuckles over a confinement in Port Clements. There was an insistent knock on the door. "Nurse, nurse. . ." came the urgent voice of the patient's mother. "I can't come now," said Mrs. Turner, "You'll have to come back later." But Grandma-to-be had a message that couldn't wait, so she poked her head in the door and said "I must talk to you, Nurse, because I want you to know that if the Lord should happen to take me tonight, I have clean stockings on."

Mr. Turner liked the Miller Creek area and pre-empted land which adjoined Tom Drain. Drain pre-empted one lot and liked the lot to the north of him (511) so well that he bought that land outright. It had a lake in the centre which became known as Drain's Lake. The idea of purchasing land seemed much less complicated than the lengthy process of pre-empting to Mr. Pitt-Turner and, learning that George McRae would sell his place near Clay Hill, he made McRae a cash offer – which was quickly accepted. "On the main road and with that ocean view – it was wonderful," says Mrs. Turner.

There were already settlers around Lawn Hill in 1909 when Robert and Mrs. Scharfee began building their store on the main road, near the intersection of the Inside Road. Charlie Nelson, Van Meter, Andy Christenson, Jim Irwin, Ralph Ward, John Bray, Arthur Fritz, Joe Renner and the Taylor brothers, had all built cabins and 1910 saw such an influx that Clement de Pape opened a hotel on the opposite side of the road to Robert Scharfee. That year C. P. Edwards, Superintendent of Dominion Wireless Service, recommended the establishment of a wireless station in the Lawn Hill area and land for the station was purchased from Dr. J. C. Spencer, who had two lots at Dead Tree Point.

On August 10, 1912 the organizational meeting for the East Coast Farmer's Institute was held. Ed Ashton was elected president; William Duncan, vice-president; Robert Scharfee, secretary; and George Ashton, treasurer. Directors were Austin Richardson, William J. Leary, Mr. Sandison and Charlie Turney. Archie Gordon was appointed auditor. Although the initial meeting was held only in August, by October they put on a big exhibition. William Manson M. P., from Prince Rupert was invited to open it with a formal address. In addition to exhibits of garden produce from up and down the coast and other attractions there was a baby contest. William Duncan was prevailed upon to be judge and with utmost diplomacy declared that the only two babies entered, Jackie Cochrane of Queen Charlotte City and Dorothy Husband of Miller Creek, were such fine ones he was going to award them both a first prize.

This organization, which is still in existence, was formed to offer practical help to settlers in obtaining ranching supplies at reduced rates, and was instrumental in having an experimental farm started. Austin Richardson was in charge of this project which was conducted on lot 273 along the North Road. It became a show-place and many methods for the best utilization of the soil were demonstrated. People who remember the farm have little patience with today's statements that the Islands will not grow excellent garden produce. When the right methods were used, results were extremely rewarding. The regular fall exhibitions held in Prince Rupert received Island entries — which took top prizes. In the 1914 exhibition the Bulloch-Webster trophy for the best collection of vegetables was won by Lawn Hill and Skidegate entries for the second time in succession, making it theirs to keep.

Perhaps it is the dances and picnics which accompanied the Institute meetings which are the most warmly remembered of its activities. They were the eagerly anticipated events of the year. Babies were put to sleep on benches as the adults two-stepped or square-danced to the violin, jews-harp, mouth-organ and accordian music. The picnics were equally popular.

The first Lawn Hill wedding took place in July 1913 when Nick Schaeffer of Southeast Harbor (a few miles north of Lawn Point) married Mrs. Lucy Bruce of Skidegate. Rev. Len Bygraves officiated for this ceremony which was held in the launch *Swan* near the Lawn Hill buoy which marks the rocks of the Haida legend about the great Chief of the Sea Otter tribe. (1) Mrs. Norman ("Ma") Fraser, Mrs. Scharfee and Harry Bruce were aboard to be witnesses, and ashore Mrs. Hunsby and Mrs. Ranch supervised the refreshments.

It was April 1911 when B. F. "Bert" Roberts arrived on the Islands. He had come to Canada in 1906 from England and during the 1907 depression had made his way to Vancouver where he chummed up with Fred Greenstreet. They were working at Stave Falls (Vancouver electricity) in 1910 at the same camp as Alf Cooke and John Ledgerwood. Cooke was anxious to get onto some land of his own. Ledgerwood had a place at Dead Tree Point, which he had proved up on, but later decided that he was not cut out to be a rancher. His description of the Islands interested the other three, especially Mr. Cooke who decided to try pre-empting. Roberts and Greenstreet went also. Cooke chose the lot adjoining Andy Christenson on the Inside Road, and Bert paced out the one to the east of Mr. Cooke. Fred Greenstreet liked Tlell better.

"I think the biggest attraction for settling at Lawn Hill," says Mr. Roberts, "were those two very pretty girls, Marie de Pape and Marie Scharfee." Mr. Roberts recalls that one of the items Robert Scharfee sold in his store — from under the counter — was Black and White whisky. "It cost $1.75 a bottle and was put on your bill as 'one shirt — $1.75'."

Women were scarce in this batchelor's world of pre-empting and no chance was lost to make a good impression whenever an unattached lady came into the region. William Leary, who loved a good joke, couldn't resist having some fun

(1) See Appendix One.

274

with a few of the more gullible batchelors. He had done a bit of "staking" – locating land for prospective buyers – as a sideline. One day he gathered a few batchelors and told them confidentially that he had a letter from a young widow, Mrs. O'Flanagan, who insisted she wanted to go farming on the Queen Charlotte Islands. The only place he could locate for her was lot 518. It was a long way in, with only a poor trail, and no cabin of any sort. What a shock it would be to the poor widow! . . . and so on. "In some strange manner," recalls Charlie Hartie who tells the story now, "a neat log cabin appeared on the place in a few weeks. Mrs. Flanagan never appeared – and no one ever learned who the would-be swain was."

A different sort of cabin episode happened to Bert's friend, Alf Cooke. "Alf was a very industrious man," says Bert "He built a nice log cabin of squared timbers, carefully fitted together. Then he took a trip home to England and stayed for a year or two. When he came back he found his cabin had completely vanished. There was no sign of a fire or vandalism – just an empty spot. Some time later he discovered his cabin on another man's land four miles away. This new settler thinking Alf had left the country for good, took the cabin apart and re-erected it on his own land."

William Prettyjohn was one of the first of Lawn Hill settlers and one of the last to leave. "William wasn't too much for looks," says one of his former neighbors, "he was about five foot five, very bowlegged and had to wear heavy lensed spectacles to see at all. But he must have had the heart of a lion. His lot was next to Ed Hyder's and he farmed on a small delta that had formed in the Tlell river. Every few years the river would overflow and wash most of his farm away, but he rebuilt all the dams and ditches and began again. He made some of his income by working on the roads, but his main source of money was from the sale of vegetables and fruit which he peddled at the south end – walking the twelve miles each way to do this." Mr. Prettyjohn lived on his land for twenty years and claimed he was one settler who had made farming pay. He had come there with fifty dollars in his pocket and when he left he had one thousand dollars "clear profit". "Of course," said another, "he was a saving man. One of the first things he did was to save all his flour sacks as a sort of dowry for the bride he hoped to find. And at Dominion Day picnics he would salvage all the little flags." Originally from Devon, he loved to sing – always the song, "The Honey and the Bee," over and over.

Camille Peters boarded with Mr. and Mrs. Grey at the Dead Tree Wireless Station when she taught school in Lawn Hill. Mrs. Grey's sister, Mary Sinclair (who became Mrs. Bert Roberts) came that year from Scotland to visit and remembers Prettyjohn coming to court Miss Peters. "I felt sorry for the little fellow and didn't think the others should laugh at his eccentricities. I was determined that I wouldn't. But when he brought out one of those Dominion Day flags one evening to use for his handkerchief . . . it was too much!"

Tom Hearn, whose property was across the road from Mr. and Mrs. Bob Wilkie's about a mile from the Lawn Hill store, had been married five times. "He loved to drag out his old snapshot album," says Charlie Hartie, "and then leafing through the pages would say, 'that's one of my wives, she's dead, here's an old flame, this is a racehorse – isn't she a beauty' another old flame, a wife, more horses. .' and so on, as though it were all one and the same." Deaf as a post, Tom nevertheless put bells on all his sheep, to the amusement of his friends. Tom's son still owns his father's land although no one has lived on it for years.

By 1920 it was obvious that a school was needed and arrangements were made to use the Farmer's Institute building temporarily — until the government could be prodded into building a schoolhouse. During the coal drilling by Wright and Green in 1912 the English company backing the operation had built a home for Frank Wright on land purchased from John Bray. It reverted for non-payment of taxes when the firm ran out of money and was purchased by the trustees of the Farmer's Institute as headquarters for meetings. For a short period around 1919 or 1920 it was occupied by Mr. and Mrs. Jory. Jory was supervising the drilling for oil with some geological outfit, and a man named Smith was the driller. "It was of course another piece of bunkum," say oldsters. "The only way to get the suckers to bite was to advertise that there was a drill working on the property. They explored and made tests along the coast and on the Inside Road — no oil. They never got through the gravel and glacial clay."

"School opened in the Institute in the fall of 1920," says Dorothy Richardson, who was in that first class. "Helen Graham was the teacher. They had a big basket social to raise funds to convert the Institute building into a school. A skylight had to be put in to improve the light and my Dad (1) did that. Mrs. Ralph Ward's basket went for a fabulous price at the social as a bottle of her home-made parsnip wine was showing at one corner."

By September 1922 the government had built a school on land which Joe Molitor, father of eleven children, donated near Dead Tree. This school was in use until the early nineteen-thirties when it was closed for lack of pupils.

The first world war took many of the settlers from the East Coast — as it did elsewhere on the Islands. William J. Leary's fears that unless Islanders could control their own natural resources revenue they would be drained financially were borne out, and the depression years which aggravated the poor economic outlook caused most of the remaining pioneers to leave — some to live in established centers elsewhere on the Islands and others to return to the mainland. A few of the sites were taken up later, such as the homesteads of John Higney, the tall, partly deaf gunner from the English army and his Scots neighbor, Jim Reid. Gus Ross ranched on their sites for years, (2) with his wife and two sons, Eric and Fred, until his sudden death. Old timers remember when the creek near Mr. Ross's farm was called Higney's Creek.

Mr. Ross was a brother of Mrs. Bob Wilkie who, with her husband and daughter, Charlotte, lived on the pre-emption adjoining the Hubley place about a mile inland from Scharfee's store. Bob Wilkie was one of the last of the pioneer ranchers still working his land when he died — his strawberry patch was known to all East Coasters. This land was recently purchased by Mr. John Marks, a newcomer to the Islands, who says he plans to start ranching.

The Scharfee store and post office were taken over in 1924 by Mrs. Eric Richardson; her daughter, Doris, was the Islands' first lady mail carrier. The old site of the de Pape hotel is now the home of Mr. Sears, but there is no sign of the old government stables where Frank Mallory kept the horses he used when

(1) Dick Husband
(2) More about Gus Ross under Tlell.

276

keeping the roads in good condition. The stables were across the road from de Papes.

Captain Hubley died on his place and was buried there. For awhile Mrs. Hubley and her son, Julius, ran the ranch until in a few years Mrs. Hubley married her pioneer neighbor, Joe Renner, and they went to ranch on Maude Island.

The Dead Tree Wireless Station is now the United Church Recreation Camp and the land William Duncan farmed until the end is today the site of an automatic beacon and range lights. Mrs. Scharfee's brother, Billy Bruckener, left but her sister, Mrs. Henry Fersch and her husband stayed with their land long enough for their two sons to go to Lawn Hill's first school. Nick and Mrs. Schaeffer farmed their land until a disastrous fire robbed them of everything. It was too late in life to begin again and the Schaeffers moved to Queen Charlotte City near many of their former pioneering friends.

During the depression years the old homesite of Mr. McNaughton, near Miller Creek, achieved some notoriety when two friends, Billy Burke and Pete Monchal, built a cabin and started what was known locally as the Monte Carlo club. There were some lively evenings — and even livelier tales told of the poker games held every Saturday night at that secluded cabin. It was standing room only.

The cabins which dotted the region have fallen down except for the four which are maintained by the Queen Charlotte Rod and Gun Club. The roads are little more than trails and in some cases have been obliterated. It is hard to believe that this was once a busy pioneering area.

Fish bite as well as ever in Ed Anderson's Lake (1) — where he said, "You have to hide behind a tree to bait your hook the fish are so thick." Between Lawn Hill and Lawn Point and about two hundred feet south of Ed Ashton's old house there is a spring which runs through a fault in the land. Named St. Mary's Spring by Mrs. Annie L. Richardson of Tlell for a similar spring she had known in her native England, it is said that whoever drinks from the pure water of this spring will return to the Islands.

(1) This lake lies partly on the northwest portion of lot 1842, and partly in Township 6.

CHAPTER FORTY-FOUR

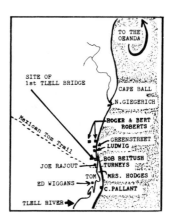

TLELL

Mid-way between Cape Ball and Clay Hill lies the mouth of the meandering Tlell River which gives its name to a large section of the land. Known as Ti-el by early settlers, Tlell is a corruption of an ancient Haida word meaning "land of plenty", "land of berries", or "place of the big surf". All three descriptions fit this picturesque place equally well, but a fourth, "good fishing river", should be added.

Mexican Tom, Tlell's first settler, was running one hundred and sixty head of cattle — and this included three registered bulls — when Cecil Pallant, George Sharp and Perry Parker chose sites adjoining him in 1908. They were, together with Nick Geigerich who was at Cape Ball that year, the forerunners of the score who would take up land along the river bank and ocean front of this region.

In the fall of 1911, Bert Roberts, who had been living for a brief period behind Lawn Hill, was eager to own a place of his own where the sound of the surf was within earshot. Learning that there was a site north of his friend, Fred Greenstreet, three-quarters of a mile beyond the mouth of the river, Bert too, became a Tlell pre-emptor. Two years later he had his treasured Crown Grant. Mr. Roberts was more fortunate than his earlier neighbors in Tlell, for in the fall of 1911 the first bridge across the Tlell River was completed — making travel much more convenient. It was erected near the mouth of Geike Creek, close to Sam Raybold's cabin on the west side and crossed to the east bank to land which in March of 1912 was pre-empted by one of Tlell's best known pioneers, Robert Paul "Bob" Beitush.

Bob had come to the United States from his native Russia in 1907, moving shortly afterwards to Alberta where he became a Canadian citizen. From Alberta he came to Tlell to live for the rest of his life. Following the example of his neighbor, Charles Turney, Bob went into sheep-raising and had a fine vegetable garden and fruit farm which drew visitors and customers from all over the Islands. Generous with the use of his land, he permitted picnics and ball games whenever people requested and few large gatherings at Tlell were held anywhere except "down at Bob's". When he died in January 1964 he left his land to his

279

son. Bob, junior, making it one of the few pioneer farms to bear the original family name today.

Bob's neighbor, Charles Turney, had come to Tlell in 1909. (1) He chose a site on the east bank of the river, across from Joe Rajout, who had his cabin at the Tlell end of the Mexican Tom trail. Mrs. Turney and her sister, together with Charlie Turney "Junior" arrived soon after to help Mr. Turney with the sheep ranch he established that summer. The first post office in Tlell was in their home, as was the first place of worship — the Turney home was the scene of many impromtu services for five or six years — and were usually held without a minister present in those roadless days.

Charlie Turney, junior, chose a small lot to the south of what is now the farm of Lionel Andrews and his mother, and built a cabin on it. He had the unusual foresight to obtain a strip of land running inland from his lot to behind the Andrews property which gave him an access road to the bank of the Tlell — a favored fishing spot.

Mr. Turney, senior, felt that the temperature and conditions around Tlell might be ideal pheasant country. In the spring of 1913 he imported a number of birds, hand-raising the young and releasing them in the fall. They thrived and multiplied for years until someone introduced raccoons to the Islands, which also thrived and did well — at the expense of the pheasants which were wiped out. (2)

Joe Rajout — or "French Joe" as his neighbors called him — had come shortly before the Turney family. When Mrs. Hodges died and Joe bought the property from her son, Byron, he felt that such an important landowner as he was then, should have a wife. Accordingly he set off to find one in Belgium. Joe had an old 18-foot boat which had been built by guesswork and was so much wider on one side than the other that it had to be heavily ballasted to be reasonably safe even in calm waters. He decided to sail this craft to Prince Rupert to economize on his fare to Europe. Somehow he persuaded Bob Beitush, his neighbor to accompany him. "Perfectly safe," he assured the hesitant Bob. "We'll have life jackets." Joe, a former tinsmith, had his own idea of a good life jacket. He plugged the holes of empty milk cans, then arranging them in a row, sewed them into a strip of canvas which he fastened around the wearer's waist. Joe, himself, didn't need one he said — he was a good swimmer.

"It was one of those flat calm evenings in August," recalls Bert Roberts, "I had gone down to Turney's after supper and they told me Bob and French Joe had left for Prince Rupert about seven that evening. My heart sank at the thought of those two out on Hecate Straits in that old boat of Joe's — even on such a quiet night. But by midnight when one of the fiercest gales I've ever known blew up — we knew Bob and Joe were lost. Oh, it was awful! The wind just laid the trees level with the ground, uprooting many of them. When word came some days later that those two were safe — it seemed a miracle."

On the other side of Hecate Straits the following day, George McRae down from Anyox, had checked into Black's Central Hotel in Prince Rupert. Taking

(1) The Turneys were from Buckinghamshire, England.
(2) In 1966 an effort to restock the region is being attempted, several pairs of pheasants have been released in widely separated parts of the Q. C. Islands.

a stroll around the docks at noon, he could hardly believe his eyes when he saw that old lopsided boat of Joe's sailing into the harbor. "Boy, we were scared alright," the two Islanders told Mr. McRae, "but there wasn't much to do but keep going. We tried to dodge the biggest waves. That wind at our backs sure sailed us over in a hurry."

"I don't think French Joe could be drowned anyway," says Mr. McRae. "One of the first things he did when he came to the Islands was to walk off the end of the dock at Skidegate in the middle of the night. No one even knew he was down there. I was staying at the boarding-house at the time. Joe came in, soaking wet. And he was swearing mad because he had lost his hat!" Mr. McRae went on to tell of the time in 1911 when Jimmy Carter and Joe had been fishing off the coast at Tlell and were caught in a sudden storm.

"The boat turned turtle about a mile off shore and apparently as it did, a big sack of salt caught Jimmy in the back. They were both thrown into the sea and as he was swept shoreward, Joe lost sight of Jimmy. He had to swim for his life in those big waves. He made it to shore, but in that heavy undertow couldn't get up on the beach. Every time he would fight his way to wading distance he would be dragged out again — over and over. Finally he was cast up on the beach by a big wave high enough to hang on. He was all in. Completely done. Luckily it was in front of my homesite near Clay Hill and I found him on the beach. His fingers were worn right to the bone trying to dig his hands into the beach to keep from being swept out again in the back-wash. Carter was drowned."

Joe's trip to Belgium was successful and he married Madame Peters, a hard-working widow with a grown son and daughter. The son, although he came to Canada with the newly-wed Rajouts, did not stay long on the Islands. When the batchelors of Tlell learned that Madame Rajout was accompanied by her daughter, Camille, who had inherited the dark beauty and chic associated with her nationality — every pair of shoes were shined and extra pomade was put on unruly heads of hair as the young men sought excuses to visit Joe and admire his step-daughter.

Joe and his wife lived in the cottage across the road from Mrs. Hodges former "Do Drop Inn" cabin. It was a stormy marriage and after a few years they agreed to part. Joe moved to Port Clements. In 1926 Madame Rajout engaged John Dover to supervise the building of the well-known "Dunes" hotel — erecting it on practically the same site of the old "Do Drop Inn". The cuisine at "The Dunes" was the attraction which brought guests back year after year to this favorite holiday spot. As the years began to catch up with Madame, she turned the hotel over to Camille and son-in-law, Jim Denholme, who ran it under her guidance for many years.

Jim Denholme attended a funeral in Queen Charlotte for one of his neighbors in the early 1940s and felt that it might be comforting for the people of Tlell to have a cemetery nearer. He talked the idea over with Madame Rajout, who agreed. She offered to donate any part of her land that he would like to choose for such a site. After consulting his neighbors, a location near the east end of the second (and present) Tlell bridge was selected, the cemetery laid out and with volunteer labor — given most especially by the Richardson family — the site was cleared and fenced.

The task was still under way when Mrs. Marian Richardson died. She had operated the store at Lawn Hill for many years and became the first person to be buried in the cemetery. Less than three months later Jim Denholme was himself laid to rest there.

After the untimely death of her husband, Mrs.Denholme moved to Vancouver with her mother and two children, selling the Dunes to Mr. and Mrs. John Slagboom. The superb fishing in the Tlell river drew guests from many places and among them were some wealthy Americans. They made John Slagboom a lucrative offer and, forming a syndicate, bought the property for a vacation club. John and his wife, Greta, were given a position on one of the member's estates in the United States and Stan Newcombe was engaged to come with his family and manage the former Dunes. Eight years later, in January 1966, a flash fire of unknown origin turned this historic landmark into a pile of rubble in less than two hours. The Newcombe's lost everything. The syndicate built a new lodge slightly to the west of the Dunes site that same year. Luxurious and comfortable it contrasts unbelievably with the humble "Inn" operated by Mrs. Hodges so many years ago on this same land.

When Simon Leiser sold the Mexican Tom ranch to Jake and Neil Walsh in 1909 the new owners made the place into everything old Tom had dreamed it might be. Neil Walsh brought his bride, the former Nettie Myers from Montana, to live in the log house that Benny Cromp and Ed Wiggans had built for Tom and Mrs. Hodges and the farm became a home ranch in the best western tradition. Guests were always welcome. However, when Nettie's family came to make an extended visit the log house would not accommodate everyone and a larger frame house was built north along the river bank, near the orchard. (Today Douglas Richardson and his family live in this house.)

The Walshes were adding to the sizeable herd Tom had been running when they took over and to obtain more grazing land for their stock they obtained a site near the Oeanda River. Two miles south of the mouth of the Oeanda the Walshes, with Dave Ruttan and Caesar Verhyden, dug a big drainage ditch ten feet wide and six hundred feet long. In that flat land it had the unexpected effect of changing the mouth of the river — which ever since has flowed out of the big ditch into the sea, two miles south of its normal course. Neil Walsh put four pairs of Belgium hares in his meadow at Tlell in April of 1913 to see how they would do. The experiment was a success and for thirty years rabbits thrived in the environment, then no more were ever seen.

On December 30, 1912 a daughter was born to Mr. and Mrs. Neil Walsh, the first baby for Tlell. In July 1913, Tlell's second baby arrived when a son was born to Mr. and Mrs. Frank Rice. Mr. Rice a B.C.L.S., had brought his family to live in the cottage which was later occupied by Madame and Joe Rajout. When the baby was born, Mrs. Rice's sister, Rose Hollingsworth, stayed with her when Frank was out on surveys. The baby was only a month old when Rose went to the river one afternoon for a swim and was drowned — the river's first fatality.

With the increase in their stock, the Walsh brothers took on help and one of their first employees was Gus Ross, the brother of Mrs. Bob Wilkie at Lawn Hill. Gus brought his twelve-year-old half-brother, Eric Cossik with him. "He was a terribly hard working boy," says Bert Roberts of Eric, "and more than did his share of any job." When Gus left later on to begin his own ranch at Southeast

282

Harbor, Eric stayed on with Nettie Walsh, who had taken a great liking to the boy, although she worried about his working so hard at such an early age. Her premonitions about the lad were born out for Eric was barely into his twenties when he died.

By the time Jake and Neil Walsh sold their ranch to Eric Richardson in 1919 there were six members of the Myers family living with them, and it was Mr. Myers, Nettie's father, who had the first car on the Islands. He brought it up from Skidegate over the rough wagon road. "Some excitement," recalls one early resident. "I think everybody all along the way came out to watch it go past — the first car most of us had seen."

Eric Richardson had been farming on the prairies when he was ordered by his doctor to leave and try living in the more temperate climate on the coast. "I'll never forget the first evening I arrived at Tlell," he recalled. "We were having supper and I could hear a continuous splashing in the river beside the house. When I asked what was making such a noise I was told it was the salmon. And it sure was salmon. The whole half-mile stretch of river was a solid mass of jumping fish!"

Mr. Richardson's appreciation of Tlell was shared by most of the members of his family. They came to visit, one by one, and remained to stay. His mother Mrs. Annie L. Richardson, and sister Sybil Mrs. de Bucy, were the first. Later another sister Mrs. Helliwell, and younger brother, Ken, joined the family group. Ken Richardson bought his own farm nearby. This was the farm that Cecil Pallant had hoped he had staked out — but which the survey revealed he had not. When Mr. Pallant went to Sandspit, a man named Aspinwall pre-empted on the newly surveyed lot.

John Allard and Ed Wiggans lived near Aspinwall, and when Allard left, Ed Wiggans bought his property to add to his own. The farm of Lionel Andrews, near Ken Richardson, was owned first by Mr. Bristoe, whose half-brother, Ed Ashton, was very well known at Lawn Hill. It was purchased next by Jack Cook, who later married Mrs. Wiggans. Lionel's father, William Andrews, bought it shortly after the first world war and brought his bride to live in the snug cabin near the bank of the river.

Mrs. Andrews was the sister of Ralph Ward, the pioneer homesteader from Lawn Hill. When Mr. Ward returned from his overseas service and learned that so many of his former Lawn Hill neighbors had gone to war — many of them never to return — he decided to make a change, and bought Charles Turney, senior, out. The Wards loved Tlell dearly, and even after Mr. Ward was appointed telegraph agent in Port Clements in 1925, he still considered Tlell his home and returned to the ranch at every chance — employing a caretaker to look after it during his absence. After his death, Mrs. Ward went to England to live and sold the place to Nelson Brothers — a well-known B.C.Cannery family who have their plant at Port Edward, near Prince Rupert. "Oh, how I remember Mrs. Ward's parsnip wine," says Bert Roberts. "Every visitor was always given a glass — and you can bet we never passed that house without making a visit, coming and going!"

The log house on the Ward property was originally built by Benny Cromp on the Walsh meadows when he was thinking of getting married. Ed Wiggans helped him. When the Cromps decided to live in Skidegate, Charles Turney, Senior, bought the squared timbered house which Benny had completed up to the rafters and gave Bert and Roger Roberts the contract to take the house apart, float the logs down the river and rebuild the house on its present site.

Roger Roberts came to visit Bert in September 1914. Like Eric Richardson, Roger was fascinated by the tremendous amount of salmon going upstream. "He would stand on that old bridge (by Bob Beitush's) and watch the fish by the hour," says his brother Bert. "I think that's what sold him on Tlell." Roger chose a lot behind Bert and obtained his Crown Grant.

Tommy Rae went inland for his pre-emption also and was about a mile in along the Mexican Tom trail from Joe Rajout's first cabin. Between Joe and Geike Creek, on the west side of the river, was a large government reserve section, not open to settlers. Sam Raybold was near the mouth of Geike, and beside Sam was Emil Ludwig, a close friend of Gus Buschel, the blacksmith from Lawn Hill. (It was Ludwig's location that Mr. Scowcroft had chosen earlier and this was where he had the big self-binder delivered in 1911.) Other settlers along here besides Bert, Roger, and Fred Greenstreet, were H. Boyle, Cristen Christenson and James Hickey for whom Hickey Lake was named.

Settlers from the Oeanda and the Blue Danube came to Tlell for mail and supplies frequently. Two of these, Bill Carr and Ernest Whittle had earned extra cash by working on the road that went to Tow Hill from the Blue Danube, and tacked a sign up, feeling that if the road was to have a name, it might as well bear theirs. For years this road was called the "Carr and Whittle Trail". It was used as extensively as its counterpart to the south, the Mexican Tom trail. Jim Broker, Victor Vigelous, Caesar Verhyden, Jimmy and Bill White, Dave Rutten and R. R. "Railroad" Smith were all well-known Tlell visitors from this region. It was Mr. Smith's initials which led to his nickname and he was "...one of the most persistent con men I've ever met," remembers Charlie Hartie. "His approach was that he was going to do you a real favor." Bert Roberts thought that the settler named Clarke who lived on the west bank of the Tlell, slightly south of the present bridge site, was Railroad's equal. "He was a physical culture expert with all sorts of formulas for diets. Then he got hold of a formula for making silver polish and talked me into going to Vancouver to peddle the stuff — until I wised up," he adds with a chuckle.

It is generally conceded that Tlell's most ardent booster was Nick Geigerich who had brought his wife and small son Napoleon from Missouri to the Cape Ball homestead in 1908. Mr. Geigerich wrote extensively of his farming experiences on the Islands for newspapers and journals for many years, telling of the possibilities he felt were open to anyone willing to go about things in the right way. Three more children were born to Mr. and Mrs. Geigerich, John, Mary and Anna. (1) When the telephone and telegraph lines were laid across the Islands in 1913, Mr. Geigerich became the first operator, taking up duties first in Queen Charlotte City, then in Masset and finally moving to the Port Clements office until 1924 when he returned with his family to the United States. In the 1940s the memories of those earlier years on the Charlottes drew him irresistibly to resume life in Tlell. He remained until advancing years made farming, even on a modest scale, too difficult and retired with his second wife to live at White Rock.

The first telephone lines were laid along the East Coast to Cape Ball, at which point they crossed overland to Mayer Lake, seven miles away. There was a fairly

(1) Mrs. Bob Beitush.

284

adequate wagon road from Mayer Lake to Kumdis Bay, so when the telephone poles and right of way were being put in, there was much urging (1) in the fall of 1912 for a road to be put in that would connect Cape Ball with Graham Centre (2) and eliminate the hopelessly difficult Mexican Tom trail, as it seemed unlikely that anything could be done to improve conditions along that type of terrain.

Today all that section north from the Beitush ranch is abandoned by settlers, nevertheless Tlell has as many residents today as it had in early days, and it is almost impossible to buy land there with waterfrontage that is accessible by road. The big ranch which was so attractive to Tom Hodges, above all other places, is still in the Richardson family, who share Tom's love for this spot. When Eric Richardson retired from active farming his son, Francis, who married the former Dorothy Husband, assumed the reins for many years. Now their eldest son Douglas and his wife Alice, run the ranch under the guiding eye of Doug's parents who still live close by. "I could never leave Tlell," says Dorothy Richardson, "I think my heart would be forever on the banks of this river." The Tlell post office is attached to her house and whenever her neighbors arrive to collect their mail they announce their presence to the busy postmistress by ringing — a cow bell.

(1) *Queen Charlotte News, August 10, 1912*
(2) *Graham Centre appeared to be the leading town for Masset Inlet in 1912.*

CHAPTER FORTY-FIVE

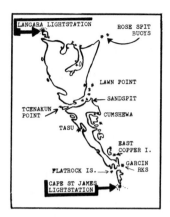

TRANSPORTATION

The announcement in 1912 that two first-order lighthouses were to be established on the Q.C.I., one at Cape St. James and the other at North Island — as well as the flashing light on a buoy off Rose Spit — was greeted with sighs of relief by all mariners who used these waters. Work began on the North Island site that year, and, in recognition of the importance of the light to all coastal navigation it was felt that a more distinctive name must be used for its location. Jacinto Caamano's old name of Langara was adopted and Dixon's North Island was dropped from the charts.

When tenders were called, the government found that it had no bids for contracts under the usual scheme. Getting men and supplies to such a rugged site would be enough of a hazard without a contractor having to worry about losing money over the venture. The only way the jobs could be done was on a cost-plus basis. Building Langara Lightstation was begun in July 1912 and in May 1913 the first lightkeeper took up his duties. During that time the *Leebro* under Captain Hunter made innumerable trips with material and men — often having to anchor off-shore for weeks at a time before he could unload in the stormy seas.

One of the first men to work on building Langara lighthouse was Mr. Lindstrom, a pioneer from Terrace. It was far too wild and lonesome for him and he came back to the mainland with the next supply ship — in less than a month. Thirty-eight years later, in 1950, his son, Otto answered an advertisement for lightkeeper at this same place, and he and his wife liked it so well they stayed for three years. "The idea of a lighthouse on an island nearly ten miles long seemed wonderful," says Mrs. Lindstrom, "most of them seem to be on such dinky little rocks. I had heard that there was a jeep out there and had visions of driving all over the place — that is until I saw the road. Two or three planks for each tire and most of it set on trestles above the muskeg."

The jeep had been left on Langara by the R.C.A.F. who had operated a radar station there from April 19, 1943, until 1945 with a complement of sixty-five men. When the station was abandoned the lightstation residents fell heir to

287

many comforts they might not other wise have had – a piano, leather easy chairs, a water system and a good supply of lumber to add cupboards and so on to the living quarters. "Our house was a large duplex on top of a two hundred foot cliff," says Mrs. Lindstrom. "Each side had three rooms down and four up. The living room had a 12 by 20 foot floor space and a big brick fireplace on the inside wall. We had a little garden with vegetables and flowers. It doesn't get very warm on Langara, but we rarely had frosts there, so quite a few things seemed to do very well."

The lighthouse, built of cement, had three floors with a steep ladder going up to the top floor and the huge reflector with a 200 watt bulb in it. The reflectors are diamond shaped pieces of glass, put together in a octagonal shape, and said to weigh three tons. It is set in a mercury bath and so delicately balanced that it can be moved with a touch of the hand. Light is thrown out through four circles, with the reflector set to turn at such a speed that at a given point there is one flash every five seconds. This is a specific signal, visible for nineteen miles, and recognizable by all who know, as the Langara Light. No other light has the same flash. "A system of weighted cords was used to wind it up and when fully wound it would operate for four and half hours," says Mrs. Lindstrom.

There was a radio operator at Langara as well as the lightkeeper and he had his own quarters in the radio "shack" surrounded by all his equipment. Otto Lindstrom was the lightkeeper and for a time he had an assistant. One was a man with five children, who enlivened the Island to quite a degree. There were few spare moments in the busy schedule so when the Department of Fisheries asked Lindstrom to take on the job of obtaining samples of sea water, it added to an already full calendar. The samples had to be taken each day within an hour of high tide, so the duty was quite demanding. Pay was twenty-five cents a day. Hoping for a raise, Otto wrote to the superintendent of fisheries saying that twenty-five cents barely covered the shoe leather he wore out walking the three-quarters of a mile, twice a day – each way – to take the samples. A message was telegraphed out from the superintendent's office asking to know what size shoes Mr. Lindstrom wore. When the supply ship arrived on its next trip there was a parcel for Otto from the Department of Fisheries – a new pair of gum boots, plus the information that he was to get a raise in pay, from twenty-five cents to twenty-seven cents a day.

Langara's counterpart – the big Cape St. James light – flashes every six seconds and can be seen for twenty-four miles. Built on bowler-shaped St. James Island in 1913, it was put into operation in February 1914 with Taylor Ash, a former quartermaster on the *Princess May,* in charge. During the second world war the R.C.A.F. had a radar station at the "Cape" comparable to the one at Langara. It was in operation from August 26, 1943 until August 10, 1945 and also had a complement of sixty-five men stationed there. (1)

Built in an era when the word transportation meant marine travel exclusively, these two lightstations now continue to serve shipping – which has grown steadily in volume – and, in addition the modern radio beacons and the meterological reports sent in to mainland headquarters are vital in the jet age of aircraft travel. So much so that in 1962 an extensive program was undertaken by

(1) *Information from Wing Commander R. V. Manning, Chief of Defence Staff, Ottawa, 1965.*

the Department of Transport for the two stations to modernize the living quarters, making them as comfortable as possible and to install every facility to enable the stations to provide up-to-date data. The old inevitable isolation factor has been decreased by the addition of a helicopter landing pad for the big Sikorski 61N which services the lighthouses from its base in Prince Rupert.

With the subsequent addition of more navigational aids in particularly hazardous locations along the shipping routes of the Charlottes, captains could breathe easier — although it was still no coast to be taken lightly. Shipwrecks with loss of life, however, have not been as great here as in other coastal regions. Two of the most notable exceptions to this were the *Galiano* and the *Clarksdale Victory*. The *Galiano*, a fisheries vessel, was doing double duty as a lighthouse tender in November 1918 when she foundered in heavy seas off Cape St. James. She was on her way to Ikeda Head from Triangle Island when her master, Captain Pope told his wireless operator to send the message, "We are sinking." No trace was ever found of the *Galiano* or her complement of twenty-six men and a lady passenger, Miss Brunton, who had embarked at Triangle Island.

In 1947 one of the Victory ships built during the second world war, the *Clarksdale Victory*, operating as a United States Transport vessel, was returning from Alaska to the United States with war surplus material when she got off course in the middle of the night and was wrecked on the west side of Hippa Island with a loss of forty men.

What might have been the scene of an equal tragedy was averted by a quick thinking skipper on April 1st, 1920 when the *Prince John* and the *Prince Albert* collided with a grinding crash in a heavy snow storm off Lawn Hill. Realizing that the *"John"* was in danger of sinking immediately, the skipper of the *"Albert"* kept his bow in the gaping hole, and ordering full steam ahead, he pushed the stricken *"John"* onto the shore near Miller Creek. Everyone was taken safely off and the damaged vessel abandoned to await rescue operations.

Of the many ships which served on the Island runs it would be difficult to single out any one as being more favored than another. The *Amur, Tees, Vadso* and *Princess Beatrice* of the first years were well-known — as was the *Henriette*, although she was not so well loved. "Oh, how she rolled!" remark people who sailed on her. A hundred and sixty feet long, the *"Hen"* was originally a French barque which had been built in 1884 at La Seyne. In 1906 her owners at that time, McKenzie Brothers, converted her into a twin-screw steamer powered by a sixteen horse engine. "In any kind of a head wind she went backwards instead of forwards, with her engines full speed ahead," recalls Mr. T. L. Williams. In 1909 she was chartered by the Grand Trunk Pacific to enable them to get the Island mail contract — for which they would receive $200 per trip. She was purchased by them the next year and put on freighting as soon as their new ship the *Bruno* arrived on the Pacific coast.

The *Bruno* was built in England in 1892 and when she made her initial trip to Masset on June 23, 1910 under Captain Cecil Wearmouth, she had been renamed the *Prince Albert*. She was given a royal welcome in that little settlement when she docked for the first time with ". . .speeches, banners flying, and suitable entertainment," according to the newspaper accounts. The 232 foot vessel plied in Island waters until 1923 when she was sold by the G.T.P. After several years as a notorious rum-runner she was purchased by John R. Morgan in 1935 and was finally scrapped in 1949.

In 1911 a new ship was purchased by the G.T.P. and remodelled especially for the Queen Charlotte Island run — and if any ship can be thought to have been truly the Islands', it was this one. Built in 1910 by Messrs. Scott and Sons of Bowling, England, for a Mr. Robertson, she had been designed for freighting around the stormy seas of the British Isles, and was named the *Amethyst*. On August 9, 1911, she began her service under her new name *Prince John*, and the honor of being her skipper for that first trip also fell to Captain Cecil Wearmouth. The *"John"* was smaller than the *"Albert"*, being 186 feet long, but she was beamy and stout and with a full load could make 12 knots. Considered by many to have been the safest boat ever to cross Hecate Straits, old-timers would say, "Well, if the old *John* can't make it, no other ship can either. . ." when she was late on her runs during winter gales. In 1941 she was sold to the Union Steamship Company and renamed the *Cassiar,* under which name she continued to do yeoman service until she was scrapped in 1951.

The aristocrat of them all was the *S. S. Prince Charles* — and she was also the largest, being 242 feet long. Built in Scotland in 1907, she was named the *Chieftain* and then the *St. Margaret.* When the G.T.P. bought her in 1925 they renamed her *Prince Charles.* Sleek and trim she was the pride and joy of Captain Neil McLean, her skipper for many years, ". . .when he wasn't high and dry on sand bars," one wag remarked. More than once she was photographed in this ignominious position on sandbars near Masset. When she landed on the Spit and some of the passengers wanted to get off to record the event on film, McLean was furious and would allow no one off the ship. She never seemed to suffer any damage in her groundings. She was sold to Union Steamships in 1940 and they renamed her *Camosun.* Five years later a Greek firm bought her and gave her her final name, *Cairo.* For several years she transported displaced persons in the Mediterranean until she was scrapped in 1952. (1)

The smallest of the *"Princes"* to be put on the Q.C.I. run was the *Prince William,* 177 feet long and barely four hundred tons gross. She had been built in Germany in 1915 and christened the *Aktion.* The C.N.R. bought her in 1930 for the Island run, but retired her the next year, and in 1937 Armour Salvage of Prince Rupert bought her for scrap.

In 1910 Thomas Deasy recorded the fact that it cost him $6 for fare and meals to go from Masset to Prince Rupert on the *Bruno,* $9 on the *"Hen"* and $10 when he went with Henry Edenshaw on the schooner *Josephine.*

One cannot go by steamer from Masset to Prince Rupert today — there is no service. Only Northland Navigation Company's *Skeena Prince* services the Islands, and she comes and goes from Vancouver, despite all protests both from the Islanders and from mainland Prince Rupert, the logical terminus for at least one end of the steamer's route.

Passenger travel to the Islands to day is mostly by aircraft. The DC 6B's of Canadian Pacific Airlines make daily stops on their Prince Rupert to Vancouver run and an office in Sandspit is maintained. North Coast Air Services have an office in Masset for charter trips to all Island and mainland points. B.C. Airlines

(1) Courtesy Mr. J. Gillan, Public Relations Department, Canadian National Steamships.

maintain offices in Masset for their scheduled Prince Rupert runs, and keep a staff in Sandspit to handle inter-Island scheduled flights and charter trips with the Beaver, Cessna and Grumman Goose amphibians based at Sandspit.

Air service to the Islands began in May, 1946, when the Queen Charlotte Airlines took over aircraft which had been operated by their predecessors Spilsbury and Hepburn, Limited. In 1947 Canadian Pacific Airlines began its daily service to Sandspit using Canso aircraft to enable them to dock at the seaplane base in Prince Rupert, until the modern airport was built on Digby Island (near Prince Rupert).

It was the advent of roads which perhaps was most eagerly looked forward to by Island residents to make life more enjoyable on the Charlottes. The rough wagon road from Skidegate to Tlell was improved enough to take cars and the first taxi on this road belonged to Al Beebe. "Fare was thirty dollars to Tlell and − hang on for dear life," say old-timers.

A road from the East Coast to Masset Inlet was urgently needed. In 1912 when the telephone line was being strung from Cape Ball to Masset Inlet by way of Mayer Lake, there was hope that a road would go that way to join with the road which it was expected would run from Mayer Lake to Kumdis Narrows where it would cross and enter Graham Centre, the candidate for the leading town on Masset Inlet at that time. When that idea didn't materialize it was back to shank's mare over the Mexican Tom trail, which was not improving with years. "...and no one could ever build a road along that route," it was said. "Why, it would cost a fortune! There isn't a speck of road material in the whole distance and it would be impossible to develop a satisfactory drainage system in that level tundra terrain."

But when Jesse Bridden conceived a method to build a road using planks to Tow Hill along the sandy soil of that region, and the cost was unbelievably low − the Minister of Public Works was persuaded to consider this type of road for the Port Clements to Tlell route. It was found that the method Mr. Bridden had devised could easily and economically − which was more important − be adapted to the muskeg. In 1920 surveyors were sent to lay out the roadway, which would nearly follow the Tom Trail.

"It was exactly eleven and one half miles from Tlell to Dyson's Corner in Port Clements," says Fred Chapman, now of Port Clements, "I remember this well, as it was my job to write the distance numbers on pegs which were set in place every hundred feet along the route." Ralph Ward, Bob Rudd, and Dave Tuft were also in that first survey party. "Dave Tuft was the cook and Ralph Ward volunteered to carry the stove," Mr. Chapman recalled.

After the preliminary survey, slashing and stumping began. "The camp was a cookhouse and a bunkhouse built on skids, and we dragged this along with us, using a donkey engine," says Fred. "Tom Pelton blew the stumps and three of his sons, Gordon, Tommy and Ralph also worked on the job. Gordon was on the rigging and the other two were packers. Jim Dunroe was hook-tender until he became boss, then Bill Vyse became hook-tender. I was the chaser and Dan May was whistle punk. We had Dave Tuft for our cook for awhile, then Bill Toop took over."

There were a number of other men who came and went as the job progressed. As soon as the route was stumped, the laying of planks commenced. This was accomplished by having crews work from both ends. Longitudinal planking was laid over pole stringers, and each wheel track consisted of two twelve-inch planks — with a gap left in the center of the road for reasons of economy. In 1928 the road was completed — two narrow ribbons of planks stretched the entire twelve miles from Port Clements to the Tlell bridge — which seemed unbelievable to residents from both ends who had watched for eight years as work went on. The bill was $8,505.72 for the whole job.

Strictly a one-lane road, two-way traffic was made possible by the construction of turn-outs. Thus a driver could pull out on a siding whenever another car was sighted and wait for it to pass. If you drove past the turn-out before you saw an on-coming car, the rule of the road was that the driver nearest the turn-out was obliged to back his car along the narrow track to the siding and allow the other car to pass. This backing up called for steady nerves and expert driving, for a slight swerve and the car was off the planks into the muskeg or straddling the stringers. And a vehicle so situated would tie up traffic whilst material was scrounged from nearby timber to prod and pry the car back up on the planks.

Driving under these conditions was extremely difficult and shortly after the opening of the road, the government authorized the addition of six-inch planks to be laid on either side of the wheel tracks — adding a foot more surface to each track. Traffic was limited to a gross load of 2.5 tons. Owing to the nature of the road and the difficulty of putting a car back on the planks once it went off, careful driving was essential. In the twenty odd years the road was in use, no one was killed or even badly injured on it — probably a highway record.

With the passage of years and increase in traffic, the maintenance cost of the road was high. Replacement of the planks by a gravel road became a necessity and beginning in 1941 the old planks were taken up section by section, and replaced by a sixteen foot graded, gravelled road — the whole undertaking being completed in 1951.

In 1966 a million dollar contract was let to pave Graham Island roads, from Skidegate Mission to Port Clements, which have been straightened and widened to a degree that would make them unrecognizable to those hardy pioneers who first traversed the distance in hiking boots, with packsaddle and a blazing-axe to mark the way.

One of the striking features of the Port Clements to Tlell road section, is its arrow-straightness. A feature which contrasts with its sister artery — the Port Clements to Masset road, officially opened on June 20, 1958. (1) It was surveyed by a local road superintendent as a reasonably straight road, but with a change in government, there was the usual change in personnel — so the story goes. "When the new man came in, he sent a bulldozer out ahead to test the terrain. Whenever the operator struck a soft spot he turned his machine and crept this way and that to find a better base, sometimes doubling back on his own tracks. Then," local residents explain, "they laid the road along his tracks." To the motorist who drives this series of horse shoe bends and curves — on perfectly level stretches in many cases — this would seem to be as logical an explanation as any. Safe to say, the job was not supervised by any Islander. Meanwhile the

(1) Date taken from the diary of Bill Vyse,
   who lived on an adjoining road.

292

survey line shown on all the maps as the road — lies untouched by any road from Purdy Creek north. It is thirty miles from Port Clements to Masset and rumor has it that when all the unnecessary bends are removed from the road — as is mooted — this will lop six miles off the present distance.

CHAPTER FORTY-SIX

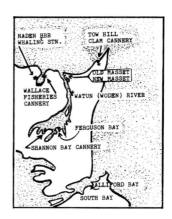

DEPRESSION YEARS

As the post war slump grew into the depression years of the 1920s and 1930s, life on the Charlottes followed a similar pattern in many respects as the rest of Canada. There was the same exodus of a segment of the population to search for better conditions elsewhere. For those who remained it meant a tightening of belts to the pre-war notch of pioneering days Money was short, but gardens grew the same fine produce, and fish and game were plentiful so no one went hungry – although diets could become monotonous during the winter months.

Perhaps it was the example of the few loggers who had decided to weather the lean times on the Islands and, missing their regular trips "to town to get oiled up," began making their own brew – but there were few homes who did not follow suit. The beverages turned out could be anything from ginger beer, wines, malt beer in many degrees of "proof", – to the moonshine specialty of those brewers who planned to commercialize their product. Yet it was rare to see drunkenness. Two policemen, one in New Masset and the other in Queen Charlotte City, handled matters for the whole of the Islands with ease.

Depression was a word which applied to financial conditions only – not morale. These were the years of strong community spirit when volunteer labor achieved wonders in the building of halls, and putting on entertainments. The thirties were the heyday of the Community Clubs, which made a valuable contribution to the social life of the settlements. Standard admission fee to dances was, "Gents – 25¢ and Ladies – Please provide". And how they provided! The tables would be loaded. Music was by an impromptu and largely volunteer orchestra or by the wind-up gramaphone. Ball games and picnics often ended with a big beach party in the evening, and one of the features was roasted potatoes – charred to a cinder on the outside and raw in the center – but pronounced delicious by all participants. And it was unthinkable for any group to go anywhere in a boat or car without singing all the way there and back.

As the depression years became more deeply ensconced, one of the most difficult problems was education. Grade eight was the end of the line for most youngsters unless they had the above average perseverance needed to wade

295

through "High School by Correspondence", from Victoria. The courses themselves were excellent — but Island mail service rendered education by this means impractical. When a student completed a paper, the equivalent of ten days work, and mailed it to be corrected — it could take two months before the youngster received the corrected paper. In the meantime he was expected to proceed with subsequent papers — not knowing whether the lesson had been understood or not. If the latter was the case, it meant complete redoing of all intervening papers. Some of the more enterprising girls found employment in cities on the mainland and, working for their board, attended high school. When mainlanders themselves began to feel the pinch too much to accommodate an extra mouth, even this avenue was closed.

For a boy, parents sent him out to school or he went fishing or logging as soon as he completed grade eight. Fishing could mean hand-trolling in an open boat unless he was lucky enough to be taken on as a helper on larger vessels. The big trolling grounds were in the Langara Island area — always called North Island by Islanders.

In 1935 prices had dropped to an all time low for the superb trolled salmon caught in this region. The fishermen, realizing that they were at the mercy of the large companies decided to form a co-operative to gain bargaining power. The first exploratory meeting was held June 15, 1935, on the beach in front of Al Peeve's cabin in Henslung Bay and a committee was formed to set up procedure for the North Island Trollers' Co-operative. A mainland company, Nelson Brothers, was contacted. They agreed to work closely with the embryo group and when the certificate of incorporation was granted to the Co-op, a vote of thanks was given to Nelson's for their part in marketing the fish with such success for the co-op that season. On August 17, 1935 — once again meeting in front of Mr. Peeve's cabin — trollers learned that the original North Island group was now enthusiastically supported by fishermen from Naden Harbor and Seven Mile Point. The North Island Trollers' Co-operative Association was born. Elected to the board of directors were: C. Eden, O. Warren, M. Hanson, E. H. Crawford (1) and K. A. Rankin. In order not to conflict with the Prince Rupert Co-op, the North Islanders' fishing grounds were carefully defined to comprise the north and west coast of Graham Island, extending from Skidegate Channel in the west to Tow Hill in the north.

In 1936 two first-class packers were purchased by the North Island Co-op for ten thousand dollars each, the *Hickey* and the *Kanawaka* — former rum-runners. The association prospered and added new members regularly until 1939 when it amalgamated with the Prince Rupert Co-op — a plan which had been under consideration for some time. The North Island Co-op was composed of men who fished at North Island, but who did not necessarily make their homes on the Islands, and the amalgamation which was welcomed by mainlanders was resented by many original founders, who felt that it was outside interference in the running of their own successful group. But it would take a large co-op to stand successful against the competition of the powerful companies and the need to pull together overcame any resentment as the two co-ops merged under the name of

---

(1) See Chapter 37, Mr. Crawford at Buckley Bay.

the Prince Rupert Fishermen's Co-operative Association. (1)

The largest fish processing plants to be established on the Islands were the whaling stations at Rose Harbor and Naden Harbor. Rose Harbor, on the north end of Kunghit Island, was built in the spring of 1910 after the site had been purchased by G. A. Huff of Alberni for a syndicate composed of business men from Vancouver and Victoria. The company, known as the Queen Charlotte Whaling Company, began operations in July 1910, and by late fall had processed eighty whales. The station employed one hundred and fifty men in the operation and was reported to have cost $270,000. It operated for nine months of the year in its early stages.

Construction of the Naden Harbor plant was begun in 1911 on land purchased by the Canadian North Pacific Fisheries, near the mouth of Germania Creek. Operations began in 1912 and in the fall of that year ownership passed into the hand of the British Empire Trust Company, who in turn sold the Naden Harbor plant to the Victoria Whaling Company in 1915. (2) In 1918 the Consolidated Whaling Incorporated (3) of Toronto bought both Naden and Rose Harbor Whaling stations and operated them almost continuously until 1943. This company went bankrupt in 1946. The next year, Western Whaling Corporation Limited, (a company in which B.C.Packers was one of three partners) acquired both properties from the trustees in bankruptcy for $7,000. Walker and Ferguson were the directors of this firm and machinery and equipment which was not obsolete was moved to the plant erected by Western Whaling at Coal Harbor on Vancouver Island. Operations were commenced at this plant in 1948. Two years later B.C.Packers purchased the interests of the other shareholders in Western Whaling, and the Naden Harbor and Rose Harbor stations, as well as the Coal Harbor station became the property of the B.C. Packers, who still own them.

Whaling was one of the resources which was exploited almost as badly as the fur seals of earlier days. By the time steps were taken to conserve remaining herds, their extinction seemed imminent. Few of today's excursionists would have the opportunity to witness the scene described by Alfred Hustwick in a 1914 article for the B.C. Magazine.

"Imagine a long wharf with a coal bunker at each end, a tramway running its full length, and its entire surface almost hidden by thousands of drums and barrels of oil awaiting shipment. To the right of the wharf, picture half a dozen factory buildings, rectangular studies in unpainted wood and corrugated iron and at the farther end a wide slipway running from a half-roofed shed down to the water. To the left of the wharf five or six bunkhouses, storehouses and office buildings with the manager's private residence showing between the trunks of great trees and through dense foliage about their roots. The background in virgin forest, sloping steeply up from the water, which is coffee-colored by a score of polluting drains.

(1) Information in this paragraph and the preceeding one from Mr. A. V. Hill, author of "Tides of Change", to be published in 1967.
(2) Land Registry Office, Prince Rupert.
(3) An American controlled company. Information courtesy Public Relations office, B.C.Packers.

The sky is grey and rainy and the air is filled with steam, smoke and a combination of abominable odors that no words can do justice to. Such was Naden Harbor Whaling Station as the engineer and I beheld it on the morning following the whale hunt. We reached the cutting shed in time to see the finback whale hauled out. A fussy winch tugged at the heavy wire which drew the lacerated carcass up the slip, and our minds, reverting to the excitement of the previous day, realizing how nearly we had escaped disaster when this huge bulk of flesh and bone so narrowly missed collision with our vessel. Hardly had the whale cleared the roller at the head of the slip than a trio of nimble Japanese had climbed on the body and commenced removal of the blubber.

The tail was made fast to the bits with a heavy chain, and the Japanese with great flensing knives cut deep incisions about a foot apart running the full length of the whale. The cable was carried to the tail end of each strip, the hook sunk deep into the blubber and the winch started. The strips, known as "blanket pieces", were ripped off with a loud crackling of the mincer, where after being cut into small squares, or "horse pieces", they were sliced up by the mincer and conveyed by a bucket chain to the drying-out house.

The blubber from the finback was about eleven inches in thickness in the center of the strip, thinning down to about eight inches where it reached the "small". It was very white, except where the cutting had flecked it with blood, and in a general appearance suggested mutton fat. It is by the means of this blubber that the whale is enabled to maintain the great blood-head which is necessary to its existence."

Three steam whaling boats operated from Naden and the catch usually consisted of sulphur-bottoms, although occasionally a sperm whale was captured. In 1914 a rare white whale was taken — and this single animal was valued at $20,000.

Canneries seem to be associated with depression days, but they were in operation some time before then. Two had a brief existence on the west coast, one in Tasu in 1911 (1) and another in Rennell Sound. The latter was an Atlin Fisheries venture. They built a ninety foot wharf in Shields Bay in 1917. Intended mainly as a collecting station it had a roof over the greater length of the wharf. Fish caught by smaller boats would be kept on ice there until the large packers arrived to transport it to the mainland. It was only used for two seasons then abandoned. Atlin Fisheries became incorporated into the Canadian Fishing Company later and the company operated the Lagoon Bay and the Lockeport plants for several years as well as the short-time operation of Alliford Bay.

One of the earliest cannery operations was the Wallace Fisheries cannery on the east shore of the entrance to Naden Harbor. (2) Operating in 1910 it prospered enough to warrant enlarging in 1912. Thomas Deasy reported that when he visited there in July of that year —

"...spring salmon were being brought into the cannery by the *Claxton.* Manager J. E. Gilmore and travelling superintendent, W. R. Lord, were there

(1) See Chapter 22.
(2) Bert Wearmouth collected fish for this cannery in 1910.

and conducted me on a tour of the plant and the fifty new dwellings which had recently been erected. It is planned to call this site by its ancient Haida name of Schahoose." (1)

Mr. Del Lutes, now of Vancouver, had been in Prince Rupert in 1906 and worked in Skeena River canneries for several years before going to Wallace Fisheries cannery in Naden Harbor in 1918. "General A. D. McRae owned it then," he recalls. "They bought a site at the mouth of Woden River in Masset Sound and in the spring of 1919 decided to move the whole operation from Naden to Woden. Everything went on rafts. Charlie Caulson started out with the big two-and-a-half-story store building with his *Quinitsa* and we dismantled the cannery to travel in sections. It went off without a hitch and we were in operation in time for the 1920 run." The Woden River cannery ran under Mr. Lutes' guidance every second summer.

The canneries along Masset Sound and Masset Inlet ran every second year — even numbered years. This is because the big run of pinks in these waters only occurs on alternate years with the heaviest run coming in the years which are divisible by four — 1940, 1944, and so on.

The epic undertaking of moving an entire cannery from one site to another along an exposed waterway was equalled in audacity of a different sort by Francis Millerd. In the early twenties he had acquired the old sailing hulk, *Laurel Whalen,* fitted her up as a floating cannery and began canning fish in Ferguson Bay, Masset Inlet. Learning that the government planned to enact legislation forbidding the use of floating canneries, Millerd engaged two crews for the season of 1926. One crew was put to work canning in the one-line cannery on the ship and the other crew went to build a one-line cannery on the near-by shoreline. "It was some cannery," recalls Albert Dalzell, fifteen years old at the time, who had gone from Prince Rupert with his father, an old-time cannery man to work for the summer. "The whole thing was built in less than two weeks — including the wharf."

Hardly had the last piling been driven when the legislation disallowing the use of floating canneries was passed. In anticipation of this, Millerd had the *Laurel Whalen* firmly lashed to the end of the dock and, asserting that she was now part of the shore operation — not a floating cannery in the accepted sense of the word — he ran both canneries, using a crew for each.

About five o'clock one morning the sleeping cannery workers on the *Laurel Whalen* were awakened by a keening wail which defied immediate identification. Going on deck with the other lads to see what was happening, Mr. Dalzell remembers a most uncommon cannery sight. The early morning sun was streaming through the ratlines on the old sailing ship and out on her bowsprit sat a young Highlander playing the bagpipes, with his very soul it seemed, serenading the tree-lined shore with haunting melodies.

Perhaps it was a swan song, for that day the big fisheries protection vessel, *Malaspina,* complete with a small gun mounted in her bow arrived to advise Millerd that he was to cease all canning operations in the *Laurel Whalen.* In vain did Millerd point out that she was part of a shore installation. So for the rest of the season he put his two crews to work in the shore cannery, running

(1) Skaös

a double shift, and the *Laurel Whalen* was used as a bunkhouse, and a storage shed for the canned fish. To make sure that the order was adhered to, the Malaspina lay off the bay for most of the season, ". . .with her gun pointed our way", says Mr. Dalzell. "It was real adventure for us boys — I think we expected warfare to break out at any moment."

Francis Millerd was to have the last word with the Fisheries Department, however. He was so positive he had not violated any laws and that he had been unjustly restrained that he took his case to court, battling for years. It finally reached the highest court in London and his plea was upheld, with the result that Inspector of Fisheries Motherwell and several officials were fined for their part in the case. The Government of Canada promptly enacted a covering legislation which eliminated any loopholes for the operation of mobile type of canneries.

The largest cannery on the Queen Charlottes was the six-line Shannon Bay cannery in Masset Inlet which was built in 1926 by the Gosse Packing Company. After the amalgamation of Gosse Packing and British Columbia Fishing and Packing Company, Shannon Bay became a B.C. Packers operation. The plant was closed from 1931 to 1935 and re-opened in 1936. After the 1940 season it was closed and all buildings demolished. B.C. Packers had also acquired ownership of Woden River cannery, Ferguson Bay and South Bay canneries and a saltery at Jedway — all of which were closed between 1928 and 1931.

One of the first fishing stations to operate on the Islands, the Pacific Coast Fisheries plant, Pacofi in Selwyn Inlet — which was in operation in February 1910 — was also the last to close down. Alvo von Alvesleben and his associates built the cold storage, reduction plant and ice plant there which was closed after one year's operation. Attempts to re-open it were made in 1913, 1916 and 1917, but for several reasons — mainly financial — were unsuccessful. It was leased by Captain E. H. Simpson for a season in 1918. During 1927 a salmon saltery was opened there which operated until 1936. In 1938 B.C. Packers purchased the plant and the old buildings and machinery were replaced by a new two-line cannery and ten-ton reduction plant, but in 1943 the cannery and reduction plant were completely destroyed by fire. Two years later B.C. Packers rebuilt the reduction plant on the same site. The plant was closed after the season of 1949 and Pacofi was finally abandoned. During 1949 and 1950 all the buildings were disposed or demolished. (1)

There were several salteries in operation during the twenties and thirties. Two of these were in Queen Charlotte City, one of which was owned by the Kobiashi family who made their home at Queen Charlotte for many years. The licence fee to operate a saltery was $300 a year — and they were not issued to Japanese. Consequently, white friends held the licences for them. There was a small saltery in Huston Inlet, to the west of Jedway as well as the one in Jedway. For a short period Japanese canned abalone near Huston Inlet. "They put up four hundred pounds the first year," recalls Mrs. E. Moore, wife of the fisheries officer in charge of the region at that time, "and you could have soled your shoes with them they were so tough," she added. Her opinion seems to have been shared by everyone.

(1) Information this paragraph is largely from the files of B.C.Packers, courtesy of their public relations office.

The story of crab canneries on the Charlottes belongs exclusively to the Simpson family — Captain and Mrs. E. H. Simpson, their son Sam and his wife Jessie, and to Sam and Jessie's son, Gene. Unlike the other cannery operators, who spent only a short season on the Islands each year to do the actual managing — the Simpson family became permanent residents.

Captain E. H. Simpson had come to the Islands in 1916 and 1917 to operate a fish-buying camp in Sedgwick Bay — buying dog-salmon which were taken by packers from there to Bellingham for processing. In 1918 he organized the first cannery at Lockeport. When this venture failed due to vanishing markets, Captain Simpson gathered his few remaining assets and, with his wife and young son, Sam, left Moresby Island for North Island where he joined forces with Captain Hume Babington. Captain Babington was no stranger to the Islands, having gone to Masset Inlet in 1907 aboard the *Rover* when he and Norman Brodhurst had accompanied Dr. Leebo and a group of cruisers to look at timber in McLinton, Juskatla and the Dinan Bay region. Babington had considered starting a fishing station on North Island and had asked Mr. Brodhurst to stake two lots for him in Henslung Bay — Lots 998 and 999 — on November 24, 1907. (1)

It was here that Simpson and Babington built the one-line cannery in the spring of 1919 to can the spring salmon which were so plentiful and cheap in that area then. "I wasn't very old at the time," recalls Sam Simpson, "but anyway I was put to work on the double seamer — and also as a fireman. North Island was a very busy place then, all sorts of people seemed to be there. A chap named Hawkinson had a store in the next bay — a queer looking contraption high up on pilings — and he was doing a roaring trade."

By the summer of 1919 it was obvious that the Babington and Simpson cannery at North Island was rapidly going bankrupt. Captain Simpson becoming desperate, piled everything left on a scow and went to Naden Harbor in the fall of 1919. The Wallace Fisheries had just vacated the site at the entrance to go into Woden. Using the standing cannery pilings, Captain Simpson, in partnership with Captain Babington, built the first crab cannery in Canada. It was, except for an abortive operation earlier at Blaine, also the first on the west coast.

"Dad had been in Japan a few years before and had learned the correct use of acids to prevent sulfide discoloration as well as other techniques," says Sam Simpson. "They built up the cannery business and were doing quite well when he found out from the Indians, who were working for him, about the razor clams (2) on the North Beach. He and Babington staked the beaches and, obtaining capital from the Everett Packing Company, built the Langara Fishing and Packing Company in New Masset in 1924. As the pilot plant at Tow Hill had proved the feasibility of this type of operation, the Tow Hill cannery was also built around this time. Clam canning, as well as fish canning, went on steadily until 1930. This was the year the largest pack ever put up in the whole of Masset Inlet was handled by all the canneries working here. The ironic part of it is that the more fish you put up in one of these big years, the more broke you become as the market price drops," explained Sam. "We did

(1) Information from Mr.Norman Brodhurst, now of Brentwood Bay, B.C.
(2) Razor clams are not affected by the "red tide" which periodically makes all other clams poisonous.

very well in this respect — we had a huge pack so we really went belly-up. We lost everything."

"Dad was always hard pressed for cash, I think," he says, "but of course no cannery manager ever lets on that he is. He used to get some of his backing from Rupert and would go to see Mr. Robertson, the manager of the Royal Bank. When Robertson asked how things were going, Dad would say, "Oh, its just doing fine — we're making money hand over fist."

About two months after this, which was in 1926, a scow came into the Masset Sound loaded with equipment and material and began to build a cannery two miles north of Captain Simpson, in Old Masset. One of the partners in the venture was Mr. Robertson, who with John Dybhaven, Olaf Hanson and Pete Lorenzon, decided that he, too, would like to make some of the "hand over fist" money. They went down in the 1930 collapse also. About six years later Nelson Brothers bought this cannery.

The autumn of 1930 marked the end of the Langara Fishing and Packing Company. During a storm the whole thing blew down in less than fifteen minutes.

"My wife and I were pretty hard up," says Sam who had married the former Jessie Stott, "but in 1933 we decided to go back into the old crab business that Dad had operated in Naden Harbor. We got financial support from Bob Johnson, the well-known manager of Inverness Cannery on the Skeena and from Alex Chamberlain, Bob's bookkeeper, as well as from Dad's former sawmill partner in Masset, Arthur Robertson. It was a pretty close operation. I would pack fish in the summer and Jessie baked bread and so on to sell to the fishermen. In 1940 we got a good offer to go up to Shannon Bay as manager and forelady. The B.C. Packers treated us very well — but I don't think either of us liked being part of a big company operation. After talking it over we decided to move our little plant from Naden Harbor into Old Masset, renting Nelson Brothers cannery, we opened Queen Charlotte Canners."

In 1942 the Simpsons took an active part in the formation of the Masset Fishermen's Co-op which was incorporated that year. The Co-op had purchased the razor clam bed leases from the Nootka Packing Company, who had inherited them when the Langara Fishing and Packing had gone bankrupt. It was planned to combine clam, crab, and fish canning so as to have all year round employment as far as possible. The Co-op was well-supported locally but were bedevilled with problems — not the least of which was during the war when prices were frozen so low operation was unprofitable.

"The Simpsons, although willing to help in every way, declined to merge their business with the Co-op, having learned very early that it takes more than good intentions to successfully operate a cannery," says Mr. A. V. Hill, author of *Tides of Change*. (1) "They urged support of the co-op plan and assisted the embryo business venture by loaning some of their own hard-come-by money to enable the initial start to be made. Asked to take over the managership of the production end of things, Mr. Simpson agreed and was one of its hardest working members. Although the Co-op was forced to cease operations eventually, it was a worthwhile project as it brought hundreds of dollars into the community under conditions which no private enterprise was prepared to tackle at that time. And it kept those dollars at home."

(1) A history of fishing co-ops in B.C.

302

In 1946 when crab prices were released, Sam and Jessie decided to make another attempt at the crab business. Sam had long had an idea that the proper place to fish crabs was out in Hecate Strait, and had sent several boats to look for likely spots, but nothing fruitful came of the expeditions. "I was so sure I was right that we took all we had in the way of capital and built a proper crab boat — with a live-well — one of the first on the B.C. coast. My son and another chap went with me and we found big crab beds off the Oeanda on the East Coast." With this promising source the Simpsons went into crab canning with renewed vigor and did well. In 1950 they built their own plant in New Masset, which has been in operation ever since and is now managed by Sam's son, Gene — who with his wife, the former Pearl Wylie, also makes his home in Masset.

The "pinks" still run every two years in Masset Inlet — and in 1966 there was such a huge run that all fishing boundary signs were removed from the mouth of the Yakoun River, the largest spawning grounds — something that has never before happened in the history of Fishery Protection. Today however, the big fishing companies find it more economical to pack the fish in mainland processing plants and not operate isolated canneries for the short season. Fish buying camps are sent to strategic locations, where the fish is bought from the boats and packed in ice for shipment to the mainland in big fish packers.

There was one business venture connected with fishing which was a wholly feminine enterprise. In 1924 or 1925 Sybil de Bucy and her friend, Mary Sinclair (who later became Mr. Bert Roberts), set up a small store and bakery on Hippa Island, on the west coast of Graham Island.

"We bought the building from a man for fifteen dollars," says Mrs. de Bucy. "He had been making a fortune out there with his bakery the year before, he told us, and it sounded pretty good to Mary and me." They only just broke even — and learned from fishermen that the former owner had sold more than bakery products. Apparently he had a still near Skidegate which he ran full blast through the winter, then peddled the product, along with bakery supplies, to the fishermen during their rough-weather layovers in the bay on Hippa Island. "It was fun, though," recalls Mrs. de Bucy, "especially the big picnic we had on July 1st that year, which included boat races and a pie-eating contest."

The twenties and thirties were the years of the small logger. As long as there were any markets, gypo logging (1) was a good way to make a living. The three logging operators of this period who rose out of the gypo category were T. A. Kelley, J. R. Morgan and A. P. Allison who all had camps on the southern part of the Islands. It was customary to build a camp, complete with bunkhouses, dining room and cookhouse, blacksmith shop, offices and living accommodations for the families of the owners — all on rafts which were lashed together to form a miniature floating village. A site would be selected for a convenient base, jill-pokes, spaced at intervals, would be connected from camp to shore and the whole affair would be securely lashed and anchored in position. When all the logging in that region was exhausted, the entire camp would be towed to the next center of action.

(1) Small independent camps.

Most logging took place within easy access of the water, using A-frames, (1) coal deck and skylining methods of operation. The exception to this was at Allison's main camp in Cumshewa Inlet (shown on maps today as Aero). Mr. Allison owned the only train ever to operate on the Islands. Tracks were laid inland to Skidegate Lake, which was crossed by a trestle bridge, and from there branch lines ran to the west, east and north — remains of this old track can still be seen.

Mr. T. A. Kelley had come to the Islands first in 1908. Mrs. Dolmage knew him well when she lived at Jedway. A tall, good-looking man, Tom Kelley was a graduate civil engineer from the United States. Although he was an excellent timber cruiser, he was not a registered B.C.L.S. and so could not register any of the surveys he made. He obtained contracts to do a great many of the early timber surveys by hiring a crew to do the work and then engaging a registered B.C. Land Surveyor to pass the work. There were few of the early timber claims around Skidegate Inlet that Tom Kelley had not done. "His secret was that he really knew how to pick good men," explained one old logger.

About the time the timber cruising slowed down, a pulp mill was started in Swanson Bay (2) by the Whalen Brothers. Kelley began logging for them on the Charlottes with machines supplied by the pulp company. This company went into the receivers hands — but as Kelley had his outfit registered as a separate company, he was able to keep his equipment. When the demand for aeroplane spruce came, he was able to supply it before any of the other outfits were started. After the war he joined the Powell River Company and leased their saw-mill to cut and market clear spruce for other purposes. Later he bought shares in an Alberta oil company and sold out at a large profit just before it went bankrupt.

"He was a good business man," says Charlie Hartie, "and managed to collect men who could make things pay. A friendly man, he was good to his employees and kept many men on the payroll after they had become too old to work. On the farm he had in Washington state most of the employees were old-time loggers who had worked for him."

John R. Morgan, the owner of another large logging camp, had come to the Islands — Masset Inlet first — to take advantage of the spruce boom. After the war he moved his operations to Skidegate Inlet, logging around the Dena River for some time before moving southward along Moresby's east coast.

In the mid-thirties he had difficulties with insurance companies about high rates and procedures for towing his Davis Rafts across Hecate Strait. Exasperated beyond endurance in 1935 he bought the *Prince Albert* and, renaming her the *J. R. Morgan*, did his own towing. "To hell with insurance — and I'm making money on the deal," he told his friends with gleeful satisfaction.

When A. P. Allison arrived on the Islands in 1926 he was a log buyer rather than an operator, and would finance men to log for him to get sufficient quantities. After more downs than ups with this method, he went into logging

---

(1) Mr. E. H. Crawford invented the A-frame when he was logging near Swanson Bay. It was so successful that loggers came from all over to watch it operate — but he never patented it.
(2) Swanson Bay is about 120 miles south of Prince Rupert.

304

for himself. The mill at Queen Charlotte City had recently closed down and Allison was able to pick up a great deal of his equipment at drastically reduced prices. He logged around Skidegate Inlet for some time before establishing his big camp in Cumshewa.

The other large logging operation of the twenties and thirties was the J. H. Baxter Pole Company, who took out poles first in Ferguson Bay, then at Mayer Lake and lastly on Kumdis Island. The Baxter Company had an especially designed carrier for this operation, the Jug-a-way, which ran on a road constructed along the same lines as a railroad. The carrier, which was motorized, had grooved wheels to fit poles, (laid end to end along the road) in much the same way as train wheels do on a track. The Baxter Pole Company is today taking out poles from Mayer Lake which were saplings during that earlier operation, and are now of commercial size.

The logger of early days was a hard-working, free-spending, easy-going man, who usually had a nickname. Who could forget Jim Kennedy's "Canada Jim", Charles Wesley's "Shy-Ann", Bill Strausman's "B. S. Bill", Ed Layton's "Cougar Bill"? Or the innumerable Shorties, Swedes, Slims, and Curlies, who later joined the settlements on the Islands to live out their days — all apparently batchelors. It was common for a logger to spend the season in the woods then during the winter, with a good-sized bankroll, go to "town" as Vancouver was always called. In less than a month he had little of his bankroll left and when time to go logging rolled around he would wire "the old man" — collect — to send his fare "so's he could go back to work".

Logging on the Charlottes, today as elsewhere, is far different from those earlier "cut and get out" policies. The big companies are keenly interested in conservation and co-operate closely with the Forestry Branch to achieve the best results. They know that there is a possibility that those splendid trees — some of which measure seventeen feet in *diameter* — and from which there is enough lumber in one tree to build five average homes, could be exhausted. Logging payrolls contribute greatly to the economy of the Islands and logging. operators, who before contributed nothing in the way of community effort, now go to great lengths to provide settlements which are conducive to permanence. Employees are encouraged to bring their wives, raise their families and live a normal life, never before possible for a logger. The old adage of each camp having three crews, "one coming, one working, and one going", seldom applies these days. Managers and superintendents as well as ordinary working men are taking part in programs for Island progress and improvement in living standards. They are on hospital boards, support the newly-formed Q.C.I.Chamber of Commerce, and take an active interest in most community efforts. Roads extend over the centre of Graham Island and the northeast part of Moresby, to facilitate the removal of logs. When a camp is not working, the public is permitted to use the roads.

Two gold mines, the Southeaster and the Hydah, were operations which were associated with the 1920 to 1930 period. Both had their beginnings several years before. The Hydah Gold Mine was located in Kootenay Inlet, on the north side of the south arm. George Chapman owned it first, in 1913. When he abandoned it, George McRae (now of Queen Charlotte City) and a man named Jones took over in 1920. Mr. Jones lost interest and Nels Larson took over

Jones's share. "We put up a little mill and got two ounces of gold for one winter's work," says Mr. McRae, "so we let the permit lapse too." In 1930 Ed Stevens and two Americans staked the claim, and when they left, Mr. Stevens fell heir to it. He interested some Vancouver business men, who brought engineer Bert Ingraham with them. Mr. Ingraham married Eddie's twin daughter, Margaret Stevens, who had been born in the big Cood house in Sandspit. The gold at the Hydah mine proved to be only surface gold, as was the case at Gold Harbor and was to be so for the Southeaster Mine also.

The Southeaster Mine site lay to the north of the Skidegate Indian Reserve. In 1910 A. J. Gordon and John McLellan, who had bought the site from the Haidas after gold-bearing quartz was discovered there, had a camp about a mile inland. They did considerable cross-cutting for the samples which assayed promisingly well. John McLellan had an interest in the Gold Harbor mine at this time also and was still working these claims in 1918, according to the mining report for that year. (1)

The Southeaster Mine was comprised of three claims, Southeaster, Sunrise and Beaconsfield. For two years 1917 and 1918, it operated under an engineer named Holmes, who employed fourteen men and a nurse — Mrs. Pitt-Turner. In 1929 it was reopened by W. G. McMorris, who earlier had been interested in coal near Cowgitz. "McMorris ran it until 1933," recalls Charlie Hartie, "and then a chap named Smith took over and ran it until 1936 when the whole thing was abandoned. Over $200,000 was put into the Southeaster Mine," and he added, "only to prove there was little of value there."

No mention of mining would be complete without the name of C.D. Emmons, who was taking men on prospecting trips on the Charlottes in 1911, and later took the sons of these same men to "scout around". For many years he prospected, surveyed and "geologized" most of Graham Island, from the oil hopes on the west coast to coal in the Yakoun Valley and gold anywhere it looked promising. "It was an education to work with the old fellow," says George Husband, whose father, Dick Husband, had been out on many trips with Mr. Emmons before George was born. Like so many men who had spent a great deal of time in solitary living in the bush, Mr. Emmons loved to talk whenever he could find an audience. He would begin a story in the morning as the crew were preparing to go out on whatever surveying he had lined up, and when they came back in the evening, would carry on with, ". . .and as I was saying." Mr. Emmons never did find the "big one" he sought for so many years, but lived such a satisfying life looking for it, that many people felt his reason for living would have been lost if Emmons had ever struck it rich and left the bush.

The wildlife which played an important role in supplementing the diet of Islanders for many years, was not all native to the Charlottes. The deer were introduced in 1910 by the Provincial Game Department and were obtained from Porcher Island, near Prince Rupert. Contracts were let by H. J. McMullin, Government Agent Prince Rupert, in May of that year and by the fall of 1911 eighteen to twenty head had been released along Masset Inlet. With no predators

(1) *The last reported shipment of gold from the Gold Harbor mine was made in 1939 by D. F. Kidd, who was leasing the Early Bird property – near the old Hudson's Bay site.*

they thrived and today there is open season on deer the year round. The Elk are a comparatively recent addition and seem to also be thriving.

It is generally believed that the black bear on the Islands originate from cubs which were brought by the Haidas as pets from the mainland in very early days. The muskrats which helped many a depression day trapper to earn a living are said to have been introduced by a settler near the McIntosh Meadows, outside Masset. Squirrels and raccoons are recent additions to animal life and not native.

The one animal which was native to the Islands is now extinct. This was the unique specie of caribou, Rangifer Dawsonii, found nowhere else in Canada. It had existed on the Charlottes since before the last glacial period which receded 10,000 years ago, according to the Provincial Museum in Victoria. When it was realized that the Q.C.I. specie of caribou was becoming extinct, the curator of the Victoria Museum, Mr. Kermode, appointed Norman Brodhurst, now of Brentwood Bay, to secure one for him in 1908. The museum had obtained a small animal in 1906, but Mr. Kermode wanted a better specimen to mount and exhibit.

"Bill Haylmore (later Gold Commissioner at Lillooet) was with me," said Mr. Brodhurst. "He was going to look at some special blue and white rock the Indians had told him about which was supposed to be below Frederick Island. We went over on the *Princess Victoria* with a Haida named Stanley, who had rigged his ship from a wrecked sealing schooner. I rented a house in Masset from Mary Ridley, whose husband, Phillip, was making a totem pole. One of the first people I met was Matthew Yeomans, who told me that he and Henry White had two caribou at his house. I was invited to have some of the meat. The animals had been skinned and slightly smoked to preserve them. The skins looked pretty good to me, but they had been cut off at the knees. However I got hold of them and wrote to Kermode, as these two Haida hunters were doubtful I would get anymore, they were so scarce." But Kermode told Brodhurst he didn't want them as they had been cut up and sent him to try to hunt some on his own. "It was hopeless," says Mr. Brodhurst. "We looked all over the Naden Harbor area where they were supposed to be — and walked down the west coast as far as the old drill at Tian Point — walking along the top of the cliffs and beaches from Kiusta."

In the end the Victoria museum took the two scorned hides and, using the small specimen secured in 1906, were able to compose the caribou now on exhibit in the Provincial Museum — three animals to make one. The caribous shot by Yeomans and White were the last ever seen on the Charlottes.

According to his book, *"In the Wake of the War Canoe,"* Archdeacon Collison had eight deer taken over on the H. B. C. supply ship to Masset in 1878. They did not survive and the surmise has been offered that they were put into someone's stew pot. Theories have been advanced that these deer may have introduced a disease to the small herd of caribou, and this is what caused their extinction after having existed on the Islands for thousands of years. But as one man said later, "It was fitting that the last of the Queen Charlotte Island caribou met their fate at the hands of the native Haida hunter and not the white."

CHAPTER FORTY-SEVEN

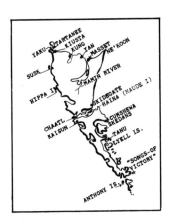

A CAPSULE OF TODAY

When John Work counted heads on the Charlottes in 1840 he estimated that there were 6693 people divided among the twelve main villages. (1) By the turn of the century this figure had dwindled to a bare six hundred, which was divided into two villages, plus a few workers in the Oilery at Sterling Bay. From that low point the population has climbed slowly but steadily until today, sixty-seven years later, there are an estimated (2) five thousand people living there — and once again there are twelve main settlements. (3)

Undoubtedly the most astounding change the years have brought — at least to pioneer settlers — would be the news that muskeg is a valuable commodity and, the purer the muskeg the more it is valued. Bering Industries of Victoria have spent a million dollars to install a peat moss processing plant at the mouth of the Nadu River. The plant went into production in early 1967 and made its first shipment of processed moss to the United States in March, where market prospects for the product are said to be excellent.

At Tian Head, the scene of early oil well hopes on the west coast of Graham Island, a mixture of water and oil bubbles merrily out of the old oil drill — now long abandoned. Interest in oil possibilities is as great today, although drillers — like earlier fur traders — are notoriously close-mouthed. However, oil

(1) Anthony Island – 308, Tasu – 196, Tanu – 545, Skedans – 439,
Cumshewa – 286, Kaisun – 329, Chaatl – 561, Skidegate – 738,
Cape Ball – 120, Rose Spit – 122, Masset – 2473 (takes in two villages)
Kiusta – 576.
(2) The reader should note the word "estimated"; the following figures
were given to the writer by residents of the settlements in
October 1966:
(3) Jedway – 278, Tasu – 1000 (expected 1967), Moresby Camp – 165,
Sandspit – 500, Q.C. City – 500, Skidegate Landing – 72
Skidegate Mission – 350, Tlell – 50, Port Clements – 210,
Juskatla Camp – 237, New Masset – 538, Old Masset – 1000.
Lighthouses, independent logging camps and prospecting camps
supply the balance.

companies in recent years have surveyed and systematically tested a large area of the Islands and the planes of their representatives are frequently seen as they unobtrusively go about their business. It is off-shore probabilities that are the center of present oil interest.

Ikeda Bay, the scene of the Islands' first productive mine, lies deserted. One small cabin can be seen which is used occasionally by prospectors who are experiencing the same lure as their predecessors. The *Dawson,* used as the Ikeda Bay Mine bunkhouse, has only her keel and part of her hull remaining – but over the hill from Ikeda, the noise of machinery working Jedway's mine can be heard for miles. From the beach in Ikeda's Cove the road from Jedway can be seen at the top of the hill, reaching down Ikeda's way for a half a mile as machines strip and clear the surface of the region for mining.

The modern amenities in Jedway, a company town which was built in 1961 are in contrast to the first Jedway which Mrs. McGregor knew in 1908 – but the wind can gust as strongly today as ever, say Jedway's residents. Copper which created such a furor in earlier years is of little interest now – instead it is the iron ore deposits of the area which are being developed. Jedway is a pretty little place with comfortable living quarters for the 278 people who make up its population. Northland Navigation's *Skeena Prince* and B. C. Airlines regular shuttle service to Sandspit help to reduce the isolation of this remote settlement.

Mr. J. C. Kay, the United Church lay minister from Sandspit, holds services in Jedway and Tasu Mine in Fairfax Inlet, on alternate weeks. Of Tasu he says, "I have watched this townsite steadily emerge, carved out of the rock and forest on Gowing Island. There was little more than a small construction crew here early in 1965 and by the fall of 1966 there were five hundred people living in modern dwellings.

One thousand people are expected to be living in Tasu by the end of 1967. The townsite is connected to the minesite on Moresby by a causeway. Sixty-two million dollars will be spent by Wesfrob-Falconbridge to develop their Tasu property. The mine here – which operates with two shifts as compared to Jedway's one shift – is mainly iron ore with some copper, and all ore is sold to Japan. A 93,000 ton ore carrier will be sent from Japan to transport the ore. Supplies are moved into Tasu by aircraft where practical, and B. C. Airlines operate a regular shuttle service from there to Sandspit. Heavy freight comes in by barge from Vancouver. To provide an alternate route for ships when gales prevent use of the west coast, Wesfrob have built a road from Sewell Inlet to the head of Newcombe Inlet with wharves at each end. This road has the honor of being the first vehicular road to the west coast salt water.

It is too soon to know whether the mining claims over the hill from Tasu have a promising future. Known as the Moresby Mines, they are still in the exploratory stage. A floating dock, tractor road and several houses have been built by the owners, Mr. and Mrs. Ronald Dale, who are full of enthusiasm about the property in their prospectus.

Logging is the reason for the settlement known as Moresby, at the head of Cumshewa Inlet. This little town of about one hundred and sixty-five people is on a tree farm licence of Rayonier of Canada. This former – and greatly modernized – J. R. Morgan Logging Camp is only a half hour's drive from Sandspit and there is frequent visiting between the two settlements.

The busy by-the-clock routine of Sandspit today, bears little resemblance to the easy-going farming days when a dozen families had the free run of the whole region. The five hundred people who call the Spit "home" live in houses which range solidly along Shingle Bay from Haans Creek to the Airport and south along the east coast to Cape Chroustcheff. Employment is largely provided by the Northern Pulpwood, a division of Crown Zellerbach Canada Limited which owns rights to ninety-nine square miles of timber in this area. (1)

Not everyone in Sandspit has been drawn there by economic prospects. Mr. and Mrs. Neil Carey and their son, Gene, came to live on the Charlottes a few years ago when Mr. Carey retired from the United States Navy. Fascinated by the rugged west coast of the Islands, which they explore at every opportunity, they are ardent beachcombers and have made a veritable museum in their garden at Sandspit.

Transportation between Moresby and Graham Island is provided by the Misty Island Transportation Limited, formerly Kendall's Water Taxi, who have a fleet of boats and barges based at Skidegate Landing for schedule and charter trips. An oilery is still located at the Landing — but today it is bulk fuel, not the dogfish oil operation of early years. Seventy-two people are located in this picturesque cove. The Thomas Dufferin Pattullo school, opened in 1926 has been closed and abandoned and all the children are taken by bus to Queen Charlotte City each day along the winding road which skirts the rock cliffs between the two communities.

In Queen Charlotte City — or "Charlotte" as it is known locally — a modern school has been constructed for students from Skidegate Mission, Skidegate Landing and Charlotte. The pupils are given instruction up to and including grade twelve.

There is still a sawmill in Charlotte, although not in the same location and of much more modest proportions than its predecessor which originated the town, and five hundred people now live along the entire length of Windy Young's "City". Logging contributes vitally to the economy of this region and fishing is also important.

Skidegate Landing is about six miles to the east of Charlotte and two miles north of the Landing is the Haida village of Skidegate Mission which has a population of about three hundred and fifty. This village is very progressive and was one of the first on the Islands to have light and water facilities. Fortunate timber sales have made this community one of the wealthiest also, and under its three man council affairs have been wisely and carefully guided. Carving of argillite is as skillful as ever there and the totem poles and curios created by these artists are in demand all over the world.

Port Clements with a population of two hundred and ten people, lies mid-way between its Tlell neighbor, to the southeast, and the Juskatla Logging Camp, on its southwest. The Tlell region takes in the coast from the mouth of the river to Clay Hill and has about fifty people living on large acreages. One of the few Provincial Park sites on the Charlottes is located at Tlell ". . .if only we had a road to get into it," say Islanders of the well-chosen, but inaccessible site on the west bank of the river. The park includes the mouth of Geike Creek, and a

(1) Information from D. H. Holden, public relations, Crown Zellerbach.

section of some of the best fishing spots on the Tlell River.

Juskatla Camp, about thirteen miles by road from Port Clements, is the headquarters of the MacMillan, Bloedel and Powell River Company's logging operation on the Charlottes. Their tree farm licence takes in the central portion of Graham Island and has necessitated the building of miles of logging roads all through the Yakoun Valley, with one branch extending to Queen Charlotte City, where they have their big booming grounds, supplementing the smaller one in Shannon Bay. Two hundred and thirty-seven people live in the modern camp facilities at Juskatla.

Tlell and Juskatla have joined with Port Clements to form a strong tri-community unit, with Port Clements — because of its central position — as the base and headquarters of the inter-community activities.

When Queen Charlotte City had successfully passed a hotly-contested by-law ruling cattle off public streets, Port Clements people — who had had their gardens broken into once too often by herds of cattle — decided to follow their southern sister's example. In 1964 they held a similar plebiscite which received a strong affirmative vote. The year before another plebiscite vote had been taken, and although it too was given assent, this was to form an Improvement District.

In 1961 the idea of electric power for the Port Clements area had been discussed but there were so many obstacles in the way of any project to obtain it, the situation seemed hopeless. Except to Stan Newcombe, who must be a second Eli Tingley, in that the tougher the odds the more he persists. Stan knew that unless power was introduced to Port Clements and later extended to Tlell — where he lived at that time — the region would be lost in a back-eddy.

"B. C. Hydro was servicing the south end at that time but said they have a firm policy that they must have at least seventy-five hook-ups before they will consider an urban area," said Mr. Newcombe. "Our trouble was that there were so few people living in Port Clements then, and no hope of new residents with things the way they were. MacBlo (1) had been scouting for a site to set up houses for their married men away from camp and indicated a preference for Port Clements — if only it had electric power. Those houses would just give us the required amount of hook-ups for B.C. Hydro. I began hounding the daylights out of everyone, and I think what really happened was that they got so sick of me in Vancouver and Victoria that the Water Resources Board finally got down to brass tacks and advised us how to go about it."

A discussion was held with representatives from MacMillan, Bloedel and Powell River ". . .and they okayed the idea all the way — of course we would be on our own to raise the money and set up the plant," said Mr. Newcombe.

In 1963 a public meeting approved the formation of the Port Clements Improvement District. A charter was obtained and by-laws enacted whereby they could borrow money by selling debentures. Not only electric power, but sewer, water and sidewalk projects may all come under the jurisdiction of an Improvement District, which is empowered to collect property taxes in connection with any approved plan (with the exception of Crown Land which is exempt from such a local improvement tax, even though they benefit from the improvement in increased land value.)

(1) MacMillan, Bloedel and Powell River Company is frequently referred to
    by this shortened version of their name.

The first Improvement Board, composed of five members, consisted of Larry Choquette, President; A. S. Ward, Secretary; and Directors, George Lee, Garry Richardson and Stanley Newcombe. $49,000 worth of debentures were issued to cover cost of the power plant installation and the bulk of the debentures were picked up by Mac-Blo. By July 24, 1964 everything was ready for operation and for the first time electric lights were turned on — and this included twenty-five street lights. Like every new plan, this one has had many problems which only trial and error could resolve, but the biggest blow came when local residents found that dealing with a multi-million dollar company can be every bit as frustrating as the government.

The Mac-Blo housing project which was the important part of the whole scheme bogged down. The site was cleared but then the Improvement Board was told that sewers and water services must be installed before the company could proceed and the townspeople were asked to have these services included with the power plans. There was nothing the Board would like to do more, but the local people who were picking up the tab were finding that the cost of having to bring in mainland electricians to do the wiring — at peak charge-out prices — plus all the modifications needed in their homes, were about all the extra costs they could absorb at that time. The company was adamant about services being installed before any houses were erected on their site.

The B. C. Hydro which was servicing the region forty miles to the south was just as adamant in refusing to take over the operation of Port Clements power plant unless there were the regulation seventy-five hook-ups. "It's a real stalemate," says Mr. Newcombe. "We can't get more customers because the rates are too high under our own set-up, and quite a few of our people are on pensions. And we can't get the rates down because we don't have enough hook-ups."

So for two and a half years while the logging company slowly drags along preparing its housing site the small community of Port Clements, caught between big business policies and the red tape of government edicts, has been paying what must be the highest electric rates in Canada. A minimum monthly charge of $20 for 200 kilowatts, and 4¢ a kilowatt for anything over the initial 200 kilowatts (as compared to the $1.50 minimum monthly charge B. C. Hydro requires of its customers a bare forty miles away). In addition $10 a year is applied to each lot for taxes, "which just about covers our interest on the debentures," said one Board member.

Although he was in Tlell when the scheme was brought into being, Mr. Newcombe has since joined the pioneering high priced electricity group himself. Resigning as manager of the wealthy Dunes club in Tlell, he built a four unit motel in Port Clements as a preliminary to the building of his proposed twenty-room Golden Spruce Hotel. It would have given Eli Tingley's heart a lift to know that in addition to these ambitious plans, Mr. Newcombe is moving his sawmill equipment from Tlell to the old Barton mill-site and once again Port Clements will hear the familiar whine of a saw.

The largest house in the hamlet today belongs to Mr. and Mrs. James Bell, who like the Careys of Sandspit, were drawn to the Islands not for economic reasons, but as an ideal place to retire to. During the many years he was a ticket agent for the C.N.R. Mr. Bell had been fascinated by stories about the

Charlottes. "My wife and I covered the Islands from one end to the other looking for a nice location. When we saw that view of the lake (1) from the mouth of the Yakoun River — we knew we'd found our spot," says Mr. Bell. Vegetables, flowers, shrubs and fruit trees flourish on soil that supported thick brush and timber a short time ago and bring back memories of the fine garden Bob Dyson and his wife had at the other end of town so many years ago, when Dyson's Corner was the object of equally admiring glances.

The unusually broad streets of New Masset and its level terrain have the same prairie atmosphere which has been prevalent from the beginning. One of the best laid out towns, Masset — with its neighbor Delkatla — decided in 1961 that the only way to move ahead was to merge and become an incorporated village. Adopting the name of the larger settlement, the Village of Masset held its first municipal election on November 7, 1961. With Mrs. Isobel Minaker as returning officer and Mrs. Muriel Anderson as poll clerk the villagers elected Sam Simpson as chairman, and four commissioners, Alex Taylor, Robert Wylie, William Hilton, and Kurt Lindner. The first village clerk was Mrs. Isobel Minaker. (2)

Although Masset made Island history by becoming the first incorporated village, its residents wanted no part of the "ban the cows" campaign waged in Island communities to the south. Bossy is free to roam the streets there at will, keeping the grass along the edge of the roads neatly clipped.

The main source of income in Masset is fishing, the crab cannery and the Navy station, where one hundred and forty-four new homes are scheduled for the near future. Several residents hold key jobs in the peat moss plant at the Nadu — which is exactly half way between Masset and Port Clements, and other men find work in nearby logging camps.

Electric power for both the Massets is supplied by Clarence Martin, son of the pioneer James Martin, who made such an important contribution to the region's early days with his well-stocked stores, ". . .and if he didn't happen to have what you wanted in stock, Jim would get it for you, no matter what it was," old-timers say of the pioneer storekeeper. Clarence was in the store with his father for years, taking over when the elder Martin died. When a fire burned the big store to the ground a few years ago, Clarence built a smaller one on the corner to the west of the site. Then when the store of Lindner and Kirmis burned a few years later, Kurt Lindner bought Clarence out, and for the first time since Masset began there was no "Martin's Store".

The busiest part of Masset and the most colorful is the fishermen's floats in Delkatla Slough — a forest of masts at tie-up time in the fall. The first sailboat of its size to be built and launched in Masset was the forty-six foot ketch, *Homeward Bound,* which slid into the water in April, 1966. A local undertaking from beginning to end, the lumber from Island trees was cut in Jeffrey White's (3) sawmill in Old Masset, and local boatbuilders did the work on her under the guidance of Alex Wylie, the veteran boatbuilder who had designed her. She was christened by a bottle of Q.C.I. champagne, smashed on the first try by the granddaughter of the owner, Sam Simpson.

(1) Masset Inlet is commonly called "the lake" by local people.
(2) Information re: election from Miss Isobel Wilson, 1966 village clerk.
(3) Son of Henry White, who with Matthew Yeomans shot
    the last caribou (Chapter 46).

The warmest glow of pride in the village is found when Ann Stewart-Burton's name is mentioned. Born in Masset in 1933, Ann, even as a little girl, dreamed of "someday being a doctor". With her three brothers she attended school in Masset when it was still the eight-grades-in-one-room. There were no extra dollars in the Stewart-Burton home to pay for high school on the mainland. "It must have been intended for Ann to achieve her wish," says her mother. "The year she was ready for high school, it was suddenly decided that Masset was big enough to warrant a high school for the youngsters here for the first time." When Ann graduated in 1951 and entered the school of medicine at U.B.C. it was also the first time this course had been added. She spent a year interning at St. Michael's Hospital in Toronto, after graduating from U.B.C., then took a four-year course in gynecology and obstetrics. In 1963 she won a fellowship in the Royal College of Surgeons and went to London's Middlesex Hospital for further training. Now practicing in Toronto Dr. Ann Stewart-Burton is rated as one of the best in her field. She financed the amazing achievement entirely on her own.

Stretched along the shoreline on the ancient site their forefathers chose is the Masset Reserve, the second largest in B.C. (1) Still listed as Old Masset in the B.C. Gazetteer, (2) a move is under way to introduce the newer designation of Haida. Comfortable homes, many of them attractively painted — and all with a superb view of the Inlet — replace the totem poles of yesterday which were a focal attraction for visitors. The nine-man village council which looks after affairs for this reserve may soon be increased to ten as band membership nears one thousand.

Not as wealthy as their Skidegate counterparts, Masset Haidas have nevertheless made tremendous strides to keep pace with their rapidly increasing population in providing adequate housing and recreational facilities. "They have the best P.T.A. I know about," said Mr. M. Tracy, principal of the school in the village which teaches youngsters up to grade three. "We had a 200% membership for this P.T.A. — a record that is unequalled to my knowledge." Enrolment stood at forty-nine pupils and P.T.A. membership, one hundred and one paid-up and active members. When the youngsters are ready for grade four they are transported by bus each day to the big modern elementary-junior-senior High School in New Masset. The plan is part of the integration program being effected by the Department of Indian affairs. "Just who is integrating who is a fine point," said one of the teachers. "We have three Haida children in the school for every white youngster. But the kids find their own level anyway once adults get out of the picture, and although it hasn't been all smooth sailing it has been of benefit to everyone in the long run."

The Old Masset carvers and engravers are unable to keep pace with the ever growing demand for their articles produced in argillite, wood, reeds, leather, silver and gold. Their talent and creative skill is as great today as ever. But perhaps the outstanding quality in this village, rarest of all in this day of speed, is the delicious tongue-in-cheek sense of humor they all have. This is also the place where people can still find time to sit awhile in the sun — to tell the yarns in the Haida tongue which is so difficult for the white man. The visitor comes away

(1) The Indian — Professor Wilson Duff, page 52.
(2) B. C. Gazetteer — page 488.

wondering what all the rush is about in the rest of the world. Basic things do not change so very much.

The Pillar, Hla-tad-zo-woh, still stands as ever in his bay near North Island, a remarkable rock, composed of columnar sandstone and conglomerate, twenty-five feet in diameter and ninety-five feet high. Perhaps the tree on top is a little taller — that is all. Hole-in-rock, in Englefield Bay, important in ancient Haida legend, has the same seas washing around and surging through the cleft which is still arched by the natural stone bridge. Perhaps the years have brought a little more erosion, but that too, is all.

The mystic spell these Islands of the Charlotte group casts on those who are attuned is as magical today as it was when the first Haida felt it centuries ago. No matter how far they travel or how many years pass, for those who have once felt even a tinge of their bewitchment — this too, can never change.

APPENDIX ONE

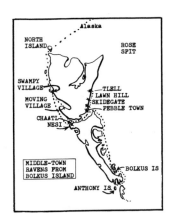

This broad and general outline of the various Haida migrations on the Queen Charlotte Islands has been condensed from information provided in Dr. J. R. Swanton's "The Haida", and applies to the three main Raven and Eagle branches. It has been divided into six parts.

Part One

GRANDCHILDREN OF THE
FOAM WOMAN

The Raven descendents of the Queen Charlotte Islands had their origin on Bolkus Island, Skincuttle Inlet. They were known as the *Middle-Town-People*.

In the early years the area around Skincuttle Inlet was supposed to have been very populous for according to legend there were ten towns there at one time. As the families grew and multiplied, migrations began to take place. Those who remained in the area became known as the *Striped-Town-People*, taking their name from a rock on Bolkus Island. Other groups of the Middle-Towns went south and west through Houston Stewart Channel to Anthony Island and the Flamingo Inlet region.

The remaining branches from Bolkus went northward along the eastern coast of Moresby Island, leaving members all along en route. Crossing Skidegate Inlet, some families went as far as Lawn Hill where they established a fair-sized village. A branch of one of these families, known as the Sea Otters (because it was said they were as numerous as the sea Otter) went north as far as Tlell where they built a small village. From the numerous artifacts found on the Richardson Ranch, it is tempting to speculate that it might have been there — but actually its definite location has been lost with the passing of years. (The large house mentioned earlier (1) belonged to the opposite Eagle tribe and was built later.)

After staying a short time in Tlell, the Sea Otters joined once more with the rest of their family at Lawn Hill, and all moved to the south of Skidegate where they established a new village which they called Small Stones. An uncle of this family, Qoona'tik, was a great hero, and after being chief on earth went to live on a reef near Lawn Hill. Known as One-Who-Makes-It-Thunder-By-His-Voice, he was called upon in storms at sea.

In the old village at Lawn Hill a big fight broke out between two remaining families and one family was forced to move out in a hurry. They bought the Small Stones village from their Sea Otter relatives and renamed it Pebble Stones. Forever after they were known as the Pebble-Stone-People. The Sea Otter tribe

(1) Chapter 9

317

moved to a new location, after the sale, to a site slightly to the north of Skidegate then, in later years when the family was reduced, they moved into Skidegate Village itself. By 1905 there was no one left of this family.

The Pebble-Stone-People had another Raven family for close neighbors — the Sqoaladas with whom they lived very harmoniously. Then one day an Eagle woman from Skidegate was mysteriously killed and it appeared that someone from one of these two Raven families was responsible. Not being able to get a satisfactory explanation — or culprit — the Skidegates declared war and a fierce fight ensued.

The Raven families had to flee for their lives to the West Coast. Here they tried to settle at Nesi (across the channel from Chaatl). At this time Chaatl was occupied by members of an Eagle family from Scotsgay Beach (near Skidegate), the Sea Lion family — the rest of the Sea Lions having gone south to live at Kaisun.

The two Raven families trying to settle at Nesi found that their site was too exposed. They bought Chaatl from the Eagle Sea Lions, who were only too happy to move to Kaisun and join the rest of their family there. (This is supposed to have happened after the time of white contact, for in the bitter fights that the Ravens had with their former Skidegate enemies, a man taken slave in one of the battles was said to have been sawn in half with a white man's saw.) (1)

In the village of Chaatl the Pebble-Towns and the Sqoaladas began a new life. For the Pebble-Towns, it was good to be able to settle down again after two earlier moves. The Sqoaladas, however, became restless before too long, and began a migration that took them northwards along the west coast of Graham Island to Hippa Passage where they built a village called Swampy Village.

Settling in there, they were joined by another group of Ravens who had come all the way round the north end of Graham Island from Rose Spit — they were some of the Rear-Town-People. These two Raven families got along well and exchanged many songs and tales. After many happy years at Swampy Village it was again time to move, but not all wanted to go the same way so the group divided. Some of them gradually went northwards to form part of the Kaigani. The big village of Tartanee (Dadens) on North Island, in which Captain Douglas had so admired the carved posts, was occupied mainly by descendents of this original Bolkus Island family.

The other members of Swampy Village went south to Rennell Sound and built a village on the south shore which they named Moving Village. However, they didn't stay long, but moved down once more to live in Chaatl. By now the decline of the whole Haida nation was rapidly setting in. Although intertribal wars contributed, it was smallpox and the diseases of civilization that were to deliver the almost knock-out blow.

In 1870 the remnants of all the west coast families, both Eagles and Ravens, began to move back to an ancient village site on Maude Island known as Haina. The first to go were the Eagles from Kaisun, whose chief became the chief of Haina. Other west coast chiefs, not wanting to be subordinate, moved back along Skidegate Inlet to sites that their ancestors had once occupied. They had hoped to draw their families with them, but Haina was abandoned only in 1893 when all moved into Skidegate.

(1) Swanton's "The Haida", page 82.

318

APPENDIX ONE

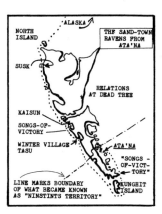

Part Two

THE SAND-TOWN-PEOPLE

The second big Raven group were the Sand-Town-People who traced their ancestry back to Ata'na (House Island) which lies adjacent to the well-known Hotspring Island. In their migrations, over a period of countless years, they gradually moved down the east side of Moresby Island and on to Kunghit. Here they divided into two sections with one part of the family settling down. Chief Koyah who had the disastrous affair with Kendrick was a Sand-Town Raven. The remains of one of his family's villages, Songs-of-Victory, south of Carpenter Bay (on southeast Moresby) could be seen with its totem poles and houses decaying in 1903. (1)

The other section of the Sand-Towns migrated, over the generations, up the rugged west coast of Moresby. Part of this migration was left at Tasu and they were known as the Pitch-Town-People. Not much is known of these Pitch-Towns, but evidently they were not considered as cultured as others. For one thing they lacked a crest system and may not have been entirely exogamic in the beginning.

Legend tells of their beginning near a small lake called Gambling Sticks, lying back from the steep part of the western coast slightly to the south of Tasu. They had two villages in Tasu Harbor called Fat Game and Winter Village. It was at Winter Village that Haida tattooing was initiated. This happened when an important Eagle woman from Cumshewa married a young Tasu Raven chief. This first Haida tattooing was done during the potlatch ceremonies to celebrate the wedding and pay for the building of the chief's new house. It was not long before the practice became an important part of Haida ritual everywhere.

Kaisun (Gold Harbor) was originally a Pitch-Town-People's village. It was later occupied by the Skidegate Inlet Eagles from Scotsgay Beach, the Sea Lions, as mentioned in Part One. However, by the time the Sea Lions moved there all the original Raven owners had died out except for one man who was so big it was said that it took "two entire bearskins to make his blanket". In fact all the Pitch-Town-People were described as being of gigantic stature and very

(1) From a report by Dr. Newcombe.

319

strong — but also extremely superstitious. They had many fears and beliefs that other Haidas regarded as quite foolish.

There were other Pitch-Town villages in that area also. One was on an island in front of Kaisun and was called Town-that-the-Sun-never-shines-upon because it faced north. A second village was on a little island they called Gūl, northwest of Hibben Island. Near Hewlett Bay (Moore Channel) they had a town "Songs-of-Victory" — which must have been a favorite name with the Sand-Towns, for there were at least two other Songs-of-Victory towns (one on Kunghit Island and one on southeast Moresby).

Thus all that wild section of coastline between Ninstints territory and Kaisun was occupied by the Pitch-Town Ravens.

As the Sand-Town migration gradually moved up past Tasu to Graham Island, some of the Sand-Towns stayed at Susk (near Frederick Island) — a village with an interesting legend about the flood. More Sand-Towns went on to North Island, settling at various spots there, one of which was the extreme northwestern tip — and they could well have been those in the group who first saw Juan Perez at Cape Santa Margarita.

Eventually all of this northern migration formed part of the Kaigani, with one branch going right up to Kasaan, in Alaska, the most northerly Haida town. As they still had relatives on Kunghit Island, they had the distinction of having Sand-Towns at either extremity of Haida territory.

DAVIS RAFTS

The Davis Raft was a large, cocoon-shaped log raft of special construction. It was built up from a floor or bottom which was made by placing logs side by side and end to end between parallel boomsticks. The boomsticks and the logs which they confined were bound together by chains and cables, woven in and out, over and under, according to an intricate design.

Into the center of this network of logs and wires, more logs were rolled, by means of a donkey engine. They were secured by wires, and the raft was built up to the desired height. More than half its contents were below the surface of the water. The towing wires were attached in such a way, that as the tug proceeded ahead with the tow, it pulled the raft together instead of asunder. A Davis Raft, when complete might be from 490 - 560 feet long, with 2 to 2½ million feet of logs in each. They were large and unwieldy to tow, and were time-consuming and expensive to build.

In 1956 log barges came into popular use, changing almost completely the long distance water transport of logs. The average log barge is about 315 feet long and has a carrying capacity of 1¼ million feet of logs. Under normal conditions a barge will travel under tow at a speed of 8 knots, compared to the speed of 2 or 3 knots for the Davis Raft — a vital factor when a gale is pending and the logs are at the point of no return in Hecate Straits.

APPENDIX ONE

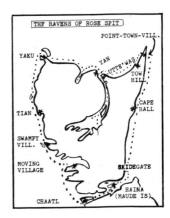

THE RAVENS OF ROSE SPIT

POINT-TOWN-VILL.

YAKU

YAN
UTTE'WAS
TOW
HILL

CAPE
BALL

TIAN

SWAMPY
VILL.

MOVING
VILLAGE

SKIDEGATE

HAINA
(MAUDE IS)

CHAATL

Part Three

THE RAVENS OF ROSE SPIT

At Rose Point on N. E. Graham Island there was a large group of Ravens who occupied a village called Point Town Village. By 1905 some two hundred feet of sand had built up in front of the ancient village which faced the eastern part of the Point.

The first Raven group to become restless and leave the Point Town Village went as far as the entrance to Masset Sound. They built a new village which they called Uttewas or White Slope and this was at the north end of what is known as Old Masset today. (1)

The chief of this village was Chief Seegay, who in later years transferred his village to the Eagle lineage of Chief Weah. (2) Although the bulk of the family settled in Uttewas, there were a few who went out to the West Coast and some to Naden Harbor where they occupied a site on a stream flowing into the harbor.

Another Point-Town family also left the village at Rose Point, and they went as far as Tow Hill where they built a village on the bank of the Hi-Ellen River. A story of what happened to this town is told in W. E. Collison's, "Teeming Waters". "In one of the few retaliatory raids ever attempted on Haida land, some of the Nisgahs and Tsimpsheans managed to land quietly near Rose Spit, then stealthily making their way to Tow Hill, descended on the town when all the men were absent, wreaking terrible vengeance on the little village. All that remained was one charred totem pole."

After the first Point-Town groups left to go into Masset and Tow Hill, a big family row broke out in the old home town on the Point. Apparently no one won this argument, though, because when the two main branches split up over the trouble, everyone there moved out abandoning the village completely.

One of the main groups taking off from the old village was the Standing-Water-People. They went a short way down the sandy east coast shoreline of Graham Island to what they called Raven Creek. They stayed there for a short

(1) Also known as Haida today.
(2) Chapter 10.

while before moving south to Cape Ball, where they settled in, establishing three small villages. Although there were actually four sites used there, one was evacuated when the waves began to wash into the base of the cliff under it. This village was called, appropriately, Town-Set-Up-High-On-A-Point, and the inhabitants moved to a more satisfactory location in the Cape Ball area. Subsequently all the Standing-Water-People moved southward to live in Skidegate.

The other group involved in the big Point Town family fracas were the Rear-Towns. They were clever and creative, but had a reputation for being hard to get along with. When the Standing-Water-People moved out of the Rose Point village in such a big huff, the Rear-Towns also took off in quite a hurry — going along to join the people in Uttewas. But it seems they didn't get along well with these relatives either.

One day on a trip up the long Masset Sound into Masset Inlet, tempers became heated and another big scrap was under way. This fight lasted hotly all the way down the Sound to Uttewas. The original inhabitants landed first — and pulled in the welcome mat. The Rear-Towns would have to build a new town. They did this at Yan, which is across the Sound from, and slightly to the north of Old Masset, and became the principal family there in after years. Yan was a large village, and for years the forest of wonderfully carved poles could be seen from the Masset side.

The people of Yan and Masset kept on fighting sporadically for years until the outbreak of smallpox proved to be a more formidable enemy than either. It marked the end of the village of Yan.

However, not all the Rear-Towns settled at Yan, for there were branches of them living at the Yakoun and also at a smaller village to the south of Yan, as well as along the rocky coast between Virago Sound and Yan. Some went to Swampy Village on the West Coast in Hippa Passage (and opposite to Hippa Island). It was here that they met the Raven family from Chaatl, the Sqoaladas. Rear-Towns were located in Tian, Yaku and, after the migration of the Kaigani, they became the principal family on the West Coast.

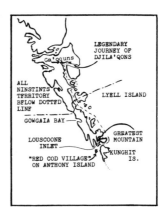

Part Four

THE EAGLES OF NINSTINTS

Around the same time as the powerful Foam Woman of the Raven Crest appeared out of the swirling waters of the Flood and came to rest on Bolkus Island — according to legend — an Eagle ancestress named Djila'qons (Dzelarhons), was brought from the mainland by the Raven, He-Whose-Voice-Is-Obeyed. She was placed in a creek called Ga'oqons which flows into the west arm of Cumshewa Inlet. Here several children were born to her, and one of these, a daughter, went to live in Ninstints territory where she was called Greatest Mountain. It was from Greatest Mountain that all the Ninstints Eagles were descended.

Ninstints territory was the area taking in the whole of the south end of the Islands from north of Gowgaia Bay on the west, then up and over to the southern part of Lyell Island on the east coast. As was usual, it acquired its name because of a powerful chief, Ninstints, of Anthony Island.

In the earliest days the Eagles of Ninstints were not nearly as numerous as the Ravens of that area. They had only one site on the east coast (in Burnaby Strait) and very few on the west coast — and even there they had to share some sites with the Ravens.

Their first main village was at the entrance to Louscoone Inlet. Later they scattered up the west coast, and Gowgaia Bay became the headquarters, for there were quite a number of Eagle villages in this bay belonging to the Ninstints. In subsequent years all the families came together on Anthony Island.

Years before, the Raven tribes from Bolkus and a few families from Kunghit had preceeded them to Anthony Island, establishing the village Qad-dad-jans on the northwest end. So the Eagles built theirs to the east and south of the Ravens — calling their town Red Cod Village after the Haida name for Anthony Island itself.

From this village came a chief, bearer of the name Ninstints which means He-Who-Is-Equal-To-Two. This chief became so powerful and rich that he was able to potlatch a full ten times — an extraordinary feat known to have been equalled by few others.

323

Although the Ravens were the more dominant tribe in the region when the first traders came for, as we know, they called the area Koyah's Place, undoubtedly Koyah's tragedy changed this situation to a marked degree. Enormous numbers of his clan were lost in battles with the whites to try to regain his prestige and in the ensuing tribal wars he conducted to build it up as well. Unlike those of other great chiefs, such as Skidegate, Skedans, Cumshewa and so on, whose names have come down in history, Koyah's has been lost. Those who succeeded him did not have the strength, or perhaps the will, to try to recoup their former glory, for his successors failed to maintain his position. In a few years it was a minor family.

At any rate by 1840 the Eagle lineage was in ascendency and by 1860 the whole area was known as Ninstints to all. The village of Red Cod was called Ninstints and became occupied (as were all the larger villages in later years) by members of both the Raven and Eagle clans, with the Eagles being the leading families. Ninstints village was the important town of the territory.

It was the Haidas of this area who were known as the fighters — for they fought everyone all down the mainland coast as well as on the Islands, where their greatest enemies were the Kloos at Tanu, but they also fought extensively with the Skidegates and the Massets. (Cumshewa and Skedans did not seem to become involved in intertribal wars to any extent.)

Perhaps it was because of the Ninstints habit of travelling to the southern mainland ports and Vancouver Island, rather than to Port Simpson to trade, which hastened their demise. It was in Victoria that they first encountered the dreaded smallpox which caused such havoc. And it was here, as well as in the Puget Sound area that they learned more of the cost of civilization in disease for their people, plus the desire and knowledge of "fire water".

In 1835 - 1840 John Wark of the H. B. C. counted 308 people living in Ninstints village. Barely fifty years later the thriving village was completely abandoned. In the 1880s the few remaining people were helped by their former enemies, the Skidegates, to pack up and move north to Skidegate to try to begin life anew. Moving with them was the aging Elijah Ninstints, successor to the great Ninstints. (1)

(1) Anthony Island, A Home of the Haidas", Wilson Duff — page 26.

Part Five

THOSE DESCENDED
FROM PROPERTY WOMAN

The Eagle descendents of Property Woman fell into some four main families: the Witch People of Cumshewa; the Eagles of Tanu and Skedans; the Eagle family in Masset; and the Sea Lion family of Scotsgay Beach near Skidegate.

The first town of all these Eagles was the old village of Djigua, on the north side of Cumshewa Inlet. This ancient site, which was demolished by fire, lay just behind a peninsula some miles west of the later village of Cumshewa.

When an important woman from the Eagle family in the town of Cumshewa married a chief of the Tasu Ravens (the Pitch-Towns) and went to Winter Village to live, her family followed her. (It was when her husband held the potlatch celebration following the building of his lodge after the wedding that the first Haida tattooing was done.) Later the Eagle family moved back to Cumshewa Inlet, settling in McKay's Harbor (now McCoy Cove).

A creek separated them from a Raven family already settled there. On the Eagle side a persistent screech owl hooted so much that they were jokingly nicknamed the Witch People. The name stuck to them even when they moved back to the main village of Cumshewa and gradually became applied to the rest of the members of that village.

The Eagles of Tanu and Skedans also came from the old village of Djigua. Skedans, traditionally a Raven village, was known as the town, "which sets new fashions." This reputation was acquired because one of the great chiefs of Skedans (the Raven who traced his origin back to Dead Tree) was very infuential in the arts of peace — rather than war. He was a great friend of the Tsimpshean chief at Kitkatla, and many crests, stories and features of the potlatch were exchanged as a result of this friendship so Skedans became known as the town of new ideas and styles.

The children of the Tanu Eagle women who married into the Skedans Ravens must have acquired some of the pace setting, for when they returned to their mothers' village of Tanu they all achieved great prominence. The real name of Skedans was Qoona, although it was popularly known as Grizzly Bear Town.

Tanu was a relatively new village and it was said that before this Eagle branch "slashed the bushes at Tanu" they had occupied several towns — the last being Chicken Hawk Town on the east side of Lyell Island. This was the town that had the large house so big that it warranted a separate name for each half.

The chief's hereditary name was Kloo, a corruption of a Haida word meaning southeast. One Chief Kloo lived at Skedans before succeeding to his chieftainship at Tanu — a highly unusual arrangement. He was later killed by some Ravens from north Louise Island and, while his successor was growing up, four chiefs from the old town of Djigua were heads there successively.

In 1878 Tanu was the most flourishing town on the Islands. When Dawson visited there that year, there were extensive preparations under way for a big celebration in connection with the post raising and building of a big house for the chief.

The quick decline of this town can be seen from the fact that when John Wark counted heads in 1840 there were five hundred and forty-five people. Dawson found it to be progressive and full of life and color as late as 1878. Yet a scant nine years later there were only eighty people and comparatively few of these were in good health. They were a dying and doomed people.

It was at this time that some of the older ones approached Rev. Thomas Crosby and begged him to help them. After careful thought he advised them to move to a new site. It was decided that they would go to a creek on the north end of Louise Island. This new village was called New Kloo. In view of the fact that a state of emergency existed — if the Kloos were to survive — these villagers now decided on a drastic action. They would adopt the way of the white man and forsake the old ways — forever.

The lived at New Kloo for about ten years during which time the new village was built and, in addition to an oilery which operated there, a church was built. (1) But in 1897 they all moved into Skidegate proper to join the rest of the people already there from other villages.

The Eagle family descended from Property Woman who went to Masset had for one of its chiefs, a Chief Weah (not Henry), whose name means — the Wind.

The Sea Lions of Scotsgay Beach, whom we have met before, when the Ravens bought the village of Chaatl from them — also came from old Djigua. In Skidegate Inlet they lived near to Pebble Town, which was largely Raven. They had a very close relationship and many intermarriages. The Sea Lions were also on good terms with the Skidegate Village Eagles. However, unexpectedly one day, a quarrel broke out with the Skidegates. Not wanting to begin a feud or have further hostilities with their former Skidegate Eagle friends, the Sea Lions went out to the West Coast. Some settled at Chaatl as mentioned earlier, but most went down to Kaisun. The Eagles at Shingle Bay (Sandspit) were also originally from old Djigua and some of them accompanied the Sea Lions from Scotsgay Beach to the West Coast. A few members of these families eventually migrated north, joining the Kaigani.

---

(1) During the second World War loggers working around this creek nicknamed it Church Creek, because of this. The name subsequently appeared on later maps.

326

Part Six

LABRET WOMAN
HAD FOUR DAUGHTERS

By far the largest group of Eagles who had a common ancestress were the Eagles descended from Labret Woman. This group would include the Gitins of Skidegate, the Gitans of Masset, the Seaward Eagles and the Stastas. Actually the connection with the Stastas is there, but they are generally thought to be almost a separate branch. The powerful chiefs of the Stastas came from the Edinshaw family.

The story of Labret Woman has at least two versions. The first is that she was born north of Dead Tree and when very young went to Masset, married and bore four daughters. Her husband died and she began to return to her old home at Dead Tree. Two of her daughters stayed behind in Masset, and one of them became an ancestress of the Stastas and the other the ancestress of the Masset Gitans. On her way back to Dead Tree, Labret Woman met and married a Raven Chief at Cape Ball. The other two daughters also formed alliances here and later went back to Dead Tree. These two daughters were the ancestresses of the Gitins of Skidegate and another group which later separated into three: Pebble Town Eagles, the Seaward Eagles and some of the West Coast Eagles.

A second version of Labret Woman agrees with the first except to say that Labret Woman was born at Masset, not at Dead Tree.

The first group mentioned, the Gitins of Skidegate, had their original town north of Dead Tree. (1) About 1750 a quarrel developed over the division of a whale and, dissatisfied with the outcome, part of the family moved away to a place in Bearskin Bay where they built a village called Dance Hat Town. In a short time they moved to Pebble Town (also occupied by a Raven family later on), and thence into Skidegate where they built a house. However, things hadn't gone well for this family and they became very poor — so much so that their house began to fall into ruin, and they became known as the Rotten-House-People.

The other part of the family who were at Dead Tree lived for a short while in Skidegate, then went to Pebble Town where they built a fine large house. So

(1) Swanton's "The Haida" – page 100.

327

imposing, in fact, that they were known as the Big-House-People. After a few years in this fine home they moved back into Skidegate, reuniting with the Rotten-House-People whose fortunes had improved. This reunited family became the ruling family of Skidegate and their chief took the hereditary name of Skidegate.

One of the most famous Chief Skidegates was Nestecanna who was a slave on the mainland in his youth but being freed by ransom was able to acquire enough wealth to remove all stigma by his lavish potlatches. He not only removed the stigma, but became great in his own right. It was under his rule that House Poles are said to have been first used. (The hereditary Chief Skidegate today is Chief Louis Collison.)

The Gitans of Masset had their family branches all over the north region, from the "land of the big cedar trees", the Mamin-Juskatla area; to the Ain River; out along the north coast between Masset and Naden Harbor; others out on the West Coast; and some who joined in the Kaigani migration.

One of the Masset Gitan families had for its chief, Chief Henry Weah, and one of his forebears had claimed descent from Property Woman also. Henry Weah, noted for his wise and competent guidance in the village was succeeded by the present Chief Weah, William Matthews — a man of great dignity and understanding.

The third group of Eagles, the Seaward Eagles, were close relatives of the Skidegate Gitins.

The last group of Eagles descended from Labret Woman were the Stastas who, although connected with her, also assigned other origins for their family. Some came from the Naas, and others from the Stikine. Chief Edenshaw said his name was of Tlingit origin and meant "nothing left of it" signifying the place where a glacier comes down to the sea — where it is melted by water.

The Stastas were along the north coast from Kiusta to Rose Spit (Lands which were acquired after the Ravens had abandoned them). They were also down the east coast as far as what was known as Low Tide River. On northwest Langara Island they had a small village which was appropriately named End of Island Town.

APPENDIX TWO

COPPERS

Coppers were pieces of native metal beaten out into flat, shaped sheets. They were imported articles from the Chil-kat country, north of Sitka. Much attention was paid to the size and make of the copper, which should be of uniform but not too great thickness, and give forth a good sound when struck by the hand. They would be about 18 inches to 2 feet long.

By 1878 spurious coppers had begun to make an appearance, and although easily detected by an expert, the value of coppers as a result became somewhat reduced. Where formerly ten slaves were paid for a good copper as a usual price, in 1878 they were being valued at from forty to eighty blankets.

It was the blanket that was becoming recognized currency when Dr. G. M. Dawson visited the Islands in 1878.

"The blankets used in trade are distinguished by points or marks on the edge, woven into the texture," he wrote, "the best being four-point and the smallest and poorest, one-point. The acknowledged unit of value is a single two and a half point blanket — now worth a little over $1.50. Everything is referred to in this unit, even a large four-point blanket is said to be worth so many 'blankets'.

Blankets, neatly folded, were stowed away in large boxes. A man of property might have several hundred. The practice of amassing wealth in blankets no doubt had its origin in the earlier one of accumulating sea otter and fur seal robes, which stood in the place of blankets in former days. This may help to explain the rich harvest of the skins which the first traders to the Queen Charlotte Islands gathered."

"1878 Geological Survey of Canada", Dr. G. M. Dawson.

APPENDIX THREE

PLACE NAMES IN THE
PORT LOUIS REGION

At Captain Musgrave's invitation, Mr. E. J. Tingley supplied the following names for the region: *Coates River* for John Coates the old prospector who had been coming to the Islands since 1896; *Virgalias Cove* (1); *Steel Creek* because it had numerous showings of iron; *Queen Island* for Eli's big sailboat *Queen; Iron Mountain* for the big area of iron colored bluff; *Blue Creek; Sea Lion Rocks* always packed with sea lions; *West River* the mouth of which was the most westerly of any river on Graham Island; and *Tingley Cove* where the cabin was.

West River is now Haines River, Sea Lion Rocks are now Tian Rocks, and Iron Mountain is now Ironside Mountain, but all the other names have remained intact. (2)

(1) Virgalias has a variety of spellings but all refer to Victor Vigelous
of page 117 and 160.
(2) All information re: names is from Mr. B. L. Tingley, Victoria.

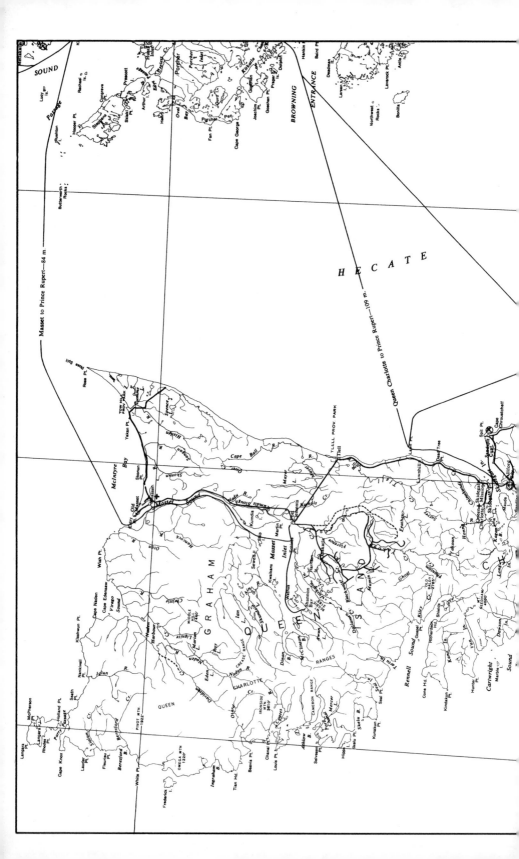

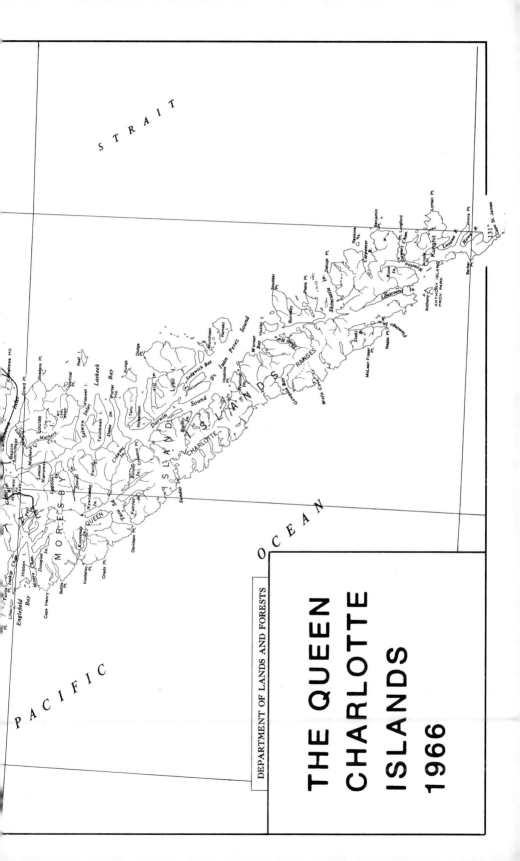

DEPARTMENT OF LANDS AND FORESTS

THE QUEEN CHARLOTTE ISLANDS 1966

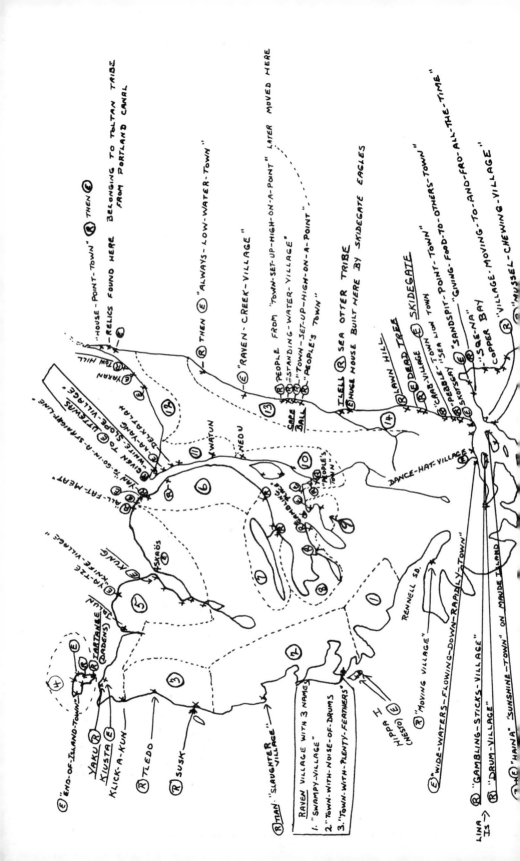

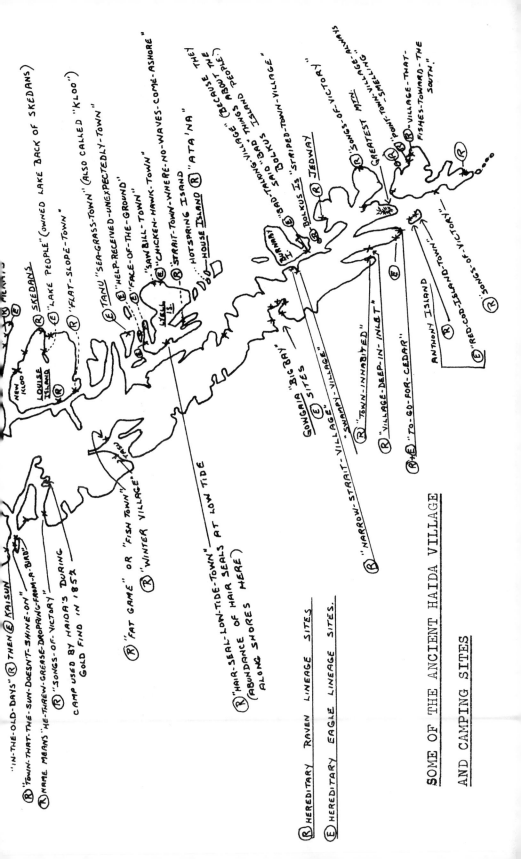

SOME OF THE ANCIENT HAIDA VILLAGE

AND CAMPING SITES

(R) HEREDITARY RAVEN LINEAGE SITES.

(E) HEREDITARY EAGLE LINEAGE SITES.

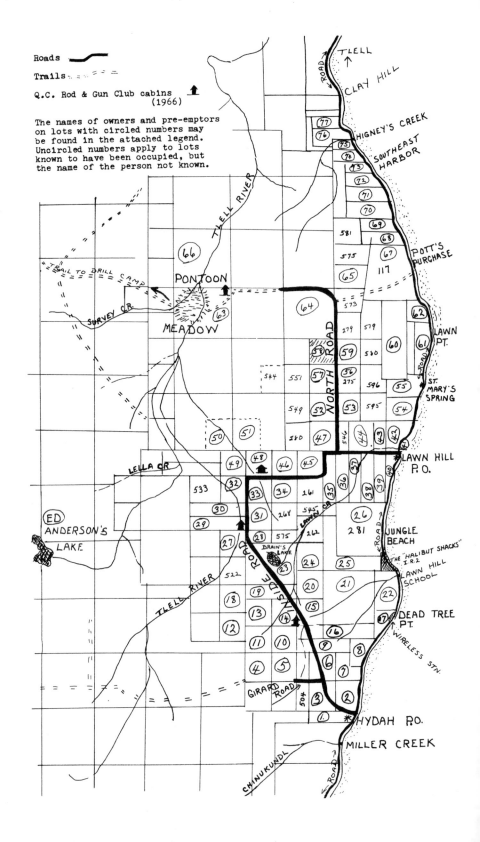

Roads

Trails

Q.C. Rod & Gun Club cabins
(1966)

The names of owners and pre-emptors
on lots with circled numbers may
be found in the attached legend.
Uncircled numbers apply to lots
known to have been occupied, but
the name of the person not known.

MAP No. 1

Legend to explain the areas containing circled numbers.
Information from Chief William Matthews of Masset, October 1965. These lands are hereditary.

1. Late James Watson's tribe, Skidegate. Solomon Wilson of Skidegate in charge, at present.
2. Chief Quince tribe. Rufus Abraham, present owner.
3. Chief Gin-na-won tribe. Geoffrey White present owner.
4. Also Chief Gin-na-won tribe. Belongs to the Point-Town Village Tribe.
5. Chief Edenso. Ruben Samuels, present owner.
6. Ya-gu-la nas tribe (meaning middle tribe). No private owner, open for Eagles and Ravens.
7. Git-ens, who are sub-tribe of Eagles. Belonged to Chief Weah and late Ed Beanlands.
8. Sub-tribe of (6), Ya-gu-la nas, a Raven Crest tribe. Present owner, Percy Brown, Point-Town-Tribe.
9. Belonged to sub-tribe of Git-ens, an Eagle Crest tribe. Was owned by the late Fred Johnson; present owner, Joseph Wiat.
10. Belongs to another sub-tribe of the Eagle Crest. Was owned by the late Ruben Spence; now is his nephew's — Wilfred Bennett.
11. Belonged to Chief Seegay of the Raven Crest. Transferred to Chief Weah's tribe, Eagles.
12. Point-Town-Village tribe. Present owner is Peter Hill.
13. Belongs to the Skidegate people.
14. Belongs to Chief Skidegate's tribe, present owner is Louis Collison

Village sites were taken in the main from J. R. Swanton's *The Haida,* supplemented by local information, gathered in 1965.

MAP No. 2

Legend for the circled numbers on Map No. 2
Information is from Mr. Charles Hartie, supplemented by data from the Prince Rupert Land Registry Office.

1. William J. Leary — residence, store and post office. Entrance to *Inside Road* was between this and (2).
2. A. McNaughton. In later years Billy Burke and Pete Monchal bought McNaughton's property and established the Notorious "Monte Carlo Club".
3. George Carmichael
4. Clarence Johnson. Frank Dix
5. George McRae. E. Girard. *Girard Road* extended from the *Inside Road* to this lot.
6. Alec McLeod.
7. R. "Scotty" Struthers.
8. Bill Lacey. George Husband.
9. Tom Anderson.
10. Norman Fraser. E. Girard.
11. Ferdinand Trappert.
12. The widowed Mrs. O'Flanagan was reported to be coming to live on this lot and a cabin mysteriously was built in anticipation.
13. Jack London.
14. William Barry.
15. Hjawkins Edwards.
16. John Ledgerwood.
17. Dr. J. C. Spencer, who sold part of this lot to the Dominion Government for the establishment of Dead Tree Wireless Station.
18. Caroline M. de Vit. Mrs. de Vit kept house for Tom Drain for a period.
19. Thomas J. Drain – who later married, and for many years was a magistrate in Haney and Maple Ridge.
20. Mr. and Mrs. George Pitt-Turner.
21. Thomas Budge bought this for $1600 in February 1911 and sold it two months later for half price to Eda Yarwood of Nanaimo.
22. Mr. Brown, whose mail-order bride was a cute little French nurse. When Mr. Brown died he was buried on his land. Joe Molitor brought his family to live on this property and it was here that the Lawn Hill school was built.
23. Thomas J. Drain, who liked this lot so well he purchased it outright, in 1911. The lake in the center was known as *Drain's Lake.*
24. Mr. McInnes.
25. Arthur C. le Plastrier Ray, who sold it a few years later to James Waddell.
26. Joseph Baker of Whitehorse bought this lot in 1910 for $1463. He sold it two months later to the law firm of Gwillim and Crisp in Vancouver for one dollar.
27. A. W. Wessels.
28. Mr. Boultbee
29. Max Ruff.

Legend for Map No. 2, continued —

30. William Prettyjohn, who said he was the only Lawn Hill pre-emptor to make farming pay.
31. James T. Erwin. Charles A. Boultbee.
32. Ed Hyder, who built a two story house — six feet square and twelve feet high.
33. James T. Erwin.
34. David A. Jones was Crown Granted this lot in 1911. Sold it to James Murray Patterson in 1920 for a tidy profit.
35. Al Daise.
36. Bill Jardine, who "baked wonderful bread".
37. Joe Renner, who afterwards had a ranch on Maude Island.
38. Bilefield. Ranch. The Ranches also lived at Clay Hill with their two sons (from an earlier marriage), Miller and C. O. Davis.
39. Tom Hearn, who put bells on all his sheep — even though he could not hear them.
40. William Switzer, Lawn Hill's first settler lived here; but the first registered owner was John Bray. When Bray subdivided the lot, one section was bought by the coal drilling company, who built a house for Frank Wright, one of their officials. This house became the well-known Farmer's Institute building. The north Section of Bray's lot was bought by Robert and Mrs. Scharfee for their store and post office which they operated in Lawn Hill until 1924, selling out to Mrs. Marian Richardson.
41. Government stables and shop, where horses and equipment were kept for maintaining the roads. Frank Mallory was in charge of this for many years.
42. J. Arthur Fritz, an early settler. Clement de Pape built his hotel on this site — Lawn Hill's only resident. Today Mr. Sears makes his home on this site — Lawn Hill's only resident. (1966)
43. Henry Grenier. Bob Wilkie.
44. Captain and Mrs. Hubley and their son Julius. Captain Hubley was buried here at his request. Later his widow married Joe Renner from across the way.
45. Roy McGillvary. B. F. "Bert" Roberts, before Bert moved to live in Tlell.
46. Al Cooke, who had his house moved, bodily, by a covetous neighbor during his absence.
47. Bill Lainey
48. Andy Christenson
49. Art Micholson. Henry Hyder.
50. Charlie Nelson.
51. Mr. Van Meter.
52. Jim Adams.
53. Mr. Hildegarde.
54. Pete Adams.
55. MacPherson on the south part, Ed Ashton on the north section. St. Mary's Spring is about 200 feet south of Ed Ashton's old house.
56. Sold in a 1927 tax sale to a company represented by Hugh M. Dignam.
57. Tom Schrouder.
58. Shaded lot — the Experimental Farm maintained by Austin Richardson.
59. Ralph Thomas Ward, an early pioneer of this area.
60. Ralph T. Ward.
61. William Duncan. Navigational beacon on this site today.
62. The blacksmith, Gus Buschel.
63. Nick Schug. Joe Darlington. Chris Hunsby.
64. Arthur Bristoe. Ed Ashton. A. Delaney.
65. Austin Richardson.
66. Chris Hunsby. Arthur Farvaque.
67. Arthur Potts bought this lot in 1909 for $1450 and sold it for $1750 three months later to J. Savannah and J. I. L. Meyer of Victoria. It was always known to the early settlers as "Pott's Purchase".
68. Ed Ashton.
69. Gus Buschel.
70. Henry Fersch. Mrs. Fersch was the sister of Mrs. Scharfee and Billy Bruckener.
71. Jack Scott.
72. Nick Schaeffer, who with his wife, farmed here for many years.
73. Billy Bruckener.
74. Jim Reid.
75. John Higney, the tall, partly deaf gunner from the English Army whose name was applied to the creek which flowed through this section of land. When Higney and Reid left, Gus Ross bought their land.
76. Bought in June 1907 by J. F. Mitchell and later sold to Fred B. Warren.
77. Purchased by Mr. G. W. Moffitt in 1907 and later sold, also, to Fred B. Warren. Today these lots are known as the "Government Gravel Pit". This was where, in 1966, huge bones were found twelve feet below the surface. Thought to have been either the bones of an ice-age mammoth, or of a whale, they were accidentally destroyed by workmen before an accurate identification could be made.

I.R. 2. refers to Indian Reservation, number 2.

335

INDEX

337